HOMECOMINGS

Studies of the Weatherhead East Asian Institute, Columbia University

Studies of the Weatherhead East Asian Institute, Columbia University

The Studies of the Weatherhead East Asian Institute of Columbia University were inaugurated in 1962 to bring to a wider public the results of significant new research on modern and contemporary East Asia.

Homecomings

THE BELATED RETURN OF JAPAN'S LOST SOLDIERS

Yoshikuni Igarashi

Columbia University Press
New York

Columbia University Press
Publishers Since 1893
New York   Chichester, West Sussex
cup.columbia.edu

Ishihara Yoshirō, "Lonely Now" (Sabishii to ima), "Song of a Ringing in My Ears" (Miminari no uta), and "Position" (Ichi) reprinted by permission of Tanaka Mironu.

Library of Congress Cataloging-in-Publication Data
Names: Igarashi, Yoshikuni, 1960– author.
Title: Homecomings : the belated return of Japan's lost soldiers / Yoshikuni Igarashi.
Description: New York : Columbia University Press, 2016. | Series: Studies of the Weatherhead East Asian Institute, Columbia University | Includes bibliographical references and index.
Identifiers: LCCN 2015050682 | ISBN 9780231177702 (cloth : alk. paper)
Subjects: LCSH: World War, 1939–1945—Forced repatriation. | Repatriation—Japan—History—20th century. | Return migration—Japan—History—20th century. | World War, 1939–1945—Prisoners and prisons, Soviet. | Prisoners of war—Japan—History—20th century. | Prisoners of war—Soviet Union—History—20th century. | Japan—Social conditions—1945–
Classification: LCC D809.J3 I35 2016 | DDC 940.54/7247089956—dc23
LC record available at http://lccn.loc.gov/2015050682

Columbia University Press books are printed on permanent and durable acid-free paper.
Printed in the United States of America

c 10 9 8 7 6 5 4 3 2 1

COVER IMAGE:
Courtesy of U.S. National Archives

CONTENTS

CONTENTS

ACKNOWLEDGMENTS

Without the generous help and intervention of so many people, it would not have been possible to complete my long journey. Here I express my deep gratitude only belatedly. I would first and foremost like to thank Kitamura Yoshihiro, an editor at Chikuma shobō, who offered me an opportunity to write a monograph for a Japanese audience. His feedback helped to sharpen the focus of this project, and his encouragement guided it to the finish line. I would also like to thank Anne Routon of Columbia University Press for patiently waiting for the English version. Her support for the project and professional guidance greatly helped me at the final stage of manuscript preparation. Whitney Johnson, also at Columbia University Press, deftly handled my questions about how I could best prepare the manuscript.

My colleagues extended helping hands at crucial points. Anne Walthall should know that her kind invitation to contribute an essay to *The Human Tradition in Modern Japan* set the project in motion. I wrote about Yokoi Shōichi for the collection and then decided to systematically examine the belated returns of Japanese soldiers. Anne continued to support my project in various ways. Frank Biese, Alan Christy, Kevin Doak, Victor Koschmann, Thomas Looser, Beatrice Trefalt, Lori Watt, and Sandra Wilson also helped me define my project in its early phase. Noriko Aso, Wesley Sasaki-Uemura, and Gerald Figal read the manuscript in part or whole and provided stylistic as well as substantive comments. Jennifer Fay read an early version of chapter 1 and helped me find a better conceptual focus for the argument. I am especially grateful that Mark Schoenfield combed through the chapter drafts line by line, critically engaging with my argument. In the final phase of the project, Faith Barter rendered much needed copyediting help, removing the holes and leaps in my argument. The two anonymous readers at Columbia University Press offered thorough and insightful comments on the manuscript. The collective wisdom of my colleagues left indelible marks on this book, but of course, all the mistakes are mine.

I also would like to express my gratitude for the hospitality and encouragement that I received in Japan. Uno Kuniichi was generous enough to discuss the Japanese version of this book in his essay on biopolitics. Igarashi Akio has long been a gracious host for numerous overseas-based researchers, including myself. Kawamura Kunimitsu and the faculty of the Japanese Studies Division of Osaka University gave me opportunities to present my ongoing research and hosted me as a visiting scholar in 2010. Nagaoka Takashi provided me with long-distance help in relation to my last-minute research needs. And on one afternoon during May 2012, Yokoi Mihoko kindly shared the personal memories of her late husband, Yokoi Shōichi.

Many people provided logistic support for the project in various forms. I thank Jim Toplon and the Interlibrary Loan staff of Vanderbilt University for handling literally hundreds of my requests; librarian Yuh-Fen Benda for helping me obtain secondary sources; Frank Lester for assisting with references; Todd Dodson of Vanderbilt University's IT department for calmly responding to my distress calls during computer emergencies; Carol Beverly, also of the IT department, for transferring scores of VHS tapes to discs; and Martin Hinze for transforming my hand-drawn maps into camera-ready versions.

I also am grateful for the generous financial support that I received for this project, which included a research fellowship from the Japan Foundation and two research scholar fellowships from Vanderbilt University. These fellowships and Vanderbilt University's generous research leave policy allowed me to focus fully on researching and writing this book for extended periods.

Finally, my thanks to Teresa, Maya, and Kaita for being the biggest source of joy in my life. Wherever you are is my home.

NOTE ON PERSONAL NAMES AND
NAMES OF WAR

In transcribing Japanese and Chinese names, I follow the local custom of placing the family name first. But when the work is written in English, the author's name (e.g., my name) is cited with the given name first.

In this book, I use the term "Asia Pacific War," rather than the conventional designations of "World War II" or "Pacific War," in order to underscore the fact that Japan had already been at war with China for several years when it attacked British Malaya, Hong Kong, and Pearl Harbor in 1941. The Asia Pacific War began with the escalation of the Sino-Japanese conflict in 1937 and ended with Japan's surrender to the Allied powers in 1945.

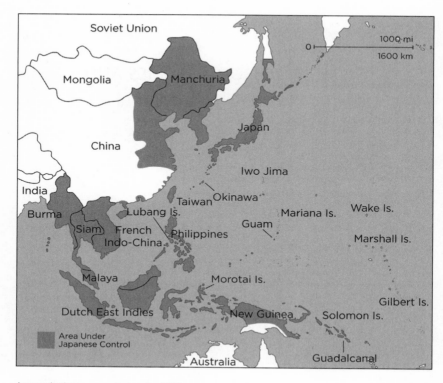

Area under Japanese control, spring 1942.

Locations of labor camps cited in the text.

HOMECOMINGS

Returnees from the Soviet Union at Maizuru Port, December 1, 1953. The original photo that appeared in the *Yomiuri shinbun* had been damaged, so another *Yomiuri* photo of the event—most likely taken a moment before or after the printed version and identical in composition—is reproduced here. (Courtesy of the *Yomiuri shinbun*)

INTRODUCTION

GOING HOME

On December 1, 1953, 811 former Japanese internees from the Soviet Union arrived in the port city of Maizuru, the site of the Japanese government's repatriation center. Of the 811, 420 were former military men, and 391 were private citizens, including 9 women and 2 toddlers. After the war, most of the civilian returnees had been detained by the Soviets in Sakhalin, the formerly Japanese northern territory that the Soviet army occupied just before Japan's surrender.[1] At the same time, hundreds of thousands of Japanese servicemen and civilians had been interned in Siberian labor camps as POWs or for various alleged crimes; more than 100,000 perished during their internment. Because their homecoming was the first repatriation from the Communist regime since April 1950, the return of these 811 internees offered hope to the families of several thousand Japanese who remained in the Soviet Union.

A photo in the *Yomiuri* newspaper's evening edition captures the arrival scene at the wharf. In the photo, the returnees are wearing heavy Russian winter coats and fur caps as they walk through the welcoming crowd of family members and relatives, some of whom are carrying Japanese flags or banners bearing the returnees' names. Even in this grainy black-and-white photo, the belated repatriates' obviously Russian appearance stands out. The accompanying article assures readers that this landing was free of the turmoil that had plagued some of the other recent returns. There were no "die-hard" Communists on board this repatriation ship as there had been when supporters of Mao Zedong were found among recent returnees from the People's Republic of China. Despite their Russian outward appearance, the 1953 returnees seemed genuinely happy to be home. The December 1 photo and article thus sent a hopeful message that notwithstanding their foreign clothing, the returnees had maintained a connection with their Japanese homeland.[2]

Of the major dailies that reported on the returnees' repatriation, the *Yomiuri*'s coverage offers perhaps the best example of the popular sentiment that awaited the returnees: while the paper acknowledged the hardships of the Soviet camps, the coverage also sought to contain the painful, lingering memories of the war. By 1953, the extreme suffering experienced by the Siberian detainees was common knowledge. As the daily noted with sensitivity in its front-page column, "These are people who lived lives of imprisonment, blindfolded to reality and separated not only from Japan but also from any 'humane life.'"[3] The *Yomiuri* nonetheless made sure to maintain an optimistic tone in discussing the returnees' reentry into Japanese society.

For example, an article on December 2 reported that some of them still felt as anxious as they had in the labor camps, even as the article suggested that reentry into Japanese society would be as straightforward as changing outfits:

> The 811 returnees who spent their first night at the repatriation assistance center have been busy since the morning of December 2 resuming life as Japanese living in Japan proper [*naichijin*]. The returnees have shed the Soviet-made winter gear, heavy and [blue-]black, to change into the suits or kimono their families brought, apparently wiping off the "stains of a foreign country" to become Japanese again overnight.[4]

The article thus makes an almost desperate attempt to convince the readers that the returnees' Russian experiences were only superficial. The article's subtext insists that beneath their layers of dark Russian clothing, the returnees nevertheless remained purely Japanese, unstained by foreign hardships. The use of the geographically defined term *naichijin* also hints at the belief that the returnees left behind the trauma of war once they crossed the border into Japan. Now that they were back in Japan proper, these returnees were expected to shed their connections with their Siberian internment in particular and with wartime violence in general "to become Japanese again overnight."

Three days after this article appeared, the *Yomiuri*'s evening edition reported that 244 of the original 811 returnees had arrived in Tokyo, as either their final destination or a relay point for further travel. The later coverage, containing a tone of relief, characterized their arrival as uneventful. The main article begins with "There were neither red flags welcoming them nor labor union members."[5] Unlike those who had returned from China several years earlier, these returnees showed no signs of feverish devotion to Communist propaganda. The returnees of 1953 were reunited only with their family members, a final, rehabilitative step toward normalcy, according to the newspaper coverage. For example, one article featured former army lance corporal Takei Takeo, whose wife and son welcomed him to their one-room home in Tokyo following his return. Noting that Takei's family could not afford to meet him in Maizuru, the article intimated that their life without him had been challenging. Almost immediately, however, Takei relaxed, and the article observes that he "began cracking jokes" while "the relatives and neighbors who surrounded the family burst into laughter." The article optimistically declares that "spring has come to the family for the first time."[6] The dark winter years that the returnee and his family had endured were finally over. The *Yomiuri* expresses the popular sentiment that just coming home was a panacea for any problems caused by the wartime separation.[7]

Yet the newspaper acknowledges that reintegration into postwar society required some effort. The future poet laureate, Ishihara Yoshirō—one of the returnees to the Tokyo area—expressed his sense of bewilderment to the *Yomiuri* reporter upon noticing how drastically the commercial district of Ginza had changed during his absence. Still wearing heavy Russian winter clothing, Ishihara stood out in the crowded shopping district. His visible difference from those around him echoed the symbolic distance that existed between him and postwar Japan. As he was getting into a taxi to return to his brother's house, Ishihara stated: "I have no idea what is going on. I will stay home quietly for a while and think about my future."[8] The *Yomiuri* article thus portrays Ishihara as a man who belonged to the past and had much to learn. But at least, according to the article, Ishihara had a secure home to which he could retreat.[9]

The title of the short article about Ishihara, "A Modern-Day Urashima Tarō's Ginza Stroll" (Ima Urashima no Ginbura), indicates the sympathetic yet patronizing attitude of contemporary society toward the returnees. In the Japanese folktale to which the title refers, Urashima Tarō returns from his pleasurable life in the palace under the sea to his home on land. Although he thinks that he has been away only a few days, it turns out that he has actually been gone for several hundred years. His village has become a completely unfamiliar place, and the people there do not recognize him. Unlike Urashima, though, Ishihara's time in Siberia was far from pleasurable. The article nevertheless transforms Ishihara into a modern-day Urashima, observing that he (Ishihara) was confused by the changes that had occurred in his absence. This cultural reference immediately rendered the strange figure of the Siberian internee into something both familiar and nonthreatening in postwar society. It also shifted the focus from what happened in Siberia to the challenge of making one's "homecoming" to a land that has become strange.

By including a brief account of the meeting between the returnees' five representatives and the minister of health and welfare, the newspaper did acknowledge that issues related to Japanese returnees had not been completely solved; the returnees' representatives urged the government to continue its efforts to bring home the Japanese who remained in the Soviet Union. Ishihara's bafflement regarding postwar society and the shadow of unresolved tension with the Soviet Union, however, only highlighted the fact that it was a privilege to be living in postwar Japan. The *Yomiuri* coverage framed the internees' belated homecoming as an occasion to celebrate their return to normal life, not as an opportunity to seriously contemplate the long, arduous years that they had survived or the difficulties that they might yet face in readjusting to postwar society. Of the major dailies, the *Yomiuri* offered the most extensive reporting on the returnees who arrived in Maizuru on December 1, 1953, although its tone catered to the strong popular desire to downplay the internees' conflicts with postwar society.

When the Empire of Great Japan collapsed, 6.88 million Japanese were living in the Japanese colonies and war fronts (equal to 9.6 percent of the population on the Japanese mainland). Of these, 3.67 million were soldiers and officers of the Japanese navy and army. It was not an easy task to move and resettle more than 6 million people in such a short span of time. The Japanese government originally contemplated having the settlers remain abroad indefinitely in order to avoid food shortages and social confusion at home. But as the former settlers' safety in Manchuria became a source of serious concern, the government soon reconsidered. Priority was given to the repatriation from Manchuria and China, and the United States' material assistance helped expedite the repatriation of 2.5 million Japanese from these regions.[10] For other areas—most notably those controlled by the Soviets—immediate repatriation was not a priority. In any event, the vast majority returned to the homeland within a few years of Japan's defeat. A total of some 6.3 million Japanese were repatriated from overseas, 97.5 percent of them (6.14 million) by the end of 1948.[11]

The early returnees came home to a war-torn nation where survival was the most pressing concern. They nevertheless had opportunities to restore their own identities as postwar citizens by participating in a process of national reconstruction.[12] However, for those who came home late—whether because they were interned in Siberia or stranded in the jungle—there were no such opportunities. When these Japanese finally returned, their country's reconstruction was well under way, and they returned to clearly crafted and well-accepted media narratives about the war and repatriation. As we have already seen in the *Yomiuri* coverage, their return home was supposed to bring closure to their long suffering. Yet as Ishihara Yoshirō later explained, homecoming turned out to be not an end but the beginning of the returnees' struggle with their past experiences. For example, many people who returned from Communist countries had difficulty finding a job because employers feared that the returnees might have become Communists during their absence and therefore would cause trouble in the workplace.

In general, postwar Japanese society showed little appetite for stories that extended beyond the days immediately before and after the returnees' homecoming. Repatriation was relegated to the past, as Japan committed itself instead to its social and cultural postwar narratives. These narratives did, however, make space for Japanese society to offer warm acceptance to those who returned home with the burdens of war. While imbued with goodwill, the project of "helping" returnees adjust to the new culture also fulfilled an ideological function: to preserve the fictional narrative that Japan, as a rescuer, was no longer afflicted by defeat. In December 1953, by the very extension of their sympathy, *Yomiuri* readers reaffirmed their good fortune at being securely ensconced in postwar Japanese society. By contrast, when the returnees emerged from their very different experience of the war, they faced a set of expectations that had already been prescribed by postwar narratives; the Japanese public expected the returnees to be the helpless yet admirable victims of circumstance.[13]

OVERVIEW OF THE PROJECT

Homecomings: The Belated Return of Japan's Lost Soldiers examines the tensions that shaped the postwar return of the "lost soldiers" of the Asia Pacific War. In particular, the book considers the return of both Japanese internees who had been detained in Siberian labor camps and soldiers who survived in the jungles of the South Pacific for more than a quarter century. These homecomings, which began in the late 1940s and continued into the 1970s, are marked by significant cultural gaps. Accordingly, I explore the cultural distance between the returnees, who bear memories of traumatic loss, and a Japanese society that assiduously sought for years to separate itself from the war. That is, I examine the struggles of these returnees to articulate "war" experiences that had the potential to disrupt Japan's carefully crafted postwar narratives.

This book was conceived as a companion to my first book, *Bodies of Memory: Narratives of War in Postwar Japanese Culture, 1945–1970*.[14] *Bodies of Memory* is a macrolevel study that generally traces collective narratives of war through postwar Japan's cultural representations. By contrast, *Homecomings* addresses the experiences of specific individuals in the postwar period, as well as these homecomings' tangled relations with larger historical narratives. I investigate here the cases of former servicemen burdened by war experiences that refused to fit neatly into the postwar narrative of Japan's war, defeat, and recovery. I focus on particular cases in which key individuals' lives received media attention not to set up a rigid binary between micro- and macrohistories that privileges the former but to investigate the tensions and interactions between these two levels of history. My goal is to illuminate the ways in which returnees negotiated such different and difficult registers of history in postwar Japan.

A basic premise of the book is that individual experiences and memories do not exist in a social vacuum. In order to make their internal struggles understandable to others, individuals must resort to socially shared images and narratives, particularly those that the media circulate in contemporary society. Because the postwar Japanese media had become entrenched as an integral part of everyday life, the process of absorbing shared images was tantamount to accepting the media's images and narratives as one's own. Anything that did not fit the modes of the mass media's representation was often disregarded as incomprehensible excess. Meanwhile, for the belated returnees abandoned after their original homecomings, the absence of in-depth media attention made it difficult for them to share their personal experiences with others or even to claim ownership of their own stories. These returnees had to contend with media-supplied narratives, whether or not they liked them, in shaping their pasts. Even though I focus on various personal experiences and memories, I believe that one can access them only by exploring their relations with media representations.

While acknowledging the importance of mass media to Japan's postwar history, I am also mindful of the limitations of those media. In disavowing the multiethnic colonial project of wartime Japan, the postwar Japanese media replicated in many ways the official discourse of repatriation based exclusively on the return of Japanese nationals to Japan proper.[15] Colonial subjects who had been mobilized for Imperial Japan's war effort completely fell out of the postwar government's scope of concern. These colonial subjects were also rendered invisible in the Japanese media discourse on repatriation. Indeed, when reporting on the 811 returnees from the Soviet Union in December 1953, the *Yomiuri* and other dailies completely omitted the fact that there were nine foreign nationals among them.[16] They supplied no information about the circumstances that brought them to Japan, much less what happened to them after they reached Japanese shores. Historian Ōkado Masakatsu offers another example of skewed representational practices: when searching through the numerous photos of Japanese repatriates archived at the *Asahi* newspaper's Osaka office, he located only one photo of a Korean repatriate, who had been called up for military service toward the end of the war and returned to Japan around 1955. Ōkado sees this dearth of representations of former colonial subjects' movements as an indictment of the media's exclusive focus on Japanese repatriation to Japan.[17]

Notwithstanding the media's complicity with official discourse, we should not underestimate their ability to produce and proliferate images beyond official prescriptions. The government's efforts to incorporate repatriates into Japanese society largely consisted of these people's physical return to the homeland; the media filled postwar society with powerful, albeit selective, images of returnees and their lives afterward. Upon arriving in Japan, the returnees encountered both official and mass media discourses about their experiences. Meanwhile, the Japanese postwar media intensified their efforts, inundating the public with more images, most of which had further incorporated the official discourse. The mirror of media representation consequently forced the belated returnees to examine themselves and also supplied a framework in which they could reconstitute their postwar selves.

In focusing on the tangled relations between individual returnees and their media images, this book is concerned with military returnees rather than their civilian counterparts. Although civilian returnees, especially women and children, initially received considerable media attention, they soon disappeared from postwar cultural representations. Their brief symbolic value seemed to end with their act of coming home. Once they had arrived, they were allowed to quietly move out of the public's view and into their domestic spaces. Even though defeat troubled the concepts of "Japan" and "the Japanese," the repatriates' strong desire to return home reconfirmed the desirability of Japan and of being Japanese. In reality, however, not everyone wanted to return to Japan. For example, *manga* artist Mizuki Shigeru (1922–2015) heard the news of Japan's defeat in Rabaul, Papua New Guinea, and hoped to settle among the local people. But on an army doctor's advice, he eventually decided to repatriate to Japan for the time being. Although he promised his local friends that he would be back in seven years, it actually took him twenty-six years to fulfill his promise. Mizuki arrived in Japan in March 1946.[18]

This ideological configuration of the returnees' images paved the way for Fujiwara Tei's memoir *Shooting Stars Are Alive* (*Nagareru hoshi wa ikiteiru*, 1949) to become a best seller in postwar Japan.[19] Fujiwara and her three children escaped Xinjing (present-day Changchun), the capital of Manchukuo, shortly after Japan's defeat, and they arrived in Japan in September 1946.[20] As historian Narita Ryūichi explains, the book's narrative of her "experiences in refugee camps and escape journey" emphasizes how Fujiwara yearns for her 'family,' how she strives to reach her 'homeland,' and how she reaffirms her identity as 'Japanese.' "[21] For example, Fujiwara offers an account of her determined effort to keep walking down the Korean Peninsula with her three young children. This characterization portrays Japan as a natural "home," and Fujiwara's testimony casts her as a heroine who struggled to protect her Japanese identity under excruciating circumstances.

But as survival ceased to be a primary concern for postwar society, the civilian returnees largely disappeared from literary and cinematic representations. Furthermore, in what little was written about them, their life after return was rarely discussed, and there was a clear gender division at work. In the popular media, the difficulties faced by the women and children who repatriated from Japan's colonies initially stood in for the entirety of the civilian returnees' experiences. These difficulties were then soon displaced in the cultural imagination by the stories of war widows and women who patiently waited for their men to return. The film version of *Shooting Stars Are Alive* (directed by Koishi Ei'ichi, 1949) illustrates this displacement. The original narrative, which ends with Fujiwara and her children arriving home, extends beyond the protagonist's and her children's homecoming to show them then waiting patiently for the return of their husband/father from the continent.[22] In the film, although their postwar life is difficult, they enjoy the security of being at home, and the heroic figure of the female returnee is reduced to a domestic figure whose hopes hinge on her man's return.[23]

In contrast, the numerous repatriated soldiers who appeared in print and visual texts represented a state of homelessness, an anxious transitional status in the postwar period. Their images were not as easily domesticated as those of the civilian repatriates because of the active role they had played in Japan's imperialism and war. The soldiers drew more media attention because they invoked the haunting presence of the past, thereby not fitting neatly into the cultural narrative of war and defeat.

My choice of former servicemen as the main subject of this book is therefore both pragmatic and strategic. While recognizing the need to recover the voices of civilian returnees, I have concentrated on those returnees who garnered the most media attention: the former soldiers. Discussion of how the returnees lived their lives after their return while burdened with their war memories—a central theme of this book—is mostly absent in what little was written at the time by and about the civilians. Rather than attempting to fill the representational void by uncovering new materials about the civilian returnees, I instead treat this lack as an important feature of postwar Japan's historical terrain, though I remain attentive to the forces that produced this terrain. I focus on what has been represented, albeit imperfectly and ideologically, about the former soldiers. Those problematic representations became part of the historical reality. In response to these representations, the former soldiers tried to articulate their sense of lateness, of having missed out on the postwar process of normalization. By reconfiguring the images of repatriated soldiers, the postwar Japanese media tamed the legacies of war and colonialism. In reality, however, some returnees were so consumed by the past that they could not or did not wish to make the transition into postwar society. This book retraces their struggles in postwar Japan, examining which parts of the returnees' experiences were accepted and which were rejected and revealing that the "postwar" was not actually the period that naturally followed the war but was instead a condition that required careful inspection and maintenance.

Media Representations of War Veterans

The optimistic outlook on postwar Japan's economic prospects that characterized the nation's high-growth era from the mid-1950s to the early 1970s greatly affected media representations of the wartime past. *Bodies of Memory* argued for the intimate relations between the war memory in postwar Japanese society and the radically changing material conditions stemming from Japan's economic recovery and growth. This book continues to emphasize the impact of Japan's economic conditions on its relationship to its history. In particular, the development of consumer society during those years greatly affected the ways in which war memories were articulated in Japanese society.

Consumerism—what was once the privilege of the urban upper and middle classes in prewar Japan—engulfed the nation by the early 1970s. Appliances and cars were not the only objects produced and consumed

Total Number of Publications and Newspaper Circulation

Year	Books	Magazines	Newspapers	Total Population
1947	53,560 (0.69)	74,870 (0.96)	19,994 (0.26)	78,101
1955	100,380 (1.12)	280,800 (3.15)	32,914 (0.37)	89,276
1973	444,436 (4.07)	1,730,560 (15.86)	39,847 (0.37)	109,104

Note: Figures are in thousands, with per capita figures in parentheses.
Source: Ministry of Internal Affairs and Communications, Statistics Bureau, Director-General for Policy Planning (Statistical Standards) & Statistical Research and Training Institute, Historical Statistics of Japan, chap. 26 (http://www.stat.go.jp/english/data/chouki/26.htm).

at a furious pace: Japan's media industry kept pace with the growth in other sectors of the economy. In 1973, for example, the residents of Japan purchased, on average, three and half times as many books and five times as many magazines as they had eighteen years earlier (see table). While newspapers maintained almost identical per capita circulation figures during those years, they also resumed printing evening editions, and each issue became three times as thick.[24] By the mid-1960s, more than 90 percent of households in Japan owned one or more television sets, with individuals watching, on average, more than 1,000 hours of television each year. Meanwhile, film attendance reached more than 1 billion from 1957 to 1960, although it fell rapidly in subsequent years as movies lost their audiences to television.[25] War proved to be an attractive theme for the rapidly expanding media. Numerous war tales and images were packaged as consumable content, creating a major boom in the second half of the 1950s.

No account of Japan's war efforts, regardless of political stance, could skirt the fact that Japan had been defeated. Nevertheless, within a decade of this defeat, Japan hit important benchmarks in reestablishing itself in the international community. It regained its independence in 1952 and acquired a seat in the United Nations four years later. Its economy reached its prewar high in 1955. Yet these gains did not nullify the new political and military arrangements that perpetuated the hierarchal relation of the vanquished to the victor. To the contrary, acceptance of the United States' hegemony in East Asia was a *sine qua non* for the nation's reconstruction and growth, and the former imperial power itself became subject to semicolonial conditions. Although war stories and accounts proliferated in print and film during this period, they did not necessarily indicate that postwar Japanese society had fully embraced its wartime past. Each work had to negotiate the tension between historical fact—Japan's defeat—and ideological imperative—Japan's national pride.

In the first part of this book, I explore visual and literary texts mainly from the late 1940s and 1950s in order to document ways in which popular media represented demobilized soldiers. These works reveal conflicting desires, on the one hand, to assimilate the men back into society and, on the other hand, to symbolically reject the men from social spaces. As Japan's economic success began to boost its national confidence, the menacing figures of former servicemen were replaced with generally more benign images. This discussion of cultural representations of former soldiers serves as the backdrop to my subsequent analyses of how former internees in the Siberian labor camps struggled to articulate their haunting memories in the media environment of the 1950s and 1960s.

The relations with the Japanese media for those men who returned from the South Pacific in the 1970s, particularly Yokoi Shōichi and Onoda Hiro'o, were radically different from those of earlier returnees. Yokoi and Onoda became media sensations the moment they left the jungle, with almost their every move and utterance under public scrutiny. The media were not willing to relinquish their celebrity status even after they returned to Japan, thereby turning them into consumable symbols of Japan's war. For Yokoi and Onoda, "home" was ironically transformed into the extremely public and unsettling state of being constantly in the spotlight. Whereas the earlier returnees had to struggle to reclaim their own voices against media representations, the 1970s returnees found that any attempt to speak about their past or current state created numerous responses in the media environment, further fueling the obsessive media coverage of their "return."

The Dangers of Turning History into a Lesson

Before turning to the individuals who belatedly returned to Japan after the war's end, I would like to explain my stance toward the subject of history and memory as it defines this book's larger framework. I have often felt uncomfortable with the moral imperative that I have heard on numerous occasions in Japan: "Do not let the war experiences [or memories] erode [*fūka saseruna*]." While sympathetic to the slogan's underlying antiwar sentiment, I am troubled by its all-knowing quality. It treats personal experiences and memories as transparent and self-explanatory, obscuring the arduous efforts required to make them one's own. Whoever voices such a call seems to treat memory as a fossilized substance to be preserved as is. To counter such a static image of history, I insist that if experience has social meaning, it must be in a constant process of transformation. It is never the case that one immediately understands a historical event's ramifications, regardless of one's proximity to it. Rather, memories are transmitted and transformed as the event acquires various meanings in society.

My point is not to insist that experiences and memories are arbitrary or untrustworthy but to underscore the need to understand them as part of a living process: their meanings are far from self-evident or easily transmittable. Even when a person survives a traumatic event, she or he cannot completely understand her or his own experience of it, let alone communicate it. The very effort to grasp the meaning of the experience in turn transforms the survivor.

This complex process is well illustrated in a case that psychiatrist Nakazawa Masao discusses in *Tracing the Psychological Wounds of Hibakusha* (*Hibakusha no kokoro no kizu o otte*, 2007). Nakao Tatsuo survived the atomic bombing in Hiroshima and subsequently led a life relatively free from traumatic memories. But once he agreed to help establish an association of *hibakusha* (atomic bomb survivors) in 2005 and began meeting other survivors, he found his psychological state becoming increasingly unstable. He lost confidence in his career, was unable to sleep, and began drinking heavily. Nakazawa explains Nakao's shaken state of mind:

Various memories came back in fragmentary form. While listening to the survivors' tales, his "framed" and unshakable still images [of the event] began to look questionable and were in some cases corrected. Mr. Nakao, whose identity grew shaky, began probing his own memories. He learned on the Internet that the account he had written long ago about his atomic bomb experiences had been filed as a public document at the Hiroshima City Office. He obtained a copy and read it, finding that it was a great deal different from his own "framed memories."[26]

Sixty years after the event, Nakao began to retrace his footsteps, and the process was so disturbing that he sought relief with alcohol. The part of himself that he had repressed returned to the present moment, and Nakao was forced to restructure his whole being in order to accommodate the undesirable past.

The passing of time did not mean that Nakao had gained distance from the original event but that he had different relations with it in his subsequent life. His account is merely a document of how he understood his experiences at a particular point in the postwar period. It is noteworthy that this document from earlier postwar days, found on the Internet, mediated his efforts to return to the past: his arrested memories gained a new life in cyberspace. In recalibrating his relationship to the past, Nakao finally let himself feel the psychological effects of the horrid event, arriving at a far more disturbing understanding of what he had experienced. This understanding, however, seems to have remained fractured and fragmented for the moment (at the time the book was written), and he lacks the means to articulate it effectively.[27]

The imperative to prohibit erosion of the past further presumes an asymmetric and hierarchical relation between those who experienced the event (the war generation) and those who did not (the postwar generations). War experiences and memories are often treated as equivalent to lessons found in history. Those who did not directly experience the war are expected to accept such lessons graciously and unquestioningly. Their charge is to receive a completed picture and pass it on to the next generation without damaging it. Meanwhile, those who personally experienced the war are given a secure position as teachers who speak the truth.[28] This notion of survivor as teacher is closely tied to another imperative, that one must learn from history so as not to repeat the same mistakes. According to this argument, in order to prevent a future war, we must learn from a past war.

By being subsumed under a future goal, personal experiences and memories are refashioned as lessons of history. But what kind of lessons can one find in the explosive power that annihilated entire communities in Hiroshima and Nagasaki? Do the humiliating experiences of the Siberian internment offer any clues to how to avoid future war?[29] What wisdom is to be found in the stragglers' prolonged struggle for survival in the South Pacific? In postwar Japan, complex historical reality and painful memories have too often been reduced to the simple and obvious mantra that we should not repeat the same miserable experiences by starting new wars. That sentiment erases the individuality of the survivors' experiences and the details of their memories. Conversely, when one refuses to examine the details, one clings to dogmatism. Survivors who do not wish to recall their difficult experiences can also block off their inward thinking by concentrating on broad lessons. However, a sensitive exploration of war experiences and memories requires avoiding such generalizations as much as possible in order to remain open to the complex and provisional status of their microlevel personal histories. These histories are too messy and unresolved to be reduced to didactic slogans.

I have no intention of abandoning a macrolevel history in this project, even though I emphasize the importance of microhistories. Jorge Luis Borges's one-paragraph story about the overzealous "Colleges of Cartographers" that made a life-size map of the unnamed "Empire" illustrates an inherent problem with microlevel descriptions. Succeeding generations deemed this map "cumbersome" and abandoned it because it offered nothing extra to their experiential knowledge.[30] In a similar vein, a life-size history that captures individual experiences in their entirety (if such an ideal were even attainable) would be useless and incomprehensible. Just as in the case of a map, history becomes readable only through the imposition of selection and reconstruction. Microhistories must also be subject to this processing in order to be intelligible. Those who explore history inevitably need a map to make sense of their segment of the world. But what if one's findings do not fit the descriptions on the popular maps? Especially when one has no power or authority to redraw them? There is yet another factor to consider in the case of postwar Japanese history: even if the returnees tried to withdraw into a private space, the media constantly bombarded them with popular versions of history. My goal is to investigate the tensions and interactions between micro- and macrohistories. I want to look at not only how several returnees experienced the war and postwar but also the ways in which they negotiated the different and difficult strata of history in postwar Japan.

My approach to the subject reflects my membership in the postwar Japanese generations that did not personally experience the Asia Pacific War (I was born in 1960). The inquiries of those in postwar generations

can—and should—be more than mere copies of what the war generations already have articulated. For that reason, I believe that war experiences need to be open to all generations. My argument is, of course, not
limited to those who were born in Japan after the war; it extends to those
who were raised in other regions. Postwar generations should not simply
adopt the same positions as those who survived the war. Rather, those
determined to pass on their experience of Japan's war must recognize not
only that postwar generations both inside and outside of Japan should
participate in the process of understanding war experiences, but also
that they have already been doing so.

Areas of Exploration and Chapter Outline

To extend my cartographical metaphor, some parts of the historical
terrain that I explore in this book have been well traversed by other researchers. On the topic of the Siberian internment of Japanese POWs, for
example, there is a sizable literature: first-person narratives, journalistic
accounts, and academic histories. Camp survivors have written thousands of books and essays about their experiences, while journalists and
academics have highlighted particular individuals' internment experiences and postrepatriation life. In addition, the opening of the Russian
archives after the Cold War has led to new research on the Japanese internment in Soviet camps.[31] The most recent English publication on the
subject, Andrew Barshay's *The Gods Left First*, synthesizes these approaches in its examination of the lives and writings of three prominent
former Siberian internees: artist Kazuki Yoshio, writer Takasugi Ichirō,
and poet Ishihara Yoshirō.[32]

By contrast, other areas of my inquiry have received far less critical
attention. For example, despite recent efforts to reevaluate the historical
impact of Japanese soldiers' belated homecomings, their stories remain
largely at the margins of scholarly discourse. Through her comprehen-
sive study of Imperial Japanese Army stragglers in Southeast Asia and
the Pacific and their subsequent journeys home, Beatrice Trefalt helps
re-situate these men in postwar Japanese history by examining the
contemporary responses to their uncanny returns and excavating their
connections with Japan's colonial legacies.[33] In Japan, journalist Kawasaki
Masumi's biography of Nakamura Teruo—a former Imperial Japanese

soldier from Taiwan who was "captured" on an Indonesian island in December 1974—discusses the historical ramifications of Nakamura's homecoming in relation to the geopolitical conditions that surrounded post–World War II Taiwan.[34] Notwithstanding these publications' analytical power, these texts seem to have had little effect on subsequent discussions about the soldier returnees, as only a few essays on the topic have appeared since the early 2000s.[35]

Even less scholarly attention has been paid to the fictional versions of these histories. Gomikawa Junpei's best-selling novel *The Human Condition* (1956–1958) has rarely been read as a historical text that resonates with its contemporary socioeconomic conditions. Indeed, the novel's very popularity seems to have discouraged scholars from discussing this text, which grapples with Japan's imperial war. The film version of the book has met a similar fate. While touted by film critics as powerful cinema, it is rarely analyzed in terms of its cultural moment. Similarly, *Yellow Crow* (1957), a film about a man who belatedly returns to Japan from the People's Republic of China, which in 1958 won the Golden Globe Award for best foreign-language film, has been mostly forgotten in Japan and the United States.[36] The absence of scholarly interest in these works does not necessarily signal their lack of historical importance. Rather, it may attest to their ability to bring closure to the historical issues that they portray.

This book traces a rough chronology from the late 1940s to the 1970s and is divided into three parts. The first part examines mass media representations of former soldiers in postwar Japan, along with one soldier's literary efforts to revise them. The middle two chapters portray individuals who returned from Soviet internment camps and their lives after their return. In the final three chapters, I describe three soldiers who returned from the South Pacific extremely late. The book's unconventional structure—it opens with the cinematic treatment of former servicemen—underscores the claim that media representations are not mere shadows of the actual events but are part and parcel of the historical process that produced the postwar conditions, the conditions to which the veterans returned.

The first chapter, "Life After the War: Former Servicemen in Postwar Japanese Film," explores media images of repatriated soldiers through two films that portray their postwar lives: *Stray Dog* (directed by Kurosawa Akira) and *Yellow Crow* (directed by Gosho Heinosuke). By exploring these two works' narrative strategies, I trace how returnees were transformed in popular imagination. Through the figures of former soldiers, the films normalized the war into quotidian human dramas. Moreover, as postwar Japanese society began to enjoy a high-growth economy, it further distanced itself from the legacies of war and its reminders: on the screen, the war veterans were transformed into law-abiding citizens, who would then be welcomed back in middle-class families.

The second chapter, "The Story of a Man Who Was Not Allowed to Come Home: Gomikawa Junpei and *The Human Condition* (*Ningen no jōken*)," examines Gomikawa Junpei's novel *The Human Condition* (1956–1958), whose six volumes sold 20 million copies combined. I show how Gomikawa's story operated in the popular imagination. He rewrote his personal experiences—he survived a battle against the Soviet army at the end of the war and returned to Japan in 1947—as a tale of heroic struggle within Japan's military regime and, in so doing, rehabilitated the images of the vanquished. In his novel, by forbidding his protagonist, Kaji, to return to postwar Japan, Gomikawa refused to replicate his culture's narrative of repatriation and Japan's normalization. Yet Kaji's absence also signaled the author's desire to erect a boundary between the war and the postwar. Gomikawa was an exceptional case among the returnees in that while he conflicted with the media's images of war, he gained the power to modify them.

The third chapter, "Longing for Home: Japanese POWs in Soviet Captivity and Their Repatriation," discusses the POWs' Siberian experiences and postwar Japan's muted response to their return. Because they lacked control over their own destiny, these soldiers did not fit the profile of tragic war heroes who willingly sacrificed their lives for the sake of nation. Whatever hardships they suffered in Siberia, they worked for the Soviet Union's—not Japan's—reconstruction efforts. Furthermore, the widespread postwar fear of the Soviet Union turned, by association, these former detainees into unmentionable beings.

The fourth chapter, "'No Denunciation': Ishihara Yoshirō's Soviet Internment Experiences," focuses on the poet Ishihara Yoshirō, who struggled to articulate his experiences through his writing. For him, poetry was the form through which he could express the whirlwind of emotions he experienced once he returned to Japan in 1953. As traumatic as his Siberian experiences were, he tried to embrace them as the basis of his postwar self. His series of highly abstract poems became the site of his struggle to bridge the past and the present. It took him more than a decade to gain enough distance from his memories of Siberia to articulate what compelled him to write these poems. Reexperiencing the past through writing was never an easy task for Ishihara, and he was condemned to live in the chasm between a successful literary career and the trauma that compelled him to write in the first place.

The final three chapters highlight former Japanese army soldiers who were "discovered" on small South Pacific islands more than a quarter century after the war's end. Chapter 5, "Lost and Found in the South Pacific: Postwar Japan's Mania Over Yokoi Shōichi's Return," and chapter 6, "Rescued from the Past: Onoda Hiro'o's Endless War," discuss Yokoi Shōichi and Onoda Hiro'o, who returned, respectively, from Guam and Lubang, in the Philippines, in the early 1970s. Their dramatic reentries into the contemporary world stirred up memories of war, revealing it to be unfinished business. The Japanese media went into representational overdrive, generating excessive coverage of their return to Japan and their subsequent lives. Yokoi and Onoda were treated as the last missing pieces of a jigsaw puzzle. With them, the process of reassembling a Japan shattered by war and defeat supposedly came to an end.

The final chapter, "The Homecoming of the 'Last Japanese Soldier': Nakamura Teruo / Shiniyuwu / Li Guanghui's Postwar," describes the chasm between Japan's national narrative of war and the lived experiences of the belated returnees, which had grown to be unbridgeable in the thirty years since defeat. This chasm was most vividly demonstrated by the case of Nakamura Teruo, an indigenous Taiwanese. His homecoming, to Taiwan, gained only modest media attention in Japan. Nakamura's multiple identities embodied in his three names—former Japanese, indigenous Taiwanese, and citizen of the Republic of China—and his return to Taiwan made it difficult to embrace his experiences as a Japanese story. Moreover, the timing of his return was unfortunate: the Japanese media were not willing to revise the formula that they had devised for covering Yokoi's and Onoda's cases. Within the narrative of Japanese repatriation that the media had forcefully brought to a close, Nakamura's case was largely disregarded as incomprehensible excess.

These chapters thus offer records of the belated returnees' difficult journeys into the uncharted territory of postwar Japan rather than heroic tales of their recovery of ownership of their own histories. These men were strangers in their homeland searching for a place they could genuinely call home. Some were more successful than others in their quests, but they all walked a common cultural terrain, one profoundly shaped by the media's representations of the earlier returnees. Finally, the epilogue shows how the narrative of lost soldiers undermined the rigid boundaries between war and postwar. While acknowledging the power of the cultural images, this book concludes by insisting that it did not subsume the lost soldiers' entire experiences.

Yoshida Ichirō (Itō Yūnosuke) returns to Japan after spending nine years in China, *Yellow Crow* (1957).

Chapter One

LIFE AFTER THE WAR

Former Servicemen in Postwar Japanese Film

Just as the past is inseparable from remembrance, it is impossible to discuss historical events apart from historical descriptions. Historical events gain the status of historical facts only by being shaped through the narrative act.

NOGE KEI'ICHI, *PHILOSOPHY OF TALES: YANAGITA KUNIO AND THE DISCOVERY OF HISTORY*
(*MONOGATARI NO TETSUGAKU—YANAGITA KUNIO TO REKISHI NO HAKKEN*)

[At a Holocaust conference in Los Angeles in 1988] I tried to explain that one has to use the information and give shape to it in order to help people understand what happened—that historians, in fact, do that as much as any artist—but that history was far too important to leave solely to historians.

ART SPIEGELMAN, *META MAUS*

POSTWAR JAPAN'S CULTURAL TERRAIN

This chapter explores the ways in which two films—Kurosawa Akira's *Stray Dog* (*Nora inu*, 1949) and Gosho Heinosuke's *Yellow Crow* (*Kiiroi karasu*, 1957)[1]—represent former servicemen during the period in which Japan was first recovering from war damages and beginning to take the path of high-growth economy. My primary aim here is to draw a rough map of postwar Japan's cultural terrain in which the belated returnees faced the challenge of forging new identities.

Although the figures of civilian repatriates disappeared from the media shortly after the war, representations of former servicemen continued to populate the Japanese cinema as stand-ins for Japan's troubled past. The problematic images of repatriated soldiers on the screen made it clear that everything did not automatically fall into place upon their return. In the film the soldiers were often portrayed as menacing figures for the postwar social order, figures that invoked dreadful images of Japan's war and defeat. They also appeared as men who desperately needed the support of family and friends. These characters often dealt with the shadow of war as well as the social tension caused by their return home, serving as the medium through which filmmakers and audiences worked out the troubling memories of the past. The evolving depictions in these films signified the growing distance between contemporary Japanese society and wartime. In the early postwar years, veterans appeared as ambivalent figures that demanded social and media attention. The two films that I discuss in this chapter remind us that the legacies of war were still a fact of life in Japanese society in the late 1940s and 1950s and that these war legacies needed to be dealt with and, if possible, embraced, regardless of the unpleasant emotions they might trigger.

I first examine the ways in which *Stray Dog* imagines the figures of former servicemen against the chaotic conditions of the late 1940s and then shift the focus to *Yellow Crow*, which places a veteran character—a man who makes a belated return from China—in a middle-class family of the mid-1950s. Whereas *Stray Dog* tries to divide and conquer the war memories through the two antithetical images of the former servicemen, *Yellow Crow* is an effort to reconcile with the wartime past by symbolically reintegrating the belated returnee into home. The following readings call attention to, along with the inner workings of each narrative, a submotif threaded throughout these two films: economic conditions used as an explanatory tool. The characters' ethical and psychological struggles are translated into their ability to adapt to the new postwar reality, in which the economy became the nation's primary concern. While they may be critical of the money-obsessed contemporary society, these films ultimately privilege the economy as a tool to explain away Japan's troubled past. Translated into economic impoverishment, the persisting memories of war register as a remediable condition in a society that had already begun to enjoy the benefits of economic recovery and growth. I chose *Stray Dog* and *Yellow Crow* to represent the periods before and after the advent of Japan's high-growth economy. The two films were part of the larger cultural landscape in which the images of former servicemen were either rehabilitated or rejected. It was this same cultural landscape that awaited the belated repatriates upon their return to Japan.

FORMER SERVICEMEN IN JAPANESE FILM

The popularity of Japanese films surged after the war as people began to seek affordable forms of entertainment in peacetime. Even though the Japanese film industry suffered setbacks before and after the defeat,

Japanese studios saw a steady increase in their annual production of films in the second half of the 1940s.[2] The industry's rapid expansion continued into the following decade, with more than 1 billion movie tickets sold annually from 1957 through 1960 (with the total population growing from 91.2 million to 93.4 million during that time).[3] The rapid rise of the film industry coincided with the upward swing of the larger Japanese economy, which began in the mid-1950s. Although attendance numbers dropped precipitously in subsequent years—as film lost much of its audience to television—Japanese film was a powerful presence in the everyday life of early postwar Japan.[4]

Watching film was more than a popular entertainment in the early postwar years, according to social critic Tsurumi Shunshuke (1922–2015). Reflecting on his own immediate postwar year experiences, Tsurumi observed:

> During the several years after Japan's defeat, juveniles and youths filled the movie theaters spared from air raids. They watched film to explore their own lives. Back then, film was the main form through which to express ideas and a forum in which the Japanese thought collectively. Looking back at the films that I watched in those years, such films as *Blue Mountains* (*Aoi sanmyaku*, 1949), *Children Hand in Hand* (*Te o tunagu kora*, 1947), *Drunken Angel* (*Yoidore tenshi*, 1948), *Carmen Comes Home* (*Karumen kokyō ni kaeru*, 1951), *Ikiru* (1952), [and] *Godzilla* (*Gojira*, 1954), I believe, were in the middle of a lively exchange between their makers and [their] viewers.[5]

To Tsurumi, viewing films in crowded theaters constituted an intensive dialogue in which the filmmakers and the audience collectively explored what it meant to live in the postwar era.

While the films that Tsurumi lists broadly focus on postwar Japanese society, other works explored the war more explicitly. When the Occupation authority's censorship was lifted in 1949 and Japan formally regained its independence in 1952, film studios began producing films based on the recent war. A number of films also portrayed soldiers who returned from the front after Japan's defeat (including, from Tsurumi's list, *Children Hand in Hand*). These war films, as well as the works that feature war veterans, offered their contemporary audience an opportunity to work through Japan's troubled relationship with its recent past. Yet the "popular" nature of this entertainment meant that the studios' commercial concerns strongly constrained each work. The shadow of the wartime past was projected onto the screen to be resolved through cinematic devices. Although no single formula or narrative could completely explain away Japan's humiliating defeat, filmmakers were compelled to offer a satisfactory closure at the end of each work, regardless of the themes and subjects they had experimented with in their films.

The numerous films that featured former servicemen collectively attested to the ambivalent attitude that prevailed in postwar Japanese society: the memories of war were simultaneously abhorred and embraced. No matter how traumatic the memories were, they were an integral part of the postwar present. A majority of these works fell on a spectrum between two extreme treatments of the returned soldiers. On one end are works that depict the returned soldier as a threat to the postwar social order; these films' narratives culminate in the protagonist's death. *Iron Claws* (*Tetsu no tsume*, directed by Adachi Nobuo, 1951), for example, is about a man who becomes psychotic after being clawed by a gorilla while fighting at the southern front:[6] whenever he consumes alcohol, he behaves like a monstrous animal. In the end, the protagonist kills himself to save his wife and protect the postwar order. On the other end of the spectrum are such stories as *No Consultation Today* (*Honjitsu kyūshin*, directed by Shibuya Minoru, 1952) in which a returnee character suffers from posttraumatic stress disorder: he believes that he is still in the war and acts out his delirium. Nonetheless, his community warmly embraces the returnee, unconditionally accepting both him and his never-ending war.[7]

Crime and Punishment: *Stray Dog*

Director Kurosawa Akira (1910–1998) oscillated between these two extreme characterizations of the repatriated soldiers in his depiction of their postwar lives in four of his early postwar films. In *One Wonderful Sunday* (*Subarashiki nichiyōbi*, 1947), the young veteran protagonist, though penniless, finds hope for the future with his girlfriend in a bombed-out city. By contrast, *Drunken Angel* (*Yoidore tenshi*, 1948) features a different type of ex-soldier character, a *yakuza* (gangster) who suffers from tuberculosis.[8] The illness serves as a marker for the disquieting wartime past that drives the soldier to self-destructive behavior. Illness as a metaphor for the historical conditions becomes a central motif again in *The Quiet Duel* (*Shizuka naru kettō*, 1949). The main character is an army doctor who accidentally contracts syphilis during an operation at a field hospital at the southern front. As in the case of *Iron Claws*, the region broadly referred as the South (*nanpō*)—a symbol of Japan's colonial expansion and war—is marked as the original site of trauma.[9] Even after being safely repatriated, the doctor suffers from the illness, unable to resume a normal life. The film nevertheless offers a hopeful ending by suggesting that despite his continuing battle against syphilis, he will fulfill his duty as a doctor and eventually overcome his adverse condition. *Stray Dog* (*Nora inu*, 1949) presents a narrative device that accommodates the conflicting images of the former servicemen by portraying two contrasting veteran characters: a criminal and a detective. Being a repatriated soldier is no longer an incurable or hard-to-treat illness but a condition that one can conquer through willpower. Kurosawa thus contained the troublesome figures of repatriated soldiers by ultimately holding them responsible for their own fate.[10]

Stray Dog domesticates the threat—criminality—of former soldiers by explaining it away as part of the economic confusion in postwar society. In the early chaotic conditions of postwar Japan, self-discipline was the greatest deterrent keeping individuals from falling into the criminal world. Whereas the film's narrative highlights individual willpower as a remedy for social problems, the images—particularly bodily images—on the screen indicate the depth and prevalence of moral confusion in society. Being liberated from oppressive wartime regulations, bodies were celebrated as sites of unbound personal desire and new sensual experiences in postwar Japan.

In *Stray Dog*, however, bodies appear mostly as conditions to be overcome. Despite their ubiquitous presence on the screen, bodies are ultimately relegated to a secondary role of highlighting the director's moral message. The possible connections between bodies—particularly sexualized bodies—and the former servicemen's alleged criminality are carefully concealed. One of the key veteran characters, for example, does not appear on the screen until the end of the film; he is reduced to a ghostlike figure in a society filled with bodily images. In other words, his struggles in postwar society are rendered invisible and register instead only as abstract criminality. His place in society becomes "visible" through his unlawful acts that cause bodily injuries to other citizens.

Despite Kurosawa's unwillingness to explore the corporeal dimension of criminality in *Stray Dog*, bodily desire was at the core of some transgressive acts in the early postwar period. A cursory look at contemporary crimes committed by former servicemen underscores the corporeal basis of social anxiety in the immediate postwar years. On October 5, 1949, less than two weeks before *Stray Dog* was released, the serial rapist-murderer Kodaira Yoshio (1905–1949) was executed at the Miyagi penitentiary. Following his arrest on August 20, 1946, Kodaira admitted having raped and killed seven women in or near Tokyo between May 1945 and August 1946 (as well as raping fifty additional victims).

Kodaira's criminal career began in, and was assisted by, the growing social chaos as Japan neared its defeat. Abandoned in a bomb shelter, the body of his first murder victim was not found for almost six weeks. And even after the military police discovered it, they lacked the resources and manpower to connect the crime to Kodaira.[11] As the psychiatrist Uchimura Yūshi suggests in his psychiatric evaluation, the combination of the reduced police capacity and the general decline of moral standards at the time may well have led to Kodaira's later crimes.[12] With the rate of serious crimes rapidly rising, his crimes became symbolic of the postwar turmoil. Kodaira's method of enticement—he lured the victims into secluded areas with the promise of food or a job—worked in immediate postwar Japan precisely because millions were scrambling to secure employment and sustenance. Kodaira thus preyed on the desperation of women in dire financial straits. Media scholar Fujitake Akira adds that Kodaira's crimes had another powerful link to postwar society: "The *Sun Photo* newspaper carried a photo of the naked victim [the first victim linked to Kodaira] as a full front-page image. That was a gruesome photo. I remember, besides being a shocking image, it also bore a strange sense of liberation, like looking at an erotic image."[13] The media's fascination with Kodaira's sex crimes had the unintended effect of confirming the new libidinal economy in postwar Japan.

For his Japanese contemporaries, Kodaira's heinous crimes also brought home the war in the most dreadful manner. Although he was not an active serviceman during the Asia Pacific War, he had been a volunteer in the Japanese Imperial Navy's land-based unit from 1923 to 1929. In 1928, he was dispatched to Shandong Province, China, as part of the military intervention to protect the Japanese residents and business in the area. According to his preliminary interrogation, while stationed in Shandong Province, Kodaira and his fellow soldiers brutally raped and killed a number of Chinese women. To the police interrogator, he calmly answered: "Robbery and rape are routines for the Japanese military. We stabbed [Chinese women] with bayonets, and sometimes stabbed pregnant women with bayonets and extracted their fetuses. I did that to five or six women. I did pretty awful things."[14] The former serviceman Kodaira was a dreadful figure precisely because his confessions reenacted war crimes in a postwar Japan.

Writing about Kodaira's crimes in 1962, the writer Esaki Masanori recalled the gruesome evidence of colonial violence he had witnessed as a serviceman in wartime China. Remembering the bodies of local women who were raped and killed by Japanese soldiers, Esaki attempted to exceptionalize what he saw during the war. Although he emphasizes the abnormal psychology of war that caused the war crimes, this psychological defense ultimately fails to distract him from the case's obvious implications: "I am horrified by the fact that a number of Japanese soldiers acted like Kodaira at the front. It means that there are countless men among us [in postwar Japan] who are like Kodaira."[15] Esaki's thinking echoes what many thought as they learned about Kodaira's crimes and personal history, and Kodaira's violent acts forced postwar Japan to confront its inconvenient truths.

It's the Economy

In many ways, *Stray Dog* was a response to the social anxiety of late 1940s Japan, with which the media coverage of Kodaira Yoshio's cases deeply resonated. Yet the filmmakers obviously took creative license in producing a narrative that transcended the immediate social conditions. In comparison to the abominable veteran—the man "with human appearance and beastly mind," in his own words[16]—the former serviceman/criminal in *Stray Dog* appears far less menacing, even though he does kill one of his victims.[17] The villain in the film—the former soldier Yusa Shinjirō (Kimura Isao)—is humanized despite the crimes that he commits.

Yusa spends his postwar days in despair, unable to adjust to a radically changed Japan. He is a loser and victim in the new postwar society—he had his rucksack stolen when he was repatriated to Japan—in which material interests dominate, having displaced the martial concerns of yesterday. To please his dancer friend, Namiki Harumi (Awaji Keiko), Yusa wishes to buy her a fancy dress, but without the money to pay for it, he turns to crime. His desire for meaningful relations with another individual drives him into antisocial behavior, further deepening his agony.

Two women who witness Yusa's distress speak on his behalf, articulating his feelings for him. His sister explains the tormented state of her brother's mind to the two detectives: "I found him here in the dark, crying with his head in his hands. He kind of scared me." Being the closest person to him, his sister correctly sensed the depth of his despair. But she can express it only as something that scares her.

By contrast, Harumi, the object of Yusa's affection, emphatically defends him: "He committed a crime for me. But I would've stolen it [the dress] myself if I'd had the guts. They deserve it for flaunting these things in the show windows. We have to do worse than steal if we want things like this." Harumi does not interpret but ventriloquizes Yusa's murmurs about his frustrated life. Her logic is so generic that it does not sufficiently explain the nature of his frustration. Yusa does not seem to have any other means but violence—the language that he learned in the war—to express his deep feelings. Decoupled from bodily desires, he exists throughout the film only as an abstract threat to society.[18] The audience does not see him for the first 111 minutes of the film, and by the time he finally appears on the screen, only 11 minutes are left.

In contrast to Yusa's body-less presence, Detective Murakami (Mifune Toshirō), also a former serviceman, appears on the screen as a man with a powerful physique and a strong sense of justice, struggling to live a principled life against postwar Japan's moral decay.[19] He is also an emasculated figure in a different way: he has his gun stolen in a crowded bus, and Yusa later commits armed robberies and murder using Murakami's stolen gun. With it, the two veterans' lives are conjoined. Murakami follows the traces left by the gun to close in on Yusa's shadowy figure. To Murakami, the confusions in the immediate postwar years are temporary: Japanese society will recover its original state by restoring law and order. As the writer Noma Hiroshi bluntly put it, the soldiers used to be "domesticated dogs" in the emperor's military. But once the war was over, they were relieved of their duties and unleashed into postwar society with little or no support.[20] Murakami appropriately finds a new home in law enforcement, which is reminiscent of the military.

The film differentiates between the two institutions—military and law enforcement—by having Murakami's police section chief correct his military manner of speech. This correction, however, only emphasizes the continuity of Murakami's transition. Murakami has not completely shaken off his military identity. His police-issued gun is a transitional object that helps him establish his footing in postwar society. But he has yet to gain a meaningful distance from the war, in which he witnessed "men turning into beasts at the slightest provocation, over and over." Murakami's words echo those of the rapist-murder Kodaira, who claimed that during the war he had seen other soldiers commit worse crimes than his own.[21]

Murakami is aware of his own impulse toward destructive behavior, though he never acts on it. In a conversation with his senior partner, Satō (Shimura Takashi), he recalls his difficult reentry into Japanese society. For instance, when he discovered that his rucksack had been stolen on the repatriation train (Yusa had the same experience), he "was outraged and could easily have pulled off a robbery." But realizing that "I was at a dangerous crossroads, I applied for my present job." Fighting crime as a member of the police force is Murakami's way of maintaining his integrity amid the moral chaos of the postwar period. Because he is honest about his own dark feelings, Murakami is both sympathetic to and resentful of Yusa, who made the opposite decision at the same crossroads.

The film intimates that the world to which the two men have come back has lost its traditional mores. While the film makes obvious sexual references in its critique of contemporary society, it stops short of directly engaging in a dialogue about sexuality. Career criminal Ogin, who steals Murakami's handgun in the opening scene, was once known by her kimono and Japanese hairstyle. But when she appears on the screen, she wears a Western summer dress, a permanent wave, and cheap perfume just like a *panpan*, a prostitute who, for many observers, epitomized the moral decay of postwar Japan. She utters a cliché phrase thrown around in the new "democratic" Japan— "I'm gonna sue you for a violation of human rights"—to fend off Murakami's persistent questioning.[22] She also gives a feisty "bye-bye" to him and his senior colleague as she walks off.

It is not her new appearance but the fact that Ogin stole the gun that amazes the senior detective: her reputation, after all, was as a specialist at pickpocketing cash. As his observation—"she must have hit the skids"— implies, she used to have a style but is now reduced to stealing anything in order to satisfy her greed. Even in the criminal world, the traditional rule of knowing one's bounds seems to have been replaced by an insatiable desire paired with the postwar habit of self-assertion. Ogin also utters words that put Japanese society's transition into a long perspective. After giving into Murakami's persistent entreaty and giving him a clue to where to find his gun, she looks up at the sky: "For the past twenty years or so, I have completely forgotten about those wonderful stars." Ogin's timeline of twenty years implicitly refers to Japan's long war, which began with the Manchurian incident in 1931, as well as to the postwar chaos. Japan is finally regaining its peace—the stars that used to adorn the servicemen's insignia are back up in the sky—but the two veterans are forced to adjust to a world without stars. The young detective's determination to restore order in Japanese society seems to help the career criminal reflect on the frenzy of the recent past.

Ogin's decision to steal the detective's gun despite the considerable risk can also be explained in economic terms. Under Japan's hyperinflation—wholesale prices increased almost seventyfold between 1945 and 1949—the currency lost its luster. Consequently, thieves, being sensitive to market trends, valued tangible objects more highly than cash. Ogin probably grew used to the new economy in the early years of the postwar period while inflation was largely curtailed by the new, austere financial policies adopted in 1949. Former Prime Minster Miyazawa Ki'ichi had an interesting exchange with Joseph Dodge, a chairman of the Detroit Bank who visited Japan in 1949 and helped implement a superbalanced budget to combat Japan's out-of-control inflation. In the fall of that year, when Miyazawa mentioned to Dodge a newspaper article about a thief who stole some cash, Dodge saw that as a good sign: the fact that the criminal chose the cash meant that inflation was under control and trust in the currency had begun to be restored.[23] Dodge's economic plan imposed fiscal discipline on Japan's economy, which was overheating under governmental policy whose priority was a swift recovery from the war's economic devastation. Within a few years of Japan's defeat, Japanese policymakers' concerns had begun to shift from the immediate survival of the people to long-term concerns about the overall health of Japan's economy.

The Heat Is On

In *Stray Dog*, Japanese society is overheating with pleasure seeking. The film slides between economic and corporeal representations when describing the lure of frivolous consumption. Throughout the film, Kurosawa uses bodily fluid—sweat—as a trope with which to visualize postwar individuals' desire, which, untethered from the wartime regime's repressive controls, filled society. The film opens with the narrator announcing, "It was a dreadfully hot day." In the hot summer days that follow, the drama unfolds, and the characters incessantly fan and wipe the sweat from their faces and necks. Sweat persists in the film and is most visible on the female dancers' faces and half-naked bodies as they rest after performing onstage. This backstage scene resonates with the film's opening image: a dog panting heavily, its tongue hanging out in the heat of the summer. From long shots to medium shots, then to medium-closeup shots, the camera incrementally focuses on panting female—animalistic—bodies covered with sweat as objects of, and the hosts for, insuppressible desire. In the heat—hustle and bustle—of the postwar period, individuals were covered with sweat—an external sign of their own lust and greed. It may be displayed inside the vaudeville theater or its dressing room, but something as intimate as sweat must be controlled once in the general public space.

Murakami has his share of sweat—he takes the heat for his mistake and runs around searching for his gun—but mostly he manages to suppress it beneath his formal appearance. He is smartly dressed in a suit and tie and, occasionally, also in a hat. He may take off his jacket but never his tie, except when he disguises himself as a destitute former serviceman, when he dons a threadbare army uniform, to search the black markets. As the mecca of legal and illegal consumption, the black markets swelter with heat.[24] After days of investigation, Murakami finally arrests a female liaison between the gun dealer and his customers (but fails to recover his gun). During this scene, Murakami appears drenched in his own sweat, a sign that he does not hesitate to dive into the slime of the underground world. Meanwhile, the woman recalls Yusa "wearing a winter suit in this heat." Yusa is unable to feel the heat in the frenzy of postwar Japanese society—he is socially dead—and seeks a hot gun as a remedy.

Interestingly, the only person who does not sweat profusely in the film is Yusa's brother-in-law, a cooper, who works on a bucket while Murakami and Satō ask his wife about Yusa. He is also the only person who engages in manual labor and produces things with use value. The impoverished life that he and his family are forced to endure attests to the injustice of the postwar economy: he is not rewarded for his honest work because his product is left behind in the fast-changing market. Meanwhile, although the dancers sweat as a result of their hard work, their labor, as part of service industry, does not produce any tangible objects. They are consumed by and with the overheated economy. Their bodies continue to produce sweat—frivolous excess—and spin out of control. Namiki Harumi's modest living reveals the large gulf between the actual impoverished condition of the Japanese economy and the glittering veneer that the dancers produce onstage. To find out Yusa's whereabouts, Murakami and Satō visit Harumi in the old, dingy one-room apartment where she and her mother live. She first appears in *yukata*, a casual summer kimono. But in defiance of Murakami's admonishing words, Harumi changes into the fancy dress that Yusa has given her. In the dress, she spins quickly in the room shouting, "This is wonderful, so wonderful, like a dream," until her mother—who is dressed in kimono—slaps her face and stops her. Harumi's working-class body is taken over by the power of consumption, ultimately surrendering control. In the absence of a father figure, the mother behaves as a guardian of social mores. By introducing a dichotomy between the Japanese kimono and Western dress, the film indicts the United States as well, the country that represents the West to the defeated nation, as the true driving force behind the superfluous economy.

Further underscoring this dichotomy is Murakami's Colt pistol, a U.S.-made gun. In 1949, Japan was still under the U.S.-led Occupation, feeling the deep effects of defeat. Murakami's gun, a property of the police that was used to commit crimes, marks the problematic presence of the United States in postwar Japanese society. On the one hand, the American weapon buttresses Murakami's postwar project of reconstituting himself as a proud Japanese man, but on the other hand, the same weapon assaults his pride as a law enforcement officer. Even with the gun in his hand, Yusa does not recover his masculine self. The firearm seems to acquire a life of its own while circulating as a commodity, and it drives the two former servicemen—its legitimate and illegitimate owners—into action. In the confusion of the postwar period, there obviously are many American guns in circulation, contributing to the underground economy. One of Murakami's senior colleagues admits as much when he tells him, "There are many Colts other than yours." Satō, meanwhile, emphasizes the interchangeability of the weapons: "If he didn't have a Colt, he [Yusa] would have done it with a Browning." These men try to absorb Murakami's guilt for having lost the particular gun by treating it much like currency—the market does not care who used to own it. The senior law enforcement officers are more concerned about there being too many guns in circulation, driving the underground economy out of control.

The film makes no mention of the possibility that in addition to his economic difficulties, the suspect might be suffering under the weight of his war experiences. This troublesome past returns in the film's climax when Murakami arrests Yusa in the nick of time before he escapes from Tokyo. In the woods on the city's outskirts, Murakami chases and confronts the suspect.[25] The muddy water on Yusa's and Murakami's clothes is a visual maker for the proximity of Japan's war and its postwar existence. The detective first identifies the suspect because of the mud splashed on his white linen suit, the outcome of the previous night's escape in the rain. In the end, both Yusa's and Murakami's smart outfits are soiled. The woods of Tokyo are transformed into a battleground where the two former servicemen engage in combat. Despite its glittering appearance, postwar society is still fighting a war. The war against the Allied powers is thus transformed into a Japanese battle in which postwar society fights its own war memories, as enacted by a former soldier. In this postwar battle, war memories—and, by extension, the veteran—must be normalized; what refuses normalization must be disciplined.

In the pairing of the two former servicemen, this tumultuous postwar society ceases to be the cause of their anguish and instead effectively disappears into the background. The cool air of the early morning and the water on the ground, rather than the oppressive summer heat, dominate the scene. The economy is reduced to the two men's more personal exchange—the barter of the weapon and the handcuffs—through which

Murakami recovers his gun and reclaims his agency. Confronted by Murakami, Yusa fires the gun with his left hand (he is left-handed), injuring the detective in his left arm. Yusa throws the gun away after using up the bullets, and Murakami recovers the long-sought object. It is not the weapon per se but the injury it causes that empowers Murakami. A close-up shot focuses on the blood that drips from his left arm after he is shot.[26] Murakami's injury is foreshadowed in an earlier scene in which he gives blood, from his left arm, to save Satō, whom Yusa has shot as well. Murakami's blood compensates for the mistake that led to his senior colleague's injury. While sweat is a sign of the postwar frenzy—the condition to be overcome—the blood that Murakami sheds establishes his innate membership in Japan's postwar society. Murakami's injury lets him stand among Yusa's victims, making up for the fact that his gun initially enabled the latter's crime spree. He is then allowed to fight on behalf of postwar society against the threat that Yusa poses.

Yusa's criminality and identity as a former serviceman are the principal drivers of the vague anxiety about the disquieting memories in postwar society. As he is symbolically removed from the current moment, Yusa carries with him the burden of history. In other words, Yusa is a veteran sacrificed for the sake of relieving postwar society of the burden of its troubled past. As such, he is not allowed to speak for himself, although the community expresses and expel its anxiety through him. When the two characters fall onto the ground side by side, finally meeting their adversaries, the film reaches its climax. At this point, the screen image and accompanying sound reveal the film's multifaceted message. The two men pant heavily on the bottom half of the screen while a group of children walk across the top half from right to left singing the song "Butterfly" (Chōcho). This visual dichotomy is a stark representation of the chasm separating the two worlds (figure 1.1).[27] As soon as the chase is over, the peaceful everyday life returns to the screen, reminding the audience of the fundamental incongruity of persistent war in the postwar world. This scene employs the method that Kurosawa called "counterpoint," denoting his strategic choice of rather mismatched music or sound to intensify the emotion of a scene through contrast.[28] Musically and visually contrasted with the peaceful order of postwar life, the struggle between the two repatriated soldiers exposes the darkness nesting inside them and postwar society. By recovering his gun and handcuffing

FIGURE 1.1 Murakami with his gun (*left*) and Yusa Shinjirō in handcuffs, *Stray Dog* (1949).

Yusa, Murakami liberates himself from the darkness while Yusa appears to sink deep into the ground under the weight of the burden, plus Murakami's and postwar society's darkness. Whereas the children's song suggests peace to the audience, Yusa's animal-like wail reveals the violent past that is still present—albeit no longer comprehensible—in postwar society.

The wounds, both physical and metaphorical, are healed in the final scene. Murakami visits Satō, who is recovering from the gunshot wound, in a hospital room. Murakami wears a white, short-sleeved, open-collared shirt. Murakami is no longer in the heat now that he has recovered his gun and arrested Yusa. Satō's room is filled with soft morning light. Although Satō gently waves a fan, the oppressive summer heat appears to have broken, and sweat has ceased to be Murakami's immediate concern. The short dialogue between the two men reveals subtle differences between the one who returned from the war and the other who stayed home. Murakami confides to Satō that arresting the suspect was not all cathartic, saying, "But I just can't get that Yusa [out of my mind]." Completely disregarding the rookie detective's sympathy for a fellow former serviceman, Satō gives him a generic response as a veteran police detective: "I remember feeling that way myself. You somehow always remember your first arrest."

Satō then proceeds to offer advice as a senior detective: "Forget about Yusa. Yes, as soon as your arm heals, you'll be busy again. You'll naturally forget all about Yusa." But the traces of a frustrated war veteran are forever inscribed on Murakami's body. To the optimistic remark by his senior colleague, Murakami remains silent, looking out a window. As if to resist the weight of Satō's words, he looks up into the sky right before the scene fades out to the closing title. As the film scholar Mitsuhiro Yoshimoto pointed out, Murakami's momentary hesitation in this scene attests to Kurosawa's emotional ties with the past.[29] In *Stray Dog*, the wartime past already has been displaced by more recent memories of postwar struggle with the past. Against Satō's straightforward logic supported by his worldly experience, these recent memories do not seem to stand a chance of lingering much longer, as they survive on the screen only as a fleeting image of Murakami's tentative gesture.

Stray Dog reveals that in 1949 Japan, former soldiers still were regarded as problematic. They were supposedly fellow citizens, though their affinities with the war and violence made them at best marginal, if not threatening, figures. Yusa's troubled existence is much like a ghost that haunts postwar society. His frustration is translated into economic hardship, and it becomes visible only through his economically motivated crimes—which are, in reality, merely a desperate effort to register his suffering. The veteran's existential angst is thus reduced to antisocial activities, which are dealt with as one of the numerous law enforcement issues facing postwar society. The detective Murakami serves as a medium who translates Yusa's frustration, but neither Murakami nor postwar Japan appears to possess the language with which to fully express that frustration.

Return to the Middle-Class Life: *Yellow Crow*

Whereas *Stray Dog* assuages the alleged criminality of the repatriated former servicemen in the social space, *Yellow Crow* (*Kiiroi karasu*, 1957) works to ameliorate the belated returnees' existential homelessness in the domestic sphere. A cartoon from an early postwar year captures the potential hazards of the late repatriations, which the mainstream media

FIGURE 1.2 Mutsu'ura Mitsuo, "Madam, Welcome Makeup," *Manga: miru jikyoku zasshi*, July 1949, 7.

often glossed over. Cartoonist Mutsu'ura Mitsuo (1913–1969), best known for his pathos-filled depictions of early postwar city scenes, published a work entitled "Madam, Welcome Makeup" (Okusama, omukae keshō) in the July 1949 issue of *Manga: Visual Magazine on Contemporary Issues* (*Manga: miru jikyoku zasshi*) (figure 1.2).[30] The repatriation from the Soviet Union that resumed in June 1949 after a six-month interruption is the subtext of Mutsu'ura's work, which portrays a worst-case scenario for the returnees: they discover the hard way that home is not what it is cracked up to be.

In Mutsu'ura's cartoon, a man stands at the house entrance facing his wife and their five children. He is only partially visible—part of his back and left arm—but it is clear from the label on his small bag, which reads "the Siberian district," that he has just returned from Siberia. The children see him as a total stranger, and his wife tries to hide her complex emotions behind her tough gaze. Her dress, permed hair, and garish makeup suggest that in his absence, she has supported the family by becoming a *panpan*. Her expression silently screams, "Why now?" which perhaps contains a mixture of sadness and a tinge of relief. The domestic space is not what it used to be: the tears in the paper screen doors show that the life with five children has obviously not been easy. The man has returned to Japan under the U.S. Occupation and to a family supported by a *panpan* mother. We do not know who her clients are, but the connection between her sex work and the U.S. presence (and Japan's defeat) is clear. The presence of *geta* footwear, however, suggests the superficiality of the Americanization. The faceless man has nonetheless lost his place at home; his belated return is more a cause of pain than a relief from it. Now that he is home, however, the arrangements made in his absence must be undone and renegotiated. It is not clear whether there will be a happy family at the end of the renegotiation.[31]

In *Yellow Crow*, in keeping with his reputation as a director of middle-class film, director Gosho Heinosuke (1902–1981) devises a happy ending to the family drama surrounding a former serviceman, who returns home belatedly.[32] By the time the film was released in 1957, returned soldiers by and large had ceased to be a menacing existence, at least on screen. With the shadows of war fast receding into the background and its economy growing quickly, Japanese society (and Gosho) could afford to be more magnanimous and patient with the estranged members of its society. Now it is up to the returnees and their families to work out whatever issues they may have among themselves.

Yellow Crow is a family drama that revolves around the former soldier Yoshida Ichirō, who in 1953 returns after a nine-year absence from China to his wife, Machiko, who has long been waiting for his return, and their nine-year old son, Kiyoshi.[33] Although it is a happy occasion, the family's reunion alone is not enough to bring normalcy to their life. The father–son rivalry constitutes the key motif for this drama, with Kiyoshi's perturbed state of mind serving as a canvas on which his father's frustration is expressed and eventually worked out.

Among the films that portray former servicemen's lives after returning home, *Yellow Crow* is exceptional in recognizing that the psychological wounds left by the war cannot be easily healed. Having managed a difficult life alone with Kiyoshi, Machiko hopes that once her husband returns home, everything will be fine. But she gradually realizes that things are not actually that easy. Toward the end of the film, Machiko quietly tells Ichirō of her new insights: "When you came back last year, I was so relieved and believed that everything was going to be fine. But then I was too optimistic. The wounds that the war left were not so easy to heal." Her words contrast with the postwar media's short-term attention to the returnees' lives and the naive popular sentiment that everything would simply fall into place once the returnees arrived back in Japan.

Notwithstanding the historical sensitivity that Machiko's sentiment suggests, Ichirō's transnational history is reduced to a domestic psycho-drama in the bubble of middle-class life, shielded from social and economic concerns. Up until the midpoint of the drama, for example, Ichirō's detainment in China remains an important element that explains the familial tension. But once the film shifts its focus to the domestic discord, the detainment disappears from the narrative. Similarly, in an early scene, Ichirō realizes that he has much to catch up on at work, although this serves only to explain his impatience with his son. The main focus of the scene is not on his social readjustment but on his domestic life. The difficult experiences of coming home late and trying to adapt to postwar Japanese society are separated from the larger historical context—Japan's war and defeat—and are satisfactorily resolved instead through the family members' emotional work. In *Yellow Crow*, that middle-class life appears as more than just an economic goal of postwar Japan; it is also an ideological apparatus through which to seal off the troubling echoes of the wartime past.

Belated Return from China: History

Ichirō returned to Japan after being away for nine years, one of more than 26,000 Japanese who repatriated from China in 1953.[34] His difference—his distance from postwar society—is marked by the dark blue Mao suit that he is wearing when he lands at the wharf. No longer the imperial soldier he once was, he now is a foreigner in his homeland. The scene of his arrival is reminiscent of the return of the 811 internees from Siberia discussed in the introduction, whose Russian appearance became a cause of concern. The tentative steps Ichirō takes and the anxious expression on his face underscore the fact that the returned soldier is no longer a threat but more like a lost animal seeking a secure home. The film hints that

Ichirō was first sent to China as a soldier right after his son was born and subsequently was detained there.[35] However, the question of what he was doing there as both a soldier and a detainee is never addressed in the film's narrative, which revolves primarily around the place he lost in Japan during his absence. The film also does not show postwar society's deep suspicion of these belated returnees, a suspicion manifested as blatant employment discrimination.

In real life, like the returnees from the Soviet Union, those who returned late from the People's Republic of China (PRC) had difficulty securing a job in Japan. In the eyes of many prospective employers, their association with the Communist regime in China had turned them into a potential problem. For example, former Imperial Army lance corporal Okumura Waichi fought for the Nationalist government forces after Japan's defeat, became a POW of the People's Liberation Army, and eventually repatriated from China in 1954. Okumura was beleaguered by security police detectives on his return. He could not get a job, even at his cousin's auto shop because the latter was suspicious of "who knows what would happen at the shop with a guy who just came back from the PRC."[36] Former army private first class Koyabu Shigeyoshi returned from China with his wife and children in 1958, and he was also excluded from many jobs because of his associations with the Communist regime. Fortunately, he inherited a tinsmith shop from his father, but he had to learn the trade from scratch in his thirties.[37] When Maeda Fujie, who returned from the PRC in 1953, tried to have her nurse's license reissued at the Fukui prefectural office, the woman at the window rejected her request on the ground that "there are some people who dare come home now and lie [about their training] in order to obtain a license."[38]

Yellow Crow omits the issues of prejudice and discrimination, intimating that the problem is less social than personal and psychological in nature. The trading company for which Ichirō used to work immediately rehires him, though it takes some time for the employer to find him an appropriate position. His reentry is not without frustration—for instance, he must receive instructions from his junior colleague, who has leapfrogged past him in promotions during Ichirō's absence—but Ichirō is ultimately spared material concerns or worries stemming from financial difficulty. His larger-than-average family house has survived the war unscathed. Machiko seems to have had hardly any trouble supporting herself and Kiyoshi in the war and postwar years, unlike so many single mothers at the time. As soon as he returns home, Ichirō easily resumes his middle-class family life, in which everything is almost normal. The family drama hence serves as the laboratory for a psychological experiment, in which all the conditions remain constant except for Ichirō's psychological state and the presence of his nine-year-old son, who was born right before he left for the war. Rather, the tension that sets the plot in motion is the rivalry between Ichirō and his son for Machiko's affection.

Oedipal Drama at Home

Ichirō's return thus begins as a Freudian drama, in which the intimate relationship between mother and son is torn apart by the husband/father's reappearance. As a child, Kiyoshi was showered with his mother's affection. But once his father returns home, he is no longer able to monopolize his mother. Meanwhile, Ichirō is unable to extend fatherly love to his son because he is preoccupied with adapting to the new postwar society. The home then becomes an especially uncomfortable place for Kiyoshi after his sister Mitsuko is born. In the postwar triad formed by the newborn baby and her parents, Kiyoshi feels he has no place at home. He is symbolically pushed out of the family, not only as the father's sexual rival, but also as a reminder of the dark past: he is a memento of what Ichirō missed while he was in China. Unlike Oedipus's tragic end, however, the film ultimately culminates in the reconciliation of the two male characters. Kiyoshi is portrayed not as an independent person but as Ichirō's alter ego, who acts out his anxious state of mind. The act of embracing his son and being accepted by Kiyoshi in return therefore amounts to Ichirō's success in symbolically subsuming his war memories beneath the postwar reality of everyday life. The film that begins as a story of sexual rivalry ends as a drama that works through the unnamed yet troubling memories of war.

The father–son conflict comes to the fore over Ichirō's unspoken experiences in China, which are manifested through the small animals that Kiyoshi keeps in the closet of his room. His father reacts strongly to the creatures, suggesting deeper psychological issues rooted in his past. Ichirō categorically rejects his son's pets because they trigger the troubling memories of his detention. Although Kiyoshi may not be able to change the larger situation surrounding him, he finds solace in protecting and providing for his pet animals. But his happy time playing with them—a form of compensatory act for his perturbed family life—is disrupted by his father. In one scene, Kiyoshi tries to start a conversation by asking his father, "Do you like white mice?" Ichirō shows absolutely no interest in them: "I don't like them. In China, it is a rule to kill animals like mice that can carry bad bacteria." Even in talking about this seemingly trivial matter, Ichirō's experiences in China appear to create a fissure in his relationship with Kiyoshi. This fissure grows into a gulf when he denies his son's little world by insisting, "These things invite pests. How unhygienic! It is like raising bad bacteria. Haven't you learned that at school?" Ichirō's almost visceral reaction to Kiyoshi's "zoo" suggests that he is still not free from his experiences in recent years—perhaps especially from China's Patriotic Hygiene Campaign.

The PRC government launched its Patriotic Hygiene Campaign in northeastern China in March 1952, insisting that the United States had used bacteriological weapons in the region during the Korean War. During the campaign, local residents were encouraged to exterminate flies, mosquitoes, rats, lice, and bedbugs.[39] As the film scholar Liu Wenbing claims, the Manchukuo Film Association film *Lice Are Scary* (*Shirami wa kowai*, directed by Katō Tai, 1943) portrays the Japanese colonial efforts to transform "the unhygienic Chinese" into modern productive workers. In light of this symbolic representation, it is possible that Ichirō does not fear an unhygienic condition per se but that his wartime experiences in China will haunt his domestic space.[40] Invisible agents of illness serve as a metaphoric connection to the abhorrent past, much as syphilis does in Kurosawa's *The Quiet Duel*. But the eight-year gap between Kurosawa's film and *Yellow Crow* was sufficient to reduce the metaphor's efficacy. Even though the fear of syphilis was real to the 1949 audience, Ichirō's fear probably looked hyperbolic in 1957 Japan, which enjoyed far better hygienic conditions and easy access to antibiotics.

For Ichirō, who seeks a fresh start in the postwar, reminders of the past—including even his own son—pose a serious challenge. Unlike his baby sister Mitsuko, who is conceived and born after Ichirō's return, Kiyoshi maintains strong associations with the wartime past. Now home, Ichirō tries to move beyond the pain of his past. But his willful son has no intention of quietly honoring his father's wish. Despite being scolded by Ichirō, Kiyoshi refuses to abandon his animals; instead, he hides them in a cellar that used to be a bomb shelter. This relic of the war serves as an asylum where Kiyoshi is shielded from his father's anger. It also takes him back to the past when no father figure threatened the mother–son dyad. Yet the same shelter also serves as a place for discipline. Later, when Ichirō mistakenly believes that Kiyoshi's mischief caused his little sister to cry, he drags his son out to the yard and confines him in the cellar as a punishment. The father's forceful act is a symbolic threat that Kiyoshi may be banished into the past if he continues to resist his father's command.

Yellow Crow: A Symbol of Reconciliation

The second half of the film introduces a young crow that Kiyoshi captures, highlighting the color scheme of black and yellow. Of the various colors used in the film, the combination of black and yellow signals the troubled state of Kiyoshi's mind, according to color psychologist Asari Atsushi, whose work the filmmakers likely consulted.[41] Asari claimed that the contrast of black and yellow represents "the absence of the father." According to the color chart provided in his article, yellow represents "the desire for affection and reminiscence, as well as an inadequate amount of love."[42] The fact that Yellow Crow was the first color film that Gosho Heinosuke directed amplifies the film's psychological bent. In order to take advantage of the colors on the screen, the director utilized contemporary psychologists' work positing correlations between children's uses of specific colors and their mental state.[43]

While colors serve as tools to visualize the internal struggles of each character, particularly that of the nine-year-old boy Kiyoshi, the reductionist interpretations of color encouraged the filmmakers to pay close attention to the individual psyche. Moreover, the characters are color coded according to their relationship with Kiyoshi. His supporters, such as his friendly neighbor and his understanding teacher, are dressed in warm colors; children, including Kiyoshi, appear in neutral colors. Kiyoshi's mother also appears in neutral colors, suggesting the psychological closeness between mother and son. Ichirō, however, wears cool colors, which hint at the psychological distance between him and his son, as well as the distance between Ichirō and the rest of the world.[44] In this film, the sign of Japan's economic progress—the use of color film—thus helps psychologize the issue of repatriation while at the same time concealing its social and historical dimensions.

Although the belated returnee is not directly compared to the crow, the bird serves an important function in Ichirō's task of working through troubling memories. On one hand, in Japanese folk belief, the black bird has strong associations with death; that is, it is often said that when crows cry over a house, someone from that house will soon die. This ominous association emphasizes the boy's connections with the abject past.[45] On the other hand, the bird is also widely recognized as a symbol of parent–child love, as evidenced in the popular children's song "Seven Crow Babies" (Nanatsu no ko), which depicts a mother crow's deep affection for her children.[46] The crow that Kiyoshi brings home is an ambiguous creature that straddles the dark past filled with destruction and the happy future that the family could have. It is thus a test that he presents to Ichirō to see if the latter is able to reconcile past and future. The father completely fails the test, however, when he displays his abhorrence toward the animal and lets the bird fly away.

The crow's escape foreshadows Kiyoshi's subsequent decision to leave his family. He runs away from home on New Year's Eve because his parents mistakenly blame him for Mitsuko's injury. Ichirō is so upset with Kiyoshi that he tells him that he will not buy him a kite, as earlier promised. In this sequence, while admonishing his son, Ichirō discovers the crow and throws it out of the house. When Kiyoshi leaves the house, he leaves behind a drawing of the crow, which is colored in yellow against the black background (figure 1.3). On the reverse side, Kiyoshi writes "Dad. You liar. Drop dead." The black-and-yellow picture expresses Kiyoshi's psychological state, in which he is defiant even as he desperately seeks his father's affection. Nonetheless, it seems that by letting the crow (a symbol of the troubling past) fly away and instead receiving the yellow crow (Kiyoshi's plea for fatherly love), Ichirō is ready to accept his son.

In order to work through the traumatic experience of returning home, Ichirō unconsciously stages a complex drama: he first transfers his own state of homelessness to Kiyoshi—his alter ego—and then embraces him, who returns home exhausted because he has nowhere else to go. As night begins to fall, Kiyoshi intently walks through a pine forest during a storm. His search for a place where he belongs serves as a visual proxy for Ichirō's homelessness in China. Ichirō searches for his son in the wind

FIGURE 1.3 The yellow crow that Kiyoshi drew, *Yellow Crow*.

and rain. His search is a belated effort to find and bring home his alter ego. Now that Kiyoshi no longer has the crow, the bird that represents his conflicting emotions toward his father, he is less threatening to Ichirō. In the end, Kiyoshi returns home of his own volition. Prompted by his son's sincere apology, Ichirō admits his own fault. The kind words that he speaks to Kiyoshi while holding him—"I am glad you have come back, glad you have come back, Kiyoshi. It must have been cold out there, Kiyoshi. Dad was worried about you. You must be hungry"—are actually directed to himself as the man who has just returned from China.[47] The cure that the film prescribes for these wounds is the individuals' (particularly the returnees') proper attitudes. In order to reach a happy ending, Kiyoshi must first apologize for his actions, even though he had been admonished on unreasonable grounds; he is denied the opportunity to explain his position and instead is required to apologize without qualification. Through his apology, Kiyoshi accepts the father's authority as well as the postwar family order that his father has created. This is a self-serving message from the filmmakers and also from the contemporary Japanese society to those who returned home belatedly: even when they receive unreasonable treatment in postwar society, returnees will be accepted only by recognizing and apologizing for their problematic status and by accepting postwar society's new order.

In the film's final sequence, everything seems to fall into its proper place. On New Year's Day, the day that symbolizes a new beginning, Kiyoshi draws a colorful crayon picture of a happy family on the beach. His representationally correct picture announces that the family crisis is now resolved. The following sequence portrays Kiyoshi happily flying his kite on the beach while his parents, smiling, watch him (Machiko is holding their baby daughter in her arms). The family has finally embraced both their wartime and their postwar child. In place of the crow, which the father let fly away, the kite securely tethered to Kiyoshi's hand—a metaphor for Kiyoshi's raised sprit and sense of security—maintains a respectable height in the clear winter sky.

One must remember, however, that in 1954, it was not cheap to reach this resolution. The traditional Japanese kite that Kiyoshi has asked for cost ¥2,000, a hefty sum considering that the average starting monthly salary at a bank in that year was ¥5,600.[48] The love and affection between father and son are thus measured in economic terms.[49] Because Japan's economy is on the path to strong expansion, Ichirō can behave as a breadwinner earning enough to buy an expensive kite for his child. His masculine pride has been restored as he has proved his productive and reproductive capacities at work and at home. This 1957 film implies that the postwar economic condition is no longer a difficult terrain for the returnees to negotiate—as portrayed in Stray Dog eight years earlier—but now serves as the ground on which to work out their readjustments. The rapid economic growth in the following years helped render more realistic the drama of Yellow Crow, which turned the issue of belated repatriation, an issue of both national and international scope, into a middle-class luxury, a psychological issue to be resolved in the security of home.

MEDIA IMAGES AND INDIVIDUAL EXPERIENCES OF THE BELATED RETURNEES

Numerous postwar films featured former servicemen as the figures that instantiate the traumatic experiences of Japan's defeat and the subsequent chaos. Among them, Kurosawa's Stray Dog and Gosho's Yellow

Crow are noteworthy for their sensitivity to the struggles that each individual faced in reestablishing his or her life in Japan's postwar society. While the focus on the returnee characters' readjustment issues adds depth to the plots, these films are ultimately uninterested in the veterans' individual backstories. Instead, the returnees are treated more as props that highlight the narratives of recovery and reconstruction. Their stories are thus told from the perspective of postwar society, fulfilling the contemporary interest in domesticating the returned former servicemen—and, by extension, their war memories.[50]

In the following chapters, I explore the ways in which some belated returnees carried the weight of war against those images in postwar Japanese society. Veterans were forced to live in a chasm between the images that society manufactured about them and their actual, lived experiences. Those who returned to Japan belatedly faced the added challenges of adjusting to a society that already had begun to radically transform itself and its relations with its wartime past.

Gomikawa Junpei, May 1959. (Courtesy of Mainichi shinbunsha)

Chapter Two

THE STORY OF A MAN WHO WAS NOT ALLOWED TO COME HOME

Gomikawa Junpei and *The Human Condition* (*Ningen no jōken*)

> When I finished writing that [*The Human Condition*], I had a desolate feeling. I should have been feeling relieved but actually felt dejected. I have never felt like that before or since. That means, regardless of its quality, the work was part of my blood and flesh.
>
> GOMIKAWA JUNPEI, "WAGA SHŌSETSU: *NINGEN NO JŌKEN*"

> I am simply a solider like you who'll now have to live with broken dreams and with pain. But, my friend, our era is finished. After this hard-won victory fighters like you, Kien, will never be normal again. You won't even speak with your normal voice, in the normal way again.
>
> BAO NINH, *THE SORROW OF WAR: A NOVEL OF NORTH VIETNAM*

THE HUMAN CONDITION: A HISTORICAL "DO-OVER"

Kurita Shigeru, better known by his pen name Gomikawa Junpei, was a soldier in the Kwantung army (a unit of the Imperial Japanese Army), stationed in the Soviet–Manchukuo border region. He survived the Soviet offensive of August 1945 and eventually returned to Japan in October 1947.[1] Even though more than two years had passed since Japan's defeat, the distance between the wartime and postwar Japan was still small compared with the chasm that those returning later encountered. When Gomikawa came back, Japanese society was still freshly recovering from the "wartime" (*senji*). Gomikawa was relatively fortunate to return at this stage of the recovery because he was able to keep pace with the radical changes around him, even while he thought about the meaning of the war that he had survived.

Gomikawa's debut work—a six-volume novel entitled *The Human Condition* (*Ningen no jōken*, 1956–1958)—was a product of his personal struggle with the trauma of war. After his repatriation, he poured his energies into reading wartime newspapers and books on military-related topics while writing plays and fiction, some of which were later incorporated into *The Human Condition*.[2] He was, however, virtually unknown to the reading public. Before *The Human Condition*, Gomikawa had had only one short story published and one play staged. Then in September 1955, he began working on a story about a young Japanese man who struggles to maintain his conscience—that is, remain human—under the extreme conditions of the Asia Pacific War.[3] Gomikawa immersed himself in his writing. According to writer Sawachi Hisae, who later worked as Gomikawa's research assistant for more than a decade, "He sat facing a wall while working on the manuscript. Floor joists actually rotted [because he sat at the same spot for so many hours everyday]."[4] He wrote his novel as if possessed. Writer Murakami Hyōe described Gomikawa's work as "a novel written with a fool's determination."[5] What Murakami saw in this novel was the author's obstinate will to grapple with his wartime past.

The success of *The Human Condition* was closely tied to Japan's media environment during that period. Gomikawa deliberately produced a fast-paced narrative in order to attract contemporary readers who were accustomed to the pace of film and television.[6] Indeed, an editor at San'ichi shobō was so impressed by Gomikawa's manuscript that he staked his career on it: "If this novel does not sell, I will quit my publishing job."[7] The first volume appeared in August 1956, immediately followed by the second. The next three volumes reached bookstores in 1957, the last in February 1958. Their initial sales—190,000 copies in total—were strong but far below the figures of national best sellers. Media exposure via a weekly magazine was thus crucial to its subsequent phenomenal success. The popular weekly *Shūkan asahi*, with a circulation of 1.5 million, ran a seven-page cover story on *The Human Condition* in February 1958, drastically improving its sales figures: by the end of that year, the combined sales of the six volumes reached 2.43 million.[8] The novel was also repackaged into different media formats: a radio series was released in 1958;[9] a six-part film version was released in 1959 and 1961; and a television series aired from 1962 to 1963. Another television series was broadcast in 1979, and two *manga* versions were published in 1983 and 1988.[10] By the end of 1979, the total sales of the original novel had surpassed 20 million.

Rather than being imprisoned by the media representations that dogged soldiers who returned in later years, Gomikawa was fortunate in that he wielded the power to redefine the media's discourse. As I demonstrated in chapter 1, the images of former servicemen were radically transformed, irrespective of what they actually experienced in postwar society. By discursively making safe these veterans—the reminder of the war—the media helped the nation work through its troubled relations with its wartime past. Although the veterans were initially seen as threats to the postwar social order, they quickly metamorphosed in popular imagination into individuals who might be troubled but ultimately were innocuous. Rather than tacitly accepting the media representations of former soldiers, Gomikawa offered an alternative narrative as a means of grappling with his own war experiences. Against the external cultural definitions of who the veterans were, he portrayed one man's internal battle to maintain his conscience in the midst of a brutal war. Whereas Japanese film used animal imagery to mark veterans' marginalized status in postwar society, Gomikawa posited that his protagonist's struggle to remain human under the inhumane conditions of war was central to postwar society's effort to work through its troubling memories of the war. Gomikawa's debut work was an intensely personal text in which he was trying to reconcile his own war experiences, and it also became part of the national endeavor as its various media incarnations were enthusiastically embraced by millions of readers and viewers.

It was not easy for Gomikawa to live a postwar existence; rather, he faced a grueling process of spiritual and psychological return from the war that he had miraculously survived. As he readily admitted, his debut novel was the means by which he strove to inch away from "that period [in the past and move] toward the present."[11] But this semiautobiographical novel also contains a dramatic narrative twist. Against Gomikawa's authorial desire to leave the past behind and move into the present, the protagonist Kaji remains ensconced in the war, never reaching the postwar period. After escaping from a Soviet staging camp for organizing and sending POWs to Siberian labor camps, Kaji walks across the vast landscape of Manchuria southward to return to his beloved wife, Michiko. He does not reach her but dies, buried under snow, unable to complete his journey. Despite his desire to return to the present, Gomikawa does not allow his protagonist to come home.

When he finished reading *The Human Condition*, writer Usui Yoshimi "caught [himself] muttering, 'Finally, a denouement.'"[12] In a brief essay that accompanied *Shūkan asahi*'s cover story, Usui discusses the ways in which the novel stirred him: "Released from being absorbed in reading the story, I returned to its beginning, recalling the whole story. In the end I was deeply impressed and moved by it. . . . *The Human Condition* offers serious emotional drama. I cannot help but think that the novel that I have been waiting for, for the past twelve years of the postwar has finally appeared."[13] Perhaps for Usui, reading the final lines was like placing the final piece of a jigsaw puzzle in its place. He suggests that Kaji's death was an appropriate end to "the whole narrative," which was filled with dramatic turns and twists, but he says nothing about its meaning. Usui is not alone in this regard: I have found no commentaries explicitly analyzing Kaji's demise.

My reading of Gomikawa's text in this chapter is prompted by questions of (1) why Kaji must die and (2) why his death has not received any sustained critical attention. The distance is obvious between the author who managed to repatriate to postwar Japan and his semiautobiographical work, which rejected his protagonist's return. This narrative distance illustrates Gomikawa's paradoxical position in postwar Japanese society. Despite encouraging his readers to relive the horror of war, Gomikawa erects a wall that separates his war experiences from the postwar by having Kaji die at the very end. By focusing on the conscientious protagonist's life during the war years, *The Human Condition* humanizes abhorrent memories of the war. In the final analysis, it is a novel written from a postwar perspective that urges its readers to break from the troubled past and move forward. *The Human Condition* is in many ways a fantasy tale of a historical "do-over," in which the protagonist lives in the way that many wished for but could not have during the repressive wartime regime. In the end, though, Kaji must die in order not to bring home the war's gruesome memories. In the *Shūkan asahi*'s cover story, which appeared right after the final volume was published, Gomikawa states: "Speaking of my own perspective, I felt I would not be able to move forward unless I dived into and reemerged from that time [of war]."[14] These words demonstrate the author's desire to settle his account with the past and look to the future. Anchored in this desire, Gomikawa's debut work resonated deeply with the large-scale shift that took place in the postwar Japanese discourse about war experiences.

As I pointed out in chapter 1, in the mid-1950s, postwar Japan was steadily distancing itself from its wartime past when the first volume of Gomikawa's novel appeared. A number of tangible signs announced that Japan was entering a new phase of the postwar. The Economic Planning Agency's white paper, issued in July 1956, famously insisted that the postwar period had ended, declaring in its conclusion that "it is no longer the postwar." The white paper's author, Gotō Yonosuke, used these words to express his concern over the future of Japan's economy: the economic system needed to be modernized because "the growth through the recovery" from war damages was over, and there was no longer a clear path to prosperity.[15] Thanks to strong economic growth in subsequent years, however, Gotō's words were popularized as a positive assessment emphasizing Japan's recovery from the devastation of war. It is a testament to Japan's radical transformation in this period that his words acquired such a different meaning from the one he intended.

Also in the mid-1950s, Japan concluded key war reparation negotiations with other Asian nations and the Netherlands, a former imperial power in Asia. As part of the postwar settlement, the Japanese government signed a peace treaty and an agreement for reparations and economic cooperation with Burma (present-day Myanmar) in November 1954.[16] That same month, Japan and the Soviet Union signed a joint declaration reestablishing diplomatic relations between the two nations. Thanks to this diplomatic breakthrough, the "last" Japanese detainees in the Soviet Union were repatriated to Japan.[17] In March 1956, the Japanese government agreed to pay a total of $10 million (¥3.6 billion) to the Netherlands as compensation for war-related damages sustained by Dutch individuals.[18] Two months later, Japan and the Philippines reached a reparations agreement.[19] Finally, in December 1956, Japan's diplomatic efforts culminated with its membership in the United Nations.

Japan was thus leaving the immediate postwar period politically as well as economically. A decade after the defeat and on the verge of the high-growth period, Japanese society was drastically changing its relation to its dreadful wartime memories. Only a few weeks after the 1956 economic white paper appeared, San'ichi shobō published the first volume of Gomikawa's *The Human Condition*. The timing was more than a coincidence.[20] Just as postwar Japan began to recover its economic power and political agency, the reading public enthusiastically embraced the heroic figure of Kaji, who strives to maintain his independence even under impossible wartime situations.

Despite the novel's almost exclusive focus on the protagonist's war experiences, Kaji's eventual death ultimately underscores the powerlessness of individuals in the face of history. In the end, the protagonist's personal struggle is resolved and absorbed into the general condition of human suffering, the "human condition" of the title. In this work, Gomikawa still explores the historical effects of individual actions, whereas his later novels highlight the despotic power of history in defining the individual's destiny.

In this chapter, I first trace Gomikawa's life history and discuss the novel version of *The Human Condition*. Then I briefly address the ways in which the film version blunts the colonial criticism of the original text. The final part of the chapter investigates Gomikawa's image of an all-too-powerful history in more detail through a reading of Gomikawa's subsequent work, "The Historical Experiment" (Rekishi no jikken, 1959).

GOMIKAWA JUNPEI'S STEPS TOWARD THE "POSTWAR"

Except for the brief references made to his war experiences in magazine articles and interviews, Gomikawa left no autobiographical writing. He discussed his past only in fictionalized form, although autobiographical details, combined with fictional elements, drive his early works. The fictional format was essential to Gomikawa's endeavor to reclaim his agency in history. By reexperiencing the past through his fictional alter ego—an intellectual endowed with the physique and courage to act according to his belief—Gomikawa purged his regret of having failed to resist the wartime regime. Yet in interviews, he offered enough information about his actual experiences to reveal what was "true" and what was "invented" in his works.

Gomikawa was a product of Japan's colonialism: he was born to a Japanese army contractor in March 1916 in an agrarian village at the outskirts of Dalian in northeastern China. Growing up in Manchuria, he often witnessed Japanese arrogance and their mistreatment of the Chinese.

Although he felt bitter about the situation, he did not feel a sense of personal culpability until he "studied social sciences [i.e., Marxism] in university."[21] He entered the Tokyo School of Foreign Studies (Tokyo gaikokugo gakkō) in 1936,[22] where he participated in a Marxist study group. Even though his affiliation with it caused him to be taken into police custody for two months, it offered him the intellectual framework through which to understand his colonial complicity. He realized that by being part of Japan's colonialism, he was guilty of colonial aggression and thus had no right to accuse others. Upon graduating from the Tokyo School of Foreign Studies and in order to be close to his parents, he began working in Shōwa Steel Works' research section in Anshan, about 160 miles northeast of Dalian. When he accepted the job, he was fully cognizant of Manchuria's exploitative economic structure. As he later wrote, "The moment I received the appointment letter from the major steel company in Manchuria, I joined the aggressors that exploited Manchurians."[23] He was eventually transferred to a mining site, where he was put in charge of managing so-called special laborers (*tokushu kōjin*, Chinese civilians arrested for their alleged crimes or supposed connections with local criminal groups).[24] His efforts to improve their working conditions led to attempted escapes and eventually to the execution of several escapees.

Soon afterward, Gomikawa lost his draft exemption status—which had earlier been arranged by his company—and was drafted into a Kwantung army unit. Once in it, however, he tried not to be completely co-opted by the inhumane organization of the Japanese military. Although he was eligible to become a noncommissioned officer, he decided instead to serve as a soldier. His decision angered the other senior soldiers, who saw his decision as arrogant and subjected him to relentless physical abuse. After an illness and subsequent stay in a military hospital, Gomikawa joined a border defense unit. When the Soviet army commenced its offensive in August 1945, he was separated from the main unit, away with a company preparing a secondary position. After exchanging fire with Soviet forces, Gomikawa's company of 158 men was reduced to 4, including himself.[25]

Miraculously surviving the battle, Gomikawa became a straggler. He tried to reach southern Manchuria on foot but was intercepted and taken into custody by the Soviet army. In late September, he was detained in an assembly camp where the Soviet authorities kept former Japanese soldiers before sending them to labor camps in Siberia. Gomikawa escaped from that camp and arrived in Xinjing (present-day Changchun), barely alive, in late December 1945. With the help of a Chinese friend, he was able to recover fully.[26] He then returned to Anshan and participated in a movement to democratize the local Japanese community. With the rapidly changing political climate during the civil war between the Nationalists and the Communists, he returned to Japan in October 1947. The real state of the democratization movement in the Japanese community and his reasons for leaving his first wife were incorporated into the story of "The Historical Experiment" (Rekishi no jikken), which was serialized in the monthly magazine *Chūōkōron* in 1959.[27] Sawachi Hisae reports that Gomikawa was unable to "gain legitimate employment" after returning to Japan because he was marked by U.S. intelligence organizations as a "suspicious man who smuggled himself back from a Communist country."[28] Living in postwar Japan under surveillance must have constantly reminded him of his connections to the continent and his wartime past.

It was miraculous that Gomikawa returned to Japan alive, but his experiences during and after the war were no more remarkable than numerous other tales of survival and return in this period. What distinguishes his story from the others is his decision to fictionalize it as a struggle of conscience against the wartime regime and to narrate it through the perspective of a man with exceptional abilities.

Kaji as Company Man as Conscientious Objector

The story of Kaji (only his family name is given in the novel) begins in March 1943 in northeast China, where he works for the research section of a steel works company. In the past, he had been interrogated by the Special Higher Police about his antiwar beliefs. The novel establishes that Kaji's way of thinking is based on reason and logic rather than the pure dogmatism of the left. In a conversation at the office with his friend Kageyama, who is about to enlist in the Kwantung army, Kaji explains that Japan has enough resources to continue its current war efforts for only three more years. He thus implies that nations' relative production capacities will determine the war's outcome, that Japan will be defeated. Although he is talking to Kageyama, his words are also directed to the other employees, and Kaji's prediction outrages one of them, Reserve Lance Corporal Ōnishi, and their exchange of sharp words almost escalates into a physical contest. Through this scene, the novel emphasizes that Kaji has not retreated into the realm of abstract ideals. As he faces the repressive regime that Lance Corporal Ōnishi symbolically represents, Kaji is ready to support his words with action (*GJC* 1:17–20).

Though courageous and a man of action, Kaji is not a superman. The novel carefully demonstrates that despite his sincere efforts, he is unable to overcome the inhumane conditions of wartime Japan. Worse, his expert knowledge, confidence, and conscience actually serve the repressive regime. The chief of his office explains: "We must beware of Kaji. But he is also a useful man. He can handle any kind of research. There are many men who can knock out a report by cutting and pasting others' research. But he is about the only guy who writes original reports using just statistical data" (*GJC* 1:21). His company superiors and the military later express the same sentiment. The harder Kaji tries to act conscientiously, the more he is co-opted by the wartime regime. The more the story emphasizes his intellectual, mental, and physical superiority, the more clearly it demonstrates the regime's ability to appropriate his talents for its own ends.

The head of his company's mining department asks Kaji if he will assume responsibility for labor management at the iron ore mine in Laohuling in southern Manchuria (located more than sixty miles away from the company's headquarters) in exchange for exemption from the draft. He initially hesitates to accept the assignment, thinking that he will be merely the company's agent of exploitation of the Chinese workers. In the end, however, he decides to work at the mine. He then tries to build a new life with Michiko in the mountains, to survive the war, and to reach the postwar period. Life with Michiko, fragile as it may be, anticipates postwar comfort and security. When he asks Michiko if she would be willing to come with him to Laohuling, Kaji half jokingly complains, "A bad girl. When I trace my chain of thought, you are always holding the other end and beckoning me there" (*GJC* 1:43). These words suggest that Kaji is motivated by the prospect of living with Michiko, and he does choose to go to Laohuling, knowing that the Chinese workers are being forced to work under wretched conditions to keep Japan's war machine running. While enjoying a sweet love life protected from the ravages of war, he still fights the injustice he encounters. Kaji's desire for a happy domestic life takes a toll on his conscience, complicating his heroic struggle against the war regime.

The fictional Shōwa Steel Works operated in real life as part of the Manchurian Industrial Development Corporation (MIDC), which was established in December 1937 to coordinate a planned development of mining and heavy industry in Manchukuo. The initial industrialization plan, however, was revised almost immediately, for two reasons. First, the MIDC failed to secure foreign investment primarily because of the worsening U.S.–Japan relations. In addition, the second Sino-Japanese War and Japan's war against the Allied nations forced the MIDC to focus on the more immediate task of running Japan's war machine. A new five-year plan that was announced in 1942 called for a simple increase in production while largely abandoning the MIDC's initial mission of building industrial structures in Manchukuo.[29] With building infrastructure quickly becoming a secondary concern, the company's production was increased by squeezing the workers. Gomikawa was dispatched to the mine to run that local operation more efficiently, even though he knew that the Chinese workers had no reason to support Japan's war. He tried to meet the challenge with what he later described contritely as "sentimental humanism," treating the workers as humans.[30]

In the relevant part of the narrative, Kaji—like Gomikawa—scores small victories in his new assignment, but that modest success only sets the scene for a larger problem. At the mine, the Chinese workers' morale is extremely low, and Kaji's remedy for the situation—treating the Chinese workers more humanely and fighting the corrupt system that exploits them—requires that he stop the subcontractors from taking a cut out of their wages. Kaji forcefully dissolves the teams whose subcontractors are egregiously exploitative and instead places their laborers under the company's direct supervision. Despite the various obstacles, Kaji is able to carry out these reforms, improving work attendance as well as the overall production of iron ore. But when the military police entrust 600 Chinese prisoners to the mine as "special laborers," Kaji's "humanism"—his ethical imperative to "treat humans as fellow humans"—faces a larger challenge. Although the military police call them prisoners of war, in reality most of them are men that the Japanese military have rounded up in areas regarded as "hostile hamlets." These men are the ultimate victims of Japan's imperialist war. Seeing the Chinese prisoners arrive in Laohuling exhausted and starved (several already dying on the way), Kaji provides them with food and rest while creating a work environment as humane as possible for them. Such considerations do not alter the fundamentally exploitative relations between the colonizer and the colonized; Kaji's reformism within the corporation ultimately benefits only the capital and the state. For example, the head of the mine forms an opinion of Kaji similar to that of the chief of the research section: "In his daily speech and behavior, he often shows the liberal proclivity, or expresses even outright leftist sentiments. But his amazing ability to send the [special] laborers to work [at the mine] has sufficiently patriotic effects"(*GJC* 1:316). These words clearly articulate the logic of the capital that takes advantage of Kaji's skills in labor management, even though his moral stance may be at odds with state politics.

The limit of Kaji's (and Gomikawa's) brand of humanism is exposed through the intellectual and tension-filled exchange between him and the former college instructor Wang Xiangli, one of the leaders of the Chinese prisoners. Although both are intellectuals, Wang cuts a contrasting figure to Kaji. His wife was raped and killed by Japanese soldiers before he was captured. Because he had the same name as a thief, Wang was suspected of stealing food and accordingly was subjected to violent interrogation, which caused him to lose all sexual potency. To Kaji, who has come to Laohuling to protect his life (including his sexual life) with Michiko, Wang appears as a man who has lost everything but his political idealism.[31] The Chinese prisoner quietly urges Kaji to break out of his inaction by reminding him that resistance is made possible only through organizing the masses. Kaji's exchange with Wang reads more like Gomikawa's plea to the reader that even the most conscientious Japanese could do little else to change the prisoners' plight.

In Gomikawa's words, "Kaji and Wang face each other, representing the Japanese and Chinese people, respectively."[32] However, their conversation is actually no more than the author's internal dialogue externalized through the character of Wang Xiangli, who acts as Kaji's conscience. While Wang's wounded and emasculated body instantiates Japan's colonial violence and China's weakened state, his intellect and independent thinking demonstrate what Japan has failed to colonize: the interior of the Chinese people. This mind–body split thus serves to lessen Kaji's and the readers' guilty consciences by underscoring the failure of Japan's colonialism. Furthermore, Wang's independent thinking, in its highly idealized form, helps humanize the colonizer, Kaji, but not necessarily the colonized. It attests to Kaji's internal agonies over his own complicity in Japan's colonial system, but not to Wang's intellectual struggle: he (Wang) always knows the answer.

By framing the dialogue between Kaji and Wang exclusively in moral terms, the novel reverses the hierarchy of the colonizer and the colonized. Kaji does everything in his power to improve the living and working conditions for all the special laborers, including Wang. But to Wang, Kaji is simply complicit with the inhumane system because his efforts ultimately aid Japanese imperialist interests. Against this sagelike Chinese character who presides as a moral judge, the Japanese protagonist is condemned to an abject position burdened with responsibility for Japan's colonialism. Kaji claims that conscientious Japanese were the first victims of Japan's imperialism: "Professor Wang, the problem is that some Japanese were invaded by the Japanese even before you Chinese were. That is, the fire that is burning us to death has spread and is now scorching your skin. . . . Being on fire now, what I am supposed to do?" (GJC 1:269). In making this plea, Kaji is concerned less with the cruel practices of Japan's colonialism than with his lack of agency to resist them. Readers are encouraged to identify with this powerless colonizer, who can only curse the circumstance in which he finds himself. Kaji later laments to Michiko that he was not able to protect a Chinese man, Chen, who worked under him: "It is not my fault that I am Japanese. But my deepest sin is that I am Japanese" (GJC 1:365). Being Japanese, Kaji remains responsible for the larger condition that surrounds him, even though he is powerless to change it.

The novel demonstrates that Kaji is trapped not just by the wartime authorities but also by the material comforts of his life. At the mine, the military police decide to execute seven Chinese prisoners on the basis of the false charge that they attempted to escape. Although he tries to stop the executions, as a mere corporate employee Kaji lacks the power to stop military action once it is set in motion. As a last resort, he considers letting the seven prisoners escape the night before their execution, but Michiko talks him out of that plan. Michiko stresses the importance of the banal values she finds in their life together: "Your action may be heroic. But what is the point of it if you are ruined? No, you will surely be ruined. What is there for me? How am I supposed to continue to live? Just the memories of our vows. Just the memories of you, no sound or shape" (*GJC* 1:408–9). Michiko is the chain that ties Kaji to the comforts of domestic life. She appears to be concerned only with life after the war— their postwar life together. Although she eventually gives in—she says, "Do as you wish"—Kaji, worried about what will happen to his life with Michiko, cannot take the decisive step.

When Kaji later changes his mind and challenges the wartime regime, his action produces a momentary catharsis and then places him in a deeper morass. On the day of the executions, a military police officer and a policeman cut off the prisoners' heads one by one. When the third prisoner is executed, Kaji, risking his life, finally steps in to stop the murderous acts. As the military police officer prepares to cut him down with his sword, events take an unexpected turn. The rest of the Chinese prisoners who are brought there to witness the executions as an object lesson, led by Wang Xinagli, begin to cry out menacingly and appear ready to rescue the remaining four prisoners by force. In order to prevent the situation from deteriorating, the military police officer cancels the remaining executions. In return, Kaji is forced to pay the price by being imprisoned and tortured by the military police.

When he is released from detention, he finds that his draft exemption has been lifted and a draft notice is waiting for him. Although he acts according to his conscience, he does not gain freedom from authority. However, when he hears that Wang was able to escape from the mine with thirty other prisoners, Kaji feels elated (*GJC* 1:466). Through Wang's liberation, Kaji's conscience is able to find new life outside the barbed wire. The narrative price of this success is that Kaji's and Wang's dialogues have ended. When he returns home for a brief visit before his enlistment, Kaji destroys the ornamental plate that he and Michiko bought together when they decided to get married—an embodiment of their love and their 200-day-long marriage (*GJC* 1:11). Protected from the ravages of war and assured of material comfort, they had been living a postwar life during the war. This illusion is broken along with the plate as the reality of war engulfs Kaji.

The climax of parts 1 and 2 is arguably the scene in which Kaji steps up to the military police officer to stop the senseless executions. But in an August 1956 article published in the weekly magazine *Shūkan shinchō*,

Gomikawa reveals that the key elements in that scene were fictional. In his actual experience, the "prisoners" of the text were a collection of desperate individuals; there was no leader like Wang Xiangli among them. Actually, nine prisoners were sentenced to death, and four of them were beheaded by a police officer before the rest of the executions were canceled. Furthermore, the company and the police choreographed the whole bloody scene. It had been arranged ahead of time that after several of them were killed, a company executive would step in to stop the killing in order to make the prisoners feel grateful for their reprieve. The colonial authorities, that is, were far more canny and calculating than the novel makes them out to be, and the scene in real life was far less dramatic.[33] In his interview with *Shūkan asahi* in February 1958, Gomikawa confided that "I enlisted in the army not because I had caused the wrath of the military police but simply because the company no longer needed me."[34] Gomikawa tries to work through the trauma of witnessing the executions by reinserting himself—through the figure of Kaji—into the scene as an agent of resistance. In so doing, he also emphasizes Kaji's powerlessness in the face of the powerful wartime regime, and he pays for his defiant act by being drafted into the army.

Kaji as Military Man and Straggler

Once he loses his identity as a company man, Kaji finds himself in another kind of company, the Kwantung army unit stationed in the Manchukuo–Soviet Union border region. To be reunited with Michiko, he must first survive the irrational organization of the Japanese military. He refuses to become an officer candidate, determined to fight instead as an infantry soldier. Kaji is an exceptional soldier—he is the best marksman in the unit and endowed with superb physical strength and endurance, besides being courageous and conscientious—a contrast with the soldiers that Gomikawa's contemporary authors typically portrayed.[35] Writers like Noma Hiroshi, Yasuoka Shōtarō, and Ōoka Shōhei also offered fictionalized accounts of their own experiences as college graduates/students joining the imperial army in the 1940s. Unlike Kaji, however, their alter egos—Soda in *Zone of Emptiness* (*Shinkū chitai*), Agi Kasuke in *Flight* (*Tonsō*), and Tamura in *Fires on the Plain* (*Nobi*)—do not distinguish themselves in their units, weighed down instead by their reflection on their inept state.[36] These other characters are keenly aware of the impossibility of maintaining agency in the military; this sense of loss, not the will for action, defines them. Meanwhile, Kaji, who is a highly skilled soldier, feels frustration because of his inability to act rather than the futility of his attempts at resistance.

Ironically, Kaji's exceptional abilities turn him into a model soldier just as they made him a superb company man in the research section at the mine. Even his determinedly uncompromising attitude is, to his superiors at the mine and in the military, something to be co-opted and turned to their advantage. For example, Kaji accuses a senior soldier of causing a fellow rookie to commit suicide. But in the eyes of the commander, such an act only proves his exceptional quality as a soldier. The commander instructs other officers: "[Kaji's act] wakes up the senior soldiers who have grown too comfortable in the military. He is a soldier we can rely on. Do not leave him out from the next promotion assessment" (*GJC* 2:197). For the military leaders, just as for the executives of the mining company, Kaji's ability to think and act on his own make him a great asset to the organization.

Gomikawa describes the process through which Kaji steadily changes within the violence-filled military organization, a process that overtakes even his strong conscience. When he is promoted to superior private (*jōtōhei*), Kaji is given the assignment of training the new recruits. Despite being determined to protect his charges from the senior soldiers' abuse, he ends up beating one of them during maneuvers. Realizing he acted like one of the long-time soldiers by resorting to violence because of a grudge, Kaji sneers at himself: "You are a superior private, no longer Kaji. The man named Kaji has dissolved in the mold of the military" (*GJC* 2:379). The harder he struggles, the more his conscience wears out inside the war machine. Nonetheless, he continues to protect the first-year soldiers, even by subjecting himself to the fourth-year and fifth-year soldiers' physical abuse. His anger reaches a limit, however, and he grabs a bayonet and tries to retaliate against his abusers.[37] Inside the perverse world of the military, Kaji's dark anger is steadily corroding his mind, leading to impulsive behavior.

Late at night on August 8, 1945, the Soviet Union broke the Soviet–Japan Neutrality Pact and joined the war against Japan. As soon as the date changed, the Red Army began its advance into Manchukuo with more than 1.5 million soldiers, 5,000 tanks, and 5,000 planes. With a few rare exceptions, the Kwantung army was unable to stop the advance. In the final years of the Asia Pacific War, its main forces and weapons had been sent out to the South Pacific, and the total number of the Kwantung army soldiers consisted mainly of new local recruits—Japanese male settlers in Manchukuo. Without enough weapons and ammunition, some recruits were trained simply for suicide missions: throwing themselves under an enemy tank with an explosive on their back. Gomikawa at least faced the enemies with his own rifle and some ammunition.

Like Gomikawa, Kaji ends up being one of the few survivors of the 158-man company dispatched to create a secondary position behind the border. The price of his survival is high: something collapses inside him. When the enemy attack dies down, he wrestles with and kills an officer who has lost his sanity in the stress of battle. This act stems not only from the practical concern that the officer will be a liability in the attempt to escape but also from the grudge Kaji holds against all the abuses that he has endured in the Kwantung army. His humanism, or determination to live as a human and treat others as fellow humans, steadily breaks down. In the end, Kaji replicates the violence of war, deteriorating into an animal-like being. Meanwhile, his conscience constantly forces him to contemplate his own acts and their consequences. Though weakened from the extreme conditions of war, Kaji is never detached from his acute self-awareness. He suffers in the war on behalf of Michiko and the readers to prove the ultimate futility of resisting one's fate.

When the Japanese Imperial government finally accepted the Potsdam Declaration on August 14, 1945, and ordered a cease-fire on the following day, the Asia Pacific War theoretically ended. The Red Army, however, continued to advance into Manchuria for approximately two weeks, in overt disregard of Tokyo's announcement of surrender. With the Kwantung army's command system disintegrated, it was impossible for the Japanese soldiers left on the fields to obtain a clear sense of the situation. In order to escape the immediate danger, Kaji and other survivors begin the long and arduous journey toward southern Manchuria; Kaji even killed Soviet soldiers and Chinese militiamen in his desperate effort to continue the journey. When Kaji and his fellow stragglers enter a thick forest, they encounter a group of Japanese civilians who have fled from the advancing Soviet army. Imagining Michiko in a similar situation, Kaji realizes that he does not have the heart to leave them behind. Although he knows that the civilians will slow his progress, he lets them join his ragtag squad (*GJC* 3:65). In the end, however, none of the civilians survive the escape journey. Kaji's act of conscience seems to make absolutely no difference in the larger context of history.

Shortly afterward, Kaji meets his archenemy Kirihara. Kirihara and two other stragglers boast that they attacked a White Russian couple in their home, raping the woman before killing them both. Kirihara and his mates next begin escorting a Japanese girl and her brother to their parents' house, only to rape her and kill them both on the way. Learning of their heinous acts, Kaji takes away their weapons and kicks them out of the abandoned army barrack that the stragglers are using as a temporary shelter. But the two men would meet each other again under completely different circumstances inside a POW detention camp. The figure of Kirihara serves as the worst example of how the Japanese soldiers behaved in Manchuria. Compared with Kirihara's heinous crimes, Kaji's behavior—even at its worst—appears restrained.

Kaji as Prisoner of War

As Kaji and the other stragglers are finally demilitarized and sent to a POW camp by the Soviet army, the fight against the personification of absolute evil—Kirihara—displaces Kaji's earlier struggle against the more general horror of military and war. Kaji finally murders Kirihara, though not to fulfill his conscience, but to retaliate for the death of a former trainee who had embodied Kaji's hope for future Japan. His grisly act confirms that there is no way out of the oppressive situation he finds himself in, and it also blots out the colonial context of this novel.

Kaji's moral descent is precipitated by the grim reality of the Soviet Union's oppressive political system that he experiences as a POW. Marxism had been an attractive political ideology to wartime Japanese intellectuals because it offered, in their eyes, a viable alternative to the exploitative capitalist system. In *The Human Condition*, the socialist regime exists as a moral support for some Kwantung army soldiers who refused to embrace Imperial Japan's war. Betting on the possibility that the Soviet Union is a promised land where individuals are allowed to enjoy political freedom, Kaji's colleague Shinjō runs away from the unit to seek refuge in the Soviet Union (*GJC* 2:75–76).[38] Private First Class Tange, whom Kaji befriended in the army hospital, declares to Kaji that he believes in the justness of the Soviet Union despite the mounting contrary evidence: the rapes and murders of Japanese civilians by Red Army soldiers (*GJC* 3:194–97).

Meanwhile, Kaji supports the Soviet political ideology and system in principle and even fantasizes about surrendering to the Red Army, but he cannot fully embrace the idealized image of the socialist regime (*GJC* 3:196). Until he witnesses the oppressive Soviet political system firsthand, Kaji maintains hope that socialism offers a just political regime in which humans are liberated from all forms of oppression. This hope, no matter how tenuous, also buttresses Kaji's conscience by providing a concrete position from which to critique Japan's present regime. His ideal is not a mere pipe dream, for it already has been realized elsewhere. But in the abusive environment of the Japanese military, his conscience has already worn thin. With his political ideals now shattered, Kaji's primary concern ceases to be the abstract condition of being a human; he can think only about how to survive the camp.

Having arrived at the camp before Kaji, Kirihara has avoided being sent to Siberia by deceiving the camp authority. He has even become an *aktiv* (party activist) there, serving as a minion of the victor.[39] To get back at Kaji, Kirihara targets a young soldier under Kaji's tutelage and eventually causes his death. The young rookie soldier, Terada, symbolizes the transformation of militaristic Japan into democratic Japan. As the son of an army major, Terada began his first-year army training as a staunch believer in Japan's imperialist cause—he was ready to die for the nation— rejecting Kaji's teaching that emphasized the value of human lives. But after surviving the battle with the Soviet forces and the escape (with Kaji's help), Terada is finally able to accept Kaji's words. By killing this character at this point in the narrative, Gomikawa denies Kaji's legacy for the postwar period, eliminating the possibility that Kaji will manage to achieve even one positive outcome from the war.

Terada's death also sets the scene for Kaji's final act of violence, which destroys what little remains of his conscience. To avenge Terada's death, Kaji kills Kirihara by beating him repeatedly with a piece of metal wire rope and throwing him into a pool of feces. Kaji thus replicates the way that Kirihara killed Terada: Terada lost consciousness while cleaning a latrine covered in feces and subsequently died. Kirihara's death also emphasizes the senselessness of Kaji's act, illustrating the depths into which he is willing to sink in the name of vengeance. Given the fact that in an earlier scene, Kaji was outraged by senior squad members' abuse of a rookie soldier, it is clear that the ultimate target of Kaji's violence was not Kirihara as an individual but the apparatus of Japanese military violence that Kirihara represents. No longer able to endure abuse and violence, Kaji finally delivers justice with his own hands. But at that moment, he also necessarily replicates the very violence of the military that he has abhorred. There is no catharsis for Kaji here. He even seems to lose his raison d'être and is reduced to an abject state: "The crime is finished. Everything may be over. There is absolutely no sense of guilt, just empty feelings. Now and here seem to have been cut off from before and after" (*GJC* 3:449).

Even though this novel is highly critical of the colonial relations between the Japanese and the Chinese, the subplot of Kirihara's abuse and Kaji's retaliation ultimately relegate it to a drama among and about Japanese characters. Kirihara killed a Japanese teenager and her brother, as well as a Russian couple; he also discloses to Kaji that he would not hesitate to rape or kill Chinese as well (*GJC* 3:163). But Kaji's retaliation responds only to the murder of the Japanese soldier Terada. He kills Kirihara not for being the worst executioner of Japan's imperial aggression but for being a man who would not think twice about sacrificing a fellow Japanese for his own advantage. Similarly, rather than problematize the criminal behavior of the Soviet soldiers—they raped numerous Japanese women as they advanced southward—and their inhumane treatment of the Japanese POWs in the Siberian camps, the story in the end focuses on Kaji's vengeance in response to Kirihara's evil deeds against his fellow Japanese. The process through which Kaji achieves resolution—enduring his adversary's abuse and humiliation to an extreme limit before finally exploding with anger—follows the dramatic convention of what the scriptwriter Kasahara Kazuo calls the "endurance play" (*gamangeki*) seen in popular kabuki plays.[40] Kaji's final act thus resolves the complex narrative of *The Human Condition* into a familiar Japanese story. *The Human Condition* could have been a drama that relentlessly dissected the colonial dynamics among China, Japan, and the Soviet Union. This ambitious story, however, situated in a complex international setting, eventually ends as a vengeance drama of the Japanese, by the Japanese, and for the Japanese. While the sufferings of the Chinese and the Russians highlight the absolute evil of the wartime Japanese regime and military, this violence is merely a backdrop for a larger story, that Japanese soldiers are expendable.

Following the gruesome murder of Kirihara, Kaji escapes the POW camp with the hope that he can return to his wife, even though he is no longer the person that Michiko once knew. Before Kaji begins his desperate journey home, Gomikawa inserts into the story contrasting scenes of Michiko's peaceful life. She is supporting herself with the help of her friends in the Chinese city where she is working for a fledgling democratization movement in the Japanese community. She thus is safely awaiting her husband's return. The contrasting situations of Kaji and Michiko attest to the enormous distance that now separates them. There is no place in the postwar era for Kaji, who, despite his efforts to denounce it, now embodies the wartime violence. With his moral self shattered, he is a zombielike being that is staggering southward, begging for food. His only hope is that Michiko can heal his battered soul. In a confused state of mind induced by extreme fatigue and hunger, Kaji talks to Michiko: "I killed so many men. But you wouldn't know that, before this, how many times I had been killed. Don't hate me, please. I am walking just to see you" (*GJC* 3:459). Michiko will not have an opportunity to hear directly from Kaji about the experience he had in the military and on the battlefield. Snow begins to fall and covers his fatigued body, inviting him to end all struggle. Once he decides to lie down on the ground, he never rises again: "Snow kept falling. Time quietly and surreptitiously passed in the dark expanse of land. Snow continued to dance and fall insentiently, eventually making a small mound in the shape of somebody lying on the ground" (*GJC* 3:463). Although Kaji tried to live as a conscientious intellectual, he realizes in the end that he has become a cog of the war machine. Only by becoming part of the war-ravaged land is he finally allowed to rest and bury the past that is imbued with unspeakable violence. His tormented soul is cleansed and redeemed in the whiteness of the snow. It is toward this tragic climax that the novel has been building.

Indeed, in a conversation with the actress Aratama Michiyo, who played Michiko in the film, Gomikawa revealed that "I was thinking about that last scene even before I started writing the very first line of the novel."[41] By ending *The Human Condition* with Kaji's death, Gomikawa refuses to replicate the stories of the returnees that filled postwar Japan, as recounted in chapter 1. Kaji's tale cannot culminate as a happy love story, or even as a story in which a former serviceman acts out his violent past in postwar society. By not letting the protagonist come home to postwar Japan, Gomikawa refuses to allow his war experiences to be assimilated into the postwar media's narratives.

In contrast to the battered figure of Kaji, Michiko remains unhurt and unshaken by the war. Gomikawa idolizes her as a "perfect and progressive woman."[42] While highly praising the novel, writer Usui Yoshimi criticized the portrayal of Michiko: "When we look at Michiko, she is not even as developed as the characters in a vulgar fiction. All the scenes in which Michiko appears are clumsy, and not worth reading."[43] Critic Hori Hidehiko similarly complained about the lack of depth in Michiko's character: "The woman named Michiko in this novel is not developed at all. She is merely a robot endowed with white flesh. . . . The author writes that he wanted to describe her as a "perfect and progressive woman." But she is neither perfect nor progressive. No, she is not even alive."[44] Both Usui and Hori dismiss Michiko as a clumsily molded figure that suggests Gomikawa's shortcomings as a writer.

But they overlook the solace that this idealized character provides in the tension-filled narrative. While feeling the pain of every step Kaji takes, the readers are safely ensconced in the postwar period through their identification with Michiko, who—like the readers—awaits Kaji's return. In contrast to the gruesome scenes that unfold in the battlefields and along the paths that Kaji and his fellow stragglers follow, his wife leads a relatively protected life in the city, which appears to be Anshan under the Soviet occupation. Never getting hurt even in the most dangerous situations,[45] Michiko symbolically represents the atmosphere in the Japan of the 1950s that eagerly embraced the phrase "It is no longer the postwar."[46] The ravages of war will never reach her because she is already living a postwar life. Michiko's raison d'être is simply to await Kaji's return. Kaji shoulders all the moral issues, whereas Michiko must exist only as an ideal, much like a beautifully decorated papier-mâché.

A Story of the Japanese, by and for the Japanese

As I pointed out earlier, *The Human Condition*'s tragic ending is part of Gomikawa's effort to rewrite his own war experience from a postwar perspective. This fictional work lays bare his past, filled with regrets, for postwar Japan. Yet by leaving Kaji in the darkness and dissolving him into the snow-covered terrain, Gomikawa suspends history right before Kaji entered the postwar period. He leaves his real self in the war, permitting his alter ego to die a symbolic death. For Gomikawa, the postwar period exists as a bonus time in which to write about his war experiences.

In thinking about what the postwar means to Gomikawa, it is useful to go back to the moment when he decided that he had to write about his war experiences. Just as he described in *The Human Condition*, he was one of the few soldiers who survived the Soviet attack. In a short essay he wrote in 1961, he recalls the revelation that he had in the battlefield:

> I was sucking on a caramel in a foxhole. The battle was practically over. After the bombardment by the enemy tanks stopped, not even a single shot was returned from our side. An overwhelming number of enemy soldiers were coming up the hill toward our position. I occasionally shot just in front of me because I didn't want them to advance straight at me. In between shootings, I sucked on a caramel. As long as I could taste its sweetness, I seemed to be all right. The enemies, when they encountered even slight opposition, avoided that spot. Since it is clear who won the battle, there was probably no need for them to take any risks. Watching their maneuver, I began to think that I might survive this battle. I felt that if I could come out of this war alive, I would live to write about the things leading up to that day, a story about expendable men.[47]

The caramel's sweet taste appears to anchor his spirit to the body of there and then. But when his body is released from immediate danger, his thoughts slip toward the future. Gomikawa must wonder why he would survive in the battlefield where the Japanese defense unit was being decimated. Rather than directly confronting that question, he decides to remain with his dying comrades, accepting that his future will be dedicated to writing about his life with them. In other words, his postwar self existed in borrowed time, crawling out of the netherworld to memorialize what he had lost in the war.

Gomikawa continues in the same essay to explain how he envisioned the story's end:

> At the end of that story [the story about expendable men], there was an extra hundred days. Wandering through fields and mountains like a starving wolf, I was reaching my physical and emotional limits. On the last night [of my journey], I was barely walking from one electric pole to the next, with a distant town's lights in sight. I thought I would die that night. Dry, powdery snow was blowing everywhere. It was certain that if I decided to rest right there, snow would pile up in the shape of a lying man. Although I had become extremely weak, I was able to imagine a man lying on the ground covered by snow.[48]

From this near-death experience emerged an author who was, like a soul detached from the body, objectively looking down at himself from a distance. Assuming the position of observer, Gomikawa transformed his suffering into the scene of a novel. In this moment, he buried his war self in the snow and was reborn as a postwar writer. His debut work, *The Human Condition*, was ultimately a magnificent tomb that he constructed to bury his past.

The protagonist Kaji must die because he is assigned the role of protecting postwar Japan from its violence-filled past. To keep the war safely at bay from the postwar period, Gomikawa sacrifices Kaji. The readers in postwar Japan are able to reexperience the wartime injustice and deception, and they also have the privilege of celebrating their survival and safe existence in the postwar era. The narrative focus on Kaji's struggle allows readers to cheer for his immediate victory over the bureaucratic evildoers that thrived in wartime Japan while also reminding them of the limits of his agency. This simultaneous empowerment and disempowerment of the hero underscores the limits of human subjectivity. The novel thus absolves the reader of responsibility: if Kaji, endowed with exceptional abilities, cannot affect the events in his life, then no ordinary reader could reasonably feel obligated to try to change the course of history.[49] The corollary is that the best choice for individuals is just to survive the war and reach the postwar period at any cost. In other words, Kaji's heroic acts are fantastical projections that enabled guilt-riddled postwar readers to reenact history and relieve their regret at failing to stop the war. The author sends Kaji back to the wartime as a representative of the author and the postwar Japanese. It is a second chance, not necessarily to change history, but to act—and die—albeit ethically this time.

THE HUMAN CONDITION ON FILM

Between 1959 and 1961, Gomikawa's novel was made into a six-part film—nine hours and thirty-one minutes in length—by the Ninjin Club, an independent production company, in collaboration with Shochiku Studios.[50] For the director, Kobayashi Masaki, The Human Condition was his story as well. Born in 1916—only a month before Gomikawa Junpei—Kobayashi's twenties were subsumed by the war; he was stationed in Manchuria as a member of a border defense unit and later was a POW in Okinawa.[51] The lead actor, Nakadai Tatsuya (b. 1932), "instinctively" realized that both Gomikawa and Kobayashi were Kaji, and he understood that he was playing Kaji on their behalf.[52] In shooting the film, Kobayashi and the cinematographer, Miyajima Yoshio (1909–1998), pursued the reality of military life, including its extreme physical aspects. The actors were required to participate in a month-long training session that simulated the Imperial Japanese army's first-year training. In the scene in which ten or so senior soldiers hit Kaji in the face, Nakadai was actually hit by other actors until his face was swollen.[53] The filmmakers' concern for historical authenticity thus helped reproduce the oppressive atmosphere of the imperial Japanese military on the screen.

By making changes in the original narrative, the protagonist in the film version is projected as an even more tragic figure than that in the book. For example, absent are the scenes in which Michiko awaits Kaji's return. This deletion creates a higher narrative tension in the final part of the film while denying the audience access to the postwar world and its psychological relief. The final sequence of Kaji's deathly journey—only a little more than six pages in The Collected Works of Gomikawa Junpei (3:457–63)—is extended to a fifteen-minute segment on the screen. This allows the hero's final demise to be depicted in detail, but it forces into the background the historical specificity that drives the rest of the film. Covered in layers of gunny sacks to fight the cold, Kaji's identity as a military man is no longer visible. With his beard, he appears more as a Christ-like figure who finally suffers and dies for the sins of Imperial Japan.

Long before reaching its conclusion, the film inadvertently softens the harsh historical reality in Japanese-controlled China by erasing the otherness of the colonial subject. As in the original story, a number of Chinese characters appear in the film, speaking in Chinese. All are played by Japanese actors and actresses who have little or no knowledge of the language. Despite their efforts to mimic Chinese sounds, their Japanese accents reproduce the structure of domination: the colonized may be represented only by or through the colonizer.[54] It was impossible to shoot the film in northeastern China, since Japan and the People's Republic of China did not have diplomatic relations then (many shooting locations were in Hokkaidō). Also, it was then a customary practice of Japanese film studios to cast Japanese actors and actresses in the roles of Chinese characters.[55] Moreover, the absence of Chinese cast members helped make the film's critique of Japanese colonial practices more palatable to a contemporary Japanese audience.

Although the Japanese film industry had already started showing signs of decline in the late 1950s, Kobayashi lined up an all-star cast to produce *The Human Condition*. This casting choice helped reduce the tension between colonizer and colonized by emphasizing the film's fundamental Japanese-ness. Wang Xiangli, the leader of the Chinese prisoners, uses penetrating logic to excoriate Japan's militarism. Despite his elegant appeal, however, contemporary audiences recognized him as the Japanese actor Miyaguchi Seiji (perhaps best known to international audiences as the stoic samurai Kyūzō in *Seven Samurai*). Also immediately recognizable was Shōchiku's biggest star, Arima Ineko, who played the prostitute Yang Chunlan, the character who openly accuses Kaji for his failure to act.[56] That is, even when they were presented with the harsh reality of Japan's imperialism on the screen, viewers were able to easily avoid its impact by recalling the glittering celebrity status embodied by these actors. Perhaps it is not fair to measure today's standards of cultural sensitivity against the Japanese film industry's practice of more than a half century ago. But it should still be noted that these casting practices helped transform the Chinese characters into vanishing signifiers of Japanese oppression.

THE TYRANNY OF HISTORY

Gomikawa Junpei hoped to distance himself from his past by sublimating his own experiences into a fictional tale. But writing one novel, even a voluminous one, was not sufficient to bring Gomikawa the distance he desired. He wrote several other fictional works, including the eighteen-volume novel *War and Humanity* (*Sensō to ningen*, 1965–1982). At a symposium, "War and Humanity" (1972), Gomikawa discussed the unrealistic expectations he had when he began to write *The Human Condition*:

> Thirteen years ago, in *The Human Condition*, I depicted my personal war experiences against the social and historical background. Back then I had a very naive idea: I was hoping to make some sense of my war experiences and move up to the present moment by writing this novel. But the moment I finished writing it, I began to feel that I had failed to write about the war and that I should revisit the war and write about it again. *The Human Condition* deals with less than two years from the end of 1943 to the war's conclusion. It was a mistake to think that I could move away from the war by writing that novel [because it covers only the final phase of the war].[57]

By leaving his own alter ego, Kaji, in the past, Gomikawa sealed himself off from his own war experiences. But more steps were needed to achieve his repatriation to postwar Japan. While "*The Human Condition* deals with less than two years from the end of 1943 to the war's conclusion," Gomikawa's later works delineate his experiences outside this time frame. In those later writings, his battlefield experiences steadily recede into the background and his connections with China receive more attention. The stage shifts from the battlefield to the Chinese city he returned to after the war, and then finally to Japan. This movement mimics the process through which Gomikawa's protagonists slowly reenter postwar Japan.

Following the completion of *The Human Condition*, Gomikawa serialized "The Historical Experiment" (Rekishi no jikken) in the popular general-interest monthly *Chūōkōron*. The protagonist, Tanami Ikutarō, walks 1,243 miles from "the north end [of the earth]" and returns in a near-death condition to his fiancée, Akiko, who lives in a Chinese city under Communist control (*GJC* 6:203). Their reunion highlights the emotional distance that Tanami's absence has created. It appears that there is not even a shared language between Tanami, who barely survives a scene of carnage, and Akiko, who lives a relatively protected life in the Japanese community. The novel does not specify the type of violence Tanami experienced, vaguely mentioning only that he was stationed as a member of the defense unit at the Manchuria–Soviet border (*GJC* 6:251). The battle against the Soviet forces is never invoked in "The Historical Experiment"; the focus remains instead on the Japanese community awaiting postwar repatriation in a Chinese city.

Carrying the weight of the war in his everyday life, Ikutarō's relations with Akiko are irreparably damaged. Gomikawa succinctly describes the situation: "Her fiancé, whose return she had long waited for, never returned" (*GJC* 6:448). By describing the difficulties of living in the postwar era and also recognizing the persistence of wartime memory in that era, Gomikawa appears to acknowledge the impossibility of completely repatriating from the war. At the end of the novel, Tanami leaves Akiko behind and tries, with other Japanese members of the democratization movement, to reach the area to which the Communist forces have retreated. Just as in *The Human Condition*, the protagonist keeps walking, wanting to return to where he belongs. His return to Japanese society, however, is perpetually deferred.[58]

The harder Gomikawa tried to reach the point at which he could be liberated from his war experiences, the more acutely he seems to have recognized the smallness of individual historical events. "The Historical Experiment" offers commentaries on its characters, including Tanami, who are tossed around in the flow of history: "There is no beginning in history. There is no end either. It somehow begins, and nobody knows when it ends. Humans find themselves somewhere in the middle of it. People may think they act on their own volition. But in most cases, people find they are actually no more than a grain or drop in the experimental material" (*GJC* 6: 229).

It appears that even though he struggled to control the flow of history, Gomikawa finally embraced the fatalistic idea that history defines individuals' behavior, not vice versa. In his later writing, he depicts history as both an accursed object and a source of salvation. While individuals are tossed around in its wake, their subjectivity is absorbed into the national history of Japan. In other words, individuals are ultimately not responsible for history's outcomes. When reversed, Kaji's earlier lamentation expresses the comfort one can find in historical determinism: "My deepest sin is the fact that I am Japanese," but "it is not my fault that I am Japanese." He should not be held accountable for the events he has no control over, however abominable their outcome may be.

The narrative of *The Human Condition* impresses on its readers the aberrant quality of the wartime, in contrast to the tranquillity of the postwar period, as represented by the idealized images of Michiko. Gomikawa treats the war years as a unique and separate period from the postwar era. That period becomes a cesspool in which everything and everybody eventually corrode and lose their shape, so the pool of feces is an apt location for Kaji's final descent into vengeance. Standing at a safe distance from history—as if looking through a protective glass—readers can cheer Kaji's struggle and small victories in wartime Japan. Kaji's death establishes the barrier between war and postwar, ensuring that the effects of war would not reach beyond Japan's defeat. Gomikawa is fundamentally uninterested in questioning how events in the past affected postwar society. In reality, the war's end was not at all clear-cut. While Kaji was supposedly heading south, tens of thousands of men were organized into transport battalions and sent to labor camps in Siberia, and millions of former servicemen were waiting to be repatriated from East Asia, Southeast Asia, and the South Pacific. Thousands from the Soviet Union and the PRC were still arriving on Japanese shores even after Gomikawa began publishing *The Human Condition* in July 1956. He dealt with the piece of war he brought home by sending it back to the past; some of these other returnees, however, did not feel secure enough in postwar Japan to relinquish their ties with the past.

The next two chapters describe the lives of those who returned late from the Soviet internment, focusing on what they had endured in the labor camps and their postrepatriation struggle to understand their experiences.

On July 21, 1949, Japanese detainees on the *Dai'iku maru*, a repatriation ship from Nakhodka, recognize and wave to their homeland in the distance. (Courtesy of U.S. National Archives)

Chapter Three

LONGING FOR HOME

Japanese POWs in Soviet Captivity and Their Repatriation

If I have to keep having dreams about the Soviet detention, I am not sure when the "I" in the dreams can finally come home. The "I" in the dreams still wants to come home as soon as possible.

ŌTSUKA SHIGERU, FORMER JAPANESE POW IN SIBERIA

"The best of us did not return." I used to feel a twinge when I read those words that Viktor Frankl used at the opening of *Man's Search for Meaning*. I can perhaps restate them in this way: "The best of myself did not return either."

ISHIHARA YOSHIRŌ, "FOR THE COLLECTED POEMS, *THE RETURN OF SANCHO PANZA*" (SHISHŪ *SANCHO PANZA NO KIKAN* NO TAMENI)

BETWEEN 700,000 AND 800,000 PRISONERS AND MORE THAN 100,000 DEATHS

After Japan accepted the terms of surrender specified in the Potsdam Declaration, between 700,000 and 800,000 Kwantung army soldiers, civilian personnel, and other noncombatants, including Japanese settlers, were transported out of Manchuria for prolonged detention in approximately two thousand Soviet labor camps dotting the vast territories of Siberia and other Soviet-controlled regions.[1] Despite their optimism that they would be immediately sent home, the majority of detainees remained in the camps for several years, with some three thousand men convicted of alleged war crimes remaining in the Soviet Union for as long as eleven years. In addition, most Japanese POWs, already suffering from malnutrition, were forced to work under the extremely treacherous conditions of the Siberian winters.[2] The hazards of camp labor caused numerous accidents and injuries, which the camps' primitive medical services were ill equipped to treat. Despite the gradual improvement in camp conditions as the Soviet Union slowly recovered from the devastation of war, life in detention caused the deaths of slightly more than 100,000 Japanese POWs.[3] Their extreme suffering led many of those who later returned to Japan to reject anything associated with the Soviet Union, and the media images of their internment eventually became a wellspring for widespread anti-Russian feelings in postwar Japan.

As the returned POWs struggled to articulate their Soviet experiences, they refused to define themselves by sheer hatred. Thousands of accounts of POW experiences in Siberia have appeared in the past seven decades, and as the former POWs reached retirement age and beyond, even more returnees have attempted to bequeath their memories to a younger generation. They have faced various challenges, however, in their attempts to relate their stories to a postwar society that was eager to brush aside its wartime past and to concentrate on national reconstruction. Many other returnees have chosen not to speak about their experiences, even to their closest kin. Consequently, as this generation dies out, so does the hope that their stories will become part of the public memory of the war. Postwar Japanese society was eager to sentimentalize, but not to sympathize with, the plight of the returned captives.

Images of Japanese POWs have nevertheless remained in Japanese popular consciousness and media representations. In the early postwar period, when the issue of the Japanese POWs in Siberia received widespread political and media attention, popular culture provided reminders of fellow Japanese who had yet to be repatriated. In 1948, the popular song "Hill in a Foreign Land" (Ikoku no oka), was framed as a message to the "friends" who still remained in a "foreign land," expressing hope that they would soon be able to return home; the following year, Shin-Tōhō Studios produced two films based on the success of this song.[4] But by the early 1950s, when the majority of POWs had returned to Japan, interest in the remaining captives waned. Then in 1956, after the final group of Siberian prisoners returned home, representations of the detainees disappeared from popular culture as Japan and the Soviet Union reestablished official diplomatic relations.

Six decades have passed since then. During this time, prisoners of war seem to have disappeared from popular consciousness. For example, in his ambitious 2002 work on popular postwar Japanese songs, Murase Manabu reads the lyrics of "Hill in a Foreign Land" as if they describe a generic battle scene, completely devoid of the song's specific historical context. The song begins:

On a hill in a foreign land where the dusk approaches again.
Friend, it must be hard and desolate.
Endure, wait, once the storm is gone,
The day to return home will come, spring will come.[5]

Murase generalizes this part of the song, claiming that it paints a "scene in which a soldier is talking to his injured friend on the battlefield at dusk."[6] Even for the commentator attempting to situate postwar Japanese popular songs in postwar history, the image of Japanese captives in Siberia is not registered.[7]

Since the late 1940s, the most common images associated with the Siberian captives have been those of the mothers and wives who waited for years in vain at the wharves of Maizuru Port for their sons and husbands to return. In the 1950s, the Japanese media "discovered" the regulars who continued to return there, portraying them as heroic figures silently enduring their suffering.[8] For example, the popular song "A Mother on the Wharf" (Ganpeki no haha, 1954) depicts a woman who waited ten years for her son's return, the tragic end of her waiting only enhancing the song's appeal in the popular imagination. Sung in the popular ballad style, the song appealed to the stock images of women suffering in silent anguish, displacing the male experiences of POWs in Siberia. The absence of a particular historical reference in the original lyric[9] helped listeners reduce specific individual suffering to general sentimentality. That generality also concealed the fact that Port Maizuru used to be one of the four major navy ports in Imperial Japan.[10] POWs thus figured in the postwar popular imagination primarily as an absence, highlighting the hardships for those *inside* the boundaries of postwar Japan. Moreover, these women also quietly disappeared from media coverage as the ships carried the final group of repatriates home in the late 1950s. The women briefly reappeared in Japanese popular imagination in the 1970s through a revival of the song, as well as a film and a television drama of the same title that capitalized on the song's popularity. These works, however, merely replayed the domestic displacement of the returned prisoners of war.[11]

This lack of interest marks a stark contrast with postwar Germany's preoccupation with their POWs who returned from the Siberian camps. As the historian Frank Biess argues, West Germany embraced the German

POWs as ideological icons of nationhood, and their images were gradually transformed in the postwar years as they were cast as both victims and survivors of totalitarianism.[12] Images of POWs proliferated in the popular media as symbolic figures whose rehabilitation became a metaphor for the reconstruction of West German society. In East Germany in the immediate postwar years, the Socialist Unity Party of Germany was eager to reintegrate the returning POWs both ideologically and economically in order to support national rebuilding and to maintain its strong political ties with the Soviet Union.[13] Unlike their Japanese counterparts, the return of German POWs from Soviet camps was laden with positive national symbolism in the ideological space of their postwar societies.

In postwar Japan, the vast majority of the returnees' personal accounts were forgotten as soon as they were published. The only exception was the brief period in the late 1940s and early 1950s. In 1949, there were numerous incidents on the repatriation vessels, at the wharves of Maizuru, and at the transfer stations of Kyoto,[14] Osaka, Ueno, and Tokyo.[15] These incidents involved Japanese returnees who had become avid Communists as a result of the Soviet "democratization" movement.[16] Many, though, soon realized the lies in their Soviet education and abandoned their Communist beliefs within several weeks of their return.[17] Nevertheless, the Japanese media covered in detail the militant attitudes of these returning POWs, calling them "Red repatriates." Even then, however, the stories of their experiences remained at the periphery of postwar social consciousness and served to reinforce Japan's negative impressions of the Soviet Union.

This chapter is an effort to articulate the difficulties that POWs experienced in getting their stories heard in postwar society, in which various social forces prevented them from gaining a wider audience. Generally, their homecomings were not as welcoming as the POWs had anticipated while in the Siberian labor camps. The former Soviet POWs became marginal and ambivalent figures, both familiar and unfamiliar reminders of a past that postwar Japan preferred to keep at bay. Perhaps their stories were too familiar, as they embodied a wartime fear of what would happen to Japan once defeated. As such, they had to be repressed. At the same time, to a Japan that had disowned its colonial past, the stories were also unfamiliar. The Siberian POWs' belated return threatened to undermine the comfortable distance from its colonial war memories that Japan had managed to attain in just a few years after defeat.

The survivors of Soviet camps faced many of the same challenges that awaited Japan's other former servicemen. Other factors, however, made the Siberian internees' transition into postwar Japan even harder. The prolonged state of forced labor under the most demanding conditions affected not just their physical well-being but also their mental state. Many POWs survived the dehumanizing conditions in Siberia by numbing their sensibility to the pain of either their own or their fellow inmates' suffering. Their plight, therefore, destroyed them twice: first by physical humiliation and then by the fact that they passively accepted their situation. Even though they made it back physically, their wounded psyches did not necessarily come home with them. Nakahara Toshio discusses his intriguing before-and-after experience. During his internment in the Sovetskaya Gavan region, he composed several *tanka* (short poems) every day, two thousand or three thousand in total, to cope with his emotions. He wrote them on the pieces of white birch bark. Then, when he returned to his barrack at the end of a workday, he recited them aloud and gave them away to whoever wanted them. Years after repatriating to Japan, he thought of publishing them and tried to recover them from his former campmates, but to no avail. Perhaps none of them had cared enough to bring them home, in defiance of the strict Soviet ban on taking anything written back to Japan. It is more surprising to hear that Nakahara was not able to recall even a single word of his poems.[18] Apparently, he left all his emotions in Siberia; the self that experienced the humiliation of Soviet detention remained in a separate space, which the postwar self could not reach.[19]

By attending to both the treacherous conditions of the internment and the specific postwar political environment that faced the Siberian returnees, this chapter underscores the entanglement of the returnees' efforts to articulate their experiences with the popular memories of war in postwar Japanese society. I begin by describing the extreme conditions of the Siberian camps to illustrate their dehumanizing effects on the internees. These are also the conditions that made it difficult for them to talk about what they experienced. I then examine the psychological and ontological challenges that the detainees faced as they later attempted to discuss their time in the Soviet Union. Finally, I turn to the political conditions that belittled the former POWs' experiences. The former POWs confronted great psychological challenges in enunciating their traumatic experiences, and only a limited number of them were willing to relive their painful past through speaking about it, either publicly or privately. Even when they did speak, their voices were subsumed by the highly charged political terrain of postwar Japan.

THE STRUGGLE FOR SURVIVAL

By the time the Soviet Union declared war against the Great Empire of Japan on August 9, 1945, the once proud Kwantung army had been reduced to a deplorable state. It had been undermined by Japan's desperate fight and its efforts to relocate units from northeast China to Southeast Asia and the Pacific. Although forces of 664,000 were stationed in Manchuria at the beginning of the conflict,[20] hardly any of the Kwantung army's original units remained. In order to maintain the facade of a functional military organization against the threat of the Soviet forces, the army absorbed some units from the China front, as well as new units from mainland Japan, where men under forty were subject to military conscription. Also called to duty were all the local Japanese males in northeast China below the age of forty-five.[21]

These measures only worsened the conditions they were meant to ameliorate. The Kwantung army did not have enough supplies and equipment for its new recruits, who had to wear worn-out uniforms covered with patches. In addition, without enough firearms to go around, some new recruits had to carry nineteenth-century rifles.[22] Fake airplanes made from plywood were stationed at airports, and logs colored with black ink were installed in place of artillery.[23] The little training the recruits received consisted mainly of learning how to throw themselves underneath Soviet tanks with explosives on their backs.[24]

Once the Red Army crossed the Soviet-Manchurian and the Soviet-Korean borders on August 9, 1945, the Kwantung army and the Seventeenth Area Army in Korea (294,000 officers and soldiers) posed only a minimal threat to the Soviet Union's superior firepower and armored units. Japanese defense lines quickly crumbled, with a few isolated exceptions. On August 15, the Japanese emperor announced on the radio that Japan had accepted the conditions specified in the Potsdam Declaration, and on August 19, the Japanese commander surrendered to the Soviet authority and ordered a cease-fire. Sporadic fighting nevertheless continued for the next two weeks.

As of August 15, there were more than 1 million Japanese officers, soldiers, and civilian personnel (mostly members of the Kwantung army and the Seventeenth Area Army) in the areas that the Soviet army would soon occupy (Manchuria, southern Sakhalin, the Kuril Islands, North Korea, and the Liaodong Peninsula).[25] A Soviet central committee organized 700,000 to 800,000 men into work battalions for transport to Soviet territories to assist in the reconstruction of the war-devastated country.[26] To fill the gaps between the lists of personnel they had obtained from the Japanese forces and the actual number of soldiers, Soviet authorities also rounded up Japanese male civilians and a small number of Japanese women (the gaps were due to the fact that some Japanese officers discharged their local recruits on their own volition, and a number of soldiers went AWOL in the postconflict confusion).[27]

For the members of the Imperial Japanese Army and Navy, becoming a prisoner of war was not an option.[28] While publicly proclaiming the value of heroic deaths, the Japanese military never bothered to teach them how to survive captivity. Even though nothing would have fully prepared the men for the fate that awaited them in the internment camps, it should be noted that the abject images of POWs, the images propagated by the military, deepened many detainees' despair when they most needed spiritual and psychological support.

Passage from the sites of demilitarization to the Soviet labor camps was treacherous and shrouded in secrecy. Detainees were forced to march, sometimes staying at transfer camps where Soviet authorities organized them into work battalions before sending them to the labor camps. En route to or at these transfer camps, many detainees were robbed of their valuables, losing nonessential items, such as watches and fountain pens, as well as blankets and woolen clothing, which were essential to cope with winter in Siberia.[29] The Soviet authorities further deceived the Japanese captives into believing that they were being transported to their native land. Numerous survivors have testified that the Soviet guards nudged them onward during the grueling marches over hundreds of miles to railways stations by telling them, "Tokio domoy" ([You are going] home, Tokyo). The POWs wished to return home desperately enough to believe what they heard. Fukui Hideo, who was later detained at a camp located near Kuybyshevka-Vostochnaya (present-day Belogorsk) in the Amur region, reported a rumor that spread while he was in Soviet custody in late August 1945: the rumor claimed that the Soviets were first transporting them to Siberia but then to Vladivostok in order to avoid local conflicts between the Nationalists and the Communists in southern Manchuria.[30] Numerous other detainees kept their hopes up with similar tales.[31] Even after realizing that they were heading in the wrong direction on the train—north and then west to the labor camps— many clung to false optimism.[32] The freight trains kept running in the opposite direction of their home, and even when seeing Lake Baikal, some detainees insisted that it was the Sea of Japan.[33]

Although individuals had varied experiences in Siberia—conditions differed from camp to camp and the period of internment[34]—a composite picture emerges from the detainees' accounts. Upon arrival at their prison camps, the soldiers were housed in crowded facilities that offered the most primitive amenities. Some battalions stayed in tents for extended periods. Others were housed in barracks called *zyemlyankye*, which were partially underground, and some had to build their own shelters. Coal-burning stoves barely heated their living quarters in the frigid Siberian winter, and the white birch bark burned for lighting produced as much soot as light, leaving the faces of the detainees smudged black by morning.[35] Tall fences surrounded the barracks, and Soviet guards with machine guns perched in watchtowers. These guards frequently shot detainees, treating as deserters anyone who came within a certain distance of the fence. The Soviet soldiers who watched over the Japanese POWs on their marches and in their camps and worksites also had the discretion to shoot any "deserters." Returnees reported many tragedies caused by trigger-happy Soviet soldiers shooting those who had slipped on the icy roads and fallen behind their fellow detainees.

The POWs' first winter in Siberia was the worst in regard to camp provisions. World War II had devastated Soviet agricultural production and distribution systems, so the food supply was inadequate even for the local population, let alone the detainees.[36] For breakfast, the detainees were normally given a slice of dark bread, water, and runny *kasha* (porridge); for dinner, another slice of bread and a small amount of cooked meat and potatoes. Although some bread was provided for their lunch in the morning before departing for their work detail, most of the POWs ate it immediately to provide temporary relief from their perpetual hunger. Even if a detainee saved his bread for lunch, it was in danger of being stolen. Dividing the rationed food among themselves was the most important business of each day. Yoshida Isamu's illustration vividly shows each man in the work unit intently watching every move of the man whose turn it was to distribute food from the kitchen so that he would not be cheated out of a tiniest crumb (figure 3.1). As Kusanagi Taiji recalled, the process was so thorough that it took one to two hours to ration out each meal at his Tayshet camp.[37] Soviet supervisors at many of the camps embezzled food and other supplies for resale, and the distribution of food was manipulated to "motivate" the prisoners.[38] Watanabe Chiguto, a doctor who was detained in a camp near Elabuga, a city about 550 miles east of Moscow, claims that until fall of 1947, the individuals in

FIGURE 3.1 Yoshida Isamu, *Divvying Up the Food*, date unknown. Each meal was a deadly serious matter, especially during the first winter of the internment. Yoshida was initially interned at Voloshilov and then was moved to various other locations. He returned to Japan in July 1947. (Courtesy of the Maizuru Repatriation Memorial Museum)

his battalion received only about 50 percent of the officially announced 2,650 calorie ration.[39]

The POWs were reduced to desperate measures. Nakamaki Yasuhiro, interned near Irkutsk, describes a man who made the fatal choice of exchanging his undergarments for bread. He died after spending a few days in just his army uniform in the extremely low temperatures of −22 to −40°F (−30 to −40°C).[40] Detainees commonly gathered wild grasses to supplement their meager meals, as shown in Tanaka Buichirō's illustration (figure 3.2). Although they were simply trying to fill their empty stomachs with any available food, the grasses were actually valuable sources of vitamins, which were otherwise low in the grain-based camp rations.[41] Pine nuts were a dependable energy source when the detainees were able to collect them.[42] Some men claimed that they chewed on pine needles[43] or drank the water after boiling them, for the same reason.[44] Many internees recall finding frozen "potatoes" on the street that when thawed on a stove, actually turned out to be horse droppings.[45] Seki

FIGURE 3.2 Tanaka Buichirō, *Inside a Labor Camp*, 1960. Evening at the cramped living quarters of a labor camp. Tanaka was interned at Abakan, the capital city of the Republic of Khakassia. He returned to Japan in October 1947. (Courtesy of Memorial Museum for Soldiers, Detainees in Siberia, and Postwar Repatriates)

Kiyoto, detained at Sverdlovsk, the largest city in the Ural Mountains region, describes how he and his fellow internees ate snakes, rats, frogs, cats, and dogs to supplement their meager diet and even hunted for potato peels in a garbage heap. They occasionally "asked Soviet soldiers to shoot dogs and cats and fought over the kill."[46] For Sakamoto Yaichi and his fellow detainees in the Karaganda region, even animal bones by the wayside provided precious sustenance, as they cracked the bones to eat the marrow inside.[47] Watanabe Tokio, who spent three years in the Komsomolsk region, recalls catching rabbits, field mice, snakes, frogs, salmon, and snakeheads.[48] Kariyuki Seiji confesses that he ate human flesh at his camp in Primorsky Kray, located across the water from Hokkaidō.[49] Other internees shared their grilled meat with him; only later did he learn that it actually had been sliced off a dead body that they had found at a work site.[50] Hiranuma Gyokutarō had similar experiences in the Krasnoyarsk region.[51] In a camp located on the lower Amur River, Murakami Yasuhiko was so hungry that he could not resist the sweet taste of the explosives used for construction. For a couple days, he sprinkled his bread with dynamite that he had stolen from a storage facility. He quickly developed jaundice and was hospitalized, although he miraculously recovered from his ill-fated experiment.[52] Physical examinations of the POWs were a simple affair: doctors pinched the prisoners' buttocks to check skin resiliency: saggy skin meant malnutrition.[53] Malnutrition and fatigue also made the internees, who also lacked adequate bathing facilities, more vulnerable to the lice that spread typhus and, especially in the older facilities, the bedbugs that came out by the hundreds at night to feast on the prisoners' warm blood. Such extreme living conditions directly contributed to a death rate in some camps that reached 30 to 50 percent during the first winter.[54]

Despite their grossly inadequate caloric intake, the POWs were forced to engage in hard and often dangerous jobs for which most had no prior training. These work assignments included general construction, railway building, mining, manufacturing, agriculture, and logging (figure 3.3). The Soviets set a strict work quota for each individual according to his assignment and health. Those who did not meet their quotas were often dealt a punitive reduction in daily rations, which further exacerbated the already dismal conditions.[55] Their prisoners' inadequate tools (e.g., dull saws) and lack of basic skills made it extremely difficult to meet these

FIGURE 3.3 Hashimoto Takuma, *Roll Call in the Morning*, date unknown. Hashimoto was detained in Nikolayevsk and returned to Japan in May 1947. (Courtesy of Hashimoto Ken'ichirō and the Maizuru Repatriation Memorial Museum)

quotas, especially in the early phase of their internment. Frigid temperatures and deep snow only exacerbated the existing challenges. For example, digging a hole in frozen ground required extra time and effort. Laborers had to burn fires on the ground repeatedly during the digging because a single fire would not melt the frozen ground to a sufficient depth.[56] Winter, however, was regarded as the best time for logging because the tree sap that clogged the saws stopped flowing in extremely low temperatures. The POWs were forced to work outside unless the outside temperature plunged below −40°F.[57] Logging was one of the most hazardous jobs for the inexperienced and malnourished detainees, and many were injured or died because their emaciated bodies were not able to move fast enough in deep snow to avoid the falling trees.[58]

While working outside in the summertime, they faced different hardships. Out in the fields or bushes, swarms of black flies mercilessly bit exposed skin.[59] The detainees learned through experience that squishing a black fly after being bitten was dangerous because the smell of blood attracted other black flies. Ishihara Yoshirō recalled that even a trace of blood on the soft part around the eye meant that in a few hours he was unable to open his eyes.[60] Working on the construction of the Baikal–Amur Mainline (BAM) in the summer of 1950, Mizutani Eiji had to wear protective gear over his head in the heat. One Georgian detainee refused to do so out of vanity but paid a high price: "Within half a day, his face was bloated like a balloon, and the black monstrosity never recovered its original shape. Horses and cows can die when attacked by swarms of mosquitoes and black flies. It was a miracle that he survived."[61] Heat and humidity also created treacherous conditions: Mizutani remembers that seven or eight men of his work unit fainted every day from heat stroke.[62] The detainees also had to cope with ticks. Watanabe Tokio recounts a case in which a tick bite produced a serious infection with high fever in another detainee, who then contracted typhus and died. While the tick bite may not have been the direct cause of death, it likely undermined his chances for survival.[63]

Although internees working in the coal or mineral mines were shielded from extreme temperatures outdoors, they faced other hazards. The shafts had no ventilation, and the men had to work without masks, and those operating the drills were constantly covered with and inhaling fine dust. Abe Yoshikuni, who worked at the tungsten mine in Bukuka, Chita, remembers leaving the mine every day covered with heavy dust: "My nostrils were stuffed with rock powder, which had turned into a dough-like substance, and, when I ground my mouth, the stuff made an unpleasant sound."[64] As a result, many of the detainees subsequently developed silicosis and died after a long struggle with the disease.[65] Moreover, a considerable number of men were misdiagnosed after returning to Japan and thus were mistakenly treated for tuberculosis because their experiences were so extreme that their illness did not conform to the postwar Japanese medical profession's diagnostic criteria.[66] The general opinion then was that silicosis developed only in individuals who worked in mines for more than ten years, whereas the detainees had worked in mines for an average of only one and a half years. The widespread occurrence of silicosis among detainees attests instead to the extreme conditions under which they strained to meet their work quotas.

Other factors also contributed to the detainees' suffering. External demands could extend their work schedules: a number of former detainees recollected that whenever a freight train arrived at the nearby station, they had to rush to unload it, regardless of the time of day.[67] During the initial stage of internment, prisoners typically worked ten to fourteen hours each day, without any days off.[68] Furthermore, the Japanese army's command system remained intact in most of the camps, reflecting the Soviet policy of controlling the POWs indirectly through the preexisting Japanese military hierarchy. Consequently, lower-ranking soldiers in the camps continued to suffer from the mental and physical abuse that had run rampant in the Japanese military. Hokari Kashio described the tyrannical behavior of the noncommissioned officers and a corporal in his work unit at a Tayshet camp. They consumed at least twice as much food as their subordinates did and subjected whoever showed the slightest sign of discontent to severe physical abuse.[69] Since there were no new recruits to take their places, the soldiers at the bottom of the pecking order could never advance. Nomura Shōtarō, who was interned in Sovetskaya Gavan, claims that the overwhelming majority of deaths—more than one hundred—were of rookies and older last-minute recruits.[70] Frustration among the rank and file eventually boiled over, fueling democratization movements at numerous camps, which I discuss later in this chapter.

Without any clear prospect for attaining freedom in the near future, the POWs' mental condition deteriorated. Many feared they might die in Siberia, a fear powerful enough to drive some to desperate acts. Kawamura Katsumi, detained in eastern Siberia, wrote about a prisoner who escaped from a coal mine in the middle of winter, only to be discovered and shot to death.[71] Kawamura himself had harbored ideas of escape. In preparation, he gradually saved up a supply of bread from the small rations he received. He even came up with a plausible plan but had to abandon it when he discovered one day that the bread he had saved had been stolen.[72]

Hiranuma Gyokutarō also engaged in acts of desperation. He was originally sentenced to death for alleged espionage activities. Since the Soviet Union had abolished the death penalty in 1947, Hiranuma's sentence was commuted to twenty-five years of forced labor. In a short account of his eleven-year Siberian experience, Hiranuma admits that he killed two Soviet foremen and seriously wounded another, being convinced that "I've gotta do something, even out of desperation, to survive. I've gotta live. . . . Since I could never go home alive, I've gotta kill even one or two."[73] In his mind, self-destructive behavior was the reason for his survival. Hiranuma's murderous rage was indeed the only leverage he had with the camp authorities, who left him alone out of fear. Hiranuma eventually made it home in 1956, but the internment took a toll on him. Upon his return in 1956, he was immediately hospitalized for an ulcer and later for tuberculosis. Believing that he was dead, his wife had remarried in the same year that he entered the camp. Despite trying to appreciate the future that he had recovered, his account is filled with pathos: he was practically a dead man in postwar Japan.

While many internees sought to maintain a sense of superiority over the Russians by focusing on their low standards of living and education, others brought back to Japan more positive impressions. As the Soviet Union gradually recovered from the devastating effects of war, the detainees' living conditions also improved in small measures. They received more food and even found the time and energy to organize various activities in their camps.[74] Security measures at some camps were also relaxed, allowing detainees to interact more with local residents outside the camps and work sites. Toward the end of his internment in the Tayshet region, Tanaka Mikio was allowed to leave the camp by himself on Sundays to go fishing at the nearby river. Happily involved in the camp theater and choral activities, he admits that he had no desire to go home when he received the repatriation order.[75]

The aforementioned Nakamaki Yasuhiro was able to sneak out of his camp because the guards were often absent from their guard station at night. His purpose was to visit houses in town to peddle toys and other wooden handicrafts that his fellow internees had produced at their job sites. Taking advantage of the elementary Russian he had taught himself at the beginning of his internment, he formed close friendships with some of the local residents.[76] While he greatly suffered in his Chuguyevka camp, about seventy miles northeast of Vladivostok, Tsuzura Gunji was proud of the work that he and his fellow Japanese prisoners did harvesting timber. In *Siberian Tales* (*Shiberia monogatari*), a collection of eleven short stories, the writer Hasegawa Shirō offers vignettes of the everyday interactions he had during his four years of internment in the Chita area. While Hasegawa suffered as many hardships in Chita as other internees did, he remembers his time there not from the position of a victim but from that of a human being; his account humanizes both detainees and the Russians living under Stalin's regime.[77]

THE PSYCHOLOGICAL AND ONTOLOGICAL
CONDITIONS OF FORMER POWS

The systematic repatriation of the POWs began in 1946, and the majority of survivors had returned to their homeland by 1950.[78] The detainees' arrival on Japanese shores, however, often did not end their struggles. The traumatic camp experiences had long-lasting effects on their postwar lives. For example, for about a year after returning to Japan in 1956, Hiranuma Gyokutarō suffered from an acute sense of paranoia, constantly feeling that he was under surveillance.[79] Ōtsuka Shigeru, who returned in 1947, had nightmares about his experiences in Siberia into the 1980s.[80] Although many tried to make sense of what they had experienced as Soviet POWs, the extreme nature of their experiences defied comprehension, and the postwar stigma attached to the former POWs made their task doubly difficult.

For many former POWs, the first hurdle to describing their traumatic internment was psychological. Only a few were willing to relive their painful memories upon returning to Japan, while many chose not to speak about them at all. When Ishimori Takeo returned from four and half years of detention, his mother cried every time she heard about his time in Siberia, so he decided never to bring up the topic again.[81] Only after some forty years did Iwamoto Masumi manage to tell a friend's bereaved family what had happened to their son; he admitted frankly that he could not bring himself to speak of the experience sooner.[82] For Ishimori, Iwamoto, and many others, silence was the only way for them to reintegrate into everyday life in postwar Japan.

Those who did decide to speak about their past in Siberia were forced to confront the humiliation that they had experienced as POWs, feelings that nevertheless varied greatly in intensity and configuration. The writings of Takasugi Ichirō as well as those of Ishihara Yoshirō, a poet whom I discuss in greater detail in chapter 4, have tremendous value for both their rarity and their insights into the nature of their degradation. What they each describe as humiliation, however, varies according to each man's experience: Takasugi distances himself from his own experiences by talking about the case experienced by another, whereas Ishihara grapples alone with his ontological crisis.

The stigma of being a POW persisted well after Japan's defeat in the Asia Pacific War. Takasugi Ichirō's 1950 account of his own Siberian experiences cites a passage from the *Field Service Code* (*Senjinkun*): "A soldier must never suffer the disgrace of being captured alive. He should not leave a shameful reputation after his death." This passage was brought to life for him when he witnessed a Russian Communist Youth member beat a Japanese POW with a stick. Through his fellow POW's pain, the passage acquired reality for him for the first time. Japanese soldiers had been taught to fear the consequence of becoming a prisoner of war, a fear realized in the Soviet camps. Although Takasugi does not subscribe to the same level of shame that another camp member expressed about becoming a POW, he does express a vague sense of humiliation for what he suffered in the camps and anticipates a feeling of desolation when he reunites with his family back in Japan.[83]

The fear of being looked down on was well justified in postwar society, as demonstrated by the experiences of those in other theaters of war. Yokota Shōhei survived the battle of Guam by surrendering to the American forces in 1944 and returned from an American POW camp in 1947 to pursue a successful career as a newspaper reporter. Though everyone in the newspaper office knew that Yokota had been a former American POW, no one, including Yokota himself, talked openly about his experiences. According to his close colleagues, even in the late 1950s, some fellow workers whispered derisively that Yokota had learned English—an advantage in his subsequent career—in a POW camp. Even though they dismissed as ridiculous the command in the *Field Service Code* to choose death over being taken captive, postwar Japanese society also celebrated Japanese servicemen's deadly sacrifices—particularly in the form of suicide missions—in the Asia Pacific War, making it extremely difficult for former POWs to discuss their experiences openly.[84]

Some returnees tried to lessen the stigma attached to their former POW status by pointing to "lesser" POWs who had surrendered to enemy forces during the war, but this psychological defense was largely unsuccessful.[85] In Siberia, some prisoners enjoyed a sense of superiority when witnessing the plight of Japanese POWs who had been captured by the Soviets in the Nomonhan incident, the large-scale conflicts between the

Soviet army and the Kwantung army in Outer Mongolia in 1939. These soldiers had been taken captive while the myth of the Kwantung army's invincibility was still intact. They suffered a far greater stigma, believing that they would be court-martialed if they returned to Japan and that their families would be disgraced. As a result, some gave up the idea of ever returning home and stayed in the Soviet Union permanently.[86] POWs who were detained after the war concluded felt superior to such unfortunate men, who had lost their sense of connection with Japan. Nevertheless, this hierarchy of disgrace did not erase the fact that regardless of when they had been detained, all the prisoners faced daily humiliation by the power structures within the Soviet labor camps.

Indeed, the price of survival in the camps was too high for some. In a series of essays published in the late 1960s and early 1970s, poet Ishihara Yoshirō contemplated the effect that Siberia had had on him. Ishihara had spent a total of eight years in confinement, five years as a prisoner of war and three additional years for his alleged anti-Soviet activities during the war. After being sentenced for his alleged crimes, Ishihara was confined for transport in a Stolypin car, a train car fitted out for transporting convicts.[87] At the beginning of their journey, each convict was given some salted sardines and bread to last for three days, with drinking water available in one barrel for each car. A second barrel was to be used for urination. Having long lost the self-control needed to save their food for the journey, the convicts immediately consumed their rations. Suffering from thirst, they gulped water from the barrel and then urinated copiously. Since the second barrel was not large enough to hold their urine, it overflowed onto the floor. Furthermore, they were allowed to use a toilet only once every twenty-four hours. "If you could not hold it and defecated on the cell floor, you were dragged into the pathway, kicked until you could not breathe any longer, and were forced to clean up the feces with your bare hands." As the journey progressed, they became soaked in their own urine, which the bread also absorbed. In order to survive, they had to stop thinking about the unsanitary conditions of the car, desensitizing themselves to their own plight. Self-preservation became the only principle of their behavior.[88] They may have survived the physical challenges, but they were reduced to shells of their former selves.

Once the Japanese suspects were convicted by the provisional court, they were separated from the other POWs and placed in the general prison population in cells on the trains. These inmates were controlled by fellow convicts, thugs called *sooka* (bitches) who served as assistants to the authorities by terrorizing their cellmates.[89] Most Japanese convicts were left on their own, with little knowledge of Russian and unable to protect themselves in a space ruled by violence. In his account of the lawless state of the Stolypin cars, Mizutani Eiji recalls how several *sooka* physically abused the helpless and monopolized the food, forcing some convicts to ingratiate themselves to the *sooka* just to receive a tiny share.[90]

With survival being the only goal, the prisoners soon lost any sense of decency. In the POW camps, many inmates, seeking reward in the form of food, informed camp authorities of their fellow captives' illicit activities, most often minor infractions of camp rules, such as the possession of contraband items like handmade sewing needles. These men traded their personal integrity for extra provisions, dragging down those who were merely trying to maintain a semblance of humanity.[91] Kamei Tsutomu, a survivor of the camps in Mongolia, offers an account that further demonstrates the primacy of self-preservation at any cost. Kamei tells of how survivors immediately stripped dead POWs of their clothes, either to keep themselves warm or to exchange them with local residents for much prized salt. With a honed sense of who was near death, the POWs monitored one another closely so as not to miss any opportunity.[92] They survived the internment by acting like scavengers, and the camp authorities treated them like herds of domesticated animals. The tales of their ignominious survival thus had little appeal for their defeated homeland as it sought to restore national dignity.

The so-called democratization movements, initiated and supported by the Soviet Ministry of Internal Affairs, brought both positive and negative changes to the camps. Democratic groups began to form in the spring of 1946, inspired by calls for democratic action that appeared in the Soviet-issued Japanese-language newspaper for the detainees.[93] In 1947, the Soviet authority began to play a more active, albeit indirect, role in providing the groups with an ideological basis.[94] Several select detainees from each camp studied Communist ideology and party history at regional centers for several months and returned as activists. In many

ways, the movements served as a school of democracy, offering an impetus for low-ranking soldiers to challenge—for the first time—the Japanese military order that continued to rule their camps.[95] Many prisoners
were empowered by their activist experience, regaining a sense of agency
in the otherwise impossible conditions of internment.

The movements, however, existed on a fraudulent basis, as the participants were prohibited from critiquing the Soviet system that had imprisoned them in the first place. Lacking genuine outlets for critique, the
activist spirit turned inward, breeding a deep sense of mutual suspicion
within the camps. In 1948 and 1949, at the height of the movements,
everyone was a potential target of collective criticism; those identified
as "anti-Soviet" were collectively denounced and forced to make public
apologies. Although many prisoners thought that the sessions of collective criticism were a farce, they refrained from saying so out of fear. Any
hint of criticism would mark them as reactionary and delay their return
to Japan, so they pretended to be serious about the collective action.[96]
Self-preservation and mutual suspicion taught the detainees to praise as
"democratization" the political system that oppressed them. Eventually,
the Japanese camp leaders organized a mass expression of gratitude to
Stalin in the form of an embroidered "letter" that took several months of
elaborate preparation and was delivered to the Kremlin in a handcrafted
ornamental casing.[97] The "voluntary" nature attributed to this farcical act
was arguably even more humiliating than direct coercion. By internaliz-
ing their captors' will, prisoners of war had to surrender their integrity and
even their resentment of the authorities that had imprisoned them. Some
transferred their anger to postwar Japan, ready to declare an ideological
war against their homeland.[98]

For the returning POWs, postwar Japanese society was not welcoming. The men were reminders of the nation's painful losses and living
proof that supported the Japanese fear of the Soviet Union. Their POWs'
survival, therefore, was never widely celebrated. It was extremely difficult for them to share their experiences under such conditions, and those
who returned from Siberia had to grapple privately with what they had
been forced to sacrifice for their own survival.[99] The stories that did
surface often complemented the widely embraced narrative in which
the Japanese were merely victims of the war. For many returned POWs,
however, the details of what they experienced in Siberia were too trau-

matic to recall. Moreover, as I show later, the highly charged politics of postwar society did not allow them to identify themselves merely as victims.

FEAR OF THE SOVIET UNION: UTOPIA OR DYSTOPIA?

The fiercely politicized atmosphere of postwar Japan ensnared former POWs who were struggling to speak about their experiences in the Siberian camps. Socialism offered an attractive political alternative for those Japanese intellectuals who detested the postwar American hegemony in Japan and East Asia. As a result, members of the Japanese Communist Party (JCP) and other leftist intellectuals vigorously protected the Soviet Union's image as the apotheosis of socialist ideology. Because the returnees' revelations were seen as damaging to the socialist cause, Soviet supporters and sympathizers in Japan made efforts to discredit the men. Representative examples of the efforts to discredit POWs are visible in the statements by progressive intellectual Kuwabara Takeo and others regarding the Soviet Union and its internment of Japanese POWs. In turn, historian Wakatsuki Yasuo offered a biting commentary on Kuwabara's claims, and Shimizu Ikutarō provided a critical self-examination of this point.[100] Their arguments inform my own analysis of the postwar Japanese discursive space, as it shaped the possibilities for speech by former Siberian detainees.

In the early postwar years, many Japanese intellectuals sympathized with the leftist positions that embraced the JCP's official stance toward the issue of Japanese POWs in Siberia. Specifically, the JCP claimed that the Soviet Union treated the detainees well and ultimately blamed the reactionary former officers of the Kwantung army for the detainees' difficult conditions and the Japanese government for not sending transport ships to bring them home.[101] In the mid-1950s, as part of its propaganda efforts, the Soviet Union invited some two hundred Japanese intellectuals to observe Soviet society.[102] As a result of the carefully staged tours, many of the guests later raved about the Soviets' economic achievements. Only a few mentioned the Japanese POWs who remained in Soviet camps. Wakatsuki notes, critically, that Kuwabara Takeo not only kept silent on the issue of the remaining POWs but even dismissed the returnees' personal accounts. Even before he had been invited to the Soviet Union,

Kuwabara was condescending in his comments on *Chūōkōron*'s January 1954 reports by returned Japanese POWs. After expressing perfunctory congratulations to the returnees, Kuwabara urged Japan to thank the Soviet Union for repatriating the POWs. He regretted that the incarceration of so many Japanese had had negative effects on international peace, not because the Soviet Union violated international law, but because the practice provided an excuse for bashing the Soviets.[103] Moreover, Kuwabara sought to protect the image of the Soviet Union by shifting the blame to the returnees themselves:

> The reports are, in a word, quite boring. Moreover, I am afraid this gets a little academic, but at the heart of the reports is the simplistic theory that since people have eyes to see, all that meets the eye must be visible. That is not true. How many times have we seen that, for example, even someone who lives in the United States for eight years has observed only a small slice? Moreover, whether or not [the reasons for their crimes were] justifiable, those who have returned at this time were incarcerated for some kind of crime. Do you look to someone who has just been released from a Japanese prison after seven years for criticism of the Yoshida cabinet?[104]

By declaring the reports "boring," Kuwabara insinuated that they were unworthy of any serious intellectual consideration. Although he was not wrong about the fallibility of human observation, such stringency should also be applied to the intellectuals, including himself, who parroted Soviet apologies without any actual experience of the system. The POWs' reports provided mostly firsthand recollections of their experiences in Siberia as political prisoners, as well as some general observations, both positive and negative, of Soviet society. But Kuwabara sought to discredit the writers for their "crimes of some kind," disregarding their imprisonment for "political crimes," many of which were trumped up by a paranoid Stalinist bureaucracy. Moreover, by shifting to a discussion of a hypothetical prisoner in Japan, Kuwabara stripped the internees' crimes of their political dimension, as if political crimes were the same as other offenses. Finally he ignored the likelihood that if political prisoners in Japan had been released in 1953 after seven years of imprisonment, their criticism of the Japanese political system responsible for their incarceration would have been highly sought after, both inside and outside Japan.

In contrast to Kuwabara's skewed reasoning, the repatriated authors of the POW reports seemed to maintain a self-reflective attitude. One such contributor, Nakai Yoshiharu, directly cautions the reader about the potential partiality of his account:

> Since we were imprisoned for war crimes, it was natural that we were treated as prisoners. Pressed into such a position, how can I correctly judge the powerful who stood in front of me? If my account contains "reactionary words," my position in the Soviet Union may have led to such judgments. At least, I now believe I am impartial [but I might be mistaken]. . . . Fair judgment may come after I have had more time, after living a while in the country called Japan.[105]

Yet despite his cautionary note, Nakai avoided sweeping remarks; his account was hardly reactionary but instead focused on what he had learned in everyday life. As was the case with many returned POWs, Nakai reported information that he gathered through conversations with local residents. He commented on ordinary Soviet citizens' lives and the effects they felt from Soviet economic policies. Kuwabara, however, takes Nakai's self-reflective statement as a sign of the partiality of all POW reports; he thus rationalizes his dismissal of the actual content in order to see what he wanted to see in *Chūōkōron*'s published reports: "I can somehow sense that the Russians have the endurance of bears, and there is absolutely no racial prejudice there. Everybody's observations are in agreement that the Soviet Union's productive power has rapidly been growing and that its living standards have been improving."[106] Kuwabara's comments are imbued with the desire of various Japanese intellectuals to see an alternative to the existing political conditions of postwar Japan—semicoloniality under U.S. hegemony—a desire powerful enough to blind them to the plight of the detainees.

Political scholar Okamoto Sei'ichi, who built his career as a progressive commentator on democratic principles, had a similar reaction to Kuwabara when remarking on *Chūōkōron*'s issue with the POW reports:

I don't think the astonishing ignorance [displayed in those returnees' writings] stems simply from the fact that they were prisoners. I suspect that they are probably the kind of people who lacked, in the first place, the sensitivity to understand such social issues properly. Of course, when they were born, they were not like that. But working for the military police, secret military agencies, or private intelligence organizations must have destroyed such sensitivity.[107]

Okamoto and others like him sought to discredit those who offered even the slightest criticism of the Soviet Union. Disparaging the returnees by speculating that they deserved to be treated as prisoners, Okamoto never acknowledged the inhumanity of their internment. He imprisons them in a tautological logic: the fact that they were prisoners disqualifies them from writing about their prison experiences. As products of a fascist regime, they are prohibited from criticizing the socialist regime.

Such categorical denials by the JCP and various other Japanese leftist intellectuals had a major impact on public debate in the early years of postwar Japan. For a window into the psychological makeup of the Japanese left at this time, we can look to the writings of Shimizu Ikutarō, a prominent leftist thinker in the early postwar period who later recanted his political beliefs in favor of a strongly nationalistic outlook. Arguing that a deep-seated fear of the Soviet Union defined their pro-Soviet attitudes, Shimizu suggests that Japanese intellectuals' preference for including the Soviet Union in the impending peace treaty stemmed from political anxieties that they actually shared with conservatives:

Many of those [leftists] who supported an overall peace [signing the peace treaty with the Socialist regimes as well]—including myself—might have been fearful of Russia. Judging from the Soviet Union's behavior at the end of World War II, we were living right near a country that was completely unpredictable in its behavior. Who knew when the United States would retreat to the other side of the Pacific once it reawakened to its isolationist instincts? Except for the Communists and Marx-Leninists who muttered, truthfully or not, that they wished to see Japan occupied by the Soviet Union, many of those who wished for an overall peace [with both the capitalist and the socialist regimes] shared a fear of Russia with those [conservatives] who supported a separate peace [with capitalist regimes]. The latter expressed their fear straight-forwardly, while the former lost that opportunity, ending up idealizing what they feared.[108]

Both groups understood that a separate peace with the United States and its allies would make Japan an enemy in the eyes of the Soviet Union; Shimizu argues that it was this very concern that led leftist intellectuals to idealize the Soviet Union as a desirable partner and a socialist utopia. Following Shimizu's logic, the Japanese POWs in Siberia embodied the unpredictable and outrageous behavior of the Soviet Union at the end of World War II.[109] Accounts of such experiences raised the specter of an invasion by the Soviet Union, which had been averted in the past but re-mained possible in the future. Accordingly, the political left repressed their fears by discrediting anything that contradicted a utopian vision of the Soviet Union, including the returnees' soul-searching accounts of their experiences. While Shimizu's analysis might have been marred by his desire to justify his conservative turn, it nevertheless offers a valuable insight into how the political reality affected Japanese intellectuals. As widely witnessed in the democratization movement in Siberian labor camps, fear was a strong impetus to embrace the Soviet political system.

The political right fared no better in accepting the returnees. Con-servatives were inclined to circulate only negative images of the Soviet system; there was no room for sympathetic description. Businesses and rural communities had deep distrust of the Soviet Union and its ideol-ogy. As a result, many returned POWs were refused employment simply because they had come back from the Soviet Union. Moreover, the me-dia's attention to the radicalized returnees did not help the other return-ees' efforts.

Historian William F. Nimmo, quoting a 1949 article in the *Nippon Times*, describes postwar Japan's general response to the former POWs who returned as staunch believers in Communism:

It is no wonder that an anguished mother welcoming her long-absent son [who, in great agitation, screamed, "Down with imperialism"] should cry out, "What have they done with my son?" Perhaps the repa-triates themselves should not be judged too severely, for they are the products of Communist training. They are the ones so well indoctrinated that the Soviets allowed them to return. They are Communists.[110]

This kind of problematic assumption—that only those who had internalized Soviet propaganda were allowed to come home—greatly hindered returnees' efforts to gain employment in postwar Japan. In 1950, three years after Fukui Hideo returned from a camp near Kuybyshevka-Vostochnaya, he applied to join the National Police Reserves, predecessor of the Self-Defense Forces, but was rejected solely because he had returned from Siberia.[111] Ishihara Yoshirō also encountered similar prejudice while seeking employment, and in the end he managed only to find a job as a translator in a business owned by another former Soviet POW.[112] Association with the "Reds" cast the returnees as potential threats to postwar society.[113]

Takasugi Ichirō relates a story that exemplifies how former POWs were caught in the political schism between the left and the right. Upon returning to Japan in 1949, he gave a talk about the Soviet Union. Takasugi soon regretted it, however, for although he tried to be honest in his account and avoid generalized descriptions, his audience listened only to confirm their preconceived notions of the Soviet Union. "Two diametrically opposite conclusions, both allegedly my own, were bounced back to me after a few days. I was surprised at how both had been transformed into something narrowly political and partisan."[114] Takasugi had tried to present a nuanced description of both his experiences in the Siberian camps and the Soviet political system. He was caught, however, in a polarized political atmosphere: both conservatives and leftists interpreted his presentation as confirming their images of Soviet society as either a totalitarian dystopia or a socialist utopia.

Another factor that worked against the POWs was the Japanese military's swift postwar transformation into a group of warmongers who had dragged the rest of Japan into a military conflict nobody else wanted. Though self-serving, this narrative played an important role in promoting postwar Japan as a desirable partner for the United States. Postwar society was eager to accept the story of Japan as rehabilitated into a potentially democratic country that had been victimized by its own military. That narrative discounted the suffering of military personnel in favor of innocent women and children, figured as victims of Japanese militarism.[115] As representatives of imperial Japan's dark past, soldiers did not have a positive role in the new national narrative, which posited the majority of Japanese as victims of militarists. POWs in Siberia could not be seen as "pure victims" in the way that the victims of Hiroshima and Nagasaki were, so the POWs' stories remained largely missing from Japan's popular consciousness.

But as Japan emerged from the Occupation and began rebuilding its national confidence in the 1950s, heroic war tales multiplied in the media and found an audience. As illustrated by the popularity of flying ace Sakai Saburō's first published memoir in 1953, it became possible to circulate images of soldiers who had enjoyed initial military success in the Pacific or who had put up a respectable fight despite their limited resources.[116] It also became possible to find an audience for stories of the suicide attacks and even the miserable deaths of Japanese soldiers in the later phases of the war.[117] Portrayals of these soldiers' desperate acts and determination to die actually preserved their agency; these soldiers controlled their destiny by sacrificing themselves for their nation. These "sacrifices" were reimagined as meaningful, even necessary for the construction of postwar democratic society.[118] Accordingly, these dead soldiers were allowed to be part of the larger postwar narrative about the new nationhood. Survivor's guilt motivated many in this process of reconstruction; war deaths would be wasted if those who remained did not produce positive outcomes.[119] The sentiment that postwar hardships could not compare with what the deceased had suffered in the battlefield demonstrated that their deaths were an integral part of Japan's postwar recovery. Moreover, the suffering of these deceased soldiers afforded them the status of victims of Japan's war efforts. The very unnecessary and wasteful nature of their deaths represented a stern indictment of the Japanese military's incompetent leadership.[120]

By contrast, there was no heroism to assign to the Japanese POWs in Siberia. They had been demilitarized after Japan's defeat by the Red Army, so Japan's military leaders could not be held responsible for what happened afterward. Efforts have been made to highlight the annihilation of the border defense units by Soviet forces[121] and the hasty retreat of the Kwantung army's leaders and their families. Moreover, many Japanese officers clung to their privileges in the prison camps, thereby exacerbating the other detainees' suffering. Nevertheless, the fact remains that

Japanese POWs lacked agency in determining their own destiny, and most of their death and suffering occurred in the Soviet prison camps. Thus they were victims not of Japanese militarism but of the Soviet system. As such, the POWs did not fit neatly into the narrative of Japan's postwar national identity that embraced death and destruction as a selfless wartime sacrifice for future generations.

THE CONTINUING STRUGGLES OF FORMER POWS

Over time, the stigma of being taken captive and the fear of the Soviet Union gradually faded from postwar Japanese society. In fact, in the peace and prosperity of postwar Japan, later generations were puzzled by the decision to choose death over capture. Meanwhile, in the 1990s, North Korea displaced the Soviet Union as an object of fear in the popular imagination.[122] Such changes in popular consciousness and political climate, along with the former detainees' awareness that their time was limited, have encouraged more of them to write about their experiences. While it was estimated that by 1976, former POWs had written around two thousand volumes about their experiences by 1976, the majority of these accounts were printed in small runs just for friends and family members.[123] Hundreds of new titles have appeared since then, though most do not make it to the shelves of ordinary bookstores.[124] Accordingly, in stark contrast with the ever popular tales of kamikaze pilots, the issue of the Japanese POWs in Siberia remains at the margins of popular imagination and scholarly consideration.

Not even the end of the Cold War or Japan's improved communications with Russia could change the situation for former POWs in Japan. In 1991, the Russian government released forty thousand names of those who had perished in Siberia, but that list aroused only modest interest in the plight of former Japanese POWs in Siberia. Although the media reported on the visits of former POWs and bereaved families to the grave sites of deceased POWs, this brief interest brought no major paradigmatic change. Japanese POWs in Siberia continued to be accorded a lukewarm sympathy reserved for the unfortunate.[125]

A recent musical production (first staged in 2001 by the theater group Shiki) sought to reintroduce the Siberian POWs into Japanese popular consciousness. Ironically, the production instead demonstrates the continuing power of certain postwar narratives that have resulted in the POWs' repeated marginalization. This musical takes its title from the 1948 popular song "Hill in a Foreign Land," and its plot is broadly based on Nishiki Masa'aki's historical fiction *Regards to Mr. Dreamface* (*Yumegao san ni yoroshiku*).[126] Nishiki's original story traces the turbulent life of Konoe Fumitaka—son of Konoe Fumimaro, the prime minister when Imperial Japan entered into hostilities with China and signed the Tripartite Pact with Italy and Germany—to his 1956 death in a Siberian camp. The musical rescues Fumitaka from historical obscurity as a nationalist who dedicated his life to arranging peace between Japan and China; he is killed by injection when he refuses to become a Soviet agent. Much like the postwar idealizations of the student soldiers, Fumitaka lives as a liberal and dies as a nationalist for his country. In contrast, the POWs' complex experiences are reduced on stage to signs of general oppression, used merely to highlight the narrative's tragic-heroic form.

The musical did succeed in generating some publicity for the returnees from the Siberian camps. Although its sentimental treatment of them as pitiful figures evokes the audience's empathy, it does little to acknowledge the POWs historical agency. The sole exception is Konoe Fumitaka; the musical's privileging of this heroic (and exceptional) nationalist figure testifies to the continuing power of the national framework to shape postwar Japan's historical consciousness. Once again, the lives of those who died or were sacrificed for the nation are valorized through a narrative of the nation's destruction and reconstruction. Meanwhile, the complex stories of the POWs themselves, all too aware of how their ties to the nation have been severed, fade from view.[127] The musical focuses on the story of the man who did not return to Japan. Fumitaka's life and death are conveniently contained in Siberia, the space that does not intersect with postwar Japan. Just as in the case of Kaji in *The Human Condition*, the audience is invited to cry over the man's tragic fate without realizing that returnees actually are living in postwar society.

The postwar narrative—positing the Japanese solely as victims in the Asia Pacific War—has been widely criticized both inside and outside Japan, particularly by highlighting Japan's imperialist aggression against other Asian countries. We must similarly resist these narratives of victimization in order to engage the stories of the Japanese POWs interned in Siberian prison camps with something more than sentimental pity.

This engagement demands a critical examination of the national image of "Japan," whose creation extends even to the control of memories. That is, we need to critique the existing paradigm through which war experiences are shared and valorized in Japanese society, though doing so means facing numerous challenges. One example of such an intellectual struggle by a former detainee, the poet Ishihara Yoshirō, is the subject of chapter 4. Thanks to Ishihara's intense reflections on his own experiences in Siberia, the Japanese POWs gained an invaluable voice, albeit at a steep cost to Ishihara himself.

Ishihara Yoshirō, May 8, 1975. (Courtesy of Mainichi shinbunsha)

Chapter Four

"NO DENUNCIATION"

Ishihara Yoshirō's Soviet Internment Experiences

In effect, after 1945 poetry is an act of defiance, a quixotic refusal to descend into silence.

JAY WINTER, *SITES OF MEMORY, SITES OF MOURNING*

Ishihara Yoshirō, he knows, more than anything else, the meaninglessness of speaking, writing, and words themselves. He is a poet who communicates in silence.

TAKANO ETSUKO, *AGE TWENTY, THE STARTING POINT (NIJUSSAI NO GENTEN)*

THE EXPERIENCES THAT ALWAYS ARRIVE LATE

In his work dealing with his own postwar Siberian internment, poet Ishihara Yoshirō forces readers to reexamine their vague conceptions of "war experience." To him, war experiences are not fossils (the dead past) waiting to be excavated; rather, they are an ongoing process of continual change that transforms the subject who encounters them. Ishihara could not fully comprehend his prison camp experiences in real time while he was in Siberia; he came to embrace these experiences only through the act of remembrance in postwar Japan. In Siberia, his life-or-death struggle crushed the subjectivity needed to process those experiences intellectually and emotionally. Only when Ishihara recovered this subjectivity was he able to feel the excruciating pain caused by the internment.

Ishihara's internal struggle with his war experiences was more than an abstract emotional process. The reconstitution of Ishihara's self took place amid the rapid and sweeping transformations under way in postwar Japanese society. During the eight years that Ishihara spent in Siberia, postwar Japan had been steadily recovering from the physical devastation of the war while gradually distancing itself from the pain of defeat. The U.S. military's special procurements for the Korean War injected a timely cash infusion into the Japanese economy in the early 1950s, paving the way for its spectacular economic growth in the following decades. Under these conditions, war experiences were accepted and honored only insofar as they did not contradict the national narrative of postwar recovery.

Even critiques of the former military regime conformed to the accepted postwar narrative, establishing a distance between postwar Japan and the war itself. While these discussions facilitated the high-handed indictment of the nation's past failure, they tended to treat personal experiences as mere by-products of larger political conditions; individual experiences registered only as examples of the regime's inhumane treatments. As demonstrated in chapter 2, Gomikawa Junpei's characterization of history—history as a gigantic flow, over which individuals have little control—nicely captures the critical premise of the discussions.

Ishihara Yoshirō refused to participate in such a categorical criticism, and he declined to cast himself as a victim of any sort. Rather than using the postwar narrative as a buoy to keep his being afloat, he chose to sink deep into the past and relive his prison camp experiences as a way of bringing the past into the present. For Ishihara, the "postwar" meant not the end but the real beginning of his internment experience. He survived the Siberian camps by destroying his own self, by completely desensitizing himself to the humiliations. In the postwar period, Ishihara first faced the task of reconstituting himself as a subject capable of confronting the humiliating experiences that threatened to overwhelm him. Ishihara confessed in his writings that the first three years after his return to Japan were the most difficult emotionally, more so even than his original experiences in Siberia (*IYZ* 2:66). During this period, he was saddened by the gulf between postwar Japanese society and the Siberian detainees, a gap that seemed only to grow wider and wider. At the same time, however, he began to confront his own experiences in the Siberian prison camps by writing poetry, for "poetry is just about the only form of expression that allows one to accept 'confusion [*konran*] as it is'" (*IYZ* 2:439).

Not until about fifteen years later did Ishihara begin to write about his internment experiences in essay form. In addition to attracting a larger audience, these essays opened the eyes of his friends and readers to the long shadows that the Siberian experiences had cast on his poetry.[1] The "confusion" that Ishihara felt about Siberia had made his poetry difficult for readers to understand. But that confusion became more ordered—

selectively abstracted and reinterpreted—in the essays. His prose tamed the deeply troubling Siberian memories while attempting to maintain the precarious balance of his reconstituted subjectivity. In his general body of work, the prose pieces did not necessarily serve as extensions of his poetic efforts but instead often offered a sharp contrast. Ishihara himself perceived a division of labor between his poetry and prose: "For a while, I felt very anxious and resistant to talking about my experiences in such [prose] form, partly because I was not able to shed my suspicion that talking [about my experiences] was futile. But above all, poetry was everything to me. I was trying to support myself at that time by, as it were, thoroughly concealing myself in poems" (IYZ 2:259). The unspoken premise in this passage is that prose gradually clarifies what poetry has hidden:[2] poetry conceals, and prose exposes. Ishihara implies that as time passed, he was eventually able to come forward with what he had been hiding, that in time, he moved from poetry to prose.

His prose, however, never fully revealed the Ishihara that was hidden in the poems. Instead, his essays were largely efforts to impose self-critical readings on the mental state that had produced his poems and to deemphasize the impact of bodily experiences. Ishihara's prose conceals the fact that in his early postwar poems, the body was not only an organ that brought tremendous suffering but also a medium through which one is able to establish meaningful relations with others. Ishihara desired, though tentatively, to reach out to others. But when he realized that his feelings were not reciprocated by postwar Japanese society, he retracted his emotional investment.

In this chapter I argue that despite Ishihara's later disavowing it, the "confusion" in his poetry was an integral part of his postrepatriation life. I also explore the divide between body and mind as a key to understanding the move from poetry to prose in Ishihara's creative career.

ISHIHARA'S SIBERIAN EXPERIENCES

Ishihara Yoshirō was born in November 1915 in Shizuoka Prefecture. Upon graduating from the Tokyo School of Foreign Studies (Tokyo gaikokugo gakkō) in 1938, he began working for Osaka Gas. In the following year, he was called up for military service and assigned to the Thirty-Fourth Infantry Regiment. In 1940, on the basis of his having studied

German at the Tokyo School of Foreign Studies, he was sent to the Army Russian Education Unit in Osaka to learn Russian. After eight months of intensive language training there, he was sent to the Tokyo Educational Unit for ten months of advanced Russian language study (*IYZ* 2:412–15). These eighteen months of language training tied Ishihara's subsequent life to the Soviet Union. Although released from official military duty after completing the advanced course, he was ordered to work for the Manchurian Telephone and Telegraph Research Bureau (Manshū den-den chōsakyoku). In fact, the bureau was a cover for the Kwantung Army Special Communication and Information Unit in Harbin.[3] Ishihara's main responsibility there was the interception and analysis of Soviet radio transmissions.

After Japan's surrender, Ishihara and his colleagues were transferred to the Manchurian Telephone and Telegraph Administration Bureau to conceal their connections with the intelligence agency. Although he lost his job in early October, Ishihara managed to survive the confusion in Harbin after Japan's defeat but was unable to repatriate directly from China. In December 1945, he and his former colleagues were rounded up by the People's Commissariat of Internal Affairs and packed into a freight train bound for the Soviet territories with other Japanese prison-ers and White Russians (*IYZ* 3:512–14).[4] Arriving in Chita the following month, the prisoners were placed in temporary units to await further transportation. Forty days after leaving Harbin, Ishihara reached Alma-Ata (present-day Almaty), the capital city of the Kazakh Soviet Socialist Republic (present-day Republic of Kazakhstan), where he was detained in Regional Camp No. 3. According to Ishihara, the prisoners' first year in the Soviet Union was "the initial period of weeding out . . . over the eight years of my internment, the largest number of Japanese detainees died during this period from fatigue from the long journey, shock from the drastic change in environment, exhaustion from labor (especially be-fore the prisoners' bodies could adjust to camp conditions), lack of food, and typhus" (*IYZ* 2:12).

The second "weeding out" took place from October 1949 to September 1950, when Ishihara was assigned to log timber in the forest area west of Lake Baikal for construction of the Baikal–Amur Mainline (BAM) rail-way. In April 1949, Ishihara was sentenced to twenty-five years of hard labor by the provisional court in Karaganda, which saw his intelligence work in Harbin as anti-Soviet activity. The court also stripped him of any (nonexistent) claims to Soviet citizenship (*IYZ* 2:12). This sentence was a political maneuver by the Soviet authorities to prosecute war crimes so that the prisoners could be used as pawns in the impending peace negotiations with Japan. The immediate result, however, was a drastic change in the treatment of the roughly 3,000 Japanese men found guilty of anti-Soviet activities.

Nishio Yasuto, who also received a twenty-five-year prison term, saw Ishihara, as both men worked on construction of the Baikal–Amur Mainline. Ishihara "looked badly bloated, and was repeatedly hospitalized" because of hunger and hard labor (*IYZ* 2:195–96). Nishio was in bad shape, too. His weight had "dipped far below ninety pounds," "his eyes unfocused, mind blurred, movement slow, and walking [was] difficult. When he fell, he could not get up without help."[5] In the fall of 1950, Japanese prisoners working in the areas along the BAM were moved through Tayshet to Khabarovsk. In the freight car, Ishihara was "mostly unconscious" (*IYZ* 2:515). In Khabarovsk, he was housed in Regional Camp No. 6 and treated like other Japanese POWs, who had not been convicted of alleged crimes. Under these new conditions, he rapidly recovered his physical health, although his mind took much longer to regain some balance. Ishihara was tormented for some time by this gap between the recovery of his body and that of his mind.

Returning from the BAM district in an emaciated state, Ishihara was initially assigned to light labor indoors at the camp. By 1951, however, his growing physical strength made it possible for him to work at a construction site in Khabarovsk City. Ishihara and the other Japanese captives also gradually began to pursue various cultural activities. As the prisoners sought outlets for self-expression, composing haiku was the most popular, and men who had been active in Harbin's haiku societies led the efforts to organize haiku gatherings (*IYZ* 2:387). Ishihara was a participant, and he later characterized the haiku at the gatherings as "nostalgic, escapist, and strangely often magnificent. . . . For the detainees who were just barely emerging from such dark conditions, even their magnificent expressions could not be but an escape from reality" (*IYZ* 2:387).

With Joseph Stalin's death in March 1953, the Soviet government softened its stance toward Japan and sought to normalize bilateral relations.[6] Repatriation of Japanese detainees, which had been suspended since

1950, thus resumed in 1953 through the mediation of the Red Cross organizations in both Japan and the Soviet Union. Ishihara Yoshirō was in the first group of 811 men who returned to Japan that year. On December 1, after twelve years on the continent, first as part of the Kwantung Army Special Communication and Information Unit in Manchuria and then as a prisoner, thirty-eight-year-old Ishihara arrived at Maizuru Port (see the introduction). The following day, a repatriation ceremony was held to mark the return of Ishihara and his fellow captives to postwar Japanese society.

THE CONFLICT BETWEEN MIND AND BODY

Immediately after his repatriation, only poetry could express the "confusion" that plagued Ishihara's memories and governed his relationship to the past. Some fifteen years after his return, his mind finally had recovered enough critical function to keep in check the brutal power of his bodily memories. Ishihara regarded the body as a negative attribute to be overcome only by the mind, and writing essays about his internment experiences was part of his effort to displace the miserable physical experiences of camp with an intellectual understanding. In an essay he published in 1971, "Longing for Home and the Sea" (Bōkyō to umi), Ishihara explains the bodily despair he felt when he was sentenced to twenty-five years of hard labor: "I *felt* that a thread of hope tugging me to the homeland was severed at that moment. That was a clearly physical feeling. Since then, I have been convinced that any mental crisis begins as a physical pain. When one talks about "actual feelings," their most important part is rooted in this physical feeling" (*IYZ* 2:196–97, italics in original). The mental anguish of losing all hope of ever going home hit him as "a physical pain." But it was not just that moment: the entire internment experience was for Ishihara a *physical* experience. Under the inhumane conditions of the prison camps, bodily needs dictated all else; the men thoroughly degraded themselves, but their minds did not have the power to support such an existence. Elsewhere, Ishihara explains the central challenge of surviving the Siberian camps:

The internment camps were where I was confronted with the mind/ body tension, that eternally old and yet new tension, in its most radical form. There the classic problematic of rivalry between mind and body was absent. Their relationship was manifested only as a futile routine in which the body disdained and constantly distanced itself from the mind. Observed from the side of the body, this routine exactly corresponded to the process through which [the internees] adjusted to the extreme conditions at the internment camps. Adjusting was "to survive" and, more than that, to surely lose one's human qualities. (*IYZ* 2:259)

No matter how humiliating the conditions were, it was necessary to obey bodily needs in order "to survive." Survival at camp meant "to surely lose one's human qualities." By subjecting individuals' bodies to pain and miserable conditions, the political authority manifested in the internment camps destroyed individual pride and spirit, annihilating agency and any possibility of resistance. To adjust to the extreme conditions was to accept them, and the self constantly had to create rationalizations for accepting such conditions.

Ishihara elaborates on this self-justification:

This self-justification under the extreme conditions by which one was trapped had to take the following clear and simple form. "It is an imperative to survive → in order to survive, I must adjust → in order to adjust, I cannot but degrade myself." Nobody has a means to resist this logic as long as it is articulated from the body. The problem is when and where this logic is inspected by our soul. When that happens, we are forced to confront for the first time our experiences in their entirety. (*IYZ* 2:260)

After the body recovered its health, inspection by the soul became possible. But a healthy body did not necessarily ensure the process of inspection; only in postwar Japan was Ishihara finally able to engage in introspection.

From his sentencing in Karaganda through his physical recovery in Khabarovsk City, Ishihara was continually confronted with conflicts between mind and body. Once the judgments were handed down in the provisional court, the handling of the prisoners immediately became even rougher. Dispatched to the BAM construction sites in a Stolypin train car fitted for convicts, the prisoners' treatment was tantamount to torture. The conditions in those train cars were so severe that prisoners had to be taken off every few days for about a week of rest at a transfer camp. Ishihara describes the journey's impact as follows: "The suffering we experienced during the mere three days in transit completely crushed the remnants of pride that we had somehow maintained in ourselves" (*IYZ* 2:58). When these conditions continued, "we grew to accept as a matter of course treatment that we would never accept under normal circumstances. The memory that we had once been humans became something beyond comprehension" (*IYZ* 2:59). In other words, without abandoning one's dignity as a human being—the basic capacity to feel humiliation as humiliation—survival under these extreme conditions was impossible. During their adjustment, all the prisoners "respond to the external environment in almost the same way and begin to behave with almost the same thoughts in their minds." Ishihara uses the term "averaging" to describe this erasure of individuality (*IYZ* 2:32). When mercilessly treated like domestic animals, individuals must behave like a herd of domestic animals in order to maximize their chances of survival. Just as in domestic animals, the subjectivity needed to process one's plight is completely lacking; language has no use at all.

In Khabarovsk City, however, the prisoners' treatment improved to the same level as that of the general POWs, and their physical recovery there was so fast that it was "violent." Witnessing the drastic change in the prisoners, a Soviet military doctor scornfully observed: "They fatten like pigs by the amount they eat." Ishihara was greatly perturbed by the doctor's words, not so much because they were derogatory, but because they accurately characterized how the prisoners had been animalized and reduced to mere physical functions (*IYZ* 2:62). Even though their health improved, the prisoners were still no more than empty shells. In October 1950, Ishihara and several other prisoners helped out with farm work at a nearby collective farm, which "consisted solely of women and children who had been forcefully moved from the Ukraine. Just because they had remained in the German-occupied area, their men had been sent away for hard labor" (*IYZ* 2:61–62). The women treated Ishihara and his fellow inmates to lunch, crying because the men reminded them of their husbands, brothers, and sons. But Ishihara, who by then had completely lost his sensitivity to others' feelings, could not comprehend the women's tears. Offered simple yet "stupefyingly" abundant food, he was ecstatic.

Even as the prisoners recovered from their chronic hunger, they lost the precarious balance of the mind/body relationship and fell into the state in which the body entirely dominates the mind. Once their appetites had been satisfied, their excessive interest in the next meal declined; without hunger to preoccupy them, they had nothing left to think about. While the mind then should have taken on the task of bringing them back to a higher plane of existence, the conditions of continued detention prevented the men from meeting this challenge. The prisoners had lost their humanity as a group, and they could recover it only as "a group of victims." Ishihara explains this process of resurfacing in the absence of individual agency:

> Such words as "we shared the meals" appeared to have brought us closer. But nobody ever asked with what kind of pain we shared the meals. We forged this tie by turning our backs to the reality that we all had threatened one another's lives. It was a solidarity to which we barely held on by placing ourselves unreservedly in the position of victims. . . . That was an unmistakably averaged, collective thinking that encouraged us to get along only by "forgetting" responsibility for our actions in the BAM district, responsibility that we needed to discuss with our neighbors. (*IYZ* 2:65)

Such solidarity was built on the belief that they all were victims, but it did not allow for individual agency or individual responsibility. By assuming the position of a victim, one absolves oneself of responsibility for one's actions—even for the action of falling from a state of humanity. Ishihara insists that one should confront one's actions as a human being, that only by so doing can one reconstruct a genuine subject from shameful experiences.

For a prisoner, refusing to accept the position of a victim meant deciding not to "denounce" the external conditions of his location. It was also a determination to maintain one's agency in the face of broader political or historical forces. The self as victim possesses only a secondary, shadowy existence produced by the larger dynamic. In contrast to this passivity, Ishihara tried to reconstruct himself as an active agent by separating his experiences from politics and history. That is, his experiences in the camps were not simply a response or a reaction to external conditions; he also exercised his agency in molding them. Ishihara's goal was to actively claim ownership of his humiliation as a means of intellectually overcoming it. Assigned to the noble task of making sense of the hardship that his body had endured, his mind was eager to rise above and beyond physical needs. Ishihara tried to unravel the hopelessly tangled relationship between mind and body by charging the former with overcoming the latter. He forgot, however, that the body existed not simply as a fetter but also as a contact point with others.

Poetry as an Appeal to Others

When Ishihara first began writing poetry in postwar Japan, it served as a form of expression through which he could depict—without reducing them to binary opposites—the tangled relations between mind and body.[7] In the "mind/body tension," Ishihara still believed in connections with others, and he did not privilege the quietude found in a solitary position.

In his essay "My Poetic Peregrinations" (Watashi no shireki, 1975), Ishihara confesses that the first three years after his homecoming were a very confusing period for him. At that time, although he wished to find a place in postwar society, he did not know how: "Looking back now, my behavior then was indeed abnormal. I was angry at everything I saw. When I got into an argument with somebody, I immediately stuttered and got into a physical fight with that person. Finally everyone ignored me. I angrily walked around the town by myself" (IYZ 2:388). As the literary critic Tsukimura Toshiyuki observed, Ishihara's emotional outbursts—sometimes in physical form—would have been tolerated in the chaos of the immediate postwar period but not in mid-1950s Japan; at that point, the nation was quickly regaining normalcy.[8]

In this time of personal crisis, poetry was the only way for Ishihara to speak from his state of "confusion" and reach out to others. Within months of his return, he sent several unsolicited poems to the poet Miyoshi Tatsuya. When Ishihara received encouraging words in return, he was grateful: "When I realized that I had a means to express myself, I felt I had barely regained a firm ground to stand on" (IYZ 2:389). Ishihara then sent his work to the literary magazine Writing Club (Bunshō kurabu), which had a section for readers' contributions. The first poem that he sent to the magazine, "The Night's Invitation" (Yoru no shōtai), won the reviewers' highest praise in the October 1954 issue (*IYZ* 2:389).[9] Ishihara was genuinely excited to see his poem in print, and he thereafter became a regular contributor to *Writing Club*. Ishihara and his fellow contributors soon formed a poetry coterie and, in April 1958, began publishing their own poetry magazine, *Rocinante*.[10] Both the group and the magazine created a space in which Ishihara felt safe expressing his confused self. He explained what the magazine meant to him: "The gloomy state of my interior was open only to *Rocinante*" (*IYZ* 2:389–90).

For Ishihara, as his early creative career demonstrates, writing poetry was not an abstract intellectual exercise but a communicative act through which to establish ties with postwar society, no matter how precarious. In 1972, he discussed his choice to write poetry, using the simile of a bridge: "The reason why I [initially] chose poetry as my primary mode of expression was that it contained at least a thread of appeal [to others]. On this thread of appeal, I thought I could hang all my hopes. I mention here a thread of appeal because I wholeheartedly believed in the possibility of something like a narrow bridge that one person could extend to reach another" (*IYZ* 2:265).

Unlike his later essays, this narrow bridge was not built toward an intellectual plane; instead, Ishihara's poetry addressed others who had lived as Ishihara did amid an anarchic chaos of mind and body. To illustrate, I turn to one of his early poems, "Lonely, Now" (Sabishii to ima), which originally appeared in *Rocinante* in April 1958:

Lonely
You said just now
Against the earthen wall, bearded
The back tightly pressed
Right behind it
Lonely
You said just now
Just there, warm like
An animal's underbelly
Shadows of hand gestures
Piling up sorrowfully
Around there
Between the curious hatred

Back to back
There was surely a guy
Who said he was lonely
There was a guy
Who heard that
Between the mouth that said that
And the ear that heard that
Unexpectedly
A lid rises
Like a joke, hot water
Boils over
To jump back
It is up to the earthen wall or me
There was surely a guy
Who said he was lonely
Insofar as there was a guy
Who heard that
That pasania tree
And that Japanese horse chestnut tree
The dusk and the lake
I own them entirely (*IYZ* 1:74–76)

Here the narrow bridge reaching for others still is present in the pathos of the poem, but the emotions are unmediated by any will or expression (both of which Ishihara valorized in later essays about his internment experiences). The poem is written mostly in *hiragana* script, whose curvy lines create a soft, serene visual impression. This impression resonates with the bodily images that the poem uses to convey the deep connections—not yet broken—between the "I" and others. The lines "Between the curious hatred / Back to back / There was surely a guy" suggest that there is no direct communication but that there is someone who speaks of loneliness, and the "I" listens to him. The neighbors pressed "back to back" have turned into the "earthen wall, bearded," an object that barely shows human traces. Nevertheless, in writing "Just there, warm like / An animal's underbelly," Ishihara leaves intact an organ with which to sense the existence of others. "Hand gestures" come closest to a form of human communication, but they are visible only as "Shadows."

They are "Piling up sorrowfully" as if perpetually frustrated. But there is still some warmth left in this pile. Passed between the one who hands it over and the one who receives it, the repressed feeling "Like a joke, hot water/Boils over." As long as some possibility for communication remains, the "I" of the poem is not completely alienated from the world, even if that possibility is remote. The two kinds of trees to which he refers in the last part, the pasania (*shiinoki*) and the Japanese horse chestnut (*tochinoki*), are deciduous broad-leaved trees that do not exist in Siberia. Ishihara thus transforms the alien landscape of coniferous forests into a familiar temperate terrain where "I" is securely rooted.

This poem depicts both Ishihara's life in the prison camps and his psychological state right after repatriation. Ishihara's journal entry on August 4, 1961, reads: "I value the period right after I repatriated, when I was enveloped in confusion but vividly in touch with [*fusetsu shiteita*] the crisis" (*IYZ* 2:148) Significantly, he coined the word *fusetsu* (which literally means "skin-touch") to express as a physical sensation the immediate aftermath of repatriation. Ishihara literally lived with the crisis "back to back," and that sensation allowed him to live "vividly."

The scene described in "Lonely, Now" is revisited in Ishihara's essay "From the Experience of a Kind of 'Symbiosis'" (Aru "kyōsei" no keiken kara, 1969). This essay—written about fifteen years after his return to Japan—foregrounds a rigorous "solitude within the solidarity" rather than the possibility in "Lonely, Now" of connecting with others. Ashamed that he had once opened up himself to others, Ishihara scrapes off all feelings other than hatred as he examines his experience with cool analytical language. He focuses on the strange symbiotic relations that developed in the first year spent in the camps, that initial period of weeding out. The symbiosis appeared in what the detainees called "food can pairs" (*IYZ* 2:6). They faced dire food shortages in the camps because the supervisor and staff systematically embezzled their provisions. Most of the internees were civilians detained for their alleged anti-Soviet activities and therefore had not carried mess tins with them into camp. Accordingly, without enough mess kits for all the prisoners, food was rationed out in one mess tin for every two men. The men expended a great deal of energy testing methods of dividing up the food in order to ensure a fair distribution for those sharing a mess tin. In other words, the members of a "food can pair" were mutual enemies who fought each other down to the last morsel of food. Yet at the work sites, they collaborated as teams to obtain the best tools for their work. "The curious hatred / Back to back," therefore, was not just a metaphor but a physical state that tethered the two men in a "food can pair" even in their sleep:

> After a day's work comes the time for sleep, the second most pleasurable activity next to eating. Even during sleep, however, the "symbiosis" continues. Especially that first year in the camp, when we each received only one blanket, we shared it with our food can mate, laying one blanket on the floor and placing the other one over us. We had no choice but to sleep with our backs pressed together firmly. This was the only way to prevent any loss of our meager warmth. The man who presses his boney back against me will try to bite off some of my life tomorrow. But at least for now, we have to warm our lives together. That is the contract. My mate must be thinking about the same thing. (*IYZ* 2:10)

In order to save their lives, they must collaborate, yet this collaboration was built on the basis of mutual enmity. The two that "sleep pressing [their] backs together firmly" share both warmth and hatred. The bonds that expose their ugliest aspects are needed also for physical survival. Despite being tethered to another human being, each individual remains in a solitary condition, the state privileged by Ishihara in his later essays. From his memories of bodily vulnerability and entangled relations with others, Ishihara reclaims only hatred. While the high ground of the mind is not explicitly articulated as such in this essay, he abandons the exploration of connections between internees reduced to bodily existence, putting aside the possibility for intimacy that he offers in "Lonely, Now."

Changing Songs

The relationship between the poet and his poetry changed over time. In the subtle shifts from "Lonely, Now," to "Song of a Ringing in My Ears" ("Miminari no uta," which appeared in *Rocinante* about a year later), to "Position" ("Ichi," published in August 1961 in the magazine *Oni*), there is a detectable, gradual dissipation of the emotions that Ishihara felt in the camps. The following is "Song of a Ringing in My Ears":

The man I left behind
For example likes a ringing in the ears
Within a ringing in the ears, for example
Likes a small peninsula
Likes the smell smoldering like a fuse cord
The sky is always on this side of
That man
The chest in which stars stir like wind
The man who is ashamed of me like a medal
When a ringing begins in my ears
Then suddenly
That man begins
Faraway wheat rings to that hair
He firmly
Looks around
The man I left behind
For example likes a mounted donkey
For example likes a red mane
For example likes copper horse shoes
Likes a gong-like setting sun
Just like introducing the back to a whip
The man who introduces me to the future
When a ringing begins in my ears
It is that man who probably begins
When that man unexpectedly begins
There further begins
Another man
Men who come back to life all together
At the end of the bloody series
Like a tube of lipstick
Gently stands a tower
Let my ringing sing in my ears
Beyond the illusory ringing
Still gently
Continues to stand the tower
Even now, firmly
Believing in it

The man
I left behind (*IYZ* 1:41–43)

In "Lonely, Now," it was possible to use even a feeble voice as a medium through which to share emotions with others. A year later, however, "Song of a Ringing in My Ears" describes the relationship between the "I [the narrator]" and another figure—the "man"—in the far more tenuous image of an "illusory ringing" in the ears. By calling the man "man" (*otoko*)—in contrast with a more informal term "guy" (*yatsu*), as in "Lonely, Now"—this poem reflects a larger distance between the "I" and the "man." The "man" is indeed "ashamed of me [the narrator] like a medal": the medal—a symbol of past exploits—has lost its luster, and the man does not want to be associated with the narrator.[11]

This man "introduces [the narrator] to the future," just as he introduces "the back to a whip." Just as it is impossible to separate action from reaction, the act of leaving the man in the past forcefully throws the narrator into the future. The meeting with a whip is violent, and so is the encounter with the future. The man—not a single, self-contained person—thus forcefully sets the narrator in forward motion:

When that man unexpectedly begins
There further begins
Another man
Men who come back to life all together.

The plurality of men suggests that the narrator was not alone in leaving the man behind. The color red is everywhere, imbuing all the things the man likes—"a red mane," "copper horse shoes," and "a gong-like setting sun." Red does not stand for rigid political ideas here but for everyday life. It also is the color of the bloody series, which suggests the violence that the "Men" might have endured. The tower here stands "gently," "Like a tube of lipstick." Compared with an intimate, feminine object, the tower is no longer the symbol of vertical power; rather, it is a device that converts the color of the bloody series into a symbol of life.

Much as "Lonely, Now" does, this highly abstract poem communicates the poet's resolve to remain hopeful in what appears to be an alien environment. There is, however, a decisive difference between the two poems: the speaker and the "guy" remain on the same plane in "Lonely Now," whereas the narrator leaves a man behind in a separate temporal space in "Song of a Ringing in My Ears." The narrator of the latter poem has evacuated the space the "man" occupies. Although the narrator expresses warm feelings toward the "man," the break was so decisive that there is no physical connection between them. The poem's nostalgic tone suggests that the return of the "I" to this side—the space that the narrator shares with the reader—was an unfortunate event that decisively broke the ties with the "man." The "man" exists only in the narrator's imagination in an idealized form. Ishihara, having buried the "man," embodies a genuine and yet naive hope in the poetic space.

When Ishihara received a copy of his first poetic anthology, *The Homecoming of Sancho Panza* (*Sancho Panza no kikyō*, 1963), he described it as his ashes (*ikotsu*).[12] For him, the act of publishing was the equivalent of incinerating and burying the vulnerable self that once embraced hope and reached out to others. While the ashes may have still felt warm in his hands, they sealed off his initial struggles with the past. Ishihara detested and rejected his struggles with remembering his past, though not the memories themselves.

The distancing of the present self from the immediate postrepatriation phase is even more clearly revealed in the lead poem, "Position" (Ichi), in *The Homecoming of Sancho Panza*:

At the quiet shoulder
It was not only the voices that line up
Closer than the voices
Enemies line up
The positions that the brave men strive for
Are not on their right, probably
not on their left either

The unprotected sky finally warps
At the position where it becomes the bow of noon
You should breathe
And greet
From your position, that is
The best posture (*IYZ* 1:5)

There is no sentimental connection with the past in this poem, which Ishihara wrote instead as a manifesto for the future. To choose a position to occupy means giving up all the other positions. As Ishihara suggests elsewhere, actively accepting the position in which he finds himself— whether in the Japanese army or the Siberian camps—is a way for him to reconstruct his agency. At the same time, it means giving up the chance to occupy another position that he could have filled by "denouncing" the external conditions of his imprisonment (*IYZ* 2:530–31).

In this poem, Ishihara thus tries to rescue himself as an active agent by relying solely on the power of the mind.[13] At the center position—neither left nor right—where the sky "becomes the bow of noon," the mind is in charge. Meanwhile, the body is fixed in the "best posture," rather like an insect mounted on a setting block. In that position, the body—which squirmed and desperately reached out for others—simply obeys the mind's command. Voice, which had a significant role in the previous two poems, is little more than noise here: "Closer than the voices / Enemies line up." Voice no longer possesses the power to maintain significant con- nections with others. To the contrary, others within the reach of voice are now regarded as enemies. Greeting here is an impersonal act, its primary function to confirm that you occupy the right position.

The first collection of Ishihara's poems was the ashes of the bodily im- ages he had abandoned, and the lead poem serves as a lid that sealed off his struggles in the immediate postrepatriation years. Having buried his vulnerable self in his poetic texts and articulated his resolve to place the mind in charge, Ishihara was by then only a short distance from the prose works that sharply severed his bodily experiences from the high ground occupied by his mind.

THE COURAGE OF PESSIMIST KANO BUICHI

Fifteen years after his homecoming, Ishihara began writing about his Siberian camp experiences in essay form. His essays explain the process that he deems necessary for confronting traumatic experiences: bodily experiences must be subjected to the mind's critical examination and judgment. The mind must retain ultimate control in order for Ishihara to attain the peace he desires from his troubling memories. He understands that it was impossible for him to reach this mental peace in the Siberian internment camps. Yet he does name one exception, Kano Buichi,[14] the only person whom Ishihara believed was able to maintain agency and an independent mind amid the dehumanizing conditions of internment. What Ishihara strove to achieve in the postwar years, his friend Kano had already achieved—in Ishihara's eyes—in the Siberian camps.

Born in 1918, Kano graduated from the Kyoto School of Pharmacology (Kyoto yakugaku senmon gakkō) in 1938. The following year, he joined the Ninth Infantry Regiment, which sent him to the Army Russian Education Unit in Nara and then to the advanced Russian course offered through the Tokyo Educational Unit. He befriended Ishihara in the advanced course. In 1942, he was released from military duty to work at the Infectious Disease Prevention Center (Tōan bōekisho). The center was a cover for the Kwantung army's intelligence work, much as the Manchurian Telephone and Telegraph Research Bureau (Manshū den-den chōsakyoku), which employed Ishihara, was. According to Ishihara, Kano also married in 1942 and in the following year "gave up his original aspiration of becoming a doctor and joined a Japanese settlement [by himself] as an ordinary settler" in rural Manchuria (IYZ 3:511).[15] When the Soviet Union declared war against Japan, Kano was recalled for military duty and traveled to Harbin to join his unit, but the chaos there prevented him from doing so (IYZ 3:512).[16]

Kano remained in Harbin to assist other Japanese settlers until his former career as a member of the Kwantung army intelligence agency was exposed by a White Russian—a former colleague at the agency.[17] The People's Commissariat of Internal Affairs detained Kano,[18] interned him at several different prison camps, and then sent him to Karaganda Camp No. 11 in 1947.[19] In 1949, Kano, like Ishihara, received the maximum sentence of twenty-five years of hard labor at Karaganda's provisional court. That August, he met Ishihara again at "a prison camp near a coal mine" (IYZ 2:41). When they bade farewell to each other, Kano told Ishihara: "If you ever return to Japan, please just tell people that Kano Buichi died on August (I forgot the exact date. But it was the day he told me this.) 1949." Seeing his friend's "strangely calm, almost peaceful expression," Ishihara was "able only to imagine that something had changed inside him" (IYZ 2:42). A month later, the two old friends ran into each other at a transfer camp in Tayshet. In his essay "The Courage of a Pessimist" (Peshimisuto no yūki ni tsuite), Ishihara describes the reunion: "Whenever we had spare time, we hung out. But we had hardly anything to talk about. The fundamental difference between us was that while I was still vaguely counting on some chance of survival, Kano clearly rejected any hope for the future. While in Tayshet, he never once uttered a word that suggested hope" (*IYZ* 2:43). Ishihara's account does not indicate that he immediately understood the difference between himself and Kano. Rather, it suggests that Ishihara came to this realization in 1970 while writing the essay, modifying his initial impressions to fit his postwar line of thought. In Ishihara's idealization, Kano stands as a heroic figure who maintained his internal peace and dignity in the Siberian camps.

Ishihara calls Kano a "pessimist," suggesting an attitude that "rejected any hope for the future." While experiencing the same extreme conditions that Ishihara and others faced, such as transport in a Stolypin car to the BAM district, Kano is described as assuming a different attitude:

> It takes amazing courage to take a clear stance as a pessimist under such difficult conditions as the regiment of hard labor in the BAM district. Superficial pessimism only destroys a person. The only choice left for anybody here is to close one's eyes to reality and become an optimist, relying on day-to-day hope. . . . Under such conditions, Kano was an exception, always behaving distinctly as a pessimist. (*IYZ* 2:44–45)

In Ishihara's discussion of Kano, the term "pessimism" acquires a more active meaning. Instead of a defeatist attitude, Kano's "pessimism" was a firm stance that refused the desperate hope that external conditions would drastically change by means of something like probation or even a special pardon. No matter how harsh the conditions, Kano would not be swayed, and he always acted according to his will. In other words, by thoroughly rejecting the optimistic prospect that he might enhance his chance of survival by outmaneuvering others, Kano became what Ishihara calls a pessimist.

To illustrate this point, Ishihara describes how the prisoners marched, in columns of five accompanied by armed guards, between the camp and the work site. During these marches, the prisoners fought among themselves for a place in the inside columns, because they could be shot as deserters if they slipped and fell behind on the icy, snow-packed paths.

Kano, however, never took part in the competition to push the weak
aside to occupy a safer spot. He always marched in an outside column.
Ishihara sees "a fundamental questioning of victimization and victimhood" in his behavior (*IYZ* 2:45). Increasing the chance of one's survival
meant "pushing the weak to a place closer to death." In so doing, one always occupies the place of a victimizer. By acknowledging and breaking
the cycle of victimization and victimhood—turning himself into his
own victimizer—Kano "clearly separated himself from the collective
way of thinking that was solely concerned about victimization and victimhood." Refusing to act as part of a herd that passively responds to
outside conditions, but rather as an individual who actively accepted
both victimization and victimhood, Kano "gained clarity and independence of mind as a pessimist" in the internment camp, where otherwise
one saw oneself as either a victimizer or a victim (*IYZ* 2:45). This was an
"almost futile action," as Ishihara admits (*IYZ* 2:45). Despite Ishihara's
emotional investment in his analysis, Kano's heroic act of always choosing the least advantageous condition may have been a means to avoid
making the choice to survive. Choosing "pessimism" against the hope
for bodily survival may have gained Kano balance in his mind, but he
remained powerless to change the material reality of the internment
camps, which constantly forced the internees into making senseless
choices.

In 1950, Ishihara was transferred to Khabarovsk, along with Kano on
the same freight train. While Ishihara experienced a period of physical
recovery, he noticed that Kano was working as if to punish himself: "Each
morning when he arrived at the construction site, he took the worst, most
painful post without waiting for his assignment. I happened to see the
way he worked at the same site. It was just painful to look at the man almost flinging himself onto the ground. I just gloomily absorbed the scene
where he worked as if he were severely punishing himself" (*IYZ* 2:46). The
man who chose the worst jobs and worked "as if he were severely punishing himself" left a deep impression on Ishihara. Rather than reflecting
Kano's mental condition during imprisonment, though, the description
of Kano reflects what Ishihara wished for when he was writing the essay.
That is, he recalled the working figure of Kano as an icon that embodied
the work of the mind in defiance of the humiliation inscribed through
bodily pain.

If Kano was a pessimist, Ishihara was an optimist who clung to the hope of going home to Japan. Ishihara's optimism ensured that he would simply endure any hardship in order to go home. He believed that once he was home, he would recover his whole self. Accordingly, Ishihara's life in the Siberian camp was always deferred and supposedly would resume in postwar Japan. Ishihara brought back this optimism only to realize that life—the process of overcoming his Siberian experiences—never really began there. Ishihara then idealized Kano to articulate his new stance of rejecting the hope that had once sustained him. He tried to show that the genuine agency that he had dreamed of actually existed in the Siberian camps, but not in postwar Japan.

In reality, though, Kano's solitary mind was completely closed to the community at the internment camp: it barely maintained its balance by completely rejecting any ties with others. In May 1952, at Khabarovsk City's Camp No. 6, Kano isolated himself in silence. A few days later, he completely stopped eating, as if to kill himself slowly (*IYZ* 2:39). By rejecting sustenance, he symbolically severed all relations with society. He was fasting to erase his social existence. Worried about his condition, other internees tried to talk him into eating. But Kano answered their concerns with silence. Ishihara's efforts to talk also failed; in the end, he tried to communicate with action instead. He wrote:

On the morning of the fourth day since he began fasting, I reluctantly made a decision. Right after I got out of the bed, I went to his barrack and simply announced to him that "I, too, will stop eating starting today," and headed for work. The foreman, who had learned of the situation, gave me a lighter set of tasks. Nevertheless, when I returned to the camp, I was utterly exhausted and collapsed into my bed. (*IYZ* 2:47)

Ishihara's action finally opened Kano's obstinately closed mind to end his fast. That night, Ishihara ate a meal with Kano at the canteen. Two days later, Ishihara finally heard from Kano his reasons for fasting:

On April 30, the day before May Day, Kano was mobilized with some other Japanese prisoners for cleaning and repair work at the "Culture and Rest Park." The Khabarovsk mayor's daughter happened to pass and was struck by the scene. She immediately fetched food from her home and personally handed it to every prisoner. Kano was one of them. To him, there was nothing more frightening than encountering the healthy warmth of a fellow human in the midst of such misery. To him, it felt almost like a fatal shock. He almost lost the will to live at that moment. (*IYZ* 2:47)

What was so frightening about encountering "the healthy warmth of a fellow human" while being interned in a prison camp? On this point, Ishihara says little, simply stating that it hit Kano "almost as a fatal shock." It is significant, however, that "the healthy warmth," something described in a bodily metaphor, was communicated through food and that Kano subsequently refused all food. For Kano, under the extreme conditions of the Soviet internment camps, food was merely a substance that reduced the inmates to the level of bare bodily existence, completely destroying their dignity. Kano may have been thrown off balance when he saw in that same substance the possibility that it could also communicate compassionate feelings.

By dismissing bodily needs, including food intake, as much as possible, Kano had closed himself off from the outside world in order to maintain his mental balance. Then "the healthy warmth" offered by a fellow human penetrated his obstinate defenses and touched his mind. That this process took place through food—that substance most intimately tied to bodily needs—must have forced Kano to fundamentally reexamine the way he had lived until then.[20] The body had to be treated with suspicion because the authorities effectively controlled it, and it also was a medium that enabled ties with others. These two contrasting aspects of the body were inseparable: pursuit of its positive possibility (ties with others) meant opening up oneself through the channel of the body to the outside world, which in turn made one vulnerable to the authorities. In the face of this unsettling possibility, Kano desperately clung to the only way of survival that he knew. By entirely rejecting food, he severed communications with the outside world in order to recover his internal quietude. In this battle for self-preservation, others existed only as enemies with whom he shared no common ground, enemies that included the daughter of the Khabarovsk mayor.

The words that Kano uttered to the prison interrogator after his fasting episode attest to the rigid boundaries he had constructed between self and other. Understanding that his fasting was a form of resistance, the prison authorities interrogated Kano afterward. They were unable to achieve any breakthrough; finally, the interrogator suggested that they talk "like humans," implicitly urging him to provide information regarding other inmates. To this, Kano answered: "If you are a human, I am not a human. If I am a human, you are not a human" (*IYZ* 2:48). His logic rejected the vertical power relations inherent in the power of the interrogator over the internees. Instead, Kano insisted that his free will was not compatible with the prison authorities and the Soviet political system that ran the prison network. Even after he explained to Ishihara what had caused his fasting, Kano adhered to this logic: had he accepted the warmth of another human, he would not have been able to maintain the inner sanctuary of his mind.

Without touching on the physical dimension of Kano's act, Ishihara valorizes it as a psychological struggle through which Kano denounced the futility of denouncing the victimizer. "I think that by maintaining his stance of refusing any kind of denunciation, he denounced the last 'empty seat.' Denunciation escapes the futility of being a denunciation only when it denounces this 'empty seat'" (IYZ 2:47–48). "Empty seat" for Ishihara is the space one can always find among the victims.[21] A refusal to comfortably sit in the last audience seat "left empty"—all the other seats but his are occupied—was how Kano preserved his clear agency as a human being. Ishihara elaborates:

> I am deeply fascinated by this man who turns his back to leave his group upon the shock of recognizing within the fluid relations between victimization and victimhood the victimizer within himself. [Solving] the problem always hinges on the solitary figure of each individual. Here, to be alienated [from the group] can no longer be a misery but the sign of a singular and hard-won courage. How does this courage then save the faceless majority? I believe it saves nothing. What his courage saves is only the clarity of his "position." This clarity alone is his assurance for complete independence and for the substance of his pessimism. There is nothing more blessed than a solitary man saving his solitary position. (*IYZ* 2:49)

In postwar Japan, Ishihara reenacts Kano's struggle, even though the courage of the solitary man saves nothing for "the faceless majority." Such pessimism, through the utter disregard of bodily needs and the refusal to connect with others, only confirms an individual's stance as a "solitary figure."

Ishihara's heroic tale of the pessimist Kano could be sustained only by concealing the inconvenient existence of the body. Ishihara never ruminates about the fact that he used his own body in a way diametrically opposite to what Kano did with his. In order to open the closed mind and body of his friend Kano Buichi, Ishihara reluctantly decided to join him in the fast. Ishihara's act was not as direct as carrying a colleague's backpack during a march, but by sharing mental pain through the bodily act of fasting, Ishihara rescued this solitary man from his self-confinement. In other words, Kano fasted for his own mental anguish, whereas Ishihara fasted for his friend. Although the treatment of the internees had greatly improved by then, Ishihara's decision to work without eating must not have been easy, since he had just emerged from a state of near-death starvation and had no idea how many days the fast might last. Nevertheless, Ishihara wagered his own body in order to bring his friend back to life. Kano was blessed to have such a friend. When compared side by side, the difference between their actions is clear: Kano abused his body as a step toward death, and Ishihara mistreated his as a step toward life. Kano aimed only at "saving his solitary position" as an individual; Ishihara's sympathetic act was not adopted in an empty, abstract space but in the context of human ties. Ishihara's action had a deeper social meaning.

Ishihara mentions his own fasting only in passing, implying that there was nothing special about what he did for his friend. Ishihara was an optimist who brought Kano back to the world of living through his bodily performance. It is not hard to see Ishihara in the character from "Lonely, Now." In turn, Kano was able to feel the warmth in Ishihara's gesture. Ishihara's early poems show his optimistic presence in the camps. As if he had become embarrassed by his hopeful self, Ishihara refuses to comment on the nature of his altruistic act, though he remains determined to idealize Kano. It is significant that Ishihara published this essay in 1970, seventeen years after his repatriation, thereby reexamining their internment experiences from a considerable distance. By striving for the high moral ground of the mind and, accordingly, condemning the open and vulnerable body for having served as a conduit for humiliating experiences, Ishihara attempts to reconstruct himself as a solitary figure. The body and the possibilities it offered—the sensitivity that he explores in his early poems—must be denied. Its very capacity to feel the warmth of others made the body a threat to the solitary mind. In his essays, Ishihara tried to transcend the here and now of the body by privileging the mind, just as he believed Kano had done during his internment.[22]

Kano Buichi, whom Ishihara so admired, died only fifteen months after they returned to Japan on the same ship. About Kano's fatal heart attack during an overnight shift at his hospital,[23] Ishihara writes: "It was a sudden death after having abused his mind and body like a madman. He allowed himself no rest until the very end" (*IYZ* 2:52). Kano seems to have come home only to complete the slow process of dying.[24] Kano's early death meant the loss of the genuine friendship that Ishihara had forged with him in the Siberian camps, but it also allowed him to idealize his dear friend.

THE FETTERS OF THE BODY

In 1959, Ishihara sent a letter to his brother, the only other surviving member of his immediate family. With this letter, he severed their relations, unleashing his deep anger and sorrow toward his brother, relatives, and a postwar Japanese society that refused to acknowledge his internment experiences. Ishihara had returned from internment "thinking that [he] was somehow shouldering the weight of 'war responsibility' that somebody else would eventually be assigned to carry." Instead, what he encountered in his homeland were attempts to make him conform to mundane communal behavioral norms, even while slighting him as a "Siberian returnee." In contrast to his later argument against denunciation, Ishihara bitterly accused those who refused to understand what he had undergone in Siberia (*IYZ* 2:161–75).

Several years after sending this letter to his brother, he wrote: "'The act that I forbade for myself' is the act of *denouncing*. By cutting off that word, I found the first line of my poem. By cutting off that word, my poem is destined to end in an assertion. That is, by stopping right before denunciation, I gained an assertion" (*IYZ* 2:157). To grasp Ishihara's seemingly contradictory claims, we must reexamine what he meant by "denunciation" and "assertion" in light of the shifts that take place in his poems. That is, how are his readers supposed to understand that he was writing poetry while driven by a persistent impulse toward denunciation? The key to solving this question can be found in the changes in the tone of his poetry that occurred around the time he sent this letter to his brother.

"No denunciation" was the mantra of Ishihara's determination to expect nothing from postwar society, even from his brother and other relatives. With this declaration, his mind abandoned any effort to appeal to others, thereby gaining a form of clarity. Finding "the first line of [his] poem" was a way toward establishing the mental clarity that he later expressed in his poem "Position." In this position, Ishihara was able to reconstruct himself as an active agent capable of assertion. The contents of the letter to his brother parallel the ways in which his poetry changed during this period. Moreover, at the strong urging of the editor Ōno Shin, the letter itself was published in 1967 in the literary magazine *Tall and Short* (*Noppo to chibi*), together with Ishihara's contemplative journal entries up to 1962. The letter reached an audience that well surpassed this magazine's regular readership, representing a turning point in Ishihara's literary career. Thereafter, he began to publish prose essays about his Siberian internment experiences. If the letter had been an instrument to sever relations with his brother in the fall of 1959, its publication eight years later constituted a symbolic act of cutting off relations with postwar Japanese society. To appeal to postwar society, to invite others in, required Ishihara to open up his wounded self, although this opening up left him extremely vulnerable. Once Ishihara realized that postwar society would not give him the desired response, he closed off the channel of his body and sought instead to secure the high ground of his mind.

It was not easy, however, for Ishihara to rip his mind away from a vulnerable body and the tangled emotions rooted in his physical being. Kasuya Ei'ichi, a close friend, described the pain as follows:

Probably dictated by his ethics, he produced a series of texts about the internment camps, starting with "From the Experience of a Kind of 'Symbiosis'" [Aru "kyōsei" no keiken kara, discussed earlier]. It could be, in my opinion, described as an ascetic act, which squeezed everything out of him. I hate to say this, but it was the act of a man who had barely escaped hell but was forcing himself to return there.[25]

The reason that Ishihara "forc[ed] himself to return there" was that the Ishihara of the present would not exist without these experiences in hell. In his afterword to *The Homecoming of Sancho Panza*, Ishihara states:

> "The best of us did not return." I used to feel a twinge when I read those words that Viktor Frankl inserted at the opening of *Man's Search for Meaning*. Or I can perhaps restate them in this way: "The best of myself did not return either." This alone is the reason why I am still obsessed about Siberia. To me, freedom exists only in Siberia (to be more precise, only in the Siberian internment camps). Only at the place where the rising and the setting of the sun are *plainly* absurd, can one freely imagine the future for the first time. It was the place where I did not stand as a human under the given conditions but, rather, crouched [*uzukumaru*] as a human. That is the meaning of Siberia to me. The memories of directly touching shoulders with myself in such a place comprise the substance of the unforgettable event of "once having been a human." (*IYZ* 1:543, italics in original)

As he read the psychiatrist Viktor Frankl's critical account of his own experiences in Nazi concentration camps, Ishihara revisited his Siberian past. What Ishihara saw in Frankl's text was his jumping-off point rather than an ironic aphorism. Ishihara perceived his time in Siberia as his most genuine human experiences, his subsequent life merely a process of figuring out how best to make sense of them.

The tension between Ishihara's early poetry and later prose may thus be rearticulated in the following way: In poetry, he is able to "crouch as a human," and in *The River That Runs Through the Sea* (*Umi o nagareru kawa*, 1974), Ishihara elaborates on what it means to crouch: "Others might ask where they then find hope. To this question, I have hardly any means to respond. All I can say . . . is that one should not run away. One should crouch wherever one is at while bearing all the burdens that one can bear. Do not talk about the future if one cannot commit to it" (*IYZ* 2:237). Ishihara continued to crouch in the early repatriation years under the enormous burden of his Siberian experiences.

By contrast, in prose, Ishihara urges himself to "stand as a human." Writing prose was a means of lifting himself up and, therefore, was an arduous battle against his memories of bodily humiliation. Once, he struggled for three months to write a single essay; on another occasion, he suffered from a mysterious fever while writing.[26] Fond of thinking while walking, he came home one time with his feet covered in bloody blisters after walking 18.75 miles.[27] Koyanagi Reiko, a fellow poet, remembers a time when Ishihara, unable to sit still, went to a graveyard in the middle of night and banged his head against a gravestone.[28] In addition to all these anecdotes, we know that Ishihara began to drink more heavily under the stress of writing essays.[29]

Thanks to the critical acclaim he earned for both his prose and poetry, Ishihara became a minor celebrity. In 1964, for *The Homecoming of Sancho Panza*, he won a Mr. H (H-shi) Prize, the most coveted prize awarded to Japanese poets. But Ishihara's playfulness in naming his first collection after Don Quixote's faithful servant—an allusion to antiheroic and everyman images—was largely lost to the young readers who discovered Ishihara in the politically charged atmosphere of the late 1960s and early 1970s. They saw in his essays a solitary intellectual who relentlessly questioned his own positionality. In one such youth's recollection, Ishihara was "cool" (*kakkoyokatta*).[30] College students flocked to his public lectures, and some even visited him at his workplace.[31] In 1973, his essay collection *Yearning for Home and the Sea* (*Bōkyō to umi*) received a Fujimura Kinen Rekitei Prize. In 1975, he became president of the Modern Japanese Poetry Association, and in the following year, he published a complete collection of his poetry (*Ishihara Yoshirō zen shishū*). Despite this success as a writer, trouble was coming to a head in his private life.

Not much has been written about the relationship between Ishihara and his wife, Kazue, a war widow whom he married in 1956. She had lost her first husband in the Siberian internment, and it is very likely that Ishihara's existential reexamination of his past experiences deeply affected his wife as well.[32] Even when he achieved professional success, his drinking problem worsened, and Kazue was hospitalized with a mental breakdown in 1973. Exhausted from looking after his wife and lonely during her hospitalization, Ishihara increasingly depended on alcohol. In 1976, Ishihara and Kazue descended into deeper mental and physical crisis: during his wife's rehospitalization in October, Ishihara fainted from anemia, and he too was admitted to a hospital to treat his alcohol addiction (*IYZ* 2:538). After his release, he continued treatment as an outpatient. But with Kazue in and out of the hospital throughout 1977, Ishihara began to exhibit increasingly bizarre, drunken behavior.

His memories of bodily pain corroded Ishihara from the inside out, eventually manifesting as acts of self-injury. At the end of his published conversation with the magazine *Ryūdō* (October 1977), Ishihara told Shimizu Akira that he had tried twice to cut his belly open. While showing the scars from these attempts, he explained his acts:

> One of the two incisions is almost gone, but the other one won't go away. I guess I really cut deep. Check out Kiya [the name of a well-known knife shop] in front of Mitsukoshi Department store [in Nihonbashi]. They have really beautiful short-bladed knives. I paid a fortune for one. While looking at them, I got an itch for one. That same night, I cut my belly. Then when my wife was hospitalized, I cut it again. Just mimicry. I just mimicked the real hara-kiri. (*IYZ* 3:427)

Ishihara's bodily performance may have been a farcical mimicry of a heroic act, but it also was a desperate expression of his inner pain.

It was obvious to the people around him that he needed serious medical intervention once more, but time had run out.[33] On November 14 of that year, at age sixty-two, Ishihara died of heart failure while taking a bath. Despite his effort to use his mind to overcome his bodily trauma in the internment camps, his body retaliated in the end. Although Ishihara's mind processed his bodily experiences into a series of essays, the humiliation that had been inscribed on his body continued to torment him.

WHAT ISHIHARA YOSHIRŌ LEFT BEHIND

Several months after Ishihara's death, the literary and social critic Yoshimoto Taka'aki criticized Ishihara's apparently apolitical attitude in a published conversation with Ayukawa Nobuo:

> Particularly when I read his essays I feel this, but Mr. Ishihara has no protection against such collective entities as state and society. Even though he spent a long time in the Soviet internment camps, he has none of that. I wonder about that. What about the fact that unlike Uchimura [Gōsuke], this issue never figures in his writing? I would say this is a point with which I feel dissatisfaction.[34]

Uchimura Gōsuke (1920–2009), whom Yoshimoto mentions here as a counterexample, also received a twenty-five-year prison sentence for his alleged anti-Soviet activities and was not allowed to repatriate until 1956. After returning to Japan, Uchimura continued to vigorously critique Stalinism and the Soviet society that maintained this inhumane internment system.[35] In contrast to Uchimura's combative attitude, Yoshimoto criticizes Ishihara's lack of "protection against such collective conditions as state or society" as unsatisfactory. That is, Yoshimoto criticizes Ishihara for what he did *not* say, arguing that "it is rather lazy that he [Ishihara] did not think" about the social and political conditions.[36] Ishihara, however, was neither lazy nor careless. What Yoshimoto misses is that Ishihara's stance of "no denunciation" meant a conscious refusal to "stand on the side of victimhood and justice." Ishihara rejected a categorical critique of the external force at work—whether Stalinism, Japan's militarism, or a combination of both (*IYZ* 2:241)—a denunciation that would turn him into a victim with no agency.

Yoshimoto's criticisms are spoken from a thoroughly postwar stance, as we see in the following:

Although we did not have such experiences [of Soviet internment], the war caused havoc, which we experienced as students. When the war was over, everything was flipped. Just by observing these changes, I believe, we thought through the question of what such collective entities as nation and society meant to individuals. Accordingly, since Mr. Ishihara was right in the middle of these things, directly experiencing the war and postwar, I think he should have wondered what the collective meant. But he thought about none of that. That is what I want to say.[37]

Yoshimoto's personal journey prevented him from comprehending Ishihara's silence. In the same conversation with Ayukawa, Yoshimoto refused to recognize Ishihara's struggle with his Siberian experiences, implying that Ishihara was just trying to escape from their weight: "In short, Mr. Ishihara wanted to live quietly and unnoticed. But even though he wanted to live quietly and unnoticed while he was writing poems or just living, his internment experiences began to surface. After they began to surface, his life was, in essence, just an extra or a remainder.

That is, I understand that this part was false."[38] In contrast to Yoshimoto, I contend that Ishihara's discussion of his internment experiences was a strategic choice, even though it may have been a self-destructive one.

Seeing the complete collapse of what Yoshimoto believed in served as an impetus for him to rethink "such collective entities as nation and society." This critical stance became possible only through Yoshimoto's dash between wartime experience and postwar life. Although Yoshimoto was able to make this transition in one swift move, the distance between war and postwar was too far for Ishihara to traverse so lightly, burdened as he was with his internment experiences. The opinion leader Yoshimoto ran like an Olympian sprinter to the postwar period, but the late-arriving Ishihara decided instead to crouch down and painstakingly creep on with his words. In the end, Yoshimoto's critique of Ishihara appears to be a demand that Ishihara stand up and start running. Instead of escaping the weight of his internment experience by dissolving himself in the discursive space of postwar Japan that Yoshimoto helped define— or by falling back on ready-made rhetoric—Ishihara tried to reconstitute himself on the basis of his trauma.

Though not completely separated from it, the late-returning Ishihara did not try to catch up with postwar Japan. The essays he wrote in the latter half of the 1960s can be seen as participating in the beginning of a more widespread reexamination of Japan's war aggression and victimhood. The emerging critique of postwar Japan's discursive embrace of victimhood offered a new perspective through which Ishihara could reflect on his experiences. Yet in the midst of spectacular economic growth, the almost universal remembrance of war suffering grew increasingly abstract, and Ishihara's tenuous desire to reach out to others dissipated.

The distinctive manner in which Ishihara describes Angkor Wat, which he visited during a trip to Cambodia in 1964, opens a window into the particular nature of his struggles in postwar Japan:

Angkor Wat stopped being an already created monument. By weathering and decaying day by day, it keeps changing and moving even now. The living are not the only things that move. What had given up life as a monument continued to move by decaying. The strangely moving sensation of discovering "it has been living" is something barely comprehensible at this point to me, who has arrived at the state of giving up. (*IYZ* 2:535)

Angkor Wat appealed to Ishihara not because it embodied past glories as a monument but because he realized it had "continued to move" and had "been living" through the very process of decay. Not simply a negative process, decay was the means by which the monument asserted its existence. His encounter with Angkor Wat assured Ishihara that he, too, could live, even though postwar Japan offered no ready place for him.

Perhaps Ishihara's tragedy was that he tried to live through that process of decay just as Japan was embracing a heady optimism inspired by the high-growth economy. In this context, Ishihara was misrecognized as a sublime monument rather than a decaying remnant. As Sumioka Takashi regretfully noted, "The more highly valued Mr. Ishihara's poems were, the farther we pushed away his figure as a human being."[39] Even Ishihara's prose—which exposes his ordinary self—only helped consolidate his heroic images. To prove that he was no hero, Ishihara could only hasten the process of his physical decay.[40]

In the material wealth of 1970s Japan, Ishihara's anguish deepened. The quintessential self-made man, Tanaka Kakuei, who became the prime minister in July 1972, perhaps best embodied the optimism of this period. After visiting the Soviet Union in 1973, Tanaka talked on television about his vision of launching a large-scale development in Siberia with Japan's capital and technological assistance.[41] To him, the enormous timber that had overwhelmed the Japanese internees in Siberia was merely a raw material waiting to be exploited by Japan's capital.[42] Although it was never fully implemented, Tanaka's ambition attested to this radical geopolitical shift, which further diminished the former internees' personal experiences. Ishihara once remembered the timber as grave markers driven into the frozen land; in the logic of capitalism, his somber recollection was mere sentimentalism (IYZ 2:428).[43]

When two stragglers returned from the southern Pacific to 1970s Japan, the nation's capitalism flexed its muscles, immediately turning the stragglers into consumable cultural icons: the wonders of their long survival and return were grist for media exploitation. In the final chapters of this book, I explore the lives of men who were forced to live as such iconic images.

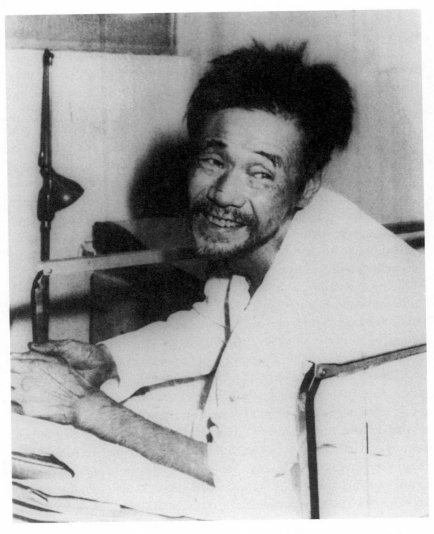

Yokoi Shōichi at Memorial Hospital in Guam, January 24, 1972. (Courtesy of Mainichi shinbunsha)

Chapter Five

LOST AND FOUND IN THE SOUTH PACIFIC

Postwar Japan's Mania Over Yokoi Shōichi's Return

I came home all right. Although I am embarrassed, I came home to tell everybody about the defeat in Guam in detail. I came home to explain the hardships that I endured to survive, the things that I cannot put in words.

YOKOI SHŌICHI, HANEDA INTERNATIONAL AIRPORT, FEBRUARY 2, 1972

To me, right now is the third jungle period. The first jungle [period] was the time I spent in poverty before I was recruited into the military. The second jungle was, of course, the time I spent in Guam. And the third is these days. This is the hardest.

YOKOI SHŌICHI, "SECOND LIEUTENANT ONODA, YOKOI SHŌICHI WILL HUMBLY TEACH YOU HOW TO RETURN TO NORMAL LIFE" (ONODA SHŌI DONO SENPAI YOKOI SHŌICHI GA SHAKAI FUKKI NO HŌHŌ O O'OSHIE SHIMASU)

RETURN FROM THE NETHERWORLD

The film *The Human Bullet* (*Nikudan*, 1968) satirizes the irrationality of Japan's war efforts through the use of silly, absurd images that verge on the surreal. The story focuses on the life of an officer candidate who is trained for and assigned to haphazardly conceived suicide missions in the final days of war. His final mission requires him to wait for enemy ships off the coast of Japan in a makeshift vessel, an oil drum tied to a torpedo, with an umbrella over his head. He never encounters any enemy ships, and in his delirium, he mistakes for a carrier a barge that carries night soil and releases the torpedo (it misses the target).[1] In this scene, while an extreme long shot highlights the absurdity of the contraption, close-up and medium-close-up shots convey the protagonist's trapped state. His sincere motive contrasts with his utter powerlessness in the situation. Although he eventually learns of Japan's defeat, he never makes it back to land; abandoned, he merely floats in his drum outside Tokyo Bay.

The scriptwriter/director Okamoto Kihachi offers a fantastic twist at the end of the film, cutting to a beach scene in the summer of 1968. The drum drifts toward what appears to be Shōnan Beach, a site of pleasure seeking and leisure.[2] In the drum are the protagonist's remains, reduced to a skeleton. The improbable return of the fallen soldier after twenty-three years highlights the unbridgeable chasm separating the past from the present, rendering Japan—both during and after the war—as an incomprehensible space. By depicting something so implausible, the scene uses the bizarre and the burlesque to shake the audience out of its complacency.

The reality proved to be at least as outlandish as what Okamoto concocted for his offbeat film. In 1972, a little over three years after the film's release, Japanese Imperial Army soldier Yokoi Shōichi emerged from twenty-eight years of hiding in the southern Pacific island of Guam. Although Guam was a coveted vacation destination for Japanese honeymooners in the late 1960s, more than 90 percent of the 21,000 Japanese defensive units had perished there in 1944 when U.S. forces took control of the island. Yokoi returned to Japan as a representative of the fallen soldiers, forcing Japanese society to revisit, albeit temporarily, the past that many considered, and wished, dead. This chapter examines the Japanese media's response to his return, as well as Yokoi's strategies for survival in both Guam and postwar Japan.

THE CAPTURE OF A STRAGGLER

On January 24, 1972, two local hunters in Guam captured a Japanese solider who had been hiding in the jungle for the twenty-seven and a half years since the Japanese defense forces were defeated in August 1944.[3] The man identified himself as Yokoi Shōichi from Aichi Prefecture in central Japan.

The Japanese news media immediately reacted to the news, initially with skepticism and then with intensity once the prefectural relief bureau confirmed Yokoi's identity. The *Asahi shinbun* briefly carried a small article, "A Former Japanese Soldier Discovered?" (Moto Nihon-hei o hakkenka?), which reported only the condition in which Yokoi was discovered. But that day's evening edition reported his discovery as a lead story on the front page. In an effort to cover every aspect of Yokoi's experiences, as many as 150 Japanese journalists descended on Guam, a southern Pacific island about one-third the size of Oahu, Hawaii. Overwhelmed by the media's aggressive approach to Yokoi, some of Guam's residents compared the Japanese reporters with kamikaze pilots.[4] For the next several weeks, millions of people around the world marveled at the story of the Japanese soldier who had continued his lone battle in the southern Pacific long after the war's end, the name of Yokoi Shōichi becoming an instantly recognizable cultural marker in Japan's postwar period.

For postwar Japan, Yokoi's emergence from the Guam jungle recalled memories of war, eliciting various reactions in Japanese society. Many former soldiers saw themselves in the emaciated figure of Yokoi, who had been an ordinary soldier from a rural community, and some bereaved family members of fallen soldiers even wondered whether their beloved sons or brothers might still be alive.[5] The younger generations who had no personal memories of the Asia Pacific War cast a curious gaze on the man who was still living under conditions of war. To many of these younger Japanese, Yokoi's behavior was simply incomprehensible. While offering an opportunity for younger generations to ruminate on Japan's postwar existence, the return of a "fallen" soldier also shook postwar Japanese society and reopened the psychological wounds of war.[6] Commenting on Yokoi's return, one young writer claimed: "I feel we owe something to them [the dead soldiers], and someday we will have to return what we owe to them. I feel we need to respond to their deaths. That is, so to speak, my sense of 'honoring history.'"[7] Another writer, Yasuoka Shōtarō, who had served in the wartime military, felt both excitement and uncanny surprise at the news. "When I first learned that Mr. Yokoi was discovered in the jungle cave, I was excited to hear that my 'war buddy' had returned alive, but at the same time caught aback as if somebody called me from the dark. What, indeed, is this frightening thing?"[8] Yasuoka admitted his shock at the way Yokoi's reappearance brought back long-repressed memories of war. At least for these writers, Yokoi Shōichi had returned from a netherworld to settle the account with the war dead.

The start of postwar Japan was premised on the clear divide between war and peace. The continuing impact of the war was underestimated in the narrative that the war had unambiguously ended and the postwar period had immediately begun in the summer of 1945. As seen in *Stray Dog*, the war was dissociated from the hardship and uncertainty of the immediate postwar years. Yokoi's twenty-eight years on Guam existed in the ambiguous space between war and postwar: his postwar began in the midst of the war, and his war continued into the postwar period. The tale of his survival was both fascinating and disturbing to his contemporaries because it destabilized the boundaries between war and postwar. Yokoi's return demonstrated, at least momentarily, the complacence of postwar Japan for not noticing its proximity to the past.

In 1972 in Japanese society—a society that had already transformed war memories into a nostalgic commodity—failed to fully comprehend the nature of the challenge posed by Yokoi's return. Like his emaciated body, the disturbing public image of the former imperial soldier underwent rehabilitation and metamorphosed into that of a more likable, even amusing, character in affluent society. As a tool for his own survival in postwar Japan, Yokoi not only acquiesced to the images generated and circulated by Japan's mass media but also hid himself among them. When Yokoi was first discovered in Guam, one of the survivors of the Second Battle of Guam lamented: "Mr. Yokoi speaks, speaks, and speaks—[look at] that manner [of his]. It is really sad to see him deceiving himself hard through his own words. We, too [other survivors of the war], continue to lie while keeping the truth to ourselves, taking it to our graves."[9] The years following Yokoi's reemergence did little to alter his approach to public commentary on his experiences. Although he continued to speak about himself and the war, his remarks followed formulaic patterns that revealed remarkably little about the effects of the war on his own personal life.

YOKOI SHŌICHI'S WAR

The first half of Yokoi Shōichi's life was as ordinary as the lives of the millions of Japanese men who had been mobilized in Japan's war efforts in the 1930s and 1940s. Indeed, Yokoi's ordinariness made him a sympathetic character in the Japanese media's retelling of his experiences. He was born in March 1915 in a rural community in Aichi Prefecture as the only son of Yamada Shōichi and Tsuru. His parents separated when he was three months old, and young Shōichi stayed with Tsuru, who eventually married Yokoi Eijirō in 1926.

At the age of sixteen, Yokoi chose to be apprenticed to a tailor shop in Toyohashi City, about forty miles from his home. His life as an apprentice to the tailor was typically grueling: In his 1974 memoir, he recalled waking up at 6:00 A.M. and working all day until his bedtime around 11:30 P.M. Because he was at the bottom of the shop hierarchy, Yokoi was not allowed to eat his full at each meal. It was by no means an easy life, but the skills he acquired at the tailor shop later proved indispensable to his survival in the Guam jungle.[10] After five years of apprenticeship and one extra year of unpaid work at the shop—a common practice at the time—Yokoi returned to his parents' house to open his own tailoring business. He maintained his business there for two years before being drafted as a soldier in the army's Third Transportation Regiment in 1938.

Like many young men before him, Yokoi planned to build a steady life on the basis of the skills acquired through his hard work. But Japan's colonial aggression forced Yokoi, like most in his generation, to interrupt his career trajectory before reaching his prime. The country was already deep into a war against China long before it declared war against the United States and the British Empire in 1941. In September 1938, Yokoi was transferred to the First Heavy Field Artillery Brigade, the Second Transportation Corps that was stationed in southeast China. The unit returned to Japan the following February, and Yokoi was discharged from service in March 1939.[11] Yokoi worked hard to rebuild his business before the Japanese military disrupted his life a second time, this time for much longer than anyone could have anticipated. In August 1941, he was called up again to serve with the Twenty-Ninth Transportation Regiment.[12] For the next two and a half years, he served as a guard in the Manchurian city of Liaoyang; being under the Kwantung army's control, the area did not experience large-scale fighting during this period.

In February 1944, Yokoi's unit relocated to the South Pacific to support the effort against the advancement of U.S. forces. The Japanese navy was steadily losing control of the region, and many transport ships had already been lost to enemy submarine attacks. Although damaged by a torpedo attack, the ship transporting Yokoi's unit managed to reach its final destination, Guam Island, in March, and by the end of April, a total of 21,000 soldiers had arrived.[13] Yokoi's unit immediately began constructing a defensive line along the island's southwestern coast and then were ordered to construct an airfield. With only limited provisions and repeated U.S. air raids under way, the soldiers had to dig the ground with only small shovels and portable pickaxes, and the airfield never became functional.[14] Facing 55,000 far better equipped U.S. invasion forces, the hastily constructed Japanese defense lines proved utterly inadequate. Bombardment by U.S. warships before the invasion had neutralized much of the already scarce Japanese firepower, and the U.S. landing lasted only a single day.

On July 21, the U.S. forces began landing on the western coast of the island; incapable of maintaining the defense line, the Japanese units retreated inland in chaos. Out of desperation, the commander of the Japanese forces, General Obata Hideyoshi, ordered the remaining soldiers to launch an all-out attack at midnight on July 25, 1944, in an effort to push the U.S. forces back to the landing points. Without the means to counter firepower and air attacks, however, the Japanese forces failed to organize an effective offensive and lost more than 80 percent of their men in the subsequent battles. After this failure, the commander mounted a defensive battle in the jungle and gathered the 3,000 soldiers left in the northern part of the island. These remaining forces were annihilated in an early August attack on U.S. tank units. General Obata committed suicide on August 11, effectively ending the Japanese forces' organized efforts to defend the island.

Life as a Straggler

Despite the annihilation of the Japanese defense forces and the collapse of General Obata's headquarters, a few thousand Japanese soldiers remained scattered throughout the Guam jungle. Communications among the defense units were disrupted in their retreat, and some units were completely left out of the command network. Yokoi's transportation platoon survived in the southern part of the island, unaware of either the all-out attack on July 25 or General Obata's death.

Without the central command system, the surviving soldiers were left to their own devices. Yokoi's platoon commander opted for guerrilla warfare rather than a desperate suicidal attack on the American stronghold, and he eventually ordered the thirty-some surviving members to divide up into small groups to avoid enemy detection.[15] Under the commander's directive, the members of Yokoi's platoon divided into three squads in early September.[16] Yokoi, whose prolonged battle experience had earned him the rank of lance corporal,[17] led one of the squads into a battle of attrition.[18] In the jungle, their focus shifted from the exchange of fire to merely survival while awaiting the arrival of friendly forces.

Yokoi and four other soldiers moved inland toward the upper reach of the Talofofo River, seeking a safer location in which to hide from the intensifying American sweeping operations. Two other soldiers soon joined the group and built a hut as a base for their activities; it was fortuitous that they were in the southern part of the island where food was more abundant. Unfortunately, they expended much of their energy in the search for sustenance, and their relationships became strained over the distribution of food.[19] These Japanese Imperial Army soldiers were reduced to a life of hunting and gathering, experimenting with local food items, and constructing crude huts with local plants. The Japanese stragglers who hid in the northern part of Guam and returned in 1951 even reported cases of cannibalism, the shooting and eating of fellow stragglers.[20] In the second half of Yokoi's memoir, *Path to Tomorrow* (*Ashita eno michi*), the section that covers his life in the Guam jungle offers details mostly about the food he and other stragglers ate and the dwellings they built (Yokoi remained in the southern part of the island).

In the early years of their struggle for survival, Yokoi and others gradually acquired valuable knowledge about local food and sustained themselves with what the jungle offered: breadfruit, coconuts, cycad nuts (*federico*), papayas, potatoes, wild grass, tree fruits, mushrooms, lizards, snails, toads, rats, cats, and deer, as well as feral populations of chickens, pigs, and cows. Some of these jungle offerings, such as cycad nuts and toads, were poisonous, so the soldiers had to learn how to prepare them properly. Later, when Yokoi lived in a smaller group, they added shrimp and eels from the Talofofo River to their dietary list.[21] They devised various ways to cook the ingredients; besides obvious boiling and grilling, they also cooked with coconut milk and deep-fried meat in coconut oil. The men even found a way to produce alcoholic beverages and vinegar by fermenting breadfruit.[22] As they spent more time in the jungle, hiding became their raison d'être. At some point, in an effort to avoid detection, Yokoi and his fellow stragglers completely stopped stealing food from the local residents' cultivated land.

For the long-term Japanese stragglers, finding a source of salt was a pressing issue. For example, Minagawa Bunzō and Itō Masashi, two soldiers who continued to hide in the Guam jungle until 1960, were desperate enough to defy the risk of detection that they made runs to collect seawater several times a year.[23] Shimada Kakuo and several other Japanese stragglers spent ten years on Manus Island in New Guinea. Though they were able to subsist on the food they prepared in the jungle, they had no source of salt. Anticipating a long-term holdout, they tried to stretch what little salt they had in their possession—mostly the Japanese army's provision of powdered soy sauce—until they finally began bartering with the local people.[24] Although Yokoi had a similarly strong yearning for salt, he neither found a supply nor dared to leave his hideout in pursuit of one. In the end, he convinced himself that if other animals could survive without salt in their diets, he could, too—and he was right.[25]

Clothing and footwear were also a central concern for the surviving soldiers, as they had no prospect of future supplies. Initially they were able to find man-made materials in war wrecks in the jungle. But once they had depleted these limited resources, they had to find alternative materials with which to repair their shoes and gear. Before long, they were wearing sandals made out of palm fiber[26] and patching their uniforms with dried toad skins.[27] One of the stragglers, Shichi Mikio, who survived until 1964, knew the basics of blacksmithing and put his knowledge to use. With Shichi's help, Yokoi produced needles from spent cases, and later—around 1959 and 1960—forged cutting tools like saws and knives.[28] Yokoi eventually devised a method to produce fabric out of *pago* (wild hibiscus trees) and tailored his own "suits."[29] When he was discovered in 1972, Yokoi was wearing his own handmade shirt and shorts, and many in Japan were amazed by the ingenuity of his creations—though it took him more than seven months to complete one of his "suits."[30] By employing their craftsmanship and the skills they had learned in the rural communities of prewar Japan, the stragglers managed to battle the natural elements.

Although Yokoi's group gained valuable survival knowledge and skills at its first settlement, they eventually decided to move farther into the jungle to hide from the American soldiers, who continued to mop up the area. With the addition of several other stragglers, the group grew to as many as eleven men in June 1945.[31] These numbers eventually dwindled, however; American soldiers shot and killed four of the stragglers in

July,[32] and Minagawa Bunzō and Umino Tetsuo (who died in July 1954)[33] left voluntarily in September because of discord within the group.[34] This personal disharmony further divided the group into smaller units: Yokoi, Shichi Mikio, and Nakahata Satoru separated from the group in 1946, and, two years later, Shichi and Nakahata deserted Yokoi in the jungle. But the three of them resumed living together the following year, frequently changing the location of their residence until 1950, when they decided to dig an underground cave and live there.

Without proper tools, digging a cave suitable for living was difficult. It took a month for Yokoi, Shichi, and Nakahata to dig their first cave— only to abandon it after spending a single month living in it. It was too small for three of them; they could not cook their food inside. It was also too close to a path popular with the local residents.[35] Several months later, they began digging a second cave at another location. It took them six months to complete this new cave, which flooded with the rising groundwater during the rainy season. Although they brought some dirt back in the cave to raise the floor above the water level, it was nevertheless an unpleasant and uncomfortable place to live. Furthermore, six months after they completed the cave, the locals burned off the surrounding area to help hunt down the Japanese stragglers.[36] At this point, the three stragglers decided to leave the cave and temporarily returned to living above ground. When his relations with the other two grew strained during this time, Yokoi chose to live alone. Unfortunately, he accidentally caused a fire and lost nearly all his possessions, including his prized handmade *pago* suits.[37]

Although he no longer shared a dwelling with the other two stragglers, the three men remained in roughly the same area and continued to help one another whenever possible. In 1959, fifteen years after they began their straggler life, they made another effort at communal living, spending three months digging a 100-foot-long cave. For about a year, living together in the cave, they maintained a relatively peaceful existence. They worked on blacksmithing projects, producing sewing needles and cutting tools, and even began to grow some potatoes.[38] Yet their relationship again soured, and in 1960, they went their separate ways one final time. Yokoi spent more than three months digging his own cave more than 1,600 feet away from the one he had shared with Shichi and Nakahata. The cave was barely large enough for one person, but Yokoi built an indoor toilet and cooking stove, dug a well, and lined the entire inside with bamboo.[39] That cave became Yokoi's permanent dwelling for the rest of his time in Guam.[40]

Despite living in separate residences, Yokoi and his companions maintained amicable relations until Shichi and Nakahata died in 1964. The cause of their deaths was a mystery to Yokoi as well as the Guam medical examiners who later examined their remains. Yokoi hypothesizes in his memoir that a natural disaster triggered a chain of events that ultimately caused their deaths. A big typhoon hit the island in 1963, decimating the vegetation there,[41] so in the aftermath, it became much harder to gather food in the jungle. In addition, when he saw Shichi and Nakahata in January 1964, Yokoi noticed that their health was visibly declining.[42] As it turned out, that encounter was Yokoi's last human contact for a very long time; ten days later he discovered their corpses in their cave, already reduced to skeletons.[43]

After discovering their dead bodies, Yokoi spent the next eight years in the jungle in total silence and seclusion. During that period, he refrained even from talking to himself for fear of being discovered by local residents. He later claimed that he never slept deeply, that even the sounds of cockroaches mating awoke him. In the middle of night, when he could not bear his complete solitude any longer, Yokoi would cry and shout, banging his head against the walls of his cave.[44] In those last years on the island, his body and mind approached the limits of endurance. In fact, his ultimate encounter with the local hunters in 1972 may have been a desperate, albeit subconsciously motivated, attempt to finally free himself from the imprisonment of isolation.

Yokoi's Choice

The Asia Pacific War ended with Japan's defeat in August 1945 (officially on September 2, 1945, with the signing of the Japanese Instrument of Surrender on the USS *Missouri*). Within a year, Yokoi apparently learned about the Potsdam Declaration and Japan's defeat from a Japanese newspaper he found in the jungle. Immediately following his reemergence, *Shūkan sankei* published an interview with Yokoi, in which he claimed: "I picked up and read a newspaper dropped from a plane. About the peace terms of Posutondaun (Potsdam) too. . . . But we were taught to honor the Yamato spirit and fall like flower petals, [that it would be] dreadful if we did not fall. That's why I could not come out."[45] Yokoi thus suggested that his decision not to surrender was motivated by a fear of sanctions from the Japanese military for surrendering to the enemy.

Two years later, however, Yokoi told a different story, maintaining instead that the war never had a clear ending for him. In his memoir, Yokoi carefully avoided stating precisely when he learned of Japan's defeat. Although his memoir mentioned the Japanese paper published in Saipan[46] that he had found before Japan's surrender, Yokoi now insisted that he had regarded the newspaper's description of the Potsdam Declaration as "an enemy deception" designed to trick Japanese soldiers into surrender.[47] He also explained that his distrust of enemies had intensified as a result of the U.S. forces' call for the Japanese to surrender, which he had heard right after Japan's surrender in 1945 and again in 1946.[48]

It now appears that in the days immediately after his emergence from the jungle, Yokoi attempted to display some knowledge of world events, perhaps out of a misplaced sense of pride. But as he spent more time in Japan, he seemed to become aware of his own mistake: he had missed his chance to return home years earlier when faced with information about Japan's defeat. In order to justify his decision not to surrender, Yokoi emphasizes in his memoir that he believed the Japanese military would surely come back to rescue him: "I did not know about Japan's defeat. Given the fact that the Sino-Japanese War and the Russo-Japanese War occurred within ten years of each other, I firmly believed that if I waited ten years at most, the Japanese forces would surely regain momentum and advance to this Guam island."[49] Yokoi then intimates that he had the ability to properly judge the situation, but he insists that although he did not want to face it, he "had an inkling of Japan's defeat."[50] He remains vague as to when precisely he first had that inkling and whether it hardened into conviction.

Once Yokoi returned to his hometown, he received numerous letters from all over Japan, many of which were encouraging. Some of them, however, accused him of cowardice and abandoning his duties as an Imperial Army soldier. For these critics, if he was indeed aware of Japan's defeat, it was fear and egoistic desire for self-preservation—not commitment to a larger nationalist cause—that animated Yokoi's decision to remain in the jungle. In response to his detractors, who demanded a clear-cut resolution—that if he knew about the war's end, he should have come out right away and that if he did not, he should have kept fighting—Yokoi insisted that battles continued in Guam even after Japan's defeat. He maintained that he continued to fight while awaiting the arrival of friendly forces. Given that his gun was not in usable condition, however, it was difficult to claim that he had survived solely to fight in the jungle. As if to address this particular point, he emphasized in his accounts that the ferocious U.S. sweeping operations and his deep suspicion of Americans made it impossible to surrender.

I do not cite these inconsistencies in his explanations to discredit his accounts in any way. Rather, they attest to the unique challenges that Yokoi faced, the challenges of living a wartime existence in the postwar period. Living in both wartime and postwar conditions, Yokoi faced two incompatible ethical demands: first, to be a brave, fearless soldier and, second, to hate war. Directly answering the question of when he learned about Japan's defeat—the question that most interested his contemporaries—would have forced Yokoi either to admit cowardice or to glorify war. If he had known of Japan's defeat, he would be a disgrace, according to the social mores of wartime Japan. If he had not been aware of Japan's defeat at all, he would be no more than an anachronistic relic of wartime Japan, a soldier with no place in the postwar era. In an effort to avoid this dilemma, Yokoi told his readers that he had only gradually come to realize Japan's defeat. For the large majority of Japanese who made the transition from wartime to postwar relatively easily, there was no need for a complicated explanation.

There are other explanations for why Yokoi remained in the jungle for so long. For example, some media reporters directly attributed his behavior to the *Field Service Code* (*Senjinkun*), the document that Tōjō Hideki, then minister of the army, issued to Japanese soldiers in January 1941.[51] It specifically prohibits them from becoming POWs: "A soldier must never suffer the disgrace of being captured alive. Do not leave [behind an] ignominious reputation after your death." The passage was widely cited to explain the behavior of the Japanese soldiers who refused to surrender, and shortly after his exodus, Yokoi himself began blaming it for his own behavior.

It was more likely, though, that fear, rather than an abstract army instruction, kept Yokoi in the jungle for so long. As the writer Yasuoka Shōtarō explains, Yokoi's elementary army training was completed long before the *Field Service Code* was issued, and even when he was called to duty, the code did not carry much weight in a soldier's education.[52] Many soldiers who fought and eventually hid in the jungle resisted surrender at least in part because they had no assurance of their subsequent safety in the hands of the enemy forces. In the case of Guam, which had been under the U.S. Navy's control since 1917, Japanese soldiers assumed that the local residents harbored pro-American sympathies. Moreover, the local residents had a tacit understanding for several years after the war that it was permissible to kill Japanese stragglers whenever they were spotted,[53] and Yokoi encountered numerous local patrols and raids. Thus Yokoi and his fellow stragglers feared both the Americans and the local residents.[54]

Yet their biggest fear was the reaction that their surrender would trigger in their own military and hometowns. Many stragglers believed that once they became POWs and were sent back home, they would be court-martialed and executed as defectors by the Japanese military authorities. Such a fate would bring disgrace to their family members and hometowns. For Yokoi and many other Japanese soldiers, surrender was simply not an option.[55]

Yokoi also refused to take his own life in Guam and later claimed that he had never thought about killing himself.[56] Yokoi's antiheroic action of hiding in the Guam jungle was a de facto objection to the army order as well as to a wartime Japanese society that belittled human lives. Social pressures forced Yokoi to choose between disgrace and death; the complete isolation that Yokoi suffered in the jungle was his answer to that choice. There was no honor in the lost battle. Only in complete isolation, wandering as the living dead, could Yokoi escape the stigma of surviving the lost battle. However, postwar Japanese society, which managed to neutralize most of the trauma of defeat by the early 1970s, failed to understand the nature of Yokoi's struggle and did not hesitate to transform him into a celebrity. By embracing his newfound celebrity in postwar Japan, Yokoi struggled to keep hidden the memories of his twenty-seven-and-a-half-year isolation, burying them instead in the collage of media images.

YOKOI SHŌICHI AND POSTWAR JAPAN

Of the 21,000 or so Japanese soldiers sent to Guam, Yokoi Shōichi was the 1,305th soldier who returned to Japan alive. Those who surrendered to or were captured by the U.S. forces were eventually sent back to Japan in the postwar period, although a number of them managed to hide in the jungle for many years. For example, Minagawa Bunzō, who spent several months with Yokoi's group in 1945, and Itō Masashi were captured by local residents and returned to Japan in 1960. Their return generated more media interest than did the stragglers who had returned to Japan from various southern Pacific islands in the 1950s.[57] But it failed to trigger any substantial media response in postwar society while the reparations of Japanese former servicemen from the Soviet Union, China, and other regions continued well into the second half of the 1950s. Public interest in the sixteen years that Minagawa and Itō spent as stragglers in Guam paled in comparison with the intense media attention surrounding Yokoi's discovery in 1972.

As Marukawa Tetsushi points out, it is noteworthy that Minagawa and Itō were hospitalized at a U.S. military hospital and placed on a U.S. military plane to the U.S. airbase in Tachikawa, Tokyo. By contrast, in 1972, Yokoi stayed in the civilian Guam Memorial Hospital, flew on a Japan Airlines special charter flight, and ultimately arrived at Haneda International Airport.[58] In 1960, Guam was not yet the island that attracted Japanese tourists with beautiful beaches; it remained a location of strategic importance, where civilian access, even American, was strictly limited.[59]

Furthermore, when Minagawa and Itō left Guam, Japan was fighting another "war"—the popular struggle over the revision of the security treaty between the United States and Japan.[60] In the weeks before the final ratification of the revised treaty on June 19, 1960, millions of Japanese rallied to express their opposition to it. This political struggle of 1960 was also a struggle with the memories of the Asia Pacific War. Most of the participants in the rallies objected less to the specific articles of the revised treaty than to the strong-arm tactics that Prime Minister Kishi Nobusuke used to push through its ratification. To the protesters, Kishi embodied the oppressive, authoritarian pre-1945 regime. He had served as a high-ranking official in the Manchukuo administration and as the minister of commerce and industry in Tōjō Hideki's administration when Japan declared war against the United States and the British Empire. Following Japan's defeat, Kishi was incarcerated as a class-A prisoner while he awaited trial at the International Military Tribunal for the Far East (Tokyo War Crimes Trials). His case never went to trial. As part of the conservative turn in the U.S. Occupation policies, the prosecution of war crimes became secondary to the fear of Communist insurgencies in East Asia. Consequently, the Tokyo War Crimes Trials did not extend past the first round, in which twenty-five defendants were sentenced to either death or a prison term. Kishi soon returned to Japanese politics and subsequently became prime minister in 1957. The 1960 opposition to the treaty revision thus served as a displaced political struggle through which protesters passed a belated critical judgment on the wartime authoritarianism, an authoritarianism that Kishi reenacted in his efforts to ratify the new treaty.[61]

Once the new treaty was ratified, Kishi resigned from office, taking responsibility for the political turmoil, and the opposition movement immediately subsided. In the 1960s, Japanese society fully embraced the conservative Liberal Democratic Party's economy-first policy, which produced unprecedented economic growth. By the time Yokoi Shōichi emerged from the Guam jungle, Japanese society and its relationship to war had been radically transformed. The postwar period began in a humiliating fashion for Japan, with the nation actively accepting the former enemy's hegemony in East Asia and transforming itself into the United States' client state. On the same day that Minagawa was "discovered," the U.S. House of Representatives passed the revised treaty that reaffirmed Japan's dependence on the U.S. military. Economic success eventually rehabilitated the nation's bruised pride, however, concealing the trauma and humiliation of defeat that Japan had suffered at the hands of the U.S. forces. Economic success also brought material wealth, which rapidly transformed the physical environment of Japan and erased the markers of the past. For example, under the urban renewal plans that various municipalities implemented in the 1960s, the black market that had sprouted in the chaos of bombed-out cities was replaced by multistory commercial buildings.[62]

On the basis of its newly found economic prosperity, postwar Japanese society celebrated two major international events in the 1960s, both of which further helped sanitize memories of war. First, in 1964, the year in which Yokoi's two remaining fellow stragglers perished, Japan proudly displayed its reconstruction to the international community by hosting the Tokyo Olympics. A few years later, when Expo 70 was held in Osaka, memories of Japan's troubled past were conspicuously absent amid the celebration of the country's economic power and future prospects. Japan's past figured only selectively in the presentations of Japan's—and humanity's—future, which were displayed for tens of millions of attend-ees.[63] Meanwhile, with the inauguration of nonstop commercial flights between Guam and Japan in 1967, Japanese tourists flooded Guam, and Japanese capital boosted the Guam tourism industry. During this pe-riod, the island was marketed as a "southern paradise," a honeymoon destination for Japanese newlyweds. Carefully curated, the idyllic images promoted by the Japanese tourism industry thus displaced the memories of fierce battles on the island and masked the continuing presence of the U.S. bases there.[64]

While Yokoi was living through his war in the Guam jungle, Japanese society steadily distanced itself from its memories of Japan's aggression and the war's destruction. In 1972, when Yokoi returned home, Japan was at the height of its optimism. Many Japanese believed that their country's political-economic environment would remain stable for the foreseeable future.[65] In this postwar atmosphere of optimism, the image of an ema-ciated Imperial Army soldier shocked Japanese society, recalling images that had long since been sanitized or forgotten. Yokoi thus reappeared as a living fallen hero of the Asia Pacific War to demonstrate that memo-ries of Japan's war could not be so easily repressed.

Yokoi Shōichi's Emergence and the Media's Competing Coverage

Yokoi felt a great amount of personal guilt for surviving the battle in which thousands of his fellow soldiers had perished. During his hospital stay in Guam, Yokoi was unable to sleep, telling reporters: "I had crazy dreams last night. They weren't exactly dreams because I didn't fall asleep. . . . Letters in the newspaper chase after me asking, Why you are going home, why are you leaving me behind?"[66] In an effort to calm the deceased soldiers' spirits, Yokoi inscribed their names on makeshift mortuary tablets at the head of his bed.[67] As he regained his physical and mental strength in Guam and Japan, the spirits ceased to torment him, and Yokoi was eventually rehabilitated as a living member of Japanese society.

The letters in Yokoi's "crazy dreams" were symbolic of his fraught relationship with the media. The Japanese mass media mercilessly covered every single word he uttered and every move he made. According to accounts in Japanese print media, Yokoi experienced an extreme surge of emotions following his capture, alternating between mania and depression. The fear of execution by the enemy stayed with him for several weeks, and he was unable to trust anyone. The reporters from Japanese newspapers and magazines who swarmed Yokoi's hospital and aggressively approached him were not sympathetic to his plight. The logic of capitalism drove their behavior and their determination to obtain a story at any cost. As Yasuoka Shōtarō observed, "The situation was like a hushed voice that, intensely reverberated, grows into an enormous noise."[68] The newspaper and weekly reporters who arrived in Guam surrounded the hospital where Yokoi was staying and used myriad tricks to interview and photograph him. For example, *Asahi shinbun* reporter Kōyō Emori climbed a palm tree to "meet" Yokoi in his room at the hospital.[69] Other reporters attempted to stage "moving reunions" by flying Yokoi's acquaintances and relatives to Guam. *Shūkan shinchō*'s exposé article described the fierce competition among the newspapers and newsweeklies during one particularly chaotic scene in Yokoi's hospital room:

> Among them, the worst was when a certain newspaper reporter brought Mr. Minagawa [Bunzō] from Tokyo and tried to arrange an exclusive interview [with Yokoi]. While they were jostling with other reporters who tried to stop their "scoop," a nurse accidentally opened the door. Mr. Minagawa poked his head in, and Mr. Yokoi turned to him. "Hey, Mr. Yokoi, I am Minagawa." The moment Mr. Yokoi recognized him, he shed some tears. One of the reporters watching their exchange shouted, "Oh, crying, he is crying. Look, he is crying . . ."[70]

In their unrelenting scrutiny, the media treated Yokoi much like the pandas that arrived at the Ueno Zoo several months later that same year. Besides the *Yomiuri shinbun*, the "certain newspaper" in the quotation, the *Sankei shinbun* brought Itō Masashi to Yokoi's hospital room in Guam.[71] *Shūkan shinchō*'s exposé article continues:

> The "No Visitors" sign meant nothing for a while because some reporters brought his [Yokoi's] relatives from Nagoya, using them as an excuse to barge into his room. . . . According to one Japanese reporter, who "objectively observed," "It was all chaotic until the associate director of Tokyo National First Hospital, Koyama Yoshiyuki, arrived on the 29th [of January]."[72]

Once he arrived at the Memorial Hospital, Koyama assumed responsibility for Yokoi's health, shutting out all media personnel. While the print media reporters were fighting for direct access to Yokoi, some of the Japanese television stations used different tactics. They had Yokoi's relatives appear on their television shows and, in some cases, brought them to Guam but limited their contact with the outside world.[73] Initially, Yokoi was happy to see his former comrades and relatives, but he gradually grew suspicious of their motives as he learned that the media had arranged their visits.[74]

Many of the articles about Yokoi explained his bizarre behavior as the result of his psychological difficulty in readjusting to the modern world, though they paid little regard to the larger historical forces at work behind his particular experiences.[75] Yokoi was caught between two worlds—the pre-1945 Japan he had defended and the postwar society he now lived in. The reporters made little effort to imagine that the world that Corporal Yokoi Shōichi had defended in Guam was as real to him as the affluent Japanese society into which he was now thrust. One writer inadvertently displayed an utter lack of will or imagination to comprehend the time Yokoi spent in Guam, writing, "Let us pray that Mr. Yokoi's new 'journey' fills the empty twenty-eight years."[76] Even though Yokoi's life in Guam had been far from "empty," this newsweekly reporter revealed his desire to evacuate Yokoi's actual lived experiences from the "miracle" of his reemergence into postwar society. The comment rendered incomprehensible and invisible the ambiguous space between war and postwar that Yokoi inhabited.

Most of the reports proceeded from the perspective of 1972 Japanese society, and the Japanese media were eager to "assimilate" Yokoi. Many reports treated him as a hometown hero, tracing his family history and his hometown roots in an effort to offer a "human interest" portrait of him. These pieces sidestepped Yokoi's struggle between surrender and death. When a few young reporters carried out their curiosity-seeking projects of staying overnight inside or in the vicinity of his cave, they wrote merely about how scary the complete darkness of the jungle would be for their contemporaries.[77] Their articles then praised Yokoi for his endurance and ingenuity while avoiding the ethical and political implications of his belated return.

Even before he returned to Japan, Yokoi's trauma received less and less attention in the media in favor of stories that chronicled his rehabilitation into postwar Japanese society. Completion of the rehabilitation process would require Yokoi to follow the "normal" life course of marriage and childrearing, thus placing his sexual "functionality" under additional scrutiny. As soon as he was discovered, there were reports about Yokoi's deceased "fiancée,"[78] followed by the media's speculations about his future marriage.[79] Reporters even asked the man who had been tortured by unbearable loneliness how he dealt with his sexual desire.[80] The fascination with Yokoi's sexual life persisted even after he married in November 1972, nine months after his return to Japan, fueling additional efforts to scoop his wife's pregnancy. Yokoi was not shy about their intention to have children, and reporters tried not to miss even the slightest change in his wife's appearance. But the couple never conceived a child.[81]

Yokoi faced a new game of survival once he reemerged from the Guam jungle, and he learned to adapt to and play his assigned role with skill. He began to assemble his own images, like a mosaic within the perimeters of media discourse. In the initial confusion of reentry into postwar Japan, Yokoi claimed that he had fought the war for the sake of the emperor and expressed a desire to see him in person once he returned Japan.[82] Many commentators argued, however, that Yokoi's statement was not typical of noncommissioned officers of the Japanese Imperial Army, for whom a meeting with the Supreme Commander would be unthinkable.[83] Yokoi lamented the state of the imperial family in postwar Japanese society—they now appeared in mass-produced magazines as popular icons, an unimaginable prospect in prewar Japan. He readily and deftly exploited the emperor's prewar authority to rationalize his own struggle.[84] Insofar as he could claim he was fighting a war for a larger pre-1945 cause—for the emperor—Yokoi could retroactively locate value in the twenty-eight years he had spent in Guam.

When he arrived at Tokyo's Haneda International Airport on February 2, 1972, Yokoi addressed 4,000 people who welcomed him there, as well as millions of Japanese watching him on television. The crowd was reportedly far bigger than that welcoming the emperor and empress back from their royal tour of Europe in 1971.[85] Yokoi's first words were: "I came home all right. *Although I am embarrassed*, I came home to tell everybody about the defeat in Guam in detail. I came home to explain the hardships that I endured to survive, the things that I cannot put in words" (italics added). The subordinate clause "Although I am embarrassed" immediately became popular among Japanese. Many prefaced their statements with it without concern for the source of the original speaker's embarrassment; Yokoi was less embarrassed by his abandonment of the war dead in Guam than by the realization that he had been hiding too long for no good reason. At the time of his reentry in 1972, Yokoi was already speaking from the postwar perspective, that his twenty-seven and a half years of hiding were meaningless because he had missed the opportunity to enjoy Japan's postwar peace and prosperity.

Despite having become a national celebrity, Yokoi Shōichi fought embarrassment in returning Japan. When he tried to project more masculine images of himself several weeks after his return, it backfired. Taunted by letters accusing him of inaction in Guam, Yokoi confessed to reporters that he had killed two local residents several years before his capture. But then, seeing the negative peacetime reaction to his story of killing, Yokoi immediately backtracked, claiming that it was merely a story "that I heard from Shichi and Nakahata, and I didn't actually do anything."[86] He eventually recanted his story completely, and the Japanese media's investigation in Guam failed to produce any concrete evidence in support of his original claim.

Many reporters were immediately skeptical of his story of murder because of his inconsistencies—Yokoi varied his accounts of the event's timing, sometimes claiming that it occurred immediately after the war, at other times claiming that it happened ten or fifteen years before his reemergence.[87] Reporters also doubted Yokoi's claims because his rusty rifle was unusable when he emerged from the jungle, the wooden component having disintegrated.[88] In the end, the fiasco over his "murders" served to dampen the "Yokoi boom" in Japanese society—for example, tourist buses ceased to stop in front of his home—and through this experience, Yokoi learned to exercise greater caution in using his celebrity status.

Marriage and Running for a House of Councillors Seat

During his life in postwar Japan, Yokoi had few financial worries. By May 1972, well-wishers throughout the country had reportedly sent at least ¥31 million ($102,836)[89] to him through the Ministry of Health and Welfare, media companies, and charity organizations. The gifts included nonmonetary items as well: one ramen producer even sent fifteen boxes of ramen to Yokoi's home immediately after his discovery in Guam, and a soy sauce company pledged to send him a ten-year supply of soy sauce. Publishers were bidding for his memoir, ready to offer him a large advance. It was rumored that he would inherit a large piece of land in his hometown, worth tens of millions of yen. Exploiting his celebrity status, Yokoi launched his career as a public speaker, commanding hefty appearance fees.[90] Although he had picked a name, Tailor Yokoshō,[91] for the tailor shop that he hoped to open at his newly constructed house, media demands and frequent lecture tours left no time for attending to his home business.

With his sound financial prospects and bachelor status, he attracted the attention of mostly middle-aged unmarried women and their relatives. Many sent letters to him,[92] and some even knocked on his door, offering themselves as his future bride.[93] Although he initially enjoyed the attention, Yokoi soon realized that much of it was merely media hype. Yet even in his discouraged state of mind, Yokoi's acquaintances managed to introduce him to some eligible prospects, and he ultimately decided to marry Hatashin Mihoko, a forty-four-year-old woman from a well-to-do family in Kyoto. The couple married in November 1972, when Yokoi was fifty-seven years old. The couple immediately expressed their intention to have a baby, though they were never successful. They canceled their planned honeymoon in light of the news of another straggler, Kozuka Kinshichi, who had been killed in the Philippines in October. In March 1973, they visited Guam on their honeymoon to fulfill Mihoko's wish "to check out with my own eyes the 'cave' where my husband spent long arduous years."[94] Revisiting his former dwelling gave Yokoi a chance to judge it from the comfort of postwar Japan; he kept uttering to himself and his bride that he "should have come out of a place like this much earlier."[95]

Although his marriage to Mihoko received some media attention, it seems to have been the final step in Yokoi's public transition to a "normal" life in postwar Japanese society. With the help of his wife, Yokoi acquired the skills to handle the media's attention, which eventually dwindled to a manageable level. His various appearances suggest that he not only accepted his image as cast by the media but also began to enjoy and to take advantage of it. The media expected him to become an outsider critic of Japanese society, and Yokoi obliged. In May 1973, he appeared in a magazine story on a "Turkish bath," a facility offering sexual services to men. In the essay, after receiving the bathing service (excluding sexual intercourse) at an establishment in Ogoto City, Shiga, Yokoi questioned several women who worked there. His conclusion was that he preferred the more discreet prewar licensed brothels.[96] Two months later, another magazine reported that he was appearing at a local theme cabaret in Fukuoka that featured the Japanese imperial military. The female companions attending the cabaret's clients were dressed in army nurse uniforms, and the waiters wore army and navy uniforms. Yokoi appeared as several army officers of various ranks, including general.[97] By doing so, he was participating in self-caricature and parody.

In the early days after his discovery, whatever his complaints about Japan—Tokyo's polluted air or congested streets, for example—the media construed Yokoi's words as profound criticisms of Japan's current conditions and of modern civilization in general. The media thereafter made space for Yokoi's somewhat off-the-wall remarks. For his part, Yokoi seemed to take the media's interest to heart. In 1974, he ran for a seat in the House of Councillors, Japan's upper house, counting on popular support. His platform was "I will become a 'dog' and sniff around. Nobody will be alarmed by me. I will sneak into both the Liberal Democratic Party and Socialist and Communist Parties and sniff out everything from political machinations to price fixings to report to the Japanese people." He also declared that he would spend no money on his campaign.[98] In his campaign speeches, Yokoi focused on the energy crisis and high inflation that Japan society experienced after the 1973 oil shock while finding new meaning in his Guam life and urging others to practice self-sufficiency and restricted consumption.[99] He printed no campaign posters and even declined the 100,000 postcards for which each national constituency candidate was eligible. Although he was confident that he would receive at least 800,000 to as many as 1 million votes,[100] Yokoi faced disappointment on election day. Of the 55 million who actually voted, a mere 250,000 cast their ballots for him. While the number was more than that of those who bought his memoir, he fell far short of a seat in the House of Councillors. Out of 112 candidates, Yokoi ranked 73, well past the 54 available seats. In the end, his celebrity status was inadequate to sway Japanese voters.

Yokoi's political aspirations revealed his misunderstanding of or disinterest in what the public actually wanted from him. An article in *Shūkan bunshun* offers a glimpse into the audience's responses to Yokoi's public appearances:

Rather than pay attention to the contents of his talk, the audience just single-mindedly looks at Mr. Yokoi. There are so many elderly men and women who merely cry with their whole bodies like a child after uttering "Mr. Yokoi . . ." Even when the mediator tries hard to understand their questions, they continue to sob convulsively. By stitching together what the grandpas and grandmas are uttering in fragments, one begins to understand their question: "My son, my brother, the only thing I have is the official notice of war death; could he be living somewhere?" They have to mention it, even though they know there is no real point in asking about it. These people are meeting with their loved ones lost in the war, by using Mr. Yokoi, who came back from the netherworld, as a medium.[101]

Many elderly people who attended Yokoi's lectures saw him as a representative of the netherworld, and they never expected him to be a political figure. After returning to Japan, however, Yokoi never spoke about the war dead. Rather than a sign of abandonment, his silence on the matter should be seen as evidence of his struggle to move beyond the painful past and focus instead on the present. The election bid for a House of

Councillors seat must have served as the opportunity to connect the is-sues of Yokoi's present to his past experiences. But judging just from the election outcome, his personal struggle failed to have a political impact.

Life Afterward

After the 1974 election, the media's coverage of Yokoi Shōichi largely de-clined, now limited to occasional social commentaries and discussions of his and his wife's low-budget life. Aside from occasional reports on his pottery making, about which he became increasingly serious in the late 1970s, the Japanese media treated Yokoi as someone who belonged to the past, featuring him mainly in postwar retrospectives. In 1991, Yokoi briefly met Emperor Akihito, son of Hirohito, at a spring imperial recep-tion. Yet even that meeting came too late, as Hirohito had died in 1989, and the meeting received minimal media coverage.

Meanwhile, Yokoi's health steadily declined in the 1990s, as he suf-fered from various ailments—a cataract, stomach cancer, a hernia, and backaches stemming from osteoporosis. In the 1990s, his body could no longer withstand the demands of pottery making, the hobby he had grown to love, and he never realized his wish to return to the ordinary life of a tailor. Several years before his death at the age of eighty-two in 1997, he discovered that he was also suffering from Parkinson's disease. Because of the advanced nature of the disease, he was no longer able to walk.

In the end, Yokoi lived the life of a serious yet farcical character, a character behind which he hid much of himself. Yokoi camouflaged himself just as he had blended into the Guam jungle, with the images circulating in the media. Although he left many words behind, they re-vealed little of his personal struggle with the trauma of war. What hap-pened to his cave house in the Guam jungle is perhaps most symbolic of Yokoi's postwar experience: left unattended after his discovery, his cave eventually crumbled. The cave now identified as his on a Guam tourist map was actually dug later by one of Yokoi's first rescuers.[102] As of 1999, the original cave had been reduced to a foot-deep depression in the ground. Much like the cave replica that was reconstructed for tourists, Yokoi painstakingly re-created his war experiences for the postwar au-dience. Actual memories of his struggles were buried in the details of everyday life, hidden from the public's attention. No one could blame the former straggler for hiding his painful memories behind the more or less farcical persona that the Japanese media created. Despite his aversion to it, however, the past continued to haunt him. In his truncated postwar life and even on his deathbed, Yokoi experienced nightmares of being chased by enemy soldiers,[103] and he continued to apologize to his war buddies for surviving alone.[104] On September 22, 1997, twenty-five years after his dramatic exodus from the Guam jungle, Yokoi Shōichi died in a Nagoya hospital of a heart attack, finally liberated from his nightmares of the Guam years and his deep-seated guilt for coming home.

Onoda Hiro'o salutes the cameras, Lubang, Philippines, March 10, 1974. (Courtesy of Mainichi shinbunsha)

Chapter Six

RESCUED FROM THE PAST

Onoda Hiro'o's Endless War

REPORTER: When Mr. Kozuka passed away, did you particularly feel like coming down from the mountains?

ONODA: No way. On the contrary, the desire for revenge grew bigger. Somebody in front of my eyes, twenty-seven or -eight years . . . though it is said man's life is as ephemeral as morning dew . . . when he fell, I have never felt so angry and frustrated [raising his voice]. Speaking of a man's true nature or natural feelings, wouldn't everybody feel the desire for revenge grow stronger?

INTERVIEW AT HANEDA INTERNATIONAL AIRPORT, MARCH 12, 1974

Mr. Onoda Hiro'o was angry and asking: "Didn't we all sing the song of the *Field Service Code*? Didn't we swear to one another that we would die together and we would fight till the end? Have you forgotten that? Are you saying that I came down from the mountains because my man was killed?" Those who came of age during the war are sick people in some way. Mr. Onoda is a sick person, and so am I. To what extent can you deny the generations that sang the song of the *Field Service Code*?

YAMAGUCHI HITOMI, "DANSEI JISHIN," *SHŪKAN SHINCHŌ*, MARCH 28, 1974

ONODA HIRO'O: HERO OR VILLAIN?

In March 1974, former army second lieutenant Onoda Hiro'o returned to Japan from Lubang Island in the Philippines. Compared with Yokoi Shōichi, Onoda, the "last" Japanese imperial soldier, had an easier time justifying his conduct on Lubang as combat action: Onoda insisted that he had been sent there to engage in guerrilla warfare and had been fighting for the nearly thirty years since then. With Private First Class Akatsu Yūichi (who left the group in September 1949 and surrendered in June 1950), Corporal Shimada Shōichi (killed by the Philippine Constabulary in May 1954), and Private First Class Kozuka Kinshichi (killed by locals and the Philippine Constabulary in October 1972), Onoda indeed continued to engage, with "conviction," in subversive acts in enemy territory.[1]

That is, Onoda and his men shot local people and took their food. Although their family members, with the help of the Ministry of Health and Welfare, had repeatedly visited the island to rescue the two men, Onoda claimed that they believed these efforts were enemy plots designed to capture them. Indeed, he managed to live this fiction until the last moment. When communication with him was established, Onoda demanded his superior officer's official order to relieve him of the assignment. Upon receiving the notice in person, Onoda finally laid down his gun and reappeared in postwar society, acting as a soldier who at long last had accomplished his long mission. Despite the uselessness of the information he had collected in the preceding twenty-nine years, Onoda managed to give meaning to his hiding by obtaining official military recognition for his service: the strength of his conviction allowed him to return to Japan as a nationalist icon.

Various appraisals of Onoda circulated in the media, both wholehearted praise of him as a "war hero" who dutifully carried out his assignments for twenty-nine years and denunciations of him as a mere "bandit." Though numerous, those who saw him as a heroic figure were probably not in the majority.[2] In 1977, Tsuda Shin, who ghostwrote Onoda's memoir, admitted that the text was full of deception and revealed that it had been written for the purpose of justifying Onoda's actions.[3] The same year, journalist Fujinami Osamu visited Lubang to gather and report for Japanese readers the stories of the bereaved families whose loved ones had been killed by Onoda and his men.[4] These publications succeeded in unmasking Onoda, presenting him as a murderous straggler who had terrorized the locals.

Since then, however, hardly any articles or commentaries have been published that are critical of Onoda's behavior while he was on Lubang. The Japanese media, which offered a variety of commentaries on his twenty-nine-year "war," have accepted Onoda's own explanation, that he was sent to Lubang in 1944 and remained there until March 1974, continuously engaging in guerrilla warfare in preparation for the Japanese forces' return and that he did not know of Japan's defeat and was merely carrying out his original orders. The number of publications about Onoda slightly increased following Emperor Hirohito's death in 1989 and again around 1995, the fiftieth anniversary of Japan's defeat. In recent years, however, only occasional short articles about him have appeared.

For his part, Onoda repeated, and in some cases refined, the claims made in his memoir. He insisted that he bore no responsibility for his actions on Lubang and claimed instead that responsibility rested with the nation of Japan. In the forty-some years that have passed since the end of Onoda's "war," however, history has thoroughly revised the details of the events on Lubang between 1944 and 1974.

With his death in 2014, did Onoda exit life touted as a "war hero"? If the online reviews of his books and the books about him are representative of a larger audience, many people have accepted his self-justification at face value. In the first part of this chapter, I examine Onoda's tortured path leading up to his "rescue drama." Although he initially supported the production of this political drama, which celebrated the newly forged friendship between the Philippines and Japan, he eventually denounced it as he tried to justify his actions. I then shift to Onoda's postwar struggle to gain his own voice against the Japanese popular media, which circulated sanitized versions of his story. What was omitted from the media's coverage—Onoda's embrace of war violence—was part and parcel of his self-proclaimed warrior identity.

A LONG PATH TO "RESCUE"

Onoda Hiro'o took the path that was originally laid by Japan's colonial aggression, but he extended it far beyond Japan's defeat. He was born in Wakayama Prefecture in March 1922.[5] After graduating from Kainan Middle School in 1939, he began working for Tajima yōkō, a trading company, which sent him to its Hankou (present-day Wuhan) branch. Onoda had hoped for this assignment because his second-oldest brother, Tadao, was stationed in Hankou as an army accounting officer. In May 1942, Hiro'o passed the military physical examination as a first-grade conscript. He quit his job in August and returned to his hometown. In December of the same year, he joined the Sixty-First Infantry Regiment but was immediately transferred to the 218th Infantry Regiment. In early 1943, he arrived in Nanchang, where the regiment was stationed. Tadao was stationed in the same city at this time, and the two brothers reunited once more.

In Onoda Hiro'o's self-image, he was an elite officer entrusted with special missions, though in reality he was only one of the many warrant officers that the army hastily churned out (warrant officers were promoted to the rank of second lieutenant after the end of war).[6] After passing the examination, Hiro'o joined the officer candidate education unit in August 1943, and he went on to enter the reserve officer school in Kurume in January 1944. Then, once he completed the officer education there in August of the same year, Hiro'o was transferred to the Futamata campus of the Army Nakano School. The media later reported widely that Onoda's education at Futamata defined his behavior in the following years. After receiving a three-month special education at Futamata, Onoda was assigned to the Special Intelligence Squadron of the Fourteenth Area Army in Manila. From there, he reported immediately to Lubang to "lead the guerrilla warfare," where about 200 Japanese soldiers were defending the island at that time. Onoda ended up staying on Lubang until February 1974.

In late February 1945, U.S. forces commenced landing at Lubang, gaining control of the island in four days. Thereafter, the remaining Japanese forces dispersed to avoid enemy detection. Forty Japanese soldiers decided to surrender in response to the surrender leaflets the U.S. forces scattered in the immediate aftermath of the war and during the joint U.S.-Japan search in 1946.[7] However, Onoda Hiro'o, Corporal Shimada Shōichi, Private First Class Kozuka Kinshichi, and Private First Class Akatsu Yūichi, convinced that the call-outs were an enemy trap, refused to emerge from the jungle. Akatsu left the group in September 1949 and surrendered nearly a year later with information about the three other surviving soldiers, and the Philippine military then called out to them. In 1952, there ensued a round of three separate searches, two by former Japanese army officers and one by a Japanese journalist.[8] But Onoda's group never responded to these efforts either.

In 1954, soldiers of the Scout Ranger Regiment fatally shot Shimada when they encountered the Onoda group during their training. Even though Shimada's death revived the searches, they failed once more to bring back the remaining two soldiers.[9] Again in 1958 and 1959, large-scale searches were organized, but to no avail. After searching for almost seven months, crews could not even find evidence that Onoda and Kozuka were alive.[10] In 1972, thirteen years after the last search, the Philippine Constabulary shot Kozuka to death. After he was shot and fell on the ground, the constabulary men finished him off with more rounds of shots. It appears that local residents then, out of years of frustration and anger, swung their machetes into his body, leaving numerous gashes.[11]

After this incident, Japan's Ministry of Health and Welfare organized large-scale searches in coordination with Onoda's family members and his former school friends. These searches were carried out in three phases between October 1972 and April 1973. Ninety-six Japanese individuals participated in the searches, at a total cost of ¥90,215,000 ($300,326).[12] Japan's newly acquired economic power had made it possible to send a large crew for an extended period.[13] Despite the searchers' efforts—they combed through several square miles of the mountain areas—they were unable to establish communication with Onoda.

In the end, twenty-four-year-old Suzuki Norio, who had not participated in the searches, succeeded in contacting Onoda on February 20, 1974. Determined to meet Onoda, Suzuki went to Lubang by himself to the area dubbed "Wakayama Point" (Wakayama was Onoda's home prefecture) by previous search crews.[14] Once there, Suzuki simply waited. On Suzuki's fifth day at Wakayama Point, Onoda approached Suzuki's campsite and initiated a conversation. The two men talked through that night, and during their conversation, Onoda agreed to come out if Suzuki could produce an official order from Onoda's immediate superior, Major Taniguchi Yoshimi, the officer who gave the original order to fight in Lubang. Onoda further specified that the order arrive in the form of oral instructions, as prescribed by the chief of staff's headquarters.[15] Suzuki and former major Taniguchi complied with Onoda's request and waited at Wakayama Point for Onoda to return. On March 9, Taniguchi orally delivered the order from the chief of staff's headquarters, releasing Onoda from any official duties, and the following day, Onoda emerged from hiding. Almost immediately, on March 12, Onoda returned to Japan on Japan Air Lines' special charter flight.

Surrender Ceremonies

When Onoda appeared in public in 1974, his resolute figure made a strong impression. Despite his being a soldier of the vanquished nation, the Philippine Air Force and President Ferdinand Marcos welcomed Onoda with the highest honors. An article in *Shūkan bunshun* called him a "hero" and lavished praise on him: "Enduring isolation and all kinds of difficulties, the second lieutenant firmly adhered to his youthful resolution to serve his country until he passed middle age. It is possible to call him the most beautiful Japanese man living in the postwar."[16] In the midst of this enthusiastic welcome, the media frequently compared Onoda with Yokoi Shōichi, who had emerged from Guam two years earlier. In contrast with the images of Yokoi—who appeared in an emaciated state—the robust Onoda radiated with the aura of a formidable soldier.

Nonetheless, the dramatic media coverage of the "war hero's" return had less to do with Onoda's experiences on Lubang than with the desires of various political actors to control the public narrative surrounding him. For example, though mostly for media consumption, his rescuers staged a number of rituals featuring Onoda as the lead character. These events began from the moment that Suzuki photographed Major Taniguchi delivering the order to Onoda in Lubang. Except for one photograph taken over Taniguchi's shoulder, however, all of Suzuki's photos were out of focus. The rest of the published photos were actually taken when Taniguchi and Onoda reenacted the scene following day.[17] On the evening of March 31, the surrender ceremony was held at an air force radar station on Lubang. Despite having already changed into a civilian suit that his brother Toshio had brought from Japan, Onoda changed back into combat gear for the ceremony.[18] As part of the ceremony, he handed over his sword to the air force commander. The commander then immediately returned it to Onoda, honoring him as a warrior. According to the *Sandei mainichi* reporter Kaji Sōichi, the press conference after the ceremony made clear that Onoda was acting for the cameras. Kaji described the scene in which Onoda bashfully unsheathed his rusty sword with Taniguchi's permission: "Finally, Second Lieutenant Onoda placed his sword on the table and looked at the cameras. Once he received permission [from former major Taniguchi], he accommodated the cameramen's requests again and again." Even as Onoda left the press conference, "he did not break out of the salute until the cameramen quit [taking photos]."[19]

On the following day, March 11, Onoda repeated the surrender ceremony, this time with President Marcos in the Malacañang Palace. Putting his arm around Onoda's shoulders, Marcos pardoned him for everything that he had done on the island.[20] The ceremonial meeting between the vanquished Japanese straggler and the Philippine president served an obvious political purpose. In December 1973, just three months earlier, President Marcos had ratified, by executive power, the Treaty of Friendship, Commerce and Navigation as part of his effort to strengthen his country's economic ties with Japan (although it had been signed in 1960, the treaty was not ratified by the Philippine legislature owing to the country's strong anti-Japanese feelings).[21] Through Onoda's surrender ceremony, Marcos was able to rehabilitate the Philippines and Japan's dark past. By standing in front of the president in combat gear, Onoda created a visual representation of the dramatic transformation of the Philippine–Japanese relationship. He appeared in civilian clothes at a dinner party held at the Japanese embassy later that evening, marking his complete transition from belligerence to peace within hours. Having seen the advantage of the two nations' improved relations, the Japanese officials participated willingly in the Philippine government's political theater. Kashiwai Akihisa, a member of Ministry of Health and Welfare who had led the most recent searches for Onoda, carefully choreographed Onoda's speech and conduct while he was in the Philippines. Kashiwai's job was not only to bring Onoda safely back to Japan but also to monitor the images of him, as he had become a symbol of the Philippines–Japan friendship.

Not wanting to undermine the two nations' efforts to forge a new relationship, Onoda also needed to reciprocate President Marcos's goodwill. For example, after Marcos praised Onoda at the palace for carrying out his military duties, Onoda responded by apologizing for his past conduct: "I am sorry for causing great trouble to the people in the Philippines. After returning to Japan, I would like to dedicate the rest of my life to promoting friendship between Japan and the Philippines."[22] Onoda later confided to the conservative critic Aida Yūji that this response was far from his true feelings but that Kashiwai had strongly urged him to say it. As I show later, Onoda saw no reason to apologize for his conduct on the island because he believed that for twenty-nine years he had been continuously fighting a legitimate war. He said of the event that "he ha[d] never been so disgusted."[23] During the press conference following the ceremony at the palace, Kashiwai repeatedly whispered into Onoda's ear before the latter answered questions. He whispered to Onoda so often, in fact, that the reporters protested: "Mr. Kashiwai, please do not coach him."[24] Kashiwai's interruptions were another effort to control the public image of the new Philippines–Japan friendship; Kashiwai could not let Onoda speak freely lest some inconvenient truth emerge.

Former army major Taniguchi, who played a major role in Onoda's rescue, was also extremely careful in safeguarding Onoda's prescribed role. After receiving the surrender order in Wakayama Point, Onoda had stayed up all night with Taniguchi discussing the emperor and other controversial topics, but the following day, Taniguchi claimed to have forgotten the details of their conversation.[25] Onoda later admitted to a journalist his deep resentment of the emperor—he even called himself a "slave" of the recruitment system, which the emperor had ultimately cosigned.[26] Like Kashiwai, Taniguchi was keenly aware of the need to protect Onoda's image in the media.

Did Onoda Know About Japan's Defeat?

These ceremonies maintained the fundamental claim that Onoda was dutifully carrying out his military mission on Lubang and thus remained unaware of Japan's defeat until he received the order from former Major Taniguchi. If accepted at face value, this claim would justify Onoda's and his men's shooting and killing of civilians on Lubang, that they had engaged in legitimate combat as part of the war among nations. This fiction offered a convenient logic for those who were trying to avoid potentially awkward situations between Japan and the Philippines. By pardoning Onoda's actions "during the war," for example, President Marcos implied that he would put to rest the larger issue of Japan's war responsibilities.

The assaults on the islanders by Onoda's group were so fierce, however, that they threatened to undermine the fragile peace between the two nations' officials. The gruesome nature of the attacks was undeniable, regardless of whether Onoda knew about Japan's defeat. Although the exact total of the casualties remains unclear, Onoda and his men clearly injured and killed numerous local residents, often also robbing them of their belongings. Right after Kozuka Kinshichi was shot to death in October 1972, the mayor of Lubang (the municipality covering the western half of the island) and the commander of the Philippine Constabulary offered the following tentative figures: they attributed to Onoda and his men more than 30 deaths, 100 injuries, and more than 1,000 victims of robbery since 1945.[27] A Japanese newsweekly also reported that according to the mayor, the Japanese stragglers had killed fourteen locals in the previous twelve years alone.[28] When Fujinami Osamu arrived at the island in 1977 to interview the bereaved families of Onoda's victims, the mayor handed him a list of thirty-one victims.[29] Of these, fifteen had been killed and sixteen injured. Onoda himself confided to Tsuda Shin that he had shot "around one hundred people" and "[killed] around thirty people."[30] A little over one year after he returned to Japan, in an interview with writer Takagi Toshirō, Onoda insisted that he had shot about 200 people.[31]

According to Tsuda Shin's description, the Onoda group's "combat action" consisted of occupying the elevated central areas of island and shooting any local people who "trespassed into the occupied areas."[32] The island people routinely walked into the mountain areas to gather fruits and to log, and to protect themselves, they occasionally fired warning shots as they walked on the mountain paths. The locals' warning shots obviously posed no danger to Onoda's group; Onoda took pride in the local people's inability to detect his and his men's whereabouts. Even so, to punish the "impertinent islanders who provoked us," the Japanese stragglers mercilessly sniped at them.[33] Prompted by Kozuka Kinshichi's death in 1972, an article in *Shūkan sankei* quoted the following comments made by someone familiar with the BC-class war crimes trials held after the war: "If Onoda had turned himself in right after the war ended, he would have been deemed guilty. Judging from the court decisions at the time, he surely would have been hanged."[34] This deduction appears reasonable, given the gravity of Onoda's actions and the obvious identification of Onoda's group as the responsible party.[35] Whether or not they were aware of the war's end, Onoda and his men's injuring and killing civilians should fall under the category of war crimes.

But by remaining inside the "wartime"—insisting that he did not know of the war's end until former major Taniguchi orally delivered the order to him—Onoda tried to justify all of his and his men's violent actions on the island.[36] From the outset, though, a number of people questioned his claims, among them Yagi Noboru, a Social Democratic Party member of the House of Representatives and former army sergeant, offered the following comments:

> The explanation that he did not come out because of the orders is just a cover. I think the real story is different. Every Japanese soldier who was in the Philippines knew of Japan's defeat. I think Mr. Onoda certainly

knew. He did not surrender despite that because all the Japanese soldiers believed that they would be killed if they surrendered. It was only
natural, because we had killed American soldiers and Filipino soldiers.
That's why we were afraid of surrendering. The reason we came out was
that we ran out of food and started killing one another. Mr. Onoda and
his men managed to procure food. That is probably why they stayed in
the mountains.[37]

In other parts of the Philippines, food determined stragglers' fates. In
fact, when they were on the verge of starving to death, they even began
killing and eating their own men.[38] By contrast, Onoda and his men had
relatively easy access to food sources.

Many people expressed similar skepticism of Onoda's explanations.
To some, his proclaimed ignorance of the war's end was inconsistent
with another claim of his, which the media widely reported: that he was
sent to Lubang Island for intelligence work. As a reporter for *Shūkan
sankei* wrote: "Anyway, he was a former intelligence officer. It is hard to
believe he could not tell whether or not the war was continuing."[39] Given
all the information that he gathered on the island—through the transistor radio that he stole and the Japanese newspapers that the search crews
left for him—it is difficult to believe that Onoda truly did not know that
the war was over. In some respects, however, the question of his knowledge misses other, more fundamental issues. In the efforts to discredit
Onoda, there is the implicit assumption that if he had not known of the
war's end, he would not be responsible for his actions on Lubang. Because
the pundits tacitly accepted this premise, their only way to discredit Onoda
was to prove that he had specific knowledge of Japan's defeat. In other
words, the nature of the dispute—centered on Onoda's knowledge—shifts
the media's focus from the stragglers' brutal actions to Onoda's interior.
Sufficiently proving Onoda's state of mind on Lubang was obviously never
a possibility, however.

A Complex and Strange Understanding of the Situation

While on Lubang Island, Onoda and his men indeed lived in a complex
psychological state that resists any clear-cut classification. In Onoda's
memoir, his indirect explanations of what he knew are enigmatic. On

this point, Suzuki Norio noted: "It appears that he [Onoda] generally knew the war was over. But our 'generally' and his 'generally' seem to have different meanings."[40] These various meanings are key to understanding Onoda's mental state before his return to Japan.

He obtained accurate information. But because he inhabited the liminal space between war and postwar, Onoda lacked a clear temporal axis—the space was both war and postwar—with which to organize that information. The events he learned about crowded his world without providing a clear sequential order. Onoda's insistence that he kept his own accurate calendar for thirty years perhaps came from his realization that something was amiss in his understanding, and it should be read as a claim that his life on the island was in sync with the outside world. Onoda's confused state attested to the extraordinary transition from war to peace that Japan experienced and took for granted.

At the foundation of Onoda's and his men's world was strong suspicion. As soon as two months after the war ended, Onoda and his men read a flier urging the stragglers to surrender. But they found some typographical errors and unnatural expressions in it and thereby dismissed it, thinking, "This is a fake. This must be a snare set by the enemies."[41] Their suspicion misled them, and their misjudgment transformed suspicion into conviction. Later, when they found incorrect characters in the letters left behind by the Japanese search crew, Onoda's group interpreted these incorrect characters as revealing the enemy's hidden intent; Onoda believed that his family was trying to warn him by intentionally making obvious mistakes. In this apparently delusional mind-set, anything that Onoda's group learned about Japan's defeat and postwar history only reinforced their assumption that the war was continuing.

Ironically, Onoda and his men had access over the years to fairly current information about contemporary world events. For instance, search crews repeatedly left a considerable number of Japanese newspapers and magazines in the hopes that the stragglers would find and read them.[42] Furthermore, in 1965, Onoda and Kozuka robbed local residents of their transistor radio. By devising a simple antenna for it, they enhanced its reception during the rainy season and listened to the Japanese-language broadcasting from several countries.[43] But out of all the information they received, they produced a worldview that could be characterized only as complex and bizarre. According to his memoir, Onoda believed that "present-day Japan" (postwar Japan) was then under the control of a democratic regime, which worked for the "establishment of the Greater Asia Co-Prosperity Sphere." The "new national army" was in charge of military affairs, and cultural and economic exchanges with the hostile countries were maintained.[44] They arrived at this fantastic explanation to satisfy two contradictory premises: while being aware that Japan had been transformed into a democratic nation, they also sought proof that the war was still under way. The problem with this explanation is that Onoda constructed it several weeks *after* his return to Japan, with the help of writer Tsuda Shin, who ghostwrote Onoda's memoir.

According to Tsuda, Onoda originally offered an even more fantastic explanation: that the "new national military" was an organization akin to a "mercenary army." Onoda even claimed that the democratic Japan "pays that organization to fight the United States." This mercenary organization was, in Onoda's mind, "the war organization that inherited the former Japanese forces," which was in charge of defending Japan and the rest of Asia from the United States.[45]

When he first heard Onoda's explanation, Tsuda wondered "whether this man is sane." But Tsuda managed to rewrite this explanation by renaming Onoda's mercenary organization as the "new national military," defining the areas of defense as "the Greater East Asia Co-Prosperity Sphere" and supplying further details with the help of Onoda's brother, Tadao.[46] Onoda's original explanation should perhaps be called a delusion, as Tsuda suggested. But in his delusion, Onoda embraced both the democratic nation of Japan and the continuing war without resolving the contradictions between them. He thus avoided facing the ramifications of Japan's transformation into a democratic nation. That is, he simultaneously knew and did not know that the war had ended. Perhaps only vaguely aware of Japan's defeat, it is most likely that he clung to the idea of an ongoing war as a means of avoiding the task of accepting defeat.

There is another example of various, contradictory elements in Onoda's narrative. In his memoir, he claims that he kept a calendar in his head by tracking the phases of the moon and monitoring his and his men's rate of food consumption; Onoda boasts that his calendar was off by only six days at the end of his "thirty-year war."[47] He also writes that when he obtained the radio, the first thing that he heard on it was Radio Peking's announcement: "It is December 27 today. This is my last broadcast of the year. I will be back next year."[48] If true, there was absolutely no need to keep a calendar in his head because the broadcaster told him the exact date. But in his mind, keeping a precise calendar was a basic guerrilla duty and proof of his self-reliance, and for this reason, it was worth highlighting in his memoir.[49] Keeping his version of a calendar and listening to an outside voice from the receiver were two separate activities. It appears as if he lived inside a bubble in which information from outside had no practical implications.

At this point, it is helpful to look at the comments made by social critic Yamamoto Shichihei, who was an army second lieutenant at the war's end and survived as a straggler for six months in the Philippine mountains. Yamamoto offers the following reflections:

> But when it comes to the psychological state in the jungle, I don't have clues either. Not because twenty-seven years have passed, but because it becomes incomprehensible a short while after one comes out of the jungle. In the POW camp, it may be possible to talk about the strange psychological state in the jungle but impossible to go back into it. Once this short time period passes, everything [about the state of mind in the jungle] becomes completely incomprehensible. Therefore, there is no way of knowing the psychological condition of a person who continued to live in the jungle for twenty-seven years. If he came out of the jungle all right, his own psychological state in the jungle would then become something incomprehensible to him very quickly. And I get the impression that because of this [ability to forget], we humans can continue living.[50]

Here Yamamoto makes some astute observations of Onoda's shifting state of mind. When working with Tsuda, although Onoda may have retained an ability to talk about the "strange psychological state in the jungle," it definitely was impossible for him to return completely to that state of mind.[51]

Tsuda linked Onoda's strange explanations to his eccentric behavior in an effort to portray his dubious personality. But his critique of Onoda privileges his own, exclusively postwar, perspective. Tsuda and the rest of postwar Japan turned a deaf ear to Onoda's desperate explanations,

explanations Onoda himself frequently struggled to articulate. It is worth considering that the historical reality—that the United States and Japan, which, in the not so distant past, had been mutually hated enemies, became close allies—is objectively as implausible or bizarre as were Onoda's fanciful reconstructions. Shimada Kakuo, who spent ten years in the jungle of New Guinea as a straggler, recalls that he was utterly unconvinced when he learned in 1952 that the two countries were then on friendly terms: "Strange, the United States and Japan, having fought so hard, would never become friendly to each other in a few years."[52] On the basis of this completely reasonable logic, Shimada proceeded to deny Japan's surrender. Thus, the stragglers were left to their own devices to deal with the strange turn of events that had brought about a democratic Japan. Onoda's and other stragglers' confused states of mind were simply incomprehensible to those safely ensconced in postwar Japan, where the transition from the war to the postwar period was clear-cut. The question of whether or not Onoda knew of Japan's defeat therefore served as a device to scale down his straggler experiences to postwar expectations.

THE BIRTH OF THE "GUERRILLA": ONODA'S VERSION

To Onoda, postwar Japan was an extension of the battlefield, as it were, where he fought hard to control his image. In producing his memoir, he was very clear about how he wanted to represent his own "war experiences." To counter the doubts—including his own—that he should have surrendered earlier, Onoda emphasizes his pedigree as a guerrilla warrior to whom the conventional rules of the war did not apply. He was also a conventional hero driven by his sincerity.

Within a few weeks of returning to Japan, Onoda began working on his memoir with the support of the Kōdansha publishing house. As soon as he arrived in Japan, however, he became a target of the media, just as Yokoi had. Onoda avoided them by hiding in a mansion in Itō with the publisher's ghostwriter (Tsuda Shin) to write his memoir.[53] Yokoi's and Onoda's dealings with the media appear diametrically opposed, reflecting their contrasting strategies of survival during both the war and the postwar. Whereas Yokoi hid deep in the jungle carefully erasing his traces, once back in Japan (which he called his third jungle period), he camouflaged himself with his images in the media environment. By

contrast, Onoda maintained his aggressive stance against the Lubang locals and reenacted it in his interactions with the Japanese media. Instead
of passively accepting whatever narrative was presented, Onoda tried to
control his own public portrayal.

A case in point is his memoir "I Fought, and Survived" (Tatakatta,
ikita), which appeared in the weekly *Shūkan gendai* in fourteen installments starting in May 1974. The installments were then compiled into
the book *No Surrender: My Thirty-Year War* (*Waga rubangu tō no 30 nen
sensō*) published by Kōdansha in September of the same year. These stories
do not portray a man who suffers and struggles in difficult situations;
they are about a heroic officer who judges rationally and almost never
loses his cool. Onoda's stories are comparable in their hyperbole to the
Imperial Headquarters' official—and dramatically inflated—announce-
ments of Japan's war gains.

In his memoir, Onoda emphasizes that starting in September 1944, at
the newly established Futamata campus of the Army Nakano School, he
received a three-month period of special training to be a clandestine
warrior engaging in guerrilla warfare.[54] No matter how efficient the education might be, however, that time period would have been too short to
cover sufficiently the various aspects of guerrilla warfare. Furthermore,
the instructors lacked clear guidelines or knowledge of the subject. As
Onoda writes: "About a month after we started our study [at Futamata],
the instructors showed us the navy records that listed the numbers of
enemy submarines lurking in areas like the Philippines, off Taiwan's
coasts, and in the South China Sea, along with a thick book that the
governor-general of Taiwan issued about Taiwan, and then asked, 'What
are Taiwan's tactical and strategic values?'"[55] It is surprising that such
unfocused, impractical instruction was still being given at this late phase
of the war, if Japan was indeed preparing guerrilla warriors for imminent missions. As if to counter such an impression, this passage is deleted
in the book version of Onoda's memoir, replaced with the following explanation: "The instructions covered espionage, propaganda, counteres-
pionage, observation, scouting, camouflage, disguise, going underground,
killing, destruction, and even karate and swordsmanship."[56] Still, Onoda's
description of how the students received this instruction reveals little room
for practical training: "Each instructor gave us an enormous amount of
work for the subject he was in charge of. Work meant homework."[57] Given

the impossibility of providing practical training through homework, most of the three months was probably spent acquiring book knowledge of each subject. The following passage underscores the rigidity and impracticality of the curriculum: "To produce operation maps, we really needed pairs of compasses and large triangular rules. But Futamata was a small town, where it was impossible to find high-grade drafting instruments, so we had to go to Hamamatsu to purchase them."[58] Were they actually trained to fight guerrilla war with "pairs of compasses and large triangular rules"? To prepare their students for guerrilla warfare, the instructor should have taught them how to produce usable maps without "high-grade drafting instruments."[59]

If indeed "240 students were packed in a small barrack while listening to the lectures,"[60] their guerrilla training must have been akin to practicing swimming on the land. Meanwhile, to make up for these inferior instructional settings, the instructors emphasized the purity of motivation in using guerrilla warfare. Onoda writes: "Then what should those who engage in the secret warfare rely on? At the Nakano school, the instructors expressed it in one word: 'The secret warfare is sincerity' [makoto]. . . . The instructors repeatedly told us [this]. That is, whatever method we use, as long as we deal with the situation with sincerity, our actions will serve our nation and people in the end."[61] Even in the future guerrilla warriors' education, in which practical knowledge should have been the key component, the instructors reduced everything to individual determination of self-sacrifice. But it is probably more accurate to see Onoda's self-image as juxtaposed with his education at Futamata. He offers his readers the narrative that he fought for his nation with the utmost "sincerity," despite his having been transformed into a "guerrilla warrior" with special skills, one who was so hard-hearted that he would not hesitate to deceive his own men.

In one exceptional scene in his memoir, Onoda is so passionate that he loses his cool. Against the U.S. forces that began landing on February 28, 1945, the Japanese defense forces were completely powerless, and the surviving soldiers scattered. Facing a desperate situation, on the night of March 2, Onoda led a raid with fifteen or so soldiers against "the troops blocking our retreat route."[62] It appears that he was trying to compensate, through his reckless conduct, for retreating without carrying out the division headquarters' orders (to destroy the wharf and the airfield).[63] Despite his heroic resolve, however, he never experienced hand-to-hand combat with American soldiers: "If the enemies had been waiting for us at that particular moment, I surely would have died in the battle. But luckily, the enemies may have detected our night raid: they had retreated beyond our reach."[64]

According to the ghostwriter Tsuda Shin, Onoda was especially concerned about this scene. When the manuscript was being revised for the book, Onoda even rewrote it himself, elaborating on his determination to carry out the night raid. Although Onoda's revision was excluded from the book, Tsuda quotes it in its entirety in his exposé. Here is part of it:

> According to our original plan, we readied ourselves for a charge at the staging area. I took a deep breath and looked back at the line of helmets, which belonged to the soldiers quietly following me. Perhaps they felt my intense zeal. Their helmets began to sway ever so slightly in the moonlight. I did not have to think anymore. I pulled out my sword, quietly sliding the sheath in my left hand away from me toward some bushes. I took a breath one more time. I was thinking about a Japanese fencing move: jumping into point-blank range and swinging my sword down on enemy. I felt filled with vigor. I checked my men again to see if they were filled with vigor. At that point, I could count on only my own power.[65]

Tsuda wrote that he saw "the self-indulging 'intense zeal'" in these overly dramatic descriptions and "felt immense anger at his detestable bluffing and his taking all the credit for himself."[66] But in the end, he rewrote the account to accommodate Onoda's requests. For the sake of comparison, I quote the same scene from Tsuda's revised version:

> We advanced to the staging area, where I took a deep breath and turned around. The helmets of the soldiers who followed me there were slightly swaying in the moonlight. After taking another breath, I pulled out my military sword and left the sheath behind. I did not have to think anymore. When I stepped forward, gripping the hilt, I counted only on my own power.[67]

As Tsuda admits to himself, he not only failed to "eliminate Onoda's 'intense zeal'" but "actually ended up emphasizing it" by cleaning up his verbose descriptions.[68] But even this episode serves as a kind of apology from Onoda. The basic message is that he was not fighting solely out of cold-blooded calculation (to survive at all costs in order to carry out the mission as a guerrilla). Rather, he was asserting that he was ready to sacrifice himself but that he survived the war by chance.

Onoda's claims boil down to two points: first, he was willing to risk his life in the battle against the U.S. forces but happened to miss them during the planned raid, and second, he embraced his missions as a "secret warrior." His narrative is built on the combination of these two contrary elements: the identity of a calculating "guerrilla warrior" and his "sincerity" in doing everything for his nation. What matters here is not whether a raid was actually attempted but why he was so interested in talking about this episode in this way. Onoda's version claims that he was not only cool headed but also passionate. It also privileges his zeal over what he accomplished in the combat attempt. While this attitude was hardly unique to Onoda—it pervaded the Japanese military—it was the key element in his efforts to justify his twenty-nine years of hiding. His conduct on the island, like his attempted night raid, had little strategic value; in his mind, however, both were important signifiers of his determination and zeal.

SIGNS OF DISSONANCE BETWEEN ONODA AND POSTWAR JAPAN

Onoda expected that postwar Japan would naturally accept him as he was—a fearless warrior—and even embrace him. At the least, in the ceremonies after his emergence from the jungle, he recognized a tacit understanding between himself and postwar Japan. What Onoda encountered when returning to Japan, however, ranged from enthusiasm to suspicion, accusations of mental instability, and even disloyalty. He was deeply unhappy about this treatment and tried to deny that he had ever entered into this implied agreement with postwar Japan. By departing from the original script as to who actually ordered him to report to Lubang Island, Onoda signaled that he had been tricked by postwar Japan into accepting humiliating terms.

When he first met Suzuki Norio on Lubang, Onoda insisted that the order come from his superior officer, Major Taniguchi Yoshimi, and he refused to emerge from the mountains without a new order from Taniguchi. Accordingly, as Onoda specified, former major Taniguchi ordered him to abort the mission.

Onoda's memoir, however, offers a different story. There, Onoda claims that the order to "go to Lubang Island and guide the island's defense forces in the guerrilla war" came from intelligence officer Major Takahashi, who was stationed at the Eighth Division Headquarters.[69] In that account, Major Taniguchi just happened to be present and giving him some encouraging words when Major Takahashi wrote down the order and handed it to Onoda.[70] Furthermore, *My Thirty-Year War on Lubang Island* emphasizes that Onoda directly reported to neither the company commander nor the regiment commander; it states instead that his direct superior was the division commander, Lieutenant General Yokoyama Shizuo. Onoda writes that he received the following orders directly from the lieutenant general: "You are absolutely forbidden to lead or participate in a suicide attack. Three years, five years, you should hold out. We will surely come to get you. Until then, as long as even a single soldier remains, please hold out using just him, even if you have to eat coconuts. All right, I repeat: A suicide attack is not allowed. You understand?"[71] As Tsuda insists, it is highly unlikely that a division commander would have taken the trouble of delivering these orders directly to a warrant officer.[72] In addition, as Onoda acknowledges elsewhere, former lieutenant general Yokoyama later had no recollection of giving these orders.[73]

Even if Onoda's memories were correct, the reality was probably close to Yamamoto Shichihei's assessment. In his opinion, Onoda's orders were not extraordinary. Right after Kozuka Kinshichi was shot to death, Yamamoto wrote:

A newspaper stated that [Onoda was] still fighting because he had been ordered [to continue to fight even after the war ended]. This, what the source said, I think, the reporter misunderstood.. It is extremely unlikely that an officer actually commanded: "They should continue fighting even when the emperor orders a cease-fire." If he had done so, he would have been charged with the crime of defying or disobeying the orders. Probably the original instructions said, roughly, "Even when the coordinated battles come to end in the Philippines and the main forces are withdrawn to mainland Japan, you should remain here to continue the battle, cause disruptions in the enemy-occupied areas, engage in guerrilla warfare, severe the enemy's supply lines, and gather information." Second Lieutenant Onoda was not the only one who received the orders like these. We did, too. . . . In my opinion, these orders were a merely a disingenuous way of telling that the officers were "abandoning us." But since all humans try to find meaning in their conduct, we certainly tried to think "about long-term perseverance and thorough guerrilla attacks—if we hold out here until we all fall and tie down as many U.S. soldiers here as possible, we can delay the enemy advance toward the Japanese mainland and help better prepare for the mainland defense. Therefore even if we die here, our deaths would not be a waste."[74]

This passage does not directly refute Onoda's claim that he received special orders; rather, it offers an explanation of why Onoda was so fixated on the terms of his "orders." For the officers who issued them, these instructions were perhaps nothing special (hence Lieutenant General Yokoyama did not remember giving them in the first place). But some continued to fight, clinging to the fiction of extraordinary orders as a mechanism for coping with their isolation.

Meanwhile, by declaring in his memoir, "My direct superior was the regiment commander, Lieutenant General Yokoyama,"[75] Onoda completely abandoned his earlier explanation that he could not stop fighting unless he received orders to that effect from his direct superior, Major Taniguchi. This inconsistency in Onoda's testimony points to the friction developing in Onoda's relationship with postwar Japan. His new claim—that Yokoyama was his direct superior—was an attempt to break away from postwar Japan, which, he thought, had showed little effort to understand the war he had been fighting. This friction became even more evident when Onoda later complained that he was brought to Japan by deception, that is, by the fictional orders from the former major Taniguchi.[76] Onoda even said to the people close to him, "The rescue only caused trouble."[77]

This point needs some explanation. Since the chief of staff's headquarters were dismantled after Japan's surrender, former major Taniguchi's orders to Onoda had to be fictional. The officials in the search groups revived the army organization only temporarily in order to bring Onoda home. For its part, postwar Japan understood it as a temporary measure needed to expedite Onoda's return. Because he returned to Japan under the illusion that there was no significant difference between wartime and postwar Japanese society, what he soon encountered must have been a shocking reality: a postwar Japan that differed sharply from its wartime identity. Onoda appears to have expected loyalty and gratitude from the Japan that he imagined, which at this point was likely a fictional construct of his own mind. In fact, postwar Japan regarded him less as a war hero and more as a curiosity.

Onoda did not find it easy to fill the gap between the wartime Japan that he knew and the postwar Japan that he did not. About a year after returning to Japan, Onoda recalled his feelings in a conversation with Aida Yūji:

> Yes, as I wrote in the memoirs, I was fighting. But what the hell! Japan had not been doing anything. . . . Even under extremely difficult conditions, we all did it for the cause. But when I came back and was thrown into postwar Japan, which had quit fighting the war, I felt like, what the hell. That's why I was really upset, even with my father. I don't believe anything that is not clear. I don't believe even when someone says something to me.[78]

In his emotional recollections, Onoda laments the failure of postwar Japan to honor its part of the deal, not continuing to support Onoda's "war" efforts. Regardless of the actual conditions on Lubang Island, Onoda had, in his mind, fought the "war" for twenty-nine years, and he wanted postwar Japanese society to recognize his sacrifice.

Onoda's Death Threat

That Onoda lived the conditions of "war" for so many years meant that violence was at the core of his being. But his belligerence had no place in Japanese society, which at the beginning of the postwar period had denounced its own violent past. Furthermore, in the interest of maintaining the still-fragile friendship between Japan and the Philippines—a friendship that had been forged largely through the bilateral drama of Onoda's rescue—he had to suppress his inconvenient memories. According to Tsuda Shin, at the outset of Onoda's memoir-writing project, his brother announced: "The Ministry of Health and Welfare requests that we avoid mentioning, as much as possible, the wounding and killing of island people."[79] A newsweekly also reported that "the Ministry of Health and Welfare strictly ordered that 'the things that happened in the Philippines not be discussed.'"[80] In the end, Onoda preferred to reject postwar Japan rather than renounce his own violent actions on Lubang. He repeatedly told the people around him the gory details of how he had shot and killed Lubang residents, disclosures that constituted an aggressive act against the society that had newly embraced nonviolence as its founding principle.[81] Onoda's frustrations with his home country surfaced in the public eye as his uncontrollable anger toward writer Nosaka Akiyuki, who had criticized Onoda's memoirs.

After reading Onoda's account serialized in *Shūkan gendai*, Nosaka raised various issues. Onoda in turn was outraged by Nosaka's critical comments, which were published in August 1974:

> It has generally been recognized that Mr. Onoda "fought" [on Lubang Island]. But given his poor judgment of the situation, his actions do not really count as fighting. Anyway, he says that because he misjudged [the situation], this happened to Mr. Kozuka or that happened to Mr. Shimada. But insofar as his writing goes, he expresses no regrets about his misjudgment. I find this rather contemptible.[82]

Right after reading Nosaka's criticism, Onoda vented his anger to Tsuda Shin: "I will run over and kill Nosaka."[83] Eight months later, in a television interview, he declared, "I shall kill Nosaka with a sword if I ever see him"—this pronouncement, anathema to Japan's postwar self-image, was not aired.[84] An article in *Shūkan yomiuri* gave an edited version of the confusing statement that the enraged Onoda made during the interview:

> Nosaka says we were not fighting. We were fighting. When we were walking in circles on the island, we were exploring the terrain so that we would be ready to guide the Japanese forces there whenever they

arrived. Then we occasionally encountered islanders. When we encountered enemies, we occasionally killed them. We were fighting the war because of the superiors' orders. But a guy like Nosaka says we were not fighting. I will kill him with a sword. We had some information that the war may have ended. But there was no confirmation that it was really over. There was no order to stop fighting. Of course, we had to keep fighting. I did survive, not because my life was dear to me, but because I had received the order not to die.[85]

Onoda's and his men's war consisted of "walking in circles on the island" and sniping at the islanders—the perceived enemies—that they occasionally encountered. As Aida Yūji had suggested, Onoda and his men should have focused first on the propaganda promoting the islanders' support of Japan's war efforts.[86] Onoda's claim that they were preparing to "be ready to guide the Japanese forces there whenever they arrived" serves only as a specific example of his misjudgment, which Nosaka pointed out in his comments. It would not take twenty-nine years to explore the terrain of a small island (forty-eight square miles) about the size of Nantucket. Therefore, attacking islanders was the only real purpose of Onoda's war. His statement, however, slightly changed his earlier explanation. Gone was his initial claim that he did not know that the war had ended; Onoda now offered a more vague description: "We had some information that the war may have ended. But there was no confirmation it was really over." Instead, he emphasized the absolute nature of "the order that I not die." Here Onoda seems to have modified his explanation in an attempt to fortify his position: as an intelligence officer, he had gathered enough information about external conditions to surmise that the war may have ended. But without confirmation, he claimed, his misjudgment was ultimately not his fault because he was just following orders—the very point that Nosaka criticized.

Nosaka's comments angered Onoda because they challenged the premise on which he rejected postwar Japan, that for him, the postwar logic and ethics were unsuitable frameworks for judging the wartime conditions that he had experienced. Onoda had not only lived the war for twenty-nine years, but he also was continuing to live it by threatening to kill Nosaka with a sword. Takagi Toshirō, who interviewed Onoda for the television program, made the following observations about his behavior:

A coward or a weakling, people like that threaten other people with a loud voice and strong language, don't they? That is, with something like a coward's bluff. I first thought that this must be it. I then thought this way: he was mentally and physically unstable for thirty long years. Therefore, once his emotions begin to intensify, he easily became more excited than normal people would. . . . Another guess is that the name Nosaka is actually just a metaphor for his anger at the mass media and the people who work for it, including myself.[87]

As Takagi pointed out, Onoda's "coward's bluff," unstable mental condition, and "anger" at the media produced his strong emotional response. Crucially, Onoda's anger was also directed at postwar Japan at large. Onoda repeatedly tried to communicate his anger through violence, which, after all, had been his primary means of communication during his extended time on Lubang. Just as he warned the island people to get off his "territory" by firing at them, Onoda guarded the fictional wartime that he continued to inhabit by making death threats to intimidate Nosaka and the rest of postwar Japanese society.

THE MEANING OF ONODA'S RESCUE

Postwar Japan was eager to rescue Onoda because his presence gave the Japanese—who were then enjoying the fruits of their high-growth economy—a chance to rewrite the past.[88] His rescue was the antithesis of another attempt to rework on the past in *Ningen no jōken* (discussed in chapter 2). Laboring under the guilt of having failed to act during the war, Gomikawa Junpei's postwar conscience sent Private First Class Kaji back to the wartime as its representative, had his conscience battle against the impossible situation, and prohibited his return to Japan for the sake of expiation. By contrast, Onoda returned to Japan as the last Imperial Army serviceman, representing all the Japanese soldiers who had died in battle. Here I want to underscore the contrast with Yokoi Shōichi's "rescue" from Guam: Yokoi emerged, without any advance signs, from an area where everyone assumed all the Japanese stragglers were dead. While this fact played no significant role in rescuing Yokoi, postwar Japan instead assumed a lead role in Onoda's rescue.[89] By "rescuing" Onoda from the war and wartime in which he was trapped and bringing him to the postwar, postwar Japan strove to undo its past mistakes. Just before Onoda's surrender, an article in *Shūkan shinchō* stated: "In any event, the typical officer of the Imperial Army of thirty years ago will ride a time machine and arrive in this 'economic super power' shaken by the oil crisis."[90] This "time machine" image captures Onoda's move from wartime to the postwar period.

Onoda fulfilled his part of the tacit agreement by playing the role of an Imperial Army officer who still inhabited a wartime reality. Before he agreed to play his part in the drama, he and the rescuers (represented by the Ministry of Health and Welfare and the Japanese embassy in the Philippines) had to work out an implied agreement that he would not be punished for his past conduct on the island. This pact was confirmed through the surrender ceremonies and was publicized by the media.

Those who were overjoyed by the prospect of rescuing Onoda from the hell of war thought little about the past he would inevitably bring home. In 1974, Japan was interested in repatriating Onoda to postwar society, but the nation had little interest in a man who was still dragging the war along with him. Onoda thus returned to Japan, a place supposed to be a land of bliss, but instead he found it extremely uncomfortable to be there. For its part, postwar Japan struggled to manage and make sense of Onoda's story. For the man who had built his entire self-worth on his "battle" against the local residents, it must have been unbearable to see his past actions completely rejected by postwar Japan. Bitterly disappointed by the Japanese government and postwar Japan at large for failing to honor his "thirty-year war," Onoda sought refuge by emigrating in the same year to Brazil, the country where his brother Tadao was living.[91] As several newsweeklies reported, the discord with his parents, whom he met for the first time in thirty years, was also a factor in his relocation.[92] Onoda's biggest motivations for emigration, however, were his anger at Japanese society and the painful realization that he no longer had a place in it.

In 1974, Japan had an intellectual framework through which to criticize Onoda's war experiences as aggressor, but society made little attempt to acknowledge Onoda's violence as part of its past. Judging by the current popular discourse on Onoda, that public posture in Japan has generally remained,[93] and so his past has become something to silence and repress. The Japanese mass media widely circulated Onoda's narrative as a victim of the wartime regime that had abandoned him. But by contrast, his past as an aggressor (the "thirty-year war," in Onoda's words) became a taboo topic. Whereas Yokoi gave the postwar Japanese media what they wanted—the figure of a helpless victim—Onoda Hiro'o brought home something that postwar Japan did not want.

ONODA HIRO'O'S LATER YEARS

Thanks to Onoda's emigration to Brazil, postwar Japan managed to avoid what it did not want. In subsequent years, the Japanese media occasionally featured the grandfatherly Onoda as a rancher or a man who established a nature camp for children. These reports, however, made barely any effort to further explore the ramifications of his past conduct.

Meanwhile, Onoda clung to the narrative that he was merely following military orders. For example, in the essay he wrote for the August 1990 issue of the monthly magazine *Shinchō*, he reiterated the major points of his 1974 memoir, adding, "In the end, we spent twenty-nine years in the jungle of Lubang. During this time, we engaged in activities regarded as crimes in peacetime, except for rape and abductions of children. But they were within the range allowed by the international law of war."[94] His logic here is sophistry. No international law of war allows robbing, attacking, or killing civilians. Most important, the war was long over, regardless of his perception. Onoda's emphasis on the phrase "except for rape and abductions of children" resonates with the same self-serving justification that he first offered in his 1976 exchange with Sakamaki Kazuo. In it, Onoda stated: "By the way, we didn't do such things as raping women. We did absolutely no harm to women and children. That's why the local residents could feel at ease coexisting with us."[95] Contrary to Onoda's assertion, however, the island residents were fearful and resentful of the Japanese stragglers' violence. It should be self-evident that even if he refrained from certain categories of crimes, he was still responsible for all the other crimes that he did commit.

Before ending this chapter, I want to examine one more example of Onoda's self-justification. At the end of *Thirty-Year-Long Solitary War* (*Tatta hitori no 30 nen sensō*), the book that appeared in 1995, he writes: "I am grateful for the extra life I was given and will live the rest of my life with the burden of the awareness that I let my two war buddies die in battle [*senshi*] in the 'postwar.'"[96] This short sentence sufficiently captures Onoda's self-justification. By placing the "postwar" in quotation marks, Onoda suggests that thirty-some years later, he is now able to discuss calmly the illusion of an eternal war—a concept that he fervently espoused before his emergence from the jungle. However, the word *senshi* (battle death) is *not* placed in quotation marks. As the thirty-year war in the title indicates, Onoda still insists that the war was continuing during the time he spent on Lubang Island; what he questions is the "postwar" aspect of postwar Japan. Although Onoda feels responsible for letting the two men die in battle, he does not accept responsibility for letting them die in vain after the war's end.

While feeling the "burden of the awareness that I let my two war buddies die in battle in the 'postwar,'" he does not feel remorse for the people whom he and his men injured or killed in the postwar. Although the title strongly hints that Onoda fought the war by himself, one man alone cannot wage a war. Even after counting the "war buddies" who fought with him, one still needs enemies in order to fight a war. In their efforts to survive on Lubang Island, the three men forcefully dragged the local people, the Philippine Constabulary, and the Scout Ranger units into their "war." In this manner, *Thirty-Year-Long Solitary War* not only repeats but also extends the self-justifications that Onoda first offered in his 1974 memoir. The fact that his claims are often accepted at face value attests to postwar Japanese society's unwillingness to imagine the consequences of his "war."

As I pointed out in this chapter, the tacit agreement between Onoda and postwar Japan at the time of his rescue necessitated silence on his aggressive acts. But then, what should postwar Japan have done to fully embrace his past? Could Onoda have emerged from the jungle in a less restrictive way? The only possible alternative would have been requiring Onoda to testify in a Philippine court with immunity for his past deeds; in any case, he almost certainly would have refused to leave the jungle without such assurance. The court's role would not have been to pass judgment but to provide a space where multiple voices could be heard.[97] Even if he had not modified his self-justification—that he was fighting a "war"—his claim would have clashed with the local people's counterclaims. At that moment, postwar Japan should have felt the need not only to extend a helping hand to the soldier left on the island but also to contemplate the inconvenient truth that such a rescue would expose. In a public trial, it might have been possible to bring Onoda's past into the present without repressing or praising it.[98]

For a court proceeding to be feasible, all the parties must be willing to participate. Considering the political conditions in the Philippines at that time—President Marcos was far less interested in unearthing the crimes committed by stragglers than in securing economic ties with Japan and in increasing his own power—there was little impetus for holding a court procedure on behalf of the Lubang residents and Onoda Hiro'o. Lubang's residents might even have opted not to revisit the painful past, facing the imminent departure of the menace.[99] Furthermore, given the fact that Onoda called the Lubang locals *donkō*—a derogatory moniker for natives—and thoroughly despised them, he most likely would have refused to listen to what the local residents had to say.[100] Even if such a proceeding had occurred, it might have become yet another elaborate ceremony. In any event, the intense emotional responses triggered by Onoda's emergence have now dissipated with very little trace.

Onoda died from pneumonia in January 2014 at the age of ninety-one, having outlived the sporadic criticisms that the 1970s media generated. He seems to have had the last laugh. Yet I believe that it is still possible to reverse the process of sanctifying Onoda's past: by realizing that Onoda's return to Japan was a drama staged by the political forces in power, by refuting each of Onoda's past efforts to rewrite his twenty-nine years on Lubang Island, and by imagining the pain that his "war" inflicted on Lubang's residents.

Nakamura Teruo, holding the photo of the emperor and empress, at Pelni Hospital, Jakarta, Indonesia, December 30, 1974. (Courtesy of Mainichi shinbunsha)

Chapter Seven

THE HOMECOMING OF THE "LAST JAPANESE SOLDIER"

Nakamura Teruo / Shiniyuwu / Li Guanghui's Postwar

> I don't know what to think. Can't even believe it is true. Feels like I am
> dreaming. . . . He will be welcomed home no matter what. But I can't destroy
> the life with my present husband.
>
> NAKAMURA YOSHIKO / SHANBI / LI LANYING (NAKAMURA TERUO'S WIFE),
> *BISHŌ*, JANUARY 25, 1975

THIRTY-ONE YEARS AS A STRAGGLER

This final chapter focuses on Nakamura Teruo (Taiwanese name: Li Guanghui; ethnic name: Shiniyuwu), the "last Japanese soldier" who was "discovered" on Morotai Island in Indonesia less than a year after Onoda Hiro'o returned to Japan. I also discuss the case of mistaken identity of a Filipino man, whom the Japanese media briefly believed to be a long-lost Japanese straggler. Unable to provide a satisfactory closure to the narrative of repatriations, these cases quickly receded from the Japanese popular consciousness. Nonetheless, these cases exposed, albeit in different ways, the fact that as it covered the long-lost soldiers in the 1970s, the Japanese media were concerned primarily about contemporary Japan's national image.

Although the search-and-rescue crew, consisting of members of the Indonesian air force, did not take him into custody until December 18, 1974, local residents had informed the authorities four years earlier that there might be a surviving Japanese straggler on Morotai.[1] Born in Taiwan under Japanese rule, Nakamura was legally a Japanese citizen and had learned the Japanese language in elementary school. Nakamura became a member of the Imperial Japanese Army in November 1943 at the age of twenty-four, but he lost his Japanese nationality with the implementation of the Treaty of Peace between Japan and the Republic of China (Taiwan) in 1952. On January 8, 1975, after having spent a few weeks in Jakarta, the man who had lived as a Japanese soldier for thirty-one years returned to his native land as a Taiwanese citizen under the rule of the Nationalist government.

While Nakamura's case was another story of extraordinary survival and return, the Japanese media's response was lukewarm at best, with only limited coverage of the case. After Nakamura returned to his hometown and "remarried" his wife several weeks later (his second marriage is described in more detail later), there was hardly any coverage of Nakamura's subsequent life. Of the Japanese newsweeklies, only *Sandei mainichi* reported Nakamura's death in 1979—and even that report appeared almost six months after he died[2]—and the *Sankei shinbun* was the only newspaper that carried an original article written by a staff reporter (the other newspapers reprinted a short article distributed by Kyodo News).[3]

One of the reasons for the Japanese media's lukewarm response was that Nakamura was an indigenous Taiwanese who had volunteered for Japanese military service during the war. In September 1972, Japan established diplomatic relations with the People's Republic of China and severed its formal diplomatic ties with the Republic of China. All the Japanese newspapers, with the exception of the *Sankei shinbun*, then closed their bureaus in Taiwan.[4] Nakamura's return to Taiwan thus was covered by a small Japanese media contingent, which consisted of the *Sankei shinbun*, TBS (television station), Fuji Television, Tokyo 12 Channel, and several magazines, which was a far cry from the media frenzy that surrounded Yokoi's and Onoda's returns. Nakamura's discovery and homecoming challenged the Japanese media companies not only with the practical question of whether they should send their reporters to Taiwan (lest they offend Beijing) but also with the more complicated question of how they should represent Japan's colonial past in Taiwan and elsewhere.[5] The Japanese media ended up largely avoiding these questions, providing only perfunctory coverage of Nakamura's case. This absence of media images explains why the name of Nakamura Teruo disappeared quickly from Japanese popular consciousness.

As historian Narita Ryūichi pointed out, the repatriations after the Asia Pacific War were not straightforward movements to Japan's mainland from former colonies or other areas formerly under Japanese control. Instead, these repatriations consisted of complex flows of multiethnic groups between various regions, in which Japan was often not the final destination.[6] In postwar Japan, however, the multiethnic experiences of repatriations were rewritten as a national story from which the former colonial subjects were politically excluded and rendered invisible.[7] Nakamura's return to the postwar world highlighted Japan's colonial ties with Taiwan, helping propel political movements demanding that the Japanese government compensate the former Taiwanese soldiers and their bereaved families for their past sacrifices.[8] Although the movements did not lead to widespread activism in the other former imperial regions, they did stir up memories of the colonies in postwar Japan.[9]

Yet Japanese society soon consigned Nakamura's return to oblivion not only because he embodied Japan's regrettable past but also because his return—or, to be more precise, the problem that he actually had no place to return to—could disrupt the narratives of repatriation that postwar Japanese society embraced. Moreover, although the Japanese media had initially searched for stragglers as pieces of Japan lost in the jungle, their interest had reached a satisfactory resolution with the "rescues" of Yokoi and Onoda.

THE INDIGENOUS TAIWANESE VOLUNTARY ARMY SOLDIER NAKAMURA TERUO

Nakamura Teruo, a member of the Ami, one of Taiwan's indigenous peoples, was born on October 8, 1919. The recruiting system for the volunteer army began in Taiwan in April 1942 as part of Imperial Japan's effort to maintain its fighting forces. In November 1943, Nakamura volunteered for the military service and joined the Reserve Squadron of the Taiwan First Infantry Regiment.[10] After training until April of the following year, his unit departed for the South Pacific, arriving at Halmahera Island via Manila on June 14. As part of the Morotai defense plan, the men in the unit were immediately assigned to shock troops consisting of four companies, and of the 485 men in the troops, 373 were indigenous Taiwanese. On July 12, the troops landed on Morotai, relieving the 211th Infantry Regiment from its original assignment of defending the island.[11]

On September 15, the U.S. forces began landing on Morotai with overwhelming fire and manpower. Without enough resources to mount a frontal attack against the enemy, the Japanese defense forces instead tried to delay the construction of an American airfield through the shock troops' guerrilla attacks. According to the plan, three companies were organized from the main forces on Halmahera and sent to Morotai for night attacks. The 211th Infantry Regiment that had retreated from Morotai was also sent back to the island.[12] Despite their sustained efforts, however, the Japanese forces were unable to overcome their disadvantage in combat capability, with the number of casualties steadily rising.

In early 1945, the division commander issued the following order to the men who survived the final charge against the U.S. forces on Morotai: "Transition to a long-term, tenacious guerrilla warfare."[13] This order shifted the focus of the battle from killing enemies to "long-term self-sustaining efforts." The soldiers who walked into the jungle seeking food soon broke into small groups, with ten stragglers, including Nakamura, coming to live together in the end. Right after Nakamura was captured, *Shūkan asahi* printed a diagram of the process through which five subgroups merged into one.[14] According to this diagram, Nakamura left one of the subgroups in the early postwar period but rejoined the same group about one year later (by then, it had merged with another subgroup). These five subgroups eventually merged into the group of ten, which at one point cultivated as much as nine acres of land and raised thirty wild pigs.[15] Nakamura left this group in the early 1950s and remained on the island by himself while the rest of the members returned to civilization in 1956.[16] Of the remaining nine stragglers from Nakamura's group, six were from an indigenous Taiwanese group. In the press conference held in Jakarta on December 30, 1974, Nakamura remembered this final group in not-so-friendly terms (it appears that he was confused about the numbers):[17] "I was with eight war buddies until the end. There were five indigenous Taiwanese people among them. But they singled me out and bullied me. They threatened to 'kill me.' I was so scared that I ran away. I lived alone ever since. It was all their fault that I don't want to see them."[18]

Nakamura's accusation in the press conference surprised those who had lived with him on Morotai, and his indigenous Taiwanese comrades strongly denied his charges.[19] Nakamura's words also shocked the Japanese media, which expected a happy ending to the story, in which the comrades who shared Nakamura's ethnic background would warmly welcome him home. After he returned to Taiwan, Japanese reporters pressed him to talk more about the group's abuse of him, but he never offered any additional details.[20] In fact, he even began changing his testimony: Nakamura later claimed that since beginning to live alone in 1945 at the age of twenty-seven, he never had any contact with the other group members. In an interview that he gave after his return to Taiwan, Nakamura explained: "We succeeded in the attack. But when we headed back to the headquarters, we were attacked and scattered. Since then, I was alone. I never looked for my comrades."[21] He repeated basically the same story in another interview several weeks later, adding: "I don't even know the name of the people I was supposed to have been with until 1951 or 1952."[22] But his new claim obviously contradicted his listing the names of eight comrades in the December 30 press conference in Jakarta.[23] Writer Satō Aiko suggested that as an Ami man, Nakamura may have had difficulty getting along with the rest of the indigenous Taiwanese soldiers in the group because the others came from the Atayal tribe—whose cultural and linguistic heritage was different from that of the Ami.[24] Nakamura's accusation also demonstrated that the indigenous Taiwanese people had their share of internal tensions, and the colonial stereotype of "easygoing, optimistic natives" was not an adequate explanation.[25]

Whereas their Taiwanese counterparts celebrated Nakamura's return, Japanese journalists were less certain about the appropriate tone for their coverage of Nakamura. Because the Japanese media could not adopt a tone of unqualified nationalism, their coverage tended to focus on Nakamura's identity as an indigenous Taiwanese. Even so, his troubled relations with his fellow Taiwanese soldiers undermined the idyllic image of a uniformly constituted indigenous community. In the absence of a convenient nation or ethnic group, the Japanese media recast Nakamura's natural "home" as his family. Yet his family also proved to be a problematic space, which demanded additional emotional work from every member.

The Extremely Public Family Drama

Believing that her husband had died in the war, Nakamura's wife, Li Lanying (Japanese name: Nakamura Yoshiko; ethnic name: Shanbi), had married Huang Jinmu in 1953. Although the media widely disseminated this information as soon as Nakamura was discovered in Indonesia in December 1974,[26] his wife did not tell him about her second marriage until January 9, 1975. Through the media, the audience—who had no personal connections with the couple—already knew about his wife's remarriage, but Nakamura himself was kept uninformed.[27]

Arriving in Taipei from Jakarta on January 8, 1975, Nakamura had an emotional reunion with Li Lanying and their thirty-two-year-old son Li Hong (Japanese name: Nakamura Hiroshi; ethnic name: Hiroshi), the three of them staying in a hotel room in Taipei that night.[28] The following day, they flew to Taidong on a special flight and then took a minibus from Taidong to Li's home in Taiyuan Village. In the minibus, as they approached their destination, Li finally broke the news to him. Nakamura was so angry that he forced her out of the bus with all her belongings. The minibus therefore did not stop at the welcoming party venue as scheduled but instead headed for his family's house, where his two sisters welcomed him.[29] Although Li chased Nakamura in another car to his family house, he refused to let her in. A number of reporters witnessed firsthand the drama unfolding and reported the couple's reactions in detail. With his marriage at stake, the international news of Nakamura's return seemed to have deteriorated into a domestic dispute, the stuff of tabloid papers. Even the *Sankei shinbun*, which was the most eager of the Japanese newspapers to cover Nakamura's case, dropped its coverage after reporting his marital discord on January 10.[30] The Taiwanese newspapers also stopped their coverage around the same time.[31] Of the Japanese media, only a few Japanese weeklies sporadically followed his life until around March of that year.

After Nakamura's dramatic "reunion" with his wife, their relatives and tribal leaders began an intense discussion regarding their marriage. In the end, Li's second husband, Huang Jinmu, agreed to leave her on the condition that he would receive some money, a piece of land, a house, and a water buffalo.[32] Nakamura and Li married for the second time on March 6 and began their new life in the house that he had newly purchased.[33] Receiving an *ex gratia* payment from the Japanese government, money that Japanese politicians had pooled, donations from the Japanese and Taiwanese benefactors, and assistance from the Taiwanese government, he would never again have to worry about his finances.[34] Yet his everyday life turned out to be rather unfulfilling. The newsweekly *Shūkan bunshun* described Nakamura's life a month after his second marriage: "He wakes up at four thirty and spends about an hour in the bed slowly waking up. He babysits four grandchildren or watches programs on his television set—one of the two in the village. . . . The only work he does is just to go find some kindling."[35] Probably to stave off boredom, he chewed betel nuts (they have a stimulant effect) and smoked as many as sixty cigarettes a day."[36]

In the typical narrative of repatriation that Japanese society expected, the man was supposed to return to a wife who had patiently waited for him. But in Nakamura's case, his wife's marriage to another man made it clear that he had no place to return to. Ironically, the only place that he could unconditionally call "home" was the jungle of Morotai Island. In 1952 or 1953, he had built a hut on Morotai and cultivated a field from a piece of land measuring about 6,500 square feet.[37] There, Nakamura initially planted yams and later sweet potatoes and bananas.[38] He also stole seedlings of corn and fava beans from the local farms and planted them on his field.[39] He even domesticated wild fowl-like birds for meat and eggs and occasionally caught wild pigs and eels to supplement his meals.[40]

Despite his and his interviewers' tendencies to make light of the challenges he faced, it is probable that his farming life on the island was generally peaceful. He initially was afraid of being discovered by the locals, but with time, that fear receded. Unlike Yokoi on Guam, Nakamura experienced no damage from typhoons. Although he suffered from malaria early in his solitary life, it disappeared when he drank boiled water and rested. He never became sick on Morotai again, but the malaria returned and required medical treatment when Nakamura was hospitalized for various examinations in Jakarta.[41] In comparison with Yokoi, who hid in an underground dwelling during the day, and Onoda, who was constantly on the move, Nakamura's life appears to have been far less stressful. He had good reason to later recall his island life with nostalgia.

In March 1977, Nakamura began appearing in stage shows at the Ami Cultural Village, a commercial establishment in Hualian City that attracted tourists with museum displays of Ami history and lifestyle as well as a staged show of Ami songs and dances.[42] Part of the museum display was dedicated to Nakamura's life on Morotai, and he appeared onstage approximately four times a day as a part of the tourist attraction. Being nicely compensated, he liked the work, expressing his future hope to a reporter: "The contract is good until March [1978]. If possible, I would like to move here for good."[43] Being surrounded by the tourists who cheered at his mere presence on the stage, he seemed to have finally found a community that accepted him unconditionally. It was perhaps a pleasure to be himself on the stage (he neither sang nor danced but merely smiled and waved at the audience). His stage appearance had a meaning quite different from Yokoi Shōichi's performance at a military-themed cabaret. Standing on the stage in various uniforms, Yokoi played military men of various ranks, quite unlike his straggler image. By contrast, Nakamura reenacted his own life as a straggler on Morotai, reestablishing a connection with the thirty-one years that he spent there. Yokoi represented himself as something that he was not; Nakamura reenacted his own past.

Nakamura's relative peace was short-lived. He was hospitalized for treatment of his lung cancer in February 1978, and he died on June 15 of the following year at age fifty-nine.[44] Before he retreated into a hospital room, he spent his final active days like a ghost, appearing several times a day on the shoddy stage set. Since his death, his figure has largely been invisible to the media.

WAR MEMORIES AND THE MASS MEDIA

There were multiple reasons why Nakamura Teruo's name was forgotten in Japanese society almost as soon as it surfaced. As I noted, his status as a former colonial subject was one of the major factors that dampened the Japanese media's excitement; unlike their coverage of Yokoi and Onoda, reporters were not sure how to cover the man who did not fit the conventional images of returnees. Yokoi, Onoda, and Nakamura all returned extremely late, well beyond the period when the cultural and media images of expatriated former servicemen were well recognized in postwar Japanese society. By the early 1970s, stories about post-defeat repatriations and belated homecomings had long receded from the popular consciousness.

For Yokoi and Onoda, the Japanese popular media nevertheless managed to restage their stories of repatriation in a dramatic way by focusing on the extreme belatedness of their returns—as if Yokoi and Onoda were long-distance runners who had never quit running. There was no such story for Nakamura. After a long wait, he finally showed up in the arena of national history but never crossed the finish line, as he did not go home to Japan. Nobody seemed to know how to comment on Nakamura's journey, which never had a satisfactory closure. The first hurdle for the Japanese media was the troublesome fact that they could not treat Nakamura as a national hero because he was from a Japanese colony. To honor him as Japanese would have been to revive the past colonialist arrogance rather unreflectively, whereas not to accept him as Japanese meant rejecting the past completely. This quandary demonstrated that postwar Japan had not yet found a way to deal adequately with its troubled past.

Several Japanese newsweeklies commented on the Japanese government's mishandling of the situation, criticizing both the fact that Nakamura would receive a mere ¥68,000 ($267)[45] for his decades of hardship and the fact that he did not return to Japan. None of the newsweeklies, however, took a clear stance on how Nakamura should be transitioned into the contemporary world. The ones that reported on Nakamura's case tended to be equivocal about even their own opinions. A typical example was an article published in *Shūkan taishū* that accused the Japanese government for pretending to honor Nakamura's wish to return to Taiwan, all while treating him as an unwelcome guest. But the article also speculates that Nakamura, as a man of nature, would not be happy in a land polluted by industrial waste or to be caught in the media frenzy. In the end, the article dodged the political questions raised by Nakamura's case, concluding instead that it would be best for Nakamura to realize his wish "to be a farmer."[46] The site of Nakamura's return was an issue that had to be worked out between two countries that did not have formal diplomatic relations—first between Indonesia and Taiwan and then between Japan and Taiwan. The need for such separate bilateral negotiations attested to Taiwan's precarious position in Cold War Asia. Although the Japanese government insisted that it was honoring Nakamura's wish to go back to Taiwan, the final decision ultimately belonged to the three nations' officials.

The Taiwanese media treated Nakamura as a Taiwanese citizen and maintained that it was only natural for him to return to Taiwan.[47] Nonetheless, there was a great distance between Taiwanese society in 1975 and the former Japanese soldier who had spent the previous three decades cut off from civilization. For example, Nakamura communicated with most of the young Taiwanese journalists only through translators because he did not speak Mandarin Chinese (he spoke Japanese, the Ami language, and some Fukienese). He was not able to communicate even with his grandchildren, who had been educated only in Mandarin Chinese.[48] Although Nakamura might not have felt at home in Taiwan, many expected that his ethnic community and family would serve as his genuine home. But in the days following his return, he found comfort in neither his family nor his larger ethnic community. He had no physical place that felt like a true home. Only after a long search, Nakamura arrived at the stage of the Ami Cultural Village, where he finally felt comfortable, an imitation of the space of his wartime and postwar displacement.

Furthermore, the absence of public ritual in Nakamura's return separated it from Yokoi's and Onoda's. Yokoi's arrival at Haneda International Airport and the surrender ceremony for Onoda helped transform them from private individuals into media symbols. In contrast, after being captured by members of the Indonesian air force, Nakamura never faced the public until he arrived in Taiwan, where no ceremony was held for the man who had fought for Taiwan's former colonizer. Thus, he remained a private individual.

Finally, the timing of Nakamura's return largely compelled his erasure from postwar Japanese memory. By the time he emerged from hiding, the national narrative about the belated returnees had largely achieved a cultural closure. Those who were forced to return home late were assigned the role of embodying the transition from war to postwar in Japanese society. Once Japanese society recovered from the devastation of the war and regained its national confidence, there was less need to reenact the past in order to reconfirm how far Japan had come.[49] The return of Yokoi Shōichi—the living war dead—shocked postwar Japanese society and the media into realizing that their war wounds had not completely healed. By restaging the drama with the "rescue" of Onoda Hiro'o, Japanese society overcame the shock of Yokoi's unexpected return. With two symbolic closures secured for the national narrative about returnees, the media no longer needed to operate in frenzy. In the end, Japanese society demonstrated little willingness to reopen the twice-ended story just for the sake of accommodating Nakamura's unique case.

A MIDSUMMER NIGHT'S DREAM

Between Yokoi's and Onoda's return, another former Japanese soldier was found in the early 1970s on a South Pacific island, but his name disappeared from the media space as soon as the news of his discovery hit Japan. In the end, this scoop turned out to be no more than a chance resemblance between two strangers, which attested to the Japanese news media's infatuation with long-lost stragglers.

The July 17, 1973, morning edition of the *Asahi shinbun* emphatically reported that its reporter had "found" the former navy seaman Miki Ryōji on Mindanao Island in the Philippines.[50] Lest they miss the news, the other major Japanese newspapers immediately sent their reporters to the area where the alleged former Japanese soldier was located. These newspapers printed articles similar to the *Asahi*'s in their evening editions,[51] and some newsweeklies followed suit as well.[52]

Although Ryōji's biological brothers confirmed his identity, from the beginning some things about the story did not add up. For example, the man who identified himself as Tanao Tao could not speak Japanese at all and claimed to be half Japanese and half Filipino. In the interview with the *Asahi* reporter, he did not acknowledge that he was indeed Miki Ryōji. Despite the striking resemblance between him and his "twin brother" Sekizō, Tanao Tao was almost three inches taller than Sekizō (figure 7.1).[53] These incongruities raised the suspicions of a Filipino TV network, which then interviewed Tao's Filipino birth mother. In it, she unequivocally declared that Tao was born to her and a Japanese man in the local village.[54] Finally, after the interview aired, Tao announced on July 25 that he was actually not Miki Ryōji. Only then did newsweekly articles list other physical characteristics that had raised their reporters' suspicions: he did not have a mole that Ryōji had; the shape of his ears was different from Sekizō's; he was left-handed (Ryōji was right-handed); and he was fluent in English (Ryōji was not).[55]

These telltale signs were not initially challenged when the base assumption was that Tanao Tao was Miki Ryōji. Another "brother," Sōzō, explained away the fact that he was not able to speak Japanese and had no memories before 1944, insisting, "While he narrowly escaped from a small island he was defending, he suffered from malaria and an endemic disease and, as a result, had a high fever for seven months."[56] The manner in which this straggler met his Japanese family—he did not look excited at all—was interpreted as showing his fear that he might have to give up his current life on Mindanao. If the news had been shared only with Miki Ryōji's immediate family, who were strongly motivated to find him,

FIGURE 7.1 Tanao Tao (*left*) and Miki Sekizō, July 21, 1973. (Courtesy of *Yomiuri shinbun*)

it would have ended as a little tragicomedy. But the Japanese mass media reported the case of mistaken identity as a national drama, demonstrating the underlying desire of Japanese society to find and rescue the former Japanese soldiers left behind in the wartime past, a desire awakened by Yokoi Shōichi's dramatic return.

Tanao Tao's lived reality became invisible in the eyes of a society possessed by this strong desire. Considering that unlike Yokoi, Tanao Tao lived completely as a local (he had married two women and had seventeen children), it should have been obvious that the "discovery of Miki Ryōji" was far-fetched.[57] It had also been known that some former Japanese soldiers had participated in the Indonesian war of independence and subsequently settled in that country.[58] In the 1971 documentaries he directed for a Japanese television station, Imamura Shōhei interviewed several former Japanese soldiers who had settled in Thailand and Malaysia after the war ended. There appeared to be a tacit criterion as to who "deserved" to be rescued by postwar Japanese society: in order to qualify for a rescue, the lost individuals must not have had agency in the circumstances that kept them from returning to Japan after the war's end. Ironically, Tanao Tao was a perfect candidate for rescue according to this standard—it did not appear that he had consciously chosen to remain on Mindanao.

The Japanese media's frenzied reaction in the summer of 1973 also revealed the need to reconstitute the stragglers' essentially Japanese identity. For example, the *Asahi*'s special correspondent, Murakami Yoshio, who had a strong interest in finding lost Japanese soldiers in Mindanao, described his preconceived image of a typical Japanese straggler: "Barefooted. Because he ran around the mountains and fields, the soles of his feet are thick and tough. He is naked on top, carrying a machete on his hip. Shiny eyes and thick eyebrows. He uses a bow and arrows and a gun well. He has a ferocious disposition that does not allow strangers to approach. He is the leader of a fierce mountain tribe."[59]

When he talked to "Miki Ryōji" in person, however, Murakami got a completely different impression. "I thought his facial features and the aura that he somehow exuded were nothing but Japanese. As I was talking with Mr. Miki, I was secretly releasing a sigh of relief. 'He appears to be such a nice person. He is an admirable person. It is really wonderful.'"[60] Murakami appeared to have feared that some Japanese stragglers had gone native, but he was reassured by what he perceived as the unwavering Japanese characteristics in Miki's personality.[61]

In Murakami's imagination, the stragglers had also become cannibals, and he recounted the dream he had had when he visited Mindanao in the previous year:

It was a dream about the former Japanese soldiers living together as a group. I just keep walking through the jungle. Suddenly I walk into an opening, where I see several nipa palm huts and some men walk out of them. They are definitely Japanese and are carrying hand-made guns. Behind their nipa palm huts is a ranch. What they are raising in the fenced ranch are not cows or pigs but humans.

After describing the disturbing dream, Murakami immediately offered his own interpretation: "In the dream, I understood that they had eaten human flesh out of overwhelming hunger, and its taste made them cannibals."[62] While it is impossible to determine a precise source for Murakami's cannibal images,[63] his primal fear resonated with cultural stereotypes about the colonial other, images widely recognized in both Western nations and Japan.[64]

In Murakami's dream, the cannibal images also may have been shaped by the actual practices of Japanese servicemen on small Pacific islands. Being cut off from the supply lines and forced to subsist on scarce local food sources (Guam was exceptional in that regard), the Japanese soldiers experienced extreme hunger. According to historian Fujiwara Akira, more than 1,300 of the 4,000 defense forces starved to death on Wake Island, a coral atoll located between Midway Island and Guam.[65] Fujiwara also estimates that half of the 247,000 deaths in the middle Pacific islands were the result of a combination of starvation and illness.[66] On a number of islands, however, servicemen survived by consuming their fellow men and, in some cases, locals and enemy soldiers as well.[67] The instances of cannibalism at the war front may not have been openly discussed in public, but by the early 1970s, it was critically dealt with in at least two films: Ichikawa Kon's *Fires on the Plain* (*Nobi*, 1959; based on Ōoka Shōhei's 1951 novel), and Fukasaku Kinji's *Under the Flag of the Rising Sun* (*Senki hatameku motoni*, 1972).[68]

Whether it was rooted in colonial fantasies or historical events, Murakami's primitive, cannibalistic images were arguably the product of his desire to safeguard the essential Japanese identity against various historical forces: he demarcated national boundaries with these outlandish constructs of what was outside. This ideological move was part and parcel of the now infamous discourse of Japanese uniqueness, the culturalist discourse that dehistoricized the contemporary Japanese identity. Facing unprecedented affluence and the attendant social transformations in the early 1970s, Japan was experiencing a national soul-searching. Tradition was arbitrarily invoked to justify Japan's current economic success in a tautological manner: the Japanese were destined to succeed because of their tradition, and Japanese nationality was the only necessary condition for producing that success. The Japanese were therefore destined to succeed because they were Japanese. In this circuitous and essentialist logic, Japan's recent past of death and destruction conveniently disappeared, and Murakami's dreams attest to the ways in which the nation's ghostly past was externalized and demonized.

Murakami's fear therefore revealed the imaginary nature of the encounters with the long-lost stragglers. The actual encounters never happened: Japanese media and society merely saw in the stragglers' figures their own deep-seated anxiety about being Japanese in the 1970s. In this sense, the Miki Ryōji they found in the Philippines was as real as Yokoi, Onoda, and Nakamura (or, alternatively, the latter three were as illusionary as Miki). The role of the stragglers was to act as mirrors in which the media and society could see what they wished to see from a safe distance. All of the stragglers resisted this assigned role in one way or another (with the exception of Miki: his lack of agency made him the perfect mirror). Nakamura's case stands out, however, as the excess that could not be assimilated into the national narratives of belated returns, the excess that brought the terrifying consequences of war and colonialism too close to home. His homecoming also exposed home—the key concept that had anchored the narrative of repatriation and, by extension, the postwar Japanese identity—as a less secure site than the postwar Japanese media and society made it out to be: the stage home that Nakamura found was symbolic of the imaginary nature of home.

EPILOGUE

DREAMING OF HOME

Every belated return of a repatriated soldier exposed the dark shadows of the troubling past in Japan's postwar society; the transition from war to postwar was a messy and incomplete process. Yet the concept of home—the *sine qua non* for homecoming—served as a cover that concealed these shadows. The postwar popular media idealized home as a centrifugal force that would keep the rapidly transforming society together, turning the belated returns into opportunities to reconfirm that image. Decades of postwar Japan's social changes, however, effectively subverted the media's efforts to cast home in warm, nostalgic images.

Kurosawa Akira's film *Dreams* (*Yume*, 1990)—a collection of eight dream segments—dramatically demonstrates the problematic status of home. In one of the early segments, the figure of an imaginary former officer and his ghostly subordinates unexpectedly return to Japan, revealing the unwelcoming quality of home in 1990. This film offers a highly critical assessment of contemporary Japan: the wrong choices that its people have made and the dire consequences of those choices. Kurosawa's indictment incorporates the story of a man who has just returned from an apparent Soviet internment. In this segment, confronted by the ghosts of the soldiers he once commanded, the former officer orders the deceased back to the netherworld. The dream suggests that each returned serviceman has brought back dark memories of war. But in 1990, Japan had little desire to accommodate these memories, as there was no longer a familiar space—home—in which to appease the souls of the war dead. Despite Kurosawa's emotional identification with the war dead—he was deeply shaken by the writing of this section[1]—his film amounts to an announcement that Kurosawa and postwar society are finally free from the shadows of war. Having lost their emotional intensity over the intervening decades, these dark shadows are now easily eliminated. The figure of the belated returnee dutifully performs the act of exorcism on behalf of postwar Japanese society.

This short segment has two encounters with the ghosts of the fallen soldiers, each of which ends with the war dead disappearing into darkness. A former officer walks through a tunnel in the mountains that appears to be leading to his hometown. As soon as he comes out, the ghost of Private Noguchi emerges from the darkness and asks if he in fact was killed in action. Although the officer explains that Noguchi died in his arms, the private refuses to believe the truth, citing his memory of having been discharged and eating the special sweets that his mother had made for his homecoming. That "memory" was actually a dream that he had had while he was unconscious, the officer explains. Honda Ishirō, who served as the assistant director of *Dreams*, was the source of an anecdote that inspired this dying soldier's dream: at the Chinese front, Honda witnessed a soldier make a similar claim right before his death.[2] The homecoming spirit is a staple image in the realm of folk beliefs, a realm that many Japanese—including the dying soldier—once embraced. Noguchi points to the house in the mountains where his parents await his return, but only in his dream is he able to return home. Despite being released from worldly constraints, his soul is unable to defy his former superior at the tunnel, and he reluctantly returns to the darkness, disheartened.

Why can he not return to his parents and the community in which he grew up? Why does the officer insist that Noguchi return to the netherworld? Is it not a long-standing Japanese custom for his family and community to embrace and quiet the souls of the deceased? A short answer to these questions is that "home" is no longer there to ensure Noguchi's transition from war to postwar. Home—embodied in family and hometown (*kokyō, furusato*)—was an essential component of the ideological apparatus that mobilized Japanese men for Imperial Japan's military missions.[3] When the soldiers left home, they were assured that they would be taken care of when they returned, whether dead or alive. More than four decades after the war's end, Japan is a radically different place from what Noguchi remembers. Home is no longer an ideological site where sacrifice for the war is embraced and normalized. It has also lost the social and cultural basis in which Noguchi's dream was anchored: gone is the rich world of folk beliefs and customs that once existed in Japan. The dead soldier's dream of homecoming becomes nonsensical once those communally held beliefs disintegrated.[4]

Although this particular scene appears to take place several years after Japan's defeat, the film as a whole is more concerned about the state of contemporary Japanese society. The tunnel scene implies that following the end of the Asia Pacific War, Japanese society focused on the pursuit of material comfort while allowing its spiritual connections with the ancestral land to deteriorate. In 1990s Japan, many rural areas simply did not have large enough populations to maintain family traditions;[5] by contrast, most of the nuclear families in the cities lacked the means or desire to carry on these customs.[6] Material wealth may have helped produce middle-class families in postwar Japan (as seen in *Yellow Crow*), but families seem to have lost their ties with the past. The home that Private Noguchi points to is nothing more than a dim light, and he has no way of reaching it.[7] His home has become a different kind of dream: a nightmare. The film is scornful of the greed that has caused spiritual and environmental crisis in Japan. In addition to this sequence, Kurosawa also includes dreams about the nuclear disaster and aftermath triggered by the eruption of Mount Fuji.

Against this critique, Kurosawa offers an idyllic vision of what life in Japan could really be like. In his view, the Japanese people's pursuit of modern convenience has caused them to lose their connections with positive as well as negative national legacies, and the natural community imagined in the final segment serves as an antidote to all the ills portrayed in the film. "I"—the actor Terao Akira plays both "I" and the former officer—visits a hamlet commonly known as "Watermill Village," which does not even have electricity. In this peaceful setting on an island in the river, the living and the dead happily coexist. The villagers have even adopted the soul of an unknown traveler from generations ago. For them, a funeral procession is an occasion to celebrate the long and healthy life of each villager at death. The visitor speaks with a 103-year-old man, played by Ryū Chishū, who joins the procession for a woman who has just died at the age of 99. Perhaps the old man already lives among the dead, but that hardly matters because in this community, death is a natural extension of life. This delightful final segment provides a stark contrast with the gloomy images of doomsday Japan in the preceding sections. This peace is what Kurosawa wants, but he is keenly aware that it is an impossible dream that exists only in his imagination.

The tunnel segment is a critical commentary on the larger reality of postwar Japan, in which war has been relegated to distant memory. Following Noguchi's disappearance, the ghosts of the entire Third Platoon march out of the tunnel, reporting no casualties. The former officer, however, claims that the Third Platoon was annihilated, and he assumes full responsibility for the tragic outcome. He begs the dead soldiers to return to where they belong, telling them that there is no place for them among the living. But his words have no visible effect on the ghosts, who continue to stand silently at the opening of the tunnel. Realizing that his plea is not enough, the officer raises his voice and orders them to do an about-face and march back. With these commands, the ghost platoon disappears into the tunnel. In order to get the dead back to the netherworld, the officer must act as if he still commands them. By enacting the fiction that they are still at war, he manages to expel the ghosts from the present.[8] Not realizing that the war has ended, the ghosts have no choice but to accept their platoon commander's orders. They march back, not to rest in peace, but to continue their war in the netherworld.

The former officer represents Japanese society in the early 1990s (and thereafter): he reminds the ghosts that they died meaningless deaths and that they do not belong in the present. He is the first one to admit his "thoughtlessness and mistakes," and he sincerely insists that he would not evade responsibility by blaming "the irrationality of war or the inhuman nature of the military rules." But what does it really mean to assume responsibility for making an entire platoon "die like dogs"? The trickery that the officer uses seems too easy and disingenuous. Although he shows signs of emotional distress afterward by falling to his hands and knees, he effectively refuses to acknowledge the battle that the war dead would continue to wage. He insists that "I wished I could have died with you," words that sound hollow and perfunctory when he does not have a genuine desire to be among them. His final orders thus do not offer solace to the fallen soldiers because his commands clearly banish the dead from the postwar period. The officer's relationship to his platoon lacks any of the emotional ties with the war dead that many survivors felt in the early postwar years.[9] The former commander stands securely on the side of the living and performs the role expected by postwar society.[10] His associations with the war dead must be exorcised completely, however, before he will be admitted into this society.

The liminal quality of the officer's space—tucked away in the mountains—safely distances postwar social settings from his eerie encounters with the past. The tunnel appears to be a conduit connecting the war and postwar Japan. Kintoki Tunnel, however, where the scene takes place, was actually constructed in 1974.[11] It was one of thousands of concrete structures built as part of the Liberal Democratic Party's pork-barrel politics, structures that permanently changed the appearance of the Japanese countryside. The tunnel therefore would not lead the audience back to the wartime but only to the economic hustle and bustle of 1970s Japan, which transformed Yokoi Shōichi and Onoda Hiro'o—the ghastly past in human form—into usable icons.

The only sign of protest comes from a sentinel dog that growls at the former officer just before and just after he encounters the dead. The dog strongly reacts to the intruder, as if to insist that the man has no business in this space inhabited by the souls of fallen soldiers. Contrary to his expressed wish, the officer's presence (and Japan's present) prevents his subordinates from resting in peace: they will continue fighting their war and looking to him for commands. The dog's barking is a distant echo of the animal-like cry that Yusa Shinjirō makes in *Stray Dog*. Even though Yusa makes only a nonsensical sound, it expresses what little agency he retains. The ghostly soldiers of 1990, in contrast, are completely deprived of their agency. Although they may have died like dogs, they are not even allowed the dog's defiant spirit.[12]

The former officer in *Dreams* easily leaps over the chasm by severing his ties with the haunting past. Despite Kurosawa's critical intention, the tunnel scene effectively serves as a foil for the final segment in which every life is celebrated. In the film's overly didactic visions of right and wrong, gone is the dark space in the postwar period, the existence of which *Stray Dog* intimated some forty years earlier. Instead, this threatening space is banished to the darkness of the tunnel. Kurosawa's idyllic community is a beautiful ideal: a multicultural and multigenerational, if not multiracial, celebration of life. Despite his critical position toward postwar society, Kurosawa's vision is clearly an extension of postwar Japan's nostalgia for the folk communities, unspoiled by the convenience of material culture. The traumatic event in the recent past—the war—has never been part of this image. What if the ghost soldiers then arrive and demand that they be included in the festivities? Would the community be ready to embrace them and their associations with the dark past? Their presence would reveal that the celebration of life is premised on their absence, that their unnatural deaths cannot be celebrated because they represent Japanese society's catastrophic choices.

BELATED RETURNEES AND POSTWAR JAPAN

In reality, the belated returnees were the ghostly figures that arrived at postwar Japan's celebration of life (and economic prosperity) demanding to be included in it. Their tales of survival and safe return indeed deserve wide recognition. Their association with Japan's wartime past, however, destabilized the symbolic divide between the war and the postwar period, the divide that the postwar media and society strove to maintain. The belatedness of their return compounded the challenges that these returnees faced. Postwar Japan had been transformed into an unfamiliar terrain for them (when he first emerged from the Guam jungle, Yokoi Shōichi complained that the young Japanese reporters looked like Americans).[13] In this unfamiliar terrain, the men could find no effective means—a map, to use Jorge Luis Borges's literary image discussed in the introduction—with which to navigate the burden of history. Some survivors of Soviet internment, most notably Ishihara Yoshirō, struggled to devise their own navigation tools (to varying degrees of success), whereas Yokoi improvised with what the media offered. By contrast, Onoda Hiro'o rejected his status as a belated returnee altogether and left Japan.

This book is an effort to demonstrate that Japan's "postwar" period was not the temporal space that naturally emerged after the war. Rather, the concept of postwar demanded constant inspection and maintenance, and the belated return of former servicemen provided the impetus for

225

EPILOGUE

carrying out these tasks. By reenacting the rituals of homecoming, their return was supposed to reinforce the symbolic boundaries of postwar Japan. But the drama of their return did not unfold according to the media's and society's script: the ghostly echoes of the past that the former servicemen brought home revealed the dark interstices in postwar Japanese society. Despite their efforts to adjust to postwar society, the belatedly returned men never fully relinquished the darkness that defined them. Their struggles after their return attested to the fact that the "home" in their homecoming was not a clearly defined end point. They continued to search for a home, a space where they could reconcile their past and present. The belated returnees' frustrated searches, the state of their homelessness, thus ultimately exposed the tension-filled, tangled relations of the war, postwar Japan, and the in-between space.

NOTES

The following abbreviations are used in the text and notes:

GJC Gomikawa Jumpei, *Gomikawa Jumpei chosakushū*, 20 vols. (Tokyo: San'ichi shobō, 1983–1985)

HT Takahashi Daizō et al., eds., *Horyo taikenki*, 8 vols. (Tokyo: Soren ni okeru Nihonjin horyo no seikatsu taiken o kirokusuru kai, 1984–1998)

IYZ Ishihara Yoshirō, *Ishihara Yoshirō zenshū*, 3 vols. (Tokyo: Kashinsha, 1979–1980)

INTRODUCTION

1. "Fumishimeru kokoku no tsuchi," *Yomiuri shinbun*, December 1, 1953, evening 4th ed., 3.
2. Ibid.
3. "Henshū techō," *Yomiuri shinbun*, December 1, 1953, 14th ed., 1.
4. "Nuguisaru ikoku no ka," *Yomiuri shinbun*, December 2, evening 4th ed., 1953, 3.
5. "Akahata no nai ekitō: warai to namida no kangei," *Yomiuri shinbun*, December 5, evening 4th ed., 3.
6. "Aodatami o kagu," *Yomiuri shinbun*, December 5, 1953, evening 4th ed., 3.
7. The *Asahi shinbun*'s coverage was also filled with similar sentiment. The "Tensei jingo" column, for example, describes the return of the internees as "the Japanese from ten years ago, who were neither Americanized nor Sovietized, appeared unexpectedly at the port" (*Asahi shinbun*, December 2, 1953, 12th ed., 1).

In the writer's mind, their return to Japan was like pressing a reset button of history.

8. "Ima Urashima no Ginbura," *Yomiuri shinbun*, December 5, 1953, evening 4th ed., 3.

9. I discuss Ishihara's homecoming in detail in chapter 3.

10. Increasingly committed to establishing closer ties with the Nationalist government, the United States was motivated to remove the residual Japanese influence—the Japanese veterans and civilians—from the region (Katō Kiyofumi, "Dai Nippon teikoku no hōkai to zanryū Nihonjin hikiage mondai," in *Dai Nippon teikoku no hōkai to hikiage, fukuin*, ed. Masuda Hiroshi [Tokyo: Keiōgijuku daigaku shuppankai, 2012], 36–37; Katō Yōko, "Haisha no kikan," *Kokusai seiji*, May 1995, 119–20).

11. Kōseishō shakaiengo kyoku engo 50 nenshi hensan iinkai, ed., *Engo 50 nennshi* (Tokyo: Gyōsei, 1997), 729–30.

12. By the end of 1949, 6.24 million people (about 91 percent of the Japanese who were either in the colonies or at the front at the war's end) returned to Japan (Kōseishō shakaiengo kyoku engo 50 nenshi henshū iinkai, *Engo 50 nenshi*, 730–31).

13. In these narratives of war and defeat, there was little room for the colonial legacies that the *hikiagesha* (Japanese repatriates from the former colonies) carried home. Speaking more broadly about the *hikiagesha*, historian Lori Watt argues: "Defining oneself as a homeland Japanese, and not as a repatriate, was a way to place a buffer between one's self and the imperial project" (*When Empire Comes Home: Repatriation and Reintegration in Postwar Japan* [Cambridge, Mass.: Harvard East Asia Center, 2009], 97).

14. Yoshikuni Igarashi, *Bodies of Memory: Narratives of War in Postwar Japanese Culture, 1945–1970* (Princeton, N.J.: Princeton University Press, 2000).

15. Ōkado Masakatsu, *Sensō to sengo o ikiru*, vol. 15 of *Zenshū Nihon no rekishi* (Tokyo: Shōgakkan, 2009), 236.

16. Maizuru-shi shi hensan iinkai, ed., *Maizuru-shi shi*, gendai-hen (Maizuru: Maizuru shiyakusho, 1988), 263.

17. Ōkado, *Sensō to sengo o ikiru*, 239.

18. Mizuki Shigeru, *Musume ni kataru otōsan no senki: minami no shima no sensō no hanashi* (Tokyo: Shakai hyōronsha, 1999), 167: Mizuki Shigeru, *He no yōna jinsei* (Tokyo: Kadokawa shoten, 2009), 456. There were also several thousand Japanese soldiers who chose to stay in Southeast Asia for various reasons. Reporter Aonuma Yōichirō provides accounts of fourteen such Japanese veterans on the basis of his interviews with them in *Kikan sezu: zanryū Nihon-hei 60 nenme no shōgen* (Tokyo: Shinchōsha, 2006). Aonuma's work gathers together their valuable testimonies. Although not everyone in the group he interviewed had a strong emotional attachment to Japan—one of them was actually born and raised in Brazil—Aonuma declares that "they all loved Japan," despite whatever difficulties they might have experienced there. By concluding that the state of Japan betrayed those who loved their lives and Japan and therefore they were not able to go back to Japan, he downplays the diversity of reasons for which they decided not to go back (*Kikan sezu*, 330).

19. Andrew Barshay discusses Fujiwara's text against the backdrop of Japan's colonial enterprise in northeast China in *The Gods Left First: The Captivity and Repatriation of Japanese POWs in Northeast Asia, 1945–1956* (Berkeley: University of California Press, 2013), 170–82.

20. An English translation was recently published as Fujiwara Tei, *Tei: A Memoir of the End of War and Beginning of Peace*, trans. Nana Mizushima (Tonnbo Books, 2014).

21. Narita Ryūichi, "'Hikiage' ni kansuru joshō," *Shisō*, November 2003, 164. *Nagareru hoshi wa ikiteiru* has been published by various publishers in different editions. Japan's National Diet Library (NDL) holds the following versions: Hibiya shuppansha (1949), Kaisei sha (1965), Seishun shuppansha (1971), Chūōkōron (1976), Kaisei sha (1976), Chikuma shobō (1977), Saitama fukushi kai (1987), and Chūōkōron new editions (1994, 2002). The NDL also owns the versions printed as part of the following series: Gendai kyōyō zenshū (Tokyo: Chikuma shobō, 1958), vol. 4; Sekai nonfikushon zenshū (Tokyo: Chikuma shobō, 1963), vol. 46; Ai to Shinjitsu no kiroku (Tokyo: Tōto shobō, 1964), vols. 1 and 2; and Shōwa sensō bungaku zenshū (Tokyo: Shūeisha, 1965), vol. 12.

22. The film spends the first sixteen minutes (out of eighty-three) tracing the family's and their friends' difficult repatriation to Japan. The rest of the film portrays their hardship in postwar society. The story culminates with the news that the protagonist's husband is safe and about to return home.

23. When some of the Japanese women and orphans who had been left in northeastern China after the war began to return to Japan in the 1980s, the Japanese media gave considerable coverage to their homecoming and subsequent lives. I do not discuss their experiences in this book, though, because I believe these former "children" should be treated more as a new class of immigrants than as belated returnees. Although their connections with the war served as the impetus for their "returning" to Japan, their later struggles in Japanese society stemmed mainly from the fact that they had been raised linguistically and culturally as Chinese. While it would be a fascinating project to examine how their presence undermined a narrowly construed concept of Japanese-ness, it is beyond this book's primary concern, which is how such boundaries were redrawn and maintained in the first three decades of the postwar period. As for the women who returned from northeastern China, the media's focus was mostly on their return home; much as in the case of the earlier returnees, their lives in Japan have received little attention.

24. For example, in 1947 an issue of the *Asahi* newspaper was only two pages long, and no evening edition was issued. In 1955, the morning edition was eight pages long and, in 1973, twenty-four pages long. During the same period, the evening edition grew from four to twelve pages.

25. After being introduced to the Japanese market in 1953, television quickly became a fixture in everyday life, and the number of television broadcasting stations correspondingly increased from 2 in 1955 to 1,604 in 1973 (Ministry of Internal Affairs and Communications, Statistics Bureau, Director-General for Policy Planning [Statistical Standards] & Statistical Research and Training

Institute, *Historical Statistics of Japan*, chap. 26, available at http://www.stat.
go.jp/english/data/chouki/26.htm).

26. Nakazawa Masao, *Hibakusha no kokoro no kizu o otte* (Tokyo: Iwanami shoten, 2007), 3–4.

27. Ibid., 2–7.

28. As historian Fukuma Yoshiaki argues, in their 1960s political activism, the
postwar generations already rejected the war generations' higher-than-thou
attitude in discussing war experiences (*"Sensō taiken" no sengoshi: sedai,
kyōyō, ideorogii* [Tokyo: Chūōkōron shinsha, 2009], 161–62, 267; and *Shōdo
no kioku: Okinawa, Hiroshima, Nagasaki ni utsuru sengo* [Tokyo: Shinyōsha,
2011], 64–65).

29. Ishihara Yoshirō succinctly articulates this point in relation to his Siberian experiences: "The only lesson I learned is that there is no lesson to be learned in
limit situations. Individuals are not placed in limit situations [*kyokugenjōkyō*]
to learn lessons" (*IYZ*, 2:525).

30. Jorge Luis Borges, "On Rigor in Science," in *A Universal History of Infamy*,
trans. Norman Thomas di Giovanni (New York: Dutton, 1972), 141.

31. For examples of archival work, see Victor Karpov, *Sutaarin no horyotachi*,
trans. Nagase Ryōji (Sapporo: Hokkaidō shinbunsha, 2001); Elena Katasonova,
Kantōgun heishi wa naze Shiberia ni yokuryū saretaka, trans. Shirai Hisaya
(Tokyo: Shakai hyōronsha, 2004); and Tomita Takeshi, *Shiberia yokuryūsha
tachi no sengo* (Tokyo: Jinbun shoin, 2013).

32. Barshay, *Gods Left First*.

33. Beatrice Trefalt, *Japanese Army Stragglers and Memories of the War in Japan,
1950–1975* (New York: RoutledgeCurzon, 2003).

34. Kawasaki Masumi, *Kaettekita Taiwanjin Nihonhei* (Tokyo: Bungei shunjū, 2003).

35. Maruyama Tetsushi, "Liu Lianren, Yokoi Shōichi, 'Nakamura Teruo' ni totteno
sensō," in *Teikokuno sensōkeiken*, vol. 4 of Iwanami kōza Ajia Taiheiyō sensō
(Tokyo: Iwanami shoten, 2006), 323–50; Bruce Suttmeier, "Speculations of
Murder: Ghostly Dreams, Poisonous Frogs, and the Return of Yokoi Shōichi," in
Perversion and Modern Japan: Psychoanalysis, Literature, Culture, ed. Nina
Cornyetz and J. Keith Vincent (New York: Routledge, 2009), 22–38; Hayashi
Ei'ichi, "Onoda Hiro'o to Yokoi Shōichi: Yutakana shakai ni shutsugen shita
Nihon hei," in *Nihon rettō kaizō: 1970 nendai*, vol. 6 of Hitobito no seishinshi,
ed. Sugita Atsushi (Tokyo: Iwanami shoten, 2016), 217–43.

36. Watt briefly discusses *The Human Condition* and *Yellow Crow* in *When Empire
Comes Home*, 148–51, 156–57.

1. LIFE AFTER THE WAR

1. *Yellow Crow* won the 1958 Golden Globe Award for best foreign-language film,
although it does not seem to have generated much publicity in the United States
or other English-speaking countries. I have not been able to locate reviews of
Yellow Crow in contemporary English-language periodicals.

2. Allied air raids destroyed 513 movie theaters during the war, and the Japanese film industry began its postwar operation with 845 theaters (Shimizu Akira, *Sensō to eiga* [Tokyo: Shakaishisōsha, 1994], 153–54). The number of theaters peaked in 1960 at 7,457.

3. Ministry of Internal Affairs and Communications, Statistics Bureau, Director-General for Policy Planning (Statistics Standard) & Statistical Research and Training Institute *Historical Statistics of Japan*, "Chapter 26 Culture and Leisure" (http://www.stat.go.jp/english/data/chouki/26.htm): "Jinkō tōkei shiryōshū," National Institute of Population and Social Security Research (http://www.ipss.go.jp/syoushika/tohkei/Popular/Popular2013.asp?chap=0).

4. The media scholar Yoshimi Shunya, for example, maintains that film was an important cultural medium particularly for the Japanese working class in the 1950s ("Eigakan to iu sengo: henyō suru Tokyo no sakariba no nakade," in *Miru hito, tsukuru hito, kakeru hito*, ed. Kurosawa Kiyoshi et al., Nihon eiga wa ikiteiru [Tokyo: Iwanami shoten, 2010], 3:110).

5. Tsurumi Shunsuke, "Maegaki," *Sengo eiga no tenkai*, Kōza Nihon eiga (Tokyo: Iwanami shoten, 1987), 5:iii.

6. Gorillas inhabit only certain regions of Africa, not the areas where the Japanese forces fought. This imaginary encounter attests to the global flow of colonial fantasy in which Japan participated. I return to the topic of persistent colonial images in chapter 7.

7. This beloved veteran character returns to the screen as Yūichi in Imamura Shōhei's *Black Rain* (*Kuroi ame*, 1989). Ibuse Masuji's original novel (1965) does not contain this character, which was inspired by *No Consultation Today*.

8. The film provides no information about the character's past life. However, given his age and impressive physique, he must have been mobilized as a soldier during the war. Uegusa Keinosuke, who coproduced the film's script for the film with Kurosawa, recalls a conversation in which the director explained the character as a former kamikaze pilot (*Keredo yoakeni: waga seishun no Kurosawa Akira* [Tokyo: Bungei shunjū, 1978], quoted in Kawamoto Saburō, *Ima hitotabi no Nihon eiga* [Tokyo: Iwanami shoten, 1994], 45–46).

9. For a more detailed discussion about the southern Pacific as the site of Japan's colonial past as well as its postwar romanticization, see Yoshikuni Igarashi, "Mothra's Gigantic Egg: Consuming the South Pacific in 1960s Japan," in *In Godzilla's Footsteps: Japanese Pop Culture Icons on the Global Stage*, ed. William Tsutsui and Michiko Ito (New York: Palgrave Macmillan, 2006), 83–102.

10. After directing these four films back to back and containing the threatening figures of former servicemen in moralistic narratives, Kurosawa never again portrayed former servicemen, with the exception of a short segment in *Dreams* (*Yume*, 1990), a retrospective of his own life and career. I briefly analyze the relevant sections of *Dreams* in the epilogue.

11. Ban Toshihiko, "Tōji no sesō to jiken no keika o otte," *Shinpyō*, August 1971, 231.

12. Uchimura Yūshi, "Kodaira jiken," in *Nihon no seishin kantei*, ed. Fukushima Akira, Nakata Osamu, and Ogi Sadataka (Tokyo: Misuzu shobō, 1973), 237.

13. Fujitake Akira, "Sengo jikenshi no imi," *Shokun*, December 1974, 35.

14. "Kodaira Yoshio no yobichōsho," *Shinpyō*, August 1971, 236–37.

15. Esaki Masanori, "Sengo ishoku jinbutsu tanken, 2: Kodaira Yoshio, jō," *Shūkan gendai*, January 21, 1962, 72.

16. Uchimura, "Kodaira jiken," 216.

17. This murder case resembles another contemporary case, in which a medical school professor's wife was killed in Hirosaki while he was away on business. The crime was committed on August 6, 1949. The actual case gained notoriety because an innocent person (a descendant of the legendary archer Nasu no Yoichi) was accused of the crime and later exonerated (Kamata Satoshi, *Hirosaki daigaku kyōju fujin satsujin jiken* [Tokyo: Shinpūsha, 2006]; Inoue Yasumasa, *Enzai no kiseki* [Tokyo: Shinchōsha, 2011]).

18. To be precise, Yusa is not desire-less. He later spends a night with a geisha, but he needs money to satisfy his bodily desire.

19. In real life, Mifune Toshirō was an army veteran whose parents died during the war, and Kimura Isao was a navy veteran who lost both his parents in the atomic bomb raid in Hiroshima (Kawamoto, *Ima hitotabi no Nihon eiga*, 49–51).

20. Noma Hiroshi, "*Nora inu* no mondai," *Chūōkōron*, December 1949, 87.

21. However, Kodaira immediately adds, "I don't think anybody has done more horrible things than what I did in peacetime" (quoted in Uchimura, "Kodaira jiken," 217).

22. For example, a female criminal uses the same line in the film *No Patients Today* (1952).

23. Miyazawa Kiichi, *Sengoseiji no shōgen* (Tokyo: Yomiuri shinbunsha, 1991), 22.

24. The actual footage of the Ueno black markets and the Ginza streets was shot with a hidden camera and incorporated into the nine-minute scene in which Murakami desperately seeks leads. Honda Ishirō served as a stand-in for Mifune's legs (Kiridōshi Risaku, *Honda Ishirō: mukan no kyoshō* [Tokyo: Yōsensha, 2014], 211).

25. Ōizumi Gakuen Station, at the outskirts of Tokyo, was used as a shooting location where Murakami spots Yusa (Onoda Yoshiki, "*Norainu* no kinchōkan," in *Bessatsu bungei: Kurosawa Akira*, ed. Nishiguchi Tōru [Tokyo: Kawade shobō shinsha, 1998], 140).

26. There is a foreshadowing of Murakami's injury. The previous night, after Yusa shoots Satō, Murakami gives his blood to his senior colleague. He emerges from the operating room holding his left arm, literally compensating with his own blood for the fellow former serviceman's crime.

27. The song "Lightly Row" was introduced to Japan in the late nineteenth century as "Chōcho," with a new lyric about butterflies. In 1947, the line "in the flourishing emperor's reign" was changed to "from flower to flower." The audience hears the 1947 version (Takeuchi Kikuo, *Shōka, dōyō 1,000 no shinjitsu* [Tokyo: Yamaha, 2009], 12–13).

28. Kurosawa Akira, *Something Like an Autobiography* (New York: Knopf, 1982), 174.

29. Mitsuhiro Yoshimoto, *Kurosawa* (Durham, N.C.: Duke University Press, 2000), 178.

30. *Manga: miru jikyoku zasshi*, July 1949, 7.
31. Ozu Yasujirō's film *A Hen in the Wind* (*Kaze no naka no mendori*, 1948) depicts a similar situation. A man returns from the front only to discover that his wife has prostituted herself to pay for their sick boy's medical bill. The tension between the couple is finally dissolved through the enactment of violence—he pushes her down the stairs and then embraces his injured wife.
32. Mitsuyo Wada-Marciano defines the middle-class films as follows: "The films depict the newly emerging modern subject, the salaried man, and his middle-class family, and the films often present a self-reflexive stance on modern society and experience" (*Nippon Modern: Japanese Cinema of the 1920s and 1930s* [Honolulu: University of Hawai'i Press, 2008], 12). As discussed here, *Yellow Crow* displays all these characteristics.
33. The name Machiko reinforces the image of a waiting woman (*matsu*/wait). Another waiting woman with the same name appeared a few years earlier in *Kimi no na wa*, a popular radio show later turned into a film trilogy. I examine *Kimi no na wa* in detail in *Bodies of Memory: Narratives of War in Postwar Japanese Culture, 1945–1970* (Princeton, N.J.: Princeton University Press, 2000), 106–14. To the wharf of Maizuru, where Ichirō landed, a number of women descended each time repatriation ships arrived, hoping that they would see loved ones. They were locally known as *ganpeki no haha* ([waiting] mothers on the wharf) or *ganpeki no tsuma* ([waiting] wives on the wharf). In the mid-1950s, the popular Japanese media singled out one of the women, Hashino Ise, turning her into a national icon. The song "Ganpeki no haha," which dramatically portrays Hashino's determination, was released in October 1954 and became an overnight hit ("Kono haha wa mada matteiru!" *Shūkan josei*, December 23, 1972, 41; " 'Ganpeki no haha' Hashino Ise san [75 sai] mukuwareta shūnen no kiroku," *Shūkan heibon*, July 10, 1975, 55).
34. The repatriation from China resumed in 1953, and in that year alone, 26,051 people returned to Japan. Between 1954 and 1958, an additional 6,506 people repatriated from China (Kōseishō shakai engo kyoku engo 50 nenshi henshū iinkai, *Engo 50 nenshi*, 46–49).
35. In a conversation with his co-worker, for example, Ichirō states, "I was not the only person who went to the war," and his wife later mentions his "detention" in China.
36. Okumura Waichi and Sakai Makoto, *Watashi wa "ari no heitai" datta: Chūgoku ni nokosareta Nihonhei* (Tokyo: Iwanami shoten, 2006), 105–7.
37. Koyabu Shigeyoshi, "Kokoro no kokyō—Maizuru—hikiage no kiroku," in *Hikiage shuki watashi no hikiage, jō*, ed. Maizuru hikiage kinenkan (Maizuru: Maizuru hikiage kinenkan, 1992), 257.
38. NHK, "Ryūyō sareta Nihonjin" shuzai han, *Ryūyō sareta Nihonjin: Watashitachi wa Chūgoku kenkoku o sasaeta* (Tokyo: NHK shuppan, 2003), 134.
39. Ruth Rogaski discusses the local reaction to the movement in Tianjin in "Nature, Annihilation, and Modernity: China's Korean War Germ–Warfare Experience Reconsidered," *Journal of Asian Studies* 61, no. 2 (2002): 387–91. This is a superb study that situates the Patriotic Hygiene Movement in the larger

context of modern Chinese history, though it does not explore possible connections with Japanese colonial hygienic practices.

40. Liu Wenbing, "Rekishi o utsusu hizunda kagami no yōni: 'Keimin eiga" ni miru Manshūkoku no hyōshō," in *Fumikoeru dokyumentarii*, ed. Kurosawa Kyoshi et al. Nihon eiga wa ikiteiru (Tokyo: Iwanami shoten, 2010), 7:134–37.

41. Gosho acknowledges that he consulted a color psychology specialist before directing *Yellow Crow*. Although he does not cite Asari, the film faithfully replicates Asari's theory (Gosho Heinosuke, *Waga seishun* [Tokyo: Ōzorasha, 1998], 96).

42. Asari Atsushi, "Shikisai to seikaku (muishiki no gengo)," *Color*, June 1953, 9.

43. Another likely source is an essay by Kubo Sadajirō and his collaborators, which extends Asari's claim by adding the following point: "What should be noted [in the example in the text] is that the color yellow is smudged [with other colors]. When yellow is clear, the father's love is not absent" ("Chichioya no ketsujo matawa fuzai," in *Shikisai no shinri: kodomono eno shinriteki kiroku*, ed. Kubo Sadajirō et al. [Tokyo: Dai Nihon shuppan, 1956], 18). As figure 1.3 demonstrates, yellow is not smudged with other colors. By embracing the opinion of Kubota and his collaborators, *Yellow Crow* seems to suggest that the problem is not the lack of Ichirō's love for his son but his inability to express it.

44. Tamura Hideo, "Gakusei no eigashitsu: Kiiroi karasu," *Kōkō jidai*, March 1957, 211.

45. The crow was traditionally regarded as a divine messenger in Japan, but the contrary negative image has also been embraced (Fukuda Ajio et al., *Nihon minzoku dai-jiten* [Tokyo: Yoshikawa kōbunkan, 1999], 419–20).

46. The song was first published in *Kin no fune* in 1921 (lyrics, Noguchi Ujō; music, Moto'ori Nagao).

47. Just as the scene of the father–son reconciliation ends, the sound of a nearby temple bell announces that a new year has arrived, marking the new phase of their relationship.

48. *Shūkan asahi*, ed., *Sengo nedan shi nenpyō* (Tokyo: Asahi shinbun shuppan, 1995), 61.

49. The film *Green Light to Joy* (*Chichiko gusa*, directed by Maruyama Seiji, 1967) is a latter-day reincarnation of the story, in which the man who has belatedly been repatriated finally finds a connection with postwar society through money. After years of internment in Siberia, Hirai Yoshitarō (Atsumi Kiyoshi) returns only to find that his wife has married his brother. He leaves his home brokenhearted and moves around from one construction site to another. One day, he becomes acquainted with Nishimura Shigeru (Ishidate Tetsuo), a young man who is supporting himself while preparing for college entrance examinations. Hirai then decides to financially support Nishimura so that he can concentrate on his studies. This is a beautiful, sentimental story with a happy ending: Nishimura passes the entrance examination for what appears to be the University of Tokyo. It is noteworthy that the fictitious father–son relation that the two men create is mediated by money. This is a story in which an exchange of money is synonymous with an expression of love (Hirai refuses the money that

his father offers when he leaves home), a story suitable for a capitalist society with a rapidly growing economy.

50. Repatriated former servicemen continued to haunt the screens in the 1950s and even later. Dr. Serizawa in *Gojira* (directed by Honda Ishirō, 1954) is a man who was injured in the war and subsequently severed all his social ties with the postwar society. He sacrifices his life to prevent his secret weapon from proliferating and possibly to join (belatedly) the community of war dead. As if to seal off the wartime past once and for all, the television drama *I Want to Be a Shellfish* (*Watashi wa kai ni naritai*, 1958, remade as a film in 1959) tells the story of a man who returns to postwar Japan but eventually is executed for his alleged war crimes (it also was remade into a TV drama in 1994 and a feature film in 2008).

The 1960s saw few changes in the two contrasting ways in which veterans were represented on screen: they were either assimilated into or ousted from society in the end. On the screen, the status of former servicemen was reduced to an explanatory tool, with information included to explain their marginal status in postwar society rather than to invoke the traumatic memories of the war. *Legend of Showa Yakuza* (*Shōwa zankyōden*, directed by Saeki Kiyoshi, 1965) is a story of male bonding in the *yakuza* world between two war veterans who are unable to return fully to postwar society. It is clear that this film uses the frustrated figures of veterans to dramatize the final scene of violence in which one of them dies and the other is put behind bars. *Dear Venerable Emperor* (*Haikei tennō-heika sama*, directed by Nomura Yoshitarō, 1969) is another film from the same decade, in which a veteran disappears from postwar society. The protagonist (Atsumi Kiyoshi) is an illiterate soldier who admires the emperor and loves his life in the military (which teaches him how to read and write). Several years after the war's end, he is about to marry a war widow. But right before their wedding, he is run over by a truck and dies.

2. THE STORY OF A MAN WHO WAS NOT ALLOWED TO COME HOME

1. According to his first wife (she is quoted in a newsweekly article that was probably based on an interview with her), Gomikawa returned to her and their children in Japan in October 1947 ("Bestoseraa no kakureta jōken," *Shūkan shinchō*, August 18, 1958, 35). *Asahi jinbutsu jiten* (Tokyo: Asahi shinbunsha, 1990) and *Gendai jinmei jōhō jiten* (Tokyo: Heibonsha, 1990) give 1948 as the year of his return. It is not clear from what source they derive this information. A weekly magazine article that appeared right after Gomikawa completed *Ningen no jōken* states that he returned to Japan in late 1947. The information in that article seems to be based on an interview with Gomikawa ("Kakureta besutoseraa 'Ningen no jōken,'" *Shūkan asahi*, February 16, 1958, 8).

2. "Kaji no ikikata to shi: Gomikawa Ningen no jōken to sono dokusha," *Nihon dokusho shinbun*, June 16, 1958, 1.

3. "Kakureta besutoseraa 'Ningen no jōken,'" 8.

4. Sawachi Hisae and Sataka Makoto, *Sedai o koete kataritsugitai sensō bungaku* (Tokyo: Iwanami shoten, 2009), 16.

5. Murakami Hyōe, "*Ningen no jōken* ron: jinseiteki kandō to bungakuteki kandō to," *Shin Nihon bungaku*, June 1958, 158.

6. "Kakureta besutoseraa 'Ningen no jōken,'" 8–9.

7. Ōgiya Shōzō, "Gendai besutoseraa monogatari 46: Gomikawa Junpei *Ningen no jōken*," *Asahi jaanaru*, September 4, 1996, 37.

8. Ibid., 36. At the gathering held on June 10, 1958, to celebrate *Ningen no jōken*'s success, the publisher, San'ichi shobō, announced that the total sales of the six volumes had reached 1,423,500 (*Nihon dokusho shinbun*, June 16, 1958). More recently, *Mainichi shinbun*, in an interview with Gomikawa's daughter, Kurita Ikuko, reported that the hexalogy sold more than 13 million copies in total (*Mainichi shinbun*, July 5, 2005). Takemura Hajime, an editor at San'ichi shobō who decided to publish *The Human Condition*, gave a much higher and more reliable sales figure: "The total sales reached twenty million copies by late 1979" (quoted in Shiozawa Minoru, "Shiozawa Minobu no 'Bestuoseraa no haikei' yomigaetta *Ningen no jōken*," *Gekkan BOSS*, November 2011, 115).

9. "Gomikawa-ke honjitsu tabō: wadai no 'Ningen no jōken' sonogo," *Shūkan asahi*, March 16, 1958, 113.

10. Tachibana Seitarō, *Ningen no jōken*, 4 vols. (Tokyo: Horupu shuppan, 1983); Ishinomori Shōtarō, *Ningen no jōken*, 4 vols. (Tokyo: Bukkusu Tokyo, 1998).

11. Gomikawa Junpei, "Waga shōsetsu: *Ningen no jōken*," *Asahi shinbun*, December 25, 1961, 12th ed., 6.

12. Usui Yoshimi, "Tsuini deta sensō bungaku: *Ningen no jōken* o yonde," *Shūkan asahi*, February 16, 1958, 9.

13. Ibid.

14. "Kakureta besutoseraa 'Ningen no jōken,'" 8.

15. Kishi Nobuhito, *Keizai hakusho monogatari* (Tokyo: Bungei shunjū, 1999), 62–71. The entire text of 1956 *Keizai hakusho* (the official title is *Nenji keizai hōkoku*) is available through the Cabinet Office, Government of Japan home page, http://www5.cao.go.jp/keizai3/keizaiwp/index.html.

16. The reparation agreement stipulated that "Japan shall supply the Union of Burma by way of reparations with the services of Japanese people and the products of Japan" the annual value of $20 million (¥7.2 billion) for the next ten years. Japan would also annually contribute additional $5 million (¥1.8 billion) worth of services and products toward the two nations' joint enterprise for the same period. See Agreement for Reparations and Economic Co-operation Between Japan and the Union of Burma, signed at Rangoon, November 5, 1954. The full text of the bilateral agreements cited in this chapter is available at the Ministry of Foreign Affairs of Japan home page, http://www3.mofa.go.jp/mofaj/gaiko/treaty/search2.php?pID=15.

17. Some detainees actually remained in the Soviet Union for much longer periods and for various reasons. For example, Hachiya Yasaburō, who had worked at a weapons factory in North Korea, was sentenced to ten years of imprisonment

for his alleged espionage activities. Although he earned probation and lived outside the prison after 1953, he was not allowed to return to Japan. Periodic interrogation and surveillance by the Soviet authority (KGB) continued, and he was not allowed to leave the city in which he resided. Because he then became a Soviet citizen to improve his living conditions, he gave up the possibility of returning to Japan in the near future. Hachiya finally returned to Japan in 1997 (Sakamoto Tatsuhiko, *Shiberia ryoshū hanseiki: minkanjin Hachiya Yasaburō no kiroku* [Tokyo: Kōbunsha, 1998]).

18. Protocol Between the Government of Japan and the Government of the Kingdom of the Netherlands Relating to Settlement of the Problem Concerning Certain Types of Private Claims of Netherlands Nationals, signed at Tokyo, March 13, 1956; Utsumi Aiko, *Sengo hoshō kara kangaeru Nihon to Ajia* (Tokyo: Yamakawa shuppansha, 2002), 31–34.

19. According to the terms of the accord, the Japanese government agreed to supply the Philippines with a total of $55 million (¥198 billion) in the form of services and goods over the next twenty years (Reparation Agreement Between Japan and the Republic of the Philippines, signed at the city of Manila, May 9, 1956). An additional $250 million (¥90 billion) was to be made available as a loan to the Philippines during the same period (Hayashi Risuke, "Firipin baishō," in *Nihon no sengo baishō: Ajia kyōryoku no shuppatsu*, ed. Nagano Shin'ichirō and Kondō Masaomi [Tokyo: Keisō shobō, 1999], 69–70). The Japanese government signed a peace treaty and a reparation agreement with the Indonesian government in January 1958. The total reparation was set at $223 million (¥80 billion), a level comparable to Japan's reparation to the Philippines (Reparation Agreement Between Japan and the Republic of Indonesia, signed at Djakarta, January 20, 1958). Japan and Vietnam signed the reparation agreement in May 1959, a package of $39 million (¥14 billion) of services and products and $16.6 million (¥ 5.97 billion) of loans (Accord de réparations entre le Japon et la république du Vietnam, signed at Saigon in May 19, 1959; Shinonaga Nobutaka, "Betonamu baishō," in *Nihon no sengo baishō: Ajia kyōryoku no shuppatsu*, ed. Nagano Shin'ichirō and Kondō Masaomi [Tokyo: Keisō shobō, 1999], 96).

20. Furthermore, in 1958 *Ningen no jōken* was completed and became a national best seller in Japan, which the film *ALWAYS Sanchōme no yūhi* (directed by Yamazaki Takashi, 2005) relentlessly idealized as a place filled with optimism.

21. Gomikawa Junpei, "Genten to shiteno waga 'sensō to ningen,'" *Ushio*, August 1971, 192.

22. Gomikawa first entered the Tokyo School of Commerce (Tokyo shōka daigaku) to pursue higher education in Japan, but he could not motivate himself to study; he quit the school after a year and a half. Before enrolling in the Tokyo School of Foreign Studies, he spent two years in Tokyo working at odd jobs. Gomikawa was in the humanities section of the English department. During roughly the same period, Ishihara Yoshirō was also studying at the Tokyo School of Foreign Studies (in the commerce section of the German department, from 1934 to

1938). But it appears that the two never met while they were in school. I discuss Ishihara Yoshirō's belated return to Japan in chapter 4.

23. Gomikawa, "Genten to shiteno waga 'sensō to ningen,'" 193.

24. In 1941, the Xinminhui, the paramilitary organization that engaged in propaganda as well as military actions against the Communist forces in northern China, and the commander of the Japanese Area Army established the guidelines for deploying the "special laborers" as a workforce. The guidelines defined the special laborers as (1) those who are in the custody of the military or civilian police for suspected crimes; (2) those who are suspected of being connected to the "bandits" captured in the counterbandit operations; (3) those who were captured in the counterbandit operations; and (4) those who engage in antisocial activities (Zhongyang danganguan et al., eds., *Riben diguo zhui qinhua dangan ziliao xuanbian: dongbei jingji lüedao* [Beijing: Zhonghua shuju chuban, 1991], 936).

25. "Manshū ni atta Aushubittsu," *Shūkan shinchō*, August 20, 1956.

26. Decades later, Gomikawa wrote about the final days of his escape to Anshan in one of the short stories in *Senki shōsetsu-shū* (Tokyo: Bungei shunjū, 1993), 195–205.

27. The work was later published as *Rekishi no jikken* (Tokyo: Chūōkōron, 1959).

28. Sawachi and Satake, *Sedai o koete kataritsugitai sensō bungaku*, 15. Even those who returned from the PRC after the end of the U.S. Occupation endured similar treatment. For example, in September 1954 after the former Japanese soldier Okumura Kazuichi finally returned to Japan from the PRC (he joined the Nationalist army after Japan's defeat and was captured by the People's Liberation Army), he was kept under the security police's close watch. Many people also looked at him with suspicion (Okumura Kazuichi and Sakai Makoto, *Watashi wa "arino heitai" datta: Chūgoku ni nokosareta Nihonhei* [Tokyo: Iwanami shoten, 2006], 105–7).

29. Tsukase Susumu, *Manshūkoku: "minzoku kyōwa" no jitsuzō* (Tokyo: Yoshikawa kōbunkan, 1998), 169–71.

30. Gomikawa Junpei et al., "'15 nen sensō' no imi," *Rekishi hyōron*, January 1972, 13.

31. The lack of his sexual desire enhances the image of Wang as a wise man.

32. Gomikawa Junpei, "Seishin no gan," in *Watashi to sensō*, ed. Gomikawa Junpei, Murakami Ichirō, and Yamada Munemitsu (Tokyo: Shunjūsha, 1959), 45.

33. "Manshū ni atta Aushubittsu," 93. In the 1972 roundtable discussion, however, Gomikawa suggested that the execution scene more or less accurately describes what actually happened. He used very vague language to describe the scene: "Because of the trouble at the execution ground, I was taken to the military police and interrogated hard. When I returned to the mine, a conscription notice was waiting for me there" (Gomikawa et al., "'15 nen sensō' no imi," 14). The 1958 interview article provides more specific biographical information in contrast to the vagueness of his 1972 claim, suggesting that his earlier statement is closer to the actual event.

34. "Kakureta besutoseraa 'Ningen no jōken,'" 8.

35. Kaji even hits the mark with his eyes closed in a target practice (*GJC* 2:90–91).

36. Noma Hiroshi, *Zone of Emptiness* (*Shinkū chitai*, 1952), Yasuoka Shōtarō, *Flight* (*Tonsō*, 1957), and Ōoka Shōhei, *Fires on the Plain* (*Nobi*, 1952)

37. The length of Japanese soldiers' service often carried more weight than their official rank. As Japan's undeclared war against China continued, many soldiers were forced to serve multiple years without rotating out. Senior soldiers' abuse in the army units has been widely written about. See Ichinose Toshiya, *Kōgun heishi no nichijō seikatsu* (Tokyo: Kōdansha, 2009), 77–87; and Edward J. Drea, *In the Service of the Emperor: Essays on the Imperial Japanese Army* (Lincoln: University of Nebraska Press, 1998), 82–87.

38. There was a famous defection case in 1938 involving the actress Okada Yoshiko and the theater director Sugimoto Ryōkichi, and the people in Japan did not learn for many years what actually happened to them in the Soviet Union. The Soviet authorities immediately suspected the two to be spies and subjected them to severe interrogation. Unable to withstand the interrogation, Okada confessed that they had entered the country to engage in espionage activities, but Sugimoto denied the charges. On the basis of Okada's confession, Sugimoto was executed in 1939, and Okada received a ten-year prison term (Konno Tsutomu, "Okada Yoshiko no ushinawareta 10 nen," *Chūōkōron*, December 1994, 323–41; Hirasawa Yoshihiro, *Ekkyō: Okada Yoshiko, Sugimoto Ryōkichi no dabisubitaanya* [Sapporo: Hokkaidō shinbunsha, 2000], 8–24).

39. This is the term used to designate the former Japanese soldiers who actively led the democratization movement in the Siberian camps. At this early stage of detention, however, the movement had not been organized yet. By using this term, Gomikawa is implying that Kirihara had ingratiated himself with the camp leader by appealing to his ideological correctness.

40. Kasahara Kazuo, *Hametsu no bigaku: yakuza eiga eno rekuiemu* (Tokyo: Tōgensha, 1997), 161–62.

41. Gomikawa Junpei and Aratama Michiyo, "Katsumokushite machimashō," *Chūōkōron*, May 1959, 158–59.

42. "Kakureta besutoseraa 'Ningen no jōken,'" 8.

43. Usui, "Tsuini deta sensō bungaku," 9.

44. Hori Hidehiko, "Seibugeki *Ningen no jōken*," *Shinchō*, July 1958, 68–69.

45. Even though many Japanese women were raped by Soviet soldiers, Michiko escaped a similar fate just by luck (*GJZ* 3:234–36). When three men impersonating the security officers abduct a woman who lives in her dormitory, Michiko remains safe inside (*GJZ* 3:323–24). She also earns a small cut of the money she gets from selling kimono on the street for wealthy Japanese residents. In the scene in which a Chinese man tries to swindle her kimono from her, a Soviet army officer forcefully intervenes to protect her (*GJZ* 3:332–34).

46. Kaji and Michiko's union embodies the postwar attitude that privileged love between individuals as a source of happiness, an attitude that rapidly spread in postwar Japan, contributing to the steady increase in love marriages (as opposed to arranged marriages) in the 1950s. In November 1958, the engagement between the imperial prince Akihito and Shōda Michiko (the outcome of their romance) was announced, and the subsequent media and popular frenzy

about the imperial prince-to-be further popularized the idea of love as the *sine qua non* for marriage. The two Michikos seem to have shared more than just their names (Ishida Ayuu, *Micchii būmu* [Tokyo: Bungei shunjū, 2006], 55, 72–73).

47. Gomikawa, "Waga shōsetsu," 6.

48. Ibid.

49. In discussing *Ningen no jōken*, Ōgiya Shōzō cites a popular reaction: "*Ningen no jōken* is no more than a Western. Kaji is a Superman. There is no way such a man exists" ("Gendai bestoseraa monogatari 46: Gomikawa Junpei *Ningen no jōken*." *Asahi jaanaru*, September 4, 1996, 38).

50. The Ninjin Club was established by three leading actresses: Kishi Keiko (b. 1932), Kuga Yoshiko (b. 1931), and Arima Ineko (b. 1932).

51. Kasuga Taichi, *Nakadai Tatsuya ga kataru Nihon eiga ōgonjidai* (Kyoto: PHP kenkyūjo, 2013), 44.

52. Ibid.

53. Ibid., 49.

54. Gomikawa was not pleased with the Chinese that the Japanese actors and actresses spoke in *Ningen no jōken*. Later when another novel by him, *Sensō to ningen*, was being made into a film, he asked the director, Yamamoto Satsuo, not to use the Chinese language at all, but his request was disregarded (Gomikawa et al., " '15 nen sensō' no imi," 6).

55. For example, Kitabayashi Tanie played a Burmese peddler in *Burmese Harp* (*Biruma no tategoto*, 1956) and a Korean woman in *Second Big Brother* (*Ni'anchan*, 1959).

56. One of the three executed Chinese laborers was her lover. She calls Kaji "*riben guizi*"(Japanese devil) and throws rocks at him for failing to save her lover.

57. Gomikawa et al., " '15 nen sensō' no imi," 3. At the time the symposium was held, Gomikawa was still working on *War and Humanity* (thirteen out of the total eighteen volumes had been published). The final and third part of the film was in production.

58. The setting of Gomikawa's stories steadily moves toward Japan. In *Contract with Freedom* (*Jiyū tono keiyaku*, 6 vols. [Tokyo: San'ichi shobō, 1958–1960]), the protagonist, Sengoku Kensuke, returns to Japan, even though he is not ready to give up his ties to Manchuria, and later, during the civil war, he attempts to return to China to reestablish his ties. But in the end, he is unable to leave postwar Japan.

3. LONGING FOR HOME

1. Neither the Soviet Union nor the succeeding Russian government has provided accurate statistics as to the number of people detained. Attempts to reach an accurate figure range from 540,000 to 1 million. As the historian Tomita Takeshi points out, the numbers themselves have been subject to political dynamics. For example, in October 1947, the U.S. Occupation authority forced

the Japanese government to use its extremely high estimate (469,059) for the number of Japanese soldiers under Soviet custody at that point in order to drum up anti-Soviet feelings in Japan. By contrast, the Soviet Union claimed a much lower number (95,000). The total number of the POWs was 639,776 (609,448 Japanese), and 62,068 POWs (61,855 Japanese) had died, according to the Soviet Ministry of Internal Affairs' 1956 data (Tomita Takeshi, *Shiberia yokuryūsha tachi no sengo* [Tokyo: Jinbun shoin, 2013], 66). These may be the most accurate Soviet statistics covering the Soviet territories and Mongolia. The other areas that the Soviet Union temporarily controlled—the Liaodong Peninsula and North Korea, as well as its newly acquired territories, the Sakhalin and Kuril Islands—are excluded from the tally. Victor Karpov estimates that 87,097 additional Japanese were detained in the Liaodong Peninsula and North Korea, of whom at least 31,383 died (*Sutaarin no horyotachi: Soren kimitsu shiryō ga kataru zenyō* [Tokyo: Hokkaidō shinbunsha, 2001], 21–24, 83). The numbers I cite—700,000 to 800,000 internees and at least 100,000 deaths—come from Abe Gunji, who analyzed various Japanese and Russian sources. His estimation includes the number of deaths that occurred during the initial transportation (*Shiberia kyōseiyokuryū no jittai: Nisso ryōkoku shiryō karano kenshō* [Tokyo: Sairyūsha, 2005], 148–53).

2. Some returnees (particularly members of Zenkoku kyōsei yokuryūsha kyōkai [National Association for Forced Detainees]), in order to dissociate themselves from the negative associations with the designation in Japan, insist that they were not prisoners of war. In this work, I use the terms "POWs," "detainees," and "internees" interchangeably to designate those who were in Soviet custody, following these terms' historical uses: *horyo* and *furyo* (prisoners of war) have been commonly used in postwar Japan to designate both Soviet POWs and POWs in the custody of other Allied powers.

3. This number also comes from Abe, *Shiberia kyōseiyokuryū no jittai*, 52.

4. The dearth of cinematic representations of returnees from Siberian camps contrasts with the numerous portrayals of former soldiers who returned from other regions. Film critic Satō Tadao dismisses these two films directed by Watanabe Kunio simply as "anti-Communist" films that are a "mouthpiece" for Shin-Tōhō Studios' nationalistic ideology. Satō is more concerned about the director's and the studio's politics than the quality of work that they produced (*Nihon eigashi* [Tokyo: Iwanami shoten, 1995], 2:277). For a more detailed discussion of the latter, see Kawamoto Saburō, *Ima hitotabi no Nihon eiga* (Tokyo: Iwanami shoten, 1994), 36–70.

5. "Ikoku no oka" (1948), lyrics by Masuda Kōji (revised by Satake Takao), music by Yoshida Tadashi.

6. Murase Manabu, *Naze "oka" o utau kayōkyoku ga takusan tsukurarete kitanoka* (Tokyo: Shunjūsha, 2002), 5–6.

7. Ibid., 5.

8. Maizuru hikiage kinenkan, *Maizuru hikiage kinenkan zuroku* (Maizuru: Maizuru hikiage kinenkan, 2000), 38.

9. Fujita Masato wrote the original lyrics:

Mother is here, today one more time
To this wharf, today one more time
Knowing that her wish would never come true
The thought of what if
The thought of what if brought her here
Please call me, I pray
Tell me you are glad to see me here
Like traveling a thousand miles over mountains and the sea
How far!
How far!
To this mother and her son. (Quoted in Akita Ken, *Haha no uta serekushon*
[Tokyo: Fūjinsha, 2001], 118)

10. On June 28, 1950, the Diet passed the Former Military Port City Transformation Law (Kyū gunkō-shi tenkan-hō) with the stated purpose of transforming
the four former military port cities (Yokosuka, Kure, Sasebo, and Maizuru) into
"peace industry port cities" (http://law.e-gov.go.jp/htmldata/S25/S25HO220
.html, accessed November 6, 2015). It is safe to say that of these four municipalities, Maizuru is the only city that completely shed its image as a former
military port. Maizuru Port is now associated exclusively with repatriations
rather than with the wartime act of sending soldiers overseas.
11. Singer Futaba Yuriko, who revived the song in the 1970s, added the soliloquy
part, which explicitly connects the song with the Siberian internment. She also
sang the song in *enka* style with a heavy dose of sentimentality.
12. Frank Biess, "Survivors of Totalitarianism: Returning POWs and the Reconstruction of Masculine Citizenship in West Germany, 1945–1955," in *The Miracle Years: A Cultural History of West Germany, 1949–1968*, ed. Hanna Schissler
(Princeton, N.J.: Princeton University Press, 2001), 63–64.
13. Frank Biess, "Pioneers of a New Germany: Rethinking POWs from the Soviet
Union and the Making of East German Citizens, 1945–1950," *Central European
History* 32, no. 2 (1999): 145.
14. For example, on July 4, 1949, at Kyoto Station, some Communist Party members and unionists welcoming the Soviet POWs brought home on the repatriation ship *Eitoku-maru* clashed with the police because of the police's efforts to
separate them from the returnees. As a result, two men from the welcoming
group were arrested for obstruction of police duties. Then 1,700 of the returnees refused to take the special trains prepared for them and participated instead
in a spontaneous "people's meeting" that demanded the immediate release of
the arrested men. About 200 of the returnees joined the unionists in the subsequent rally, in which the latter group clashed with a 1,000-member police force,
leading to some 10 additional arrests ("1,700 no hikiagesha jōsha o kotowaru,"
Asahi shinbun, July 5, 1949, 7th ed., 2).
15. At Ueno Station, many returnees ignored the official welcoming party and
instead participated in a welcoming event that the Japanese Communist Party
had spontaneously organized (*Asahi shinbun*, July 3, 1949, 6th ed., 3).

16. The *Asahi shinbun*'s "Tensei jingo" column (July 4, 1949, 6th ed., 1) describes the scene at the Ueno Station on July 2, 1949, as follows:

On the platform stood elementary students with the rising-sun flag in their hands. The returnees [who returned on the *Eitoku maru*] did not even look at the flowers offered by the girls. The few who accepted them suddenly threw them down to the ground. At the boys' welcoming cries of banzai, they yelled, "Too late for banzai. You should be singing labor songs."

17. According to the *Jiji shinpō*, the Shadan-hōjin yoron chōsa kenkyūjo surveyed 438 men who returned to the Tokyo metropolitan region out of the first group that repatriated to Japan in 1949. Although the paper does not specify the group's identity, it appears to be the men who returned home on the *Takasago maru* in June of that year. The survey was conducted in late August 1949. In the section titled "About the Communist Party" are the following responses: Glad that I joined (14.8%), Left it (14.8%), Want to leave it (7.4%), Thinking about [leaving it] (51.9%), No response (11.1%). At this point, only 44.2 percent of them had found a job (*Jiji shinpō*, September 9, 1949, D ed., 2).

18. He wrote the account in the early 1980s but did not specify when he tried to recover his poems.

19. Nakahara Toshio, "Watashi no Shiberia monogatari," in *HT* 4:38.

20. Kōseishō shakai engokyoku engo 50 nenshi henshū iinkai, ed., *Engo 50 nenshi* (Tokyo: Gyōsei, 1997), 11.

21. Shimada Toshihiko, *Kantō gun* (Tokyo: Chūōkōron,1965), 186.

22. Ishinomori Takeo, *Saihate no nagareboshi* (Tokyo: Kindai bungeisha, 1996), 10.

23. Ogawa Mamoru, who served in the border defense unit, recalls reapplying ink to the logs every time it rained (*Watashi no Shiberia monogatari* [Tokyo: Kōjinsha, 2011], 262).

24. As a unit leader, Katō Kyūzō was training the new recruits for suicide missions at the Korea–Soviet border area in July 1945. When a division commander advised them not to push themselves too hard, Katō could not comprehend the commander's words and only later came to realize that the commander knew about Japan's imminent surrender (*Shiberia ki* [Tokyo: Ushio shuppansha, 1980], 12).

25. Kōseishō shakai engokyoku engo 50 nenshi henshū iinkai, ed., *Engo 50 nenshi*, 10–11. Another 1,809,000 Japanese civilians were living in those areas (Abe, *Shiberia kyōseiyokuryū no jittai*, 49–50).

26. Abe, *Shiberia kyōseiyokuryū no jittai*, 232–33.

27. Takeda Masanao, who was interned in the Komsomolsk region, estimates that 5,000 women were interned, though he does not specify the source of his information (*Kokkan Shiberia yokuryūki* [Tokyo: Kōjinsha, 2001], 66).

28. Some navy unit members were among the Soviet detainees (Takahashi Daizō et al., "Jo ni kaete," in *HT* 2:vi).

29. Futaba Kaname, *Shiberia ni iru Nihonjin horyo no jitsujō* (Denver: Saikensha, 1948), 101–2. Although their original Japanese owners were able to retain some items, despite the repeated plundering, these also soon disappeared from the camps, being used to barter for food with the local residents or Soviet soldiers (104).

30. Fukui Hideo, *Seishun no nagai michi* (Tokyo: Kyōikushiryō shuppankai, 1995), 174.

31. Kawamura Katsumi, *Kuroi tora: Nihongami zukuri ichidai-ki* (Osaka: Fōramu A, 1996), 111–12.

32. Futaba Kaname's unit departed from Mudanjiang Station on a freight train on September 16, 1945, without being informed of the final destination. When they realized that the train was heading north, one of the POWs insisted, probably to shake off his own anxiety, "There is no way the rails always point south. There are some spots where we have to go north [to eventually head south]." In the end, Futaba and the other men arrived at a campsite about 120 miles west of Khabarovsk on September 22. They were moved to another camp located farther west on October 16 (Futaba Kaname, *Shiberia-horyo no shuki* [Tokyo: Ōzorasha, 1947], 50).

33. Ōtsuka Shigeru, *Damoi no michi wa tōkatta* (Tokyo: Kokusho kankōkai, 1995), 23–24; Hokari Kashio, *Shiberia furyoki: ichi heishi no kakoku naru yokuryūtaiken* (Tokyo: Kōjinsha, 2009), 65–66.

34. The eleven years that Maeno Shigeru spent in the Soviet penitentiary system from 1945 until 1956 gave him the opportunity to talk to prisoners who had lived in various labor camps. He emphasizes how much the conditions varied from camp to camp. The prisoners particularly feared the camps in the Kolyma, Nolinsk, and Vorkuta regions and the Ural Mountains, as the worst places (Maeno Shigeru, *Ikeru shikabane* [Tokyo: Shunjūsha, 1961], 3:73).

35. Kazuki Yasuo, *Watashi no Shiberia* (Tokyo: Bungei shunjū, 1970), 107.

36. Futaba Kaname, who ended up in a camp in Birobidzhan in the Amur River region, says that the food rations began to improve around March 1946. Because of inadequate transportation, his labor battalion did not receive food supplies until the beginning of December 1945. Hence, they were forced to subsist on what they arrived with—twenty days' worth of provisions—for forty days (Futaba, *Shiberia ni iru Nihonjin horyo no jitsujō*, 65–67).

37. Kusanagi Taiji, "Watashi no Shiberia-ki, shō," in *HT* 7:114.

38. With the help of a member of the Soviet Communist Party, Suzuki Shōzō's battalion successfully purged the camp supervisor who had embezzled their food supplies. Consequently, their food supply was restored to its official level, and the portion that they missed for about two and half months was added to their rations (Suzuki Shōzō, *"Raageru" no nakano seishun* [Tokyo: Akashi shoten, 1999], 30–36).

39. Watanabe Chiguto, *Aru igakuto no seishun* (Fukuoka: Kaichōsha, 1994), 202–3.

40. Nakamaki Yasuhiro, *Toraware no seishun: Mōhitotsu no Shiberia yokuryūki* (Tokyo: Chōbunsha, 1991), 13–14.

41. Hirose Saburō reports that two of his fellow detainees in the Tayshet region died from eating a poisonous plant, which they misidentified as Japanese parsley ("Jikyū jisoku ni taete," in *HT* 7:144).

42. They roasted pine cones and collected nuts (Nakane Hitoshi, "Watashi no yokuryū reki," in *HT* 4:215).

43. Kitahara Shigee claims that the swellings on his work unit members' faces and feet subsided once they started chewing pine needles (seventy per day). The unit was interned in the Raychikhinsk region. But the pine needles had few positive effects on their bodies, which by the second winter had been significantly weakened (Kitahara Shigee, *Sakufū no nakano furyo: Shiberia yokuryū-seikatsu no kiroku* [Tokyo: Kenkōsha, 1971], 93, 189). While interned in Chuguyevka region, about seventy miles northeast of Vladivostok, in an effort to cure his scurvy, Nishida Masuo chewed up pine needles until his stools turned green. The pine needles had no noticeable effects on his scurvy, but they caused serious constipation (Nishida Masuo, "Dōro sagyō taiin no kiroku," in *HT* 2:328).

44. Itō Eiji, who was interned on Popova Island southwest of Vladivostok, recalls supplementing vitamins in this way ("Watashi no taiken keika," in *HT* 2:238).

45. Saitō Kunio, *Shiberia yokuryūhei yomoyama monogatari* (Tokyo: Kōjinsha, 2006), 149.

46. However, Seki Kiyoto recalls that cat meat was not edible because of the foam it produced when cooked (*Tsuioku no hibi* [Tokyo: Bungeisha, 2001], 45–46). Meanwhile, Futaba Kaname writes that "I will never forget the delicious taste of cat meat" (*Shiberia horyo no shuki*, 63). Kazuki Yasuo also mentions that all the cats disappeared from his camp (*Watashi no Shiberia*, 133).

47. Sakamoto Yaichi, "Karaganda no tankō chiku de," in *HT* 5:123.

48. Watanabe Tokio, *Saihate no Raageru nite: Shiberia yokuryū chinkon no hi* (Kōfu: Yamanashi furusato bunko, 2008), 148.

49. Kariyuki Seiji, "Kūfuku no akumu," in *Namida ni urumu Maizurukō*, ed. Sōkagakkai hansen seinenbu hansen shuppan iinkai (Tokyo: Daisanbunmei sha, 1979). 95.

50. Kariyuki was shocked to learn that a Manchurian unit that joined his labor camp had eaten human flesh as well, but he does not offer any specific information (ibid., 95).

51. Hiranuma Gyokutarō, "30 dai to iu jinsei wa nai," in *Namida ni urumu Maizurukō*, 37. Other types of cannibalism were recorded as well. Katō Kyūzō, who was interned in the Bratsk region, reports a gruesome incident in which one of three escapees was killed and eaten by the other two (*Shiberia ki*, 188–202). Shiga Kiyoshige reports a case in which a Japanese solder subsisted on a dead fellow soldier's flesh before being captured by the Red Army (Shiga Kiyoshige et al., *Aa Hairaru, Daihachi kokkyō shubitai tenmatsuki* [Tokyo: Kōjinsha, 1992], 76).

52. Murakami Yasuhiko, "Watashi no seishun," in *Hikiage shuki: watashi no hikiage, jō*, ed. Maizuru hikiage kinenkan (Maizuru: Maizuru hikiage kinenkan, 1992), 100.

53. There are numerous accounts about this examination method. For example, see Kazuki, *Watashi no Shiberia*, 136; Morimoto Yoshio, *Shiberia horyoki: shi to zetsubō karano kikan* (Tokyo: Shunjūsha, 2001), 89; Katō Nobutada, *Watashi no Shiberia nōto* (Fujisawa: Takeda shuppan, 2007), 105; Watanabe, *Saihate no Raageru nite*, 133; Odaka Ushimatsu, *Ubawareshi waga seishun* (Tokyo: Kōyō shuppansha, 2008), 72; and Nagaoka Keiji, "300 pon no bohyō o nokoshite," in *HT* 7:282–83.

54. Karpov, *Sutaarin no horyotachi*, 107.

55. Often those who exerted themselves to receive extra food ended up being worn out (Abe, *Shiberia kyōseiyokuryū no jittai*, 220, 273).

56. Watanabe, *Saihate no Raageru nite*, 127–28.

57. Most of the accounts state that −40°F as the cutoff, as in, for example, ibid., 137. But Maeno Shigeru reports that −22°F was the limit for convicted criminals' outdoor work (*Ikeru shikabane* [Tokyo: Shunjūsha, 1961], 2:118). Each local authority was supposedly making the decision, taking into account that the Japanese internees were not used to working in extremely low temperatures. In reality, however, the camp directors made the decision for their facilities (Nagaze Ryōji, *Shiberia yokuryū zenshi* [Tokyo: Hara shobō, 2013], 240).

58. Hokari, *Shiberia furyoki*, 128. Tsutsumi Kizaburō, who led a work unit in the vicinity of Suchan (modern-day Partizansk), sought the expertise of an experienced member when they were assigned to lumbering. They cleared the snow about 6.5 feet from the tree that they were felling to facilitate their escape, but such cautionary steps were rarely taken to protect the detainees (Tsutsumi Kizaburō, "Shiberia yokuryū seikatsu," in *HT* 2:125–26).

59. Maeno, *Ikeru shikabane*, 3:111.

60. Ishihara, *Ishihara Yoshirō zenshū*, 2:21.

61. Mizutani Eiji, *Akai tōdo* (Tokyo: Hara shobō, 1969), 237.

62. Ibid., 238.

63. Watanabe, *Saihate no Raageru nite*, 33, 45–46, 115.

64. Abe Yoshikuni, "Watashi mo keihai datta: 3 nenkan kunan no yokuryū," in *Shiberia keihai: Soren yokuryū no kōishō*, ed. Yamamoto Yasuo (Tokyo: Shiberia keihai zenkoku renrakukai, 1983), 202.

65. The medical doctor Nawata Senrō is credited with first discovering the cases of silicosis among former Siberian detainees (Yamamoto, *Shiberia keihai*, 32–33).

66. Nawata Senrō reports that of the 130 cases of "Siberian" silicosis that he tracked, 76 of them (58.5%) were initially misdiagnosed with tuberculosis (Matsufuji Hajime and Nawata Senrō, *Sengo Soren de keihai ni kakatta Nihonjin furyotachi* [Tokyo: Nihon tosho kankōkai, 1997], 36–37).

67. Seno Osamu, *Shiberia Yokuryūki* (Tokyo: Kōyūsha, 1947), 19–20; Tajima Kyōji, *Shiberia no akumu* (Tokyo: Tokyo keizai, 1995), 124–25; Suzuki, *"Raageru" no nakano seishun*, 28; Saitō, *Shiberia yokuryūhei yomoyama monogatari*, 138.

68. Karpov, *Sutaarin no horyotachi*, 105.

69. Hokari, *Shiberia furyoki*, 79–84.

70. Nomura Shōtarō, "Watashi no yokuryū taikenki," in *HT* 4:10.

71. Saitō Kunio, who spent the first eighteen months of internment at a camp in the Irkutsk district, reports that two runaways were brought back to the camp and not punished (*Shiberia yokuryūhei yomoyama monogatari*, 37–40).

72. Kawamura, *Kuroi kami*, 133–34.

73. Hiranuma, "30 dai to iu jinsei wa nai," 38–39.

74. Takeda, *Kokkan Shiberia yokuryūki*, 175–76.

75. Tanaka Mikio, "Manga: 92 km Raageru no seikatsu," in *HT* 7:82–85.

76. Nakamaki, *Toraware no seishun*, 170–276.

77. Hasegawa Shirō, *Shiberia monogatari* (Tokyo: Kōdansha, 1991).

78. Andrew Barshay points out that the timing of their repatriations affected how they remembered the internment. The early returnees remember the dire shortage of food and harsh environment most vividly, but the material conditions steadily improved after the first winter. Those who returned to Japan in the late 1940s tended to have more traumatic memories of the so-called democratic movements (*minshu undō*) and the associated ideological struggles among the Japanese internees, whereas the memories of those men who returned to Japan in the 1950s were overshadowed by their longer and harsher treatment for the crimes they were accused of committing (Andrew Barshay, *The Gods Left First: The Captivity and Repatriation of Japanese POWs in Northeast Asia, 1945–1956* [Berkeley: University of California Press, 2013], 42–44).

79. Hiranuma, "30 dai to iu jinsei wa nai," 43.

80. Ōtsuka, *Damoi no michi wa tōkatta*, 255,

81. Ishinomori, *Saihate no nagareboshi*, 111.

82. Kamei Tsutomu, *Shiberia yokuryūsha to izoku wa ima* (Kyoto: Kamogawa shuppan, 1992), 176.

83. Takasugi Ichirō, *Kyokkō no kageni* (Tokyo: Iwanami shoten, 1991), 138.

84. Yokota Shōhei, *Watashi wa gyokusai shinakatta* (Tokyo: Chūōkōron shinsha, 1999), 448.

85. "Guamutō senyūkai no 'hiirō Yokoi' o mirume," *Shūkan bunshun*, February 21, 1972, 138.

86. While interned in Tayshet, Yamashita Shizuo came across a Japanese POW who had been taken captive during the 1939 military clashes with the Soviet army over the Manchukuo–Soviet border. After serving his sentence, he was released from prison camp, but he did not even know about World War II (Yamashita Shizuo, *Shiberia yokuryū 1,450 nichi* [Tokyo: Dejipuro, 2007], 253–55). Watanabe Tokio also mentions meeting a former Japanese noncommissioned officer who was taken prisoner during the Nomonhan incident and subsequently naturalized in the Soviet Union (*Saihate no shūyōjo nite*, 176). According to Shirai Hisaya, about 500 of the Japanese soldiers who became POWs in the Nomonhan incident subsequently chose to remain in the Soviet Union rather than face humiliation and dishonor in Japan (*Kenshō Shiberia yokuryū* [Tokyo: Heibonsha, 2010], 163).

87. Many Japanese who received prison sentences in the Russian courts have written about their experiences in the Stolypin cars as a kind of initiation for their long-term incarceration. See Mizutani, *Akai tōdo*, 72–76, 123–27; Takeya

Seikichi, "Shūjin ressha Sutoroipin," in *Nanae no teppi: Nihonjin horyo no Shiberia yokuryūki* (Tokyo: Nikkan rōdō tsūshinsha, 1958), 183–85; Nishio Yasuto, *Tōdo no uta: Shiberia yokuryū 8 nen, Tume de kaita kiroku* (Tokyo: Waseda shuppan, 1995), 144–48; and Maeno Shigeru, *Ikeru shikabane* (Tokyo: Shunjūsha, 1961), 1:266–85.

88. Ishihara, *Ishihara Yoshirō zenshū*, 2:56–59.

89. Uchimura Gōsuke, *Uchimura Gōsuke rongu intabyū*, ed. Suyama Ikurō (Tokyo: Keigadō shuppan, 2008), 279–86; Aleksandr I. Solzhenitsyn, *The Gulag Archipelago* (New York: Harper & Row, 1973), 559.

90. Mizutani, *Akai tōdo*, 163–73.

91. Ishihara, *Ishihara Yoshirō zenshū*, 2:207–8.

92. Kamei, *Shiberia yokurūsha to izoku wa ima*, 81–82.

93. Takahashi Daizō, "Kaisetsu: hangun, minshuka undo no keika," in *HT* 8:6–18.

94. Morisawa Hiroshi, "Daigo bunsho, tsurushi agerareru made," in *HT* 4:435.

95. Until 1947, the Soviet authority indirectly ruled the internees, maintaining the Kwantung army's chain of command in each camp.

96. For example, Takasugi Ichirō readily admits that he did not have enough courage to defend his friend who was accused of being "extremely reactionary" in a political meeting. In order to demonstrate genuine revolutionary spirit to his friend, he even joined, with self-loathing, the accusers who sang revolutionary songs (Takasugi, *Kyokkō no kageni*, 334–35).

97. Ochiai Harurō, *Shiberia no "Nihon shinbun"* (Tokyo: Ronsōsha, 1995), 229–33.

98. In the democratization movements, for example, such slogans as "landing on the enemy territory" and "landing on the Emperor's Islands" were often used to describe the impending repatriation (Takahashi, "Kikoku shūketsuchi Nahotoka no koe," 30; Tsutsumi, "Shiberia yokuryū seikatsu," 132).

99. Those who were in American POW camps in general had a much easier time. For example, in 1948, Ōoka Shōhei related his experience in a U.S. POW camp in Leyte (Philippines): "In fact, we were first-class POWs who enjoyed clean quarters and clothing, a ration of 2,700 calories a day, and ultimately even access to PX goods. Some of the men still refer to the camp as "paradise" and of the time they spent there as the best year of their lives" (*Taken Captive: A Japanese POW's Story*, trans. Wayne P. Lammers [New York: Wiley, 1996], 149).

100. Wakatsuki Yasuo, *Shiberia horyoshūyōjo* (Tokyo: Akashi shoten, 1999), 410–25.

101. "Hikiage mondai to han-So senden," *Akahata*, December 14, 1948, 1.

102. Wakatsuki, *Shiberia horyoshūyōjo*, 416–17.

103. Kuwabara Takeo, "Setsujitsuna kansō," *Chūōkōron*, January 1954, 108–9.

104. Ibid., 109.

105. Nakai Yoshiharu, "Kōshi no nakakara mita Soren," *Chūōkōron*, January 1954, 101.

106. Kuwabara, "Setsujitsuna kansō," 109.

107. Okamoto Sei'ichi, "Shuki o yonde," *Chūōkōron*, January 1954, 106–8.

108. Shimizu Ikutarō, *Shimizu Ikutarō chosakushū* (Tokyo: Kōdansha, 1993), 14:334.

109. Biess observed a similar psychological response in West Germany that cast returning German POWs as the embodiment of Soviet victory ("Survivors of Totalitarianism," 63).

110. William F. Nimmo, *Behind a Curtain of Silence: Japanese in Soviet Custody, 1945–1956* (New York: Greenwood Press, 1988), 105.

111. Fukui, *Seishun no nagai michi*, 311–12.

112. Ishihara, *Ishihara Yoshirō zenshū*, 2:168.

113. Shirai Hisaya discusses the difficult conditions in which many of the former Korean POWs found themselves after being released from Siberian prison camps and returning to South Korea. In South Korea, where anti-Communist sentiment was high, they were "ostracized" as soon as their Siberian experiences became known (Shirai, *Kenshō Shiberia yokuryū*, 240–43).

114. Takasugi, *Kyokkō no kageni*, 353.

115. For a more detailed discussion of this narrative, see Yoshikuni Igarashi, *Bodies of Memory: Narratives of War in Postwar Japanese Culture, 1945–1970* (Princeton, N.J.: Princeton University Press, 2000), chap. 1.

116. Sakai Saburō, *Sakai Saburō kūsen kiroku* (Tokyo: Kōdansha, 1992).

117. For example, the disastrous battles in Guadalcanal, northern India (the Imphal operation), and Iwo Jima occupied an important place in the dominant narrative of war that emerged in post-Occupation Japan.

118. As they headed toward their suicide mission, young officers on board the battleship *Yamato* already had expressed such a view. Lieutenant Usubuchi articulated the sentiment of the fellow officers in the wardroom:

> The side which makes no progress never wins. To lose and be brought to one's senses: that is the supreme path. Japan has paid too little attention to progress. We have been too finicky, too wedded to selfish ethics; we have forgotten true progress. How else can Japan be saved except by losing and coming to its senses? If Japan does not come to its senses now, when will it be saved? We will lead the way. We will die as harbingers of Japan's new life. That's where our real satisfaction lies, isn't it? (Quoted in Yoshida Mitsuru, *Senkan Yamato no saigo* in *"Senkan Yamato" to sengo*, ed. Hosaka Masayasu [Tokyo: Chikuma shobō, 2005], 56; and *Requiem for Battleship* Yamato, trans. Richard Minear [Annapolis, Md.: Naval Institute Press, 1999], 40)

119. For example, the founder of the Daiei supermarket chain, Nakauchi Isao (1922–2005), survived the warfare in the Philippines and later publicly admitted feeling survivor's guilt (Nakauchi Isao et al., "Onoda shōi to warera Taishō sedai no 30 nen," *Gendai*, May 1974, 113).

120. The popular film *Kumo nagaruru hateni* (directed by Ieki Miyoji, 1953) casts the whole story of kamikaze pilots in this binary, with the selfless nature of the young soldiers' sacrifice contrasted with the callous and self-serving navy leadership.

121. This renewed attention to the Soviet–Japan border conflicts is well demonstrated by Shinchōsha's—one of Japan's biggest publishing houses—decision to

publish a highly technical book on the battles on one of the Kuril Islands (Ōno Kaoru, *8 gatsu 17 nichi, Sorengun jōrikusu: saihate no yōshō Shumushu-tō kōbōki* [Tokyo: Shinchōsha, 2008]).

122. According to the 1960 survey conducted by the prime minister's office, when asked to list three countries that the respondents disliked, they gave the name of the Soviet Union most often (50.4%). South Korea (46.6%) and the People's Republic of China (39.3%) were a close second and third in this survey. But in the 1996 and 2001 surveys, the respondents answering the same question listed North Korea most often (56.7% and 61.6%, respectively). Russia was surpassed by large margins in both years (44.8% and 30.5%) (*Naikaku sōridaijin kanbō kōhōshitsu*, ed. Zenkoku yoron chōsa no genkyō, *Shōwa 35 nendo* [1960] [Tokyo: Sōrifu, 1961], 160–61; *Naikaku sōridaijin kanbō kōhōshitsu*, ed. Zenkoku yoron chōsa no genkyō, *Heisei 9 nendo* [1996] [Tokyo: Sōrifu, 1997], 546; *Naikaku sōridaijin kanbō kōhōshitsu*, ed. Zenkoku yoron chōsa no genkyō, *Heisei 14 nendo* [2001] [Tokyo: Sōrifu, 2002], 527).

123. The precise number of published Siberian internees' accounts is unknown. Although it is widely believed that about 2,000 have been published, that number was already in circulation in 1976 (Ono Takamichi, "Tōdo no yokuryūsha no omoi kanketsu," *Asahi shinbun*, August 5, 1998, 14th ed., 26).

124. On March 17, 2013, the National Diet Library's NDL-OPAC research system yielded 653 texts for the search conditions "Shiberia yokuryū," "since 1976," and "the National Diet Library and other public library holdings." Not all of them are original accounts by the survivors, but a large number of them do fall into this category. In addition, there might be other self-published books that are not housed at these libraries. The recent increased general interest in publishing one's life stories (a genre of writing called *jibunshi* [self-history]) has also encouraged this trend among the survivors of the Siberian camps. For details, see Gerald Figal, "How to *jibunshi*: Making and Marketing Self-Histories of Shōwa Among the Masses in Postwar Japan," *Journal of Asian Studies* 55, no. 4 (1996): 902–33.

125. For example, the topic of the Siberian internment is conspicuously missing from the journalistic photo collection covering the major events in the fifty years of the post–World War II period (Nishi'i Kazuo, ed., *Sengo 50 nen* [Tokyo: Mainichi shinbunsha, 1995]).

126. Nishiki Masa'aki, *Yumegaosan ni yoroshiku* (Tokyo: Bungei shunjū, 1999).

127. The movement led by the Zenkoku yokuryūsha hoshō kyōgikai (Committee for Seeking Compensation for Former Detainees) seeking official compensation for former Siberian detainees culminated in the compensation bill that passed the Diet on June 16, 2010. This movement should be seen as part of the returnees' effort to recover their political agency. Nagasawa Yoshio details the history of this movement in *Shiberia yokuryū to sengo Nihon: kikansha tachi no tatakai* (Tokyo: Yūshisha, 2011); and Kurihara Toshio discusses the issues not covered by this bill in *Shiberia yokuryū wa "kako" nanoka* (Tokyo: Iwanami shoten, 2011).

4. "NO DENUNCIATION"

1. Hataya Fumiyo, *Shiberia yokuryū towa nandatta no ka* (Tokyo: Iwanami shoten, 2009), 40.

2. For example, Anzai Hitoshi also saw similar relationships between Ishihara's poetry and prose (*Ishihara Yoshirō no shi no sekai* [Tokyo: Kyōbunkan, 1981], 113).

3. Tada Shigeharu, *Ishihara Yoshirō "Shōwa" no tabi* (Tokyo: Sakuhinsha, 2000), 10–11.

4. According to Nishio Yasuto, who was on the same train as Ishihara, "double-layered cages were built on either side of the train cars. Forty Japanese were packed in on one side, while thirty White Russians were on the other side" (*Tōdo no uta: Shiberia yokuryū 8 nen, Tsume de kaita kiroku* [Tokyo: Waseda shuppan, 1995], 15).

5. Ibid., 191, 198.

6. Victor Karpov, *Sutaarin no horyotachi*, trans. Nagase Ryōji (Sapporo: Hokkaidō shinbunsha, 2001), 320–21.

7. Ishihara had had an interest in Christianity since his youth and was baptized in 1938. Many Christian images appear in his poems as well, but it is difficult to discern how Christian teachings helped him deepen his thinking. The existing scholarship that examines Ishihara's relations with Christianity largely remains on the level of unearthing Christian images in his texts. See Anzai, *Ishihara Yoshirō no shi no sekai*; and Shibasaki Satoshi, *Ishihara Yoshirō: shibungaku no kakushin* (Tokyo: Shinkyō shuppansha, 2011). Anzai candidly admits the limitations of his methodology: "Ishihara's work, including 'The Acts of the Apostles' (Shito gyōden), is highly abstract and thus difficult to understand. . . . Even reading the Acts of the Apostles in the Bible would probably not help one's understanding of Ishihara's work" (*Ishihara Yoshirō no shi no sekai*, 121–22). These monographs demonstrate that Christianity does not offer a magic key to unlock Ishihara's challenging works. His thinking was far more complex than simply borrowing ready-made images. What should be explored is how various images (whether or not Christian) actually function in his texts.

8. Tsukimura Toshiyuki, "Ishihara Yoshirō: sono kiseki," *Gendaishi techō*, February 1978, 175.

9. Each month, the magazine received between 500 and 600 submissions for its poetry section alone (Hataya, *Shiberia yokuryū towa nandatta no ka*, 15–16).

10. Rocinante is the name of Don Quixote's horse. Ishihara was originally planning to name his first collection of poems after the fictional packhorse, but the group liked it so much that it decided to use the name for the magazine (ibid., 33–34).

11. Shindō Kenzō, who was interned about 200 miles southeast of Tayshet, writes that the camp director announced that Japanese soldiers and officers were allowed to wear whatever medals they possessed on the anniversary of the Russian

Revolution. The detainees scoffed at the announcement, seeing it as simply absurd in the camp where they were "treated like worthless beings." Shindō adds that "in the Soviet Union, where genealogy and private property were absent, medals served as the only symbol of a person's dignity" ("Watashi no Shiberia monogatari: Shuberuta shūyōjo no koro," in *HT*, 7:266).

12. Hataya, *Shiberia yokuryū towa nandatta no ka*, 49.

13. Not all of Ishihara's works fit into such a linear genealogy, however. For example, "Fernandes," a poem that he published in 1970, conveys his feelings right after repatriation:

As Fernandes
It is correct to call
The wall of a temple, a quiet
depression I named
One man leaned on the wall
the warm depression
left behind
"Fernandes." . . .

According to Ishihara's own annotation, his initial inspiration for the poem came nearly ten years before completing it (*IYZ* 2:528–49).

14. As Sawachi Hisae discovered through a bit of detective work, the official pronunciation of Kano's given name was Takekazu. For more details, see Sawachi Hisae, *Shōwa: tōihi chikaihito* (Tokyo: Bungei shunjū, 1997), 283. It appears that Kano had decided to use the name Buichi (an alternative pronunciation for the same two characters) with his friends. Tada Shigeharu, who interviewed his sister, decided to transcribe his name as Buichi, and in this chapter, I follow Tada to honor Kano's own practice.

15. When discussing Kano's life during the war, Tada Shigeharu wonders why he "gave up his aspiration of becoming a doctor to join a Japanese settlement [by himself] as an ordinary settler" in rural Manchuria. He suggests that through his intelligence work, Kano may have learned about the human experimentation carried out by Unit 731, whose headquarters were located in Harbin, or even that Kano had a more direct connection to that project (Tada Shigeharu, *Uchinaru Shiberia yokuryū taiken: Ishihara Yoshirō, Kano Buichi, Kan Sueharu no sengoshi* [Tokyo: Shakaishisōsha, 1994], 66–68). Andrew Barshay speculates that Ishihara may have been aware of Kano's connection with Unit 731 (*The Gods Left First: The Captivity and Repatriation of Japanese POWs in Northeast Asia, 1945–1956* [Berkeley: University of California Press, 2013], 152).

16. For more information about Kano's early life, see Barshay, *Gods Left First*, 150–52.

17. Sawachi, *Shōwa*, 260.

18. Tada, *Uchinaru Shiberia taiken*, 78.

19. Ibid., 92.

20. Ochiai Harurō, who was also interned in Siberia, offered the following comments on Kano's behavior:

> I think he chose death by fasting not because he was touched by "the healthy warmth" of the daughter of the Khabarovsk mayor, but because, in receiving the alms, he stooped to the mental level of the people who had completely adjusted to the internment camp, the people who in his words "demonstrated a completely naked humanity." He had always distinguished himself as a solitary figure. But, realizing that what he had protected at great cost had collapsed, he discovered himself no different from the other inmates whom he had thought so disgraceful.

As Ochiai argues, Kano's existence as a solitary figure was threatened in this incident. But Kano describes in his letter those who "demonstrated a completely naked humanity" as being better than him. It is more likely that Kano felt despair not because he accepted the alms but because he was unable to fully accept them (Ochiai Harurō, *Ishihara Yoshirō no Shiberia* [Tokyo: Ronsōsha, 1999], 199).

21. In his meditation on Alain Resnais's documentary film about Auschwitz (*Night and Fog*, 1955), Ishihara made the following observation: "The place I am still occupying in front of the screen is a comfortable seat in which I can continue to sit even after the images are gone. What needs to be denounced is that seat. Who is going to denounce? The dead. Those who died in Auschwitz" (*IYZ* 2:242–43). Yamashiro Mutsumi claimed, though without much effort to substantiate it, that "the last 'empty seat'" was "hope" (*Tenkeiki to shikō* [Tokyo: Kōdansha, 1999], 142). In refuting Yamashiro, Nakajima Kazuo refers to Marx's discussion of value-form and concludes that it is actually the "foe" that Ishihara was discussing in "From the Experience of a Kind of 'Symbiosis'" (Aru 'kyōsei' no keiken kara) (*Shūyōjo bungaku-ron* [Tokyo: Ronsōsha, 2008], 30–38). However, given the reference to his film-viewing experience in this passage, it should be clear that Ishihara is employing the "empty seat" as a more concrete image.

22. In the 1990s, Sawachi Hisae unearthed the letter that Kano had written to his wife, Kie, on the first night after his repatriation. In it, Kano explains that his fasting in Khabarovsk was a suicide attempt. He also describes having received "true, humane, warm words" from the KGB interrogators afterward (he does not relate the actual conversation). The letter candidly reveals that Kano was just as tormented by the humiliating conditions of internment—hunger and shameful actions that he committed under extreme distress—as were Ishihara and others. While he was the owner of a sensitive soul, he was not the heroic figure that Ishihara made him out to be (Sawachi, *Shōwa*, 275–76).

23. Tada, *Uchinaru Shiberia yokuryū taiken*, 176.

24. After revealing that Kano had liver problems, Tada suggests that excessive drinking may have caused them (ibid., 174).

25. Kasuya Eiichi, "Ishihara Yoshirō no omoide," in *Techō*, vol. 3 of *Ishihara Yoshirō zenshū* (Tokyo: Kashinsha, 1980), 2.

26. According to Ōno Shin, it took Ishihara about three months to write "Silence and the Loss of Words" (Chinmoku to shitsugo), which, in his *Complete Works*, is only thirteen pages long ("Ishihara Yoshirō ron," *Gendaishi techō*, September 1972, 37).

27. Kasuya, "Ishihara Yoshirō no omoide," 2.

28. Hataya, *Shiberia yokuryū towa nandatta no ka*, 132.

29. Koyanagi Reiko and Ōnishi Kazuo, "Nenpu," in *Techō*, 528. Several months before his death, Ishihara confided to the poet Nakagiri Masao the difficulty he was having in writing the essays: "I spent an agonizing three years on writing the ten essays of the first essay collection. I do not want to suffer like that. During that time, I was drinking as I wrote. Now that I think about it, I was in a perilous state" (*IYZ* 3:282). In the essay titled "My Drinks" (Watashi no sake, 1973), Ishihara describes his struggle to control his daily consumption of alcohol. Around this time, he had a three-stage ritual when he went to bed, drinking about seven cups of saké (1.33 qt./1,260 ml) in total. But he admits that the ritual often failed and that he drank an amount far exceeding the self-imposed limit (*IYZ* 2:319–20).

30. Hataya, *Shiberia yokuryū towa nandatta no ka*, 120.

31. Ibid.

32. Tada, *Ishihara Yoshirō "Shōwa" no tabi*, 181. Given Ishihara's deep concern with his own experiences in the Siberian camps, Kazue's loss was likely part of their bond. When Ishihara published his letter to his brother in 1967, his decision had unfortunate implications. Kazue was enraged at the editor Ōno Shin for publishing this letter in its original form. Her mental state, which already was beginning to show signs of decline, then worsened precipitously (Hataya, *Shiberia yokuryū towa nandatta no ka*, 63).

33. Tada, *Ishihara Yoshirō "Shōwa" no tabi*, 250. Eleven months before Ishihara's death, the poet Anzai Hitoshi helped him take Kazue to the hospital. In his poem "One Day with Clear Wind" (Aru harete kaze no aruhi), Anzai describes Ishihara's rather precarious condition: " 'Quick, take him to the hospital' urged the wife, who was supposed to be hospitalized /'Please buy me a can of beer' begged the poet in the car" (*Yuriika*, February 1978, 23).

34. Ayukawa Nobuo and Yoshimoto Taka'aki, "Ishihara Yoshirō no shi: sengo-shi no kiki," *Jiba*, spring 1978, 136.

35. Later, in his book *Losing Words and Resignation* (Shitsugo to dannen), Uchimura Gōsuke strongly criticized Ishihara for "lacking the perspective to look straight into the twentieth-century slaves at the internment camps" (*Shitsugo to dannen: Ishihara Yoshirō ron* [Tokyo: Shichōsha, 1979], 201).

36. Ayukawa and Yoshimoto, "Ishihara Yoshirō no shi: sengo-shi no kiki," 145.

37. Ibid., 145–46.

38. Ibid., 146.

39. Sumioka Takashi, "Shi to nichijō to: Ishihara Yoshirō san no koto," in *Techō*, 4.

40. Later in his career, Ishihara produced highly aestheticized poetry with religious undertones in haiku and *tanka* form. In these works, his Siberian internment experiences are still detectable, but the ghastly process of decay he was undergoing seems to be displaced by beautiful snapshots (*Ishihara Yoshirō kushū* [Tokyo: Shinya sōshosha, 1974]; *Kita Kamakura* [Tokyo: Kashinsha, 1978], in *IYZ* 3:3–54).

41. Tanaka's ultimate goal was the reversion of the northern four islands that the Soviet Union had been occupying since the end of World War II. In their meeting, Tanaka and the Soviet leader, Leonid Brezhnev, confirmed that these islands were one of the unresolved issues between the two nations. The issue of internment was clearly not part of Tanaka's strategic thinking (Hayano Tōru, *Tanaka Kakuei* [Tokyo: Chūōkōron shinsha, 2012], 274).

42. Tsukimura, "Ishihara Yoshirō," 173.

43. Tsukimura Toshiyuki contrasts Tanaka's TV discussion with the ways in which Ishihara talks about the timber in the Siberian taiga, but he refrains from making a larger claim about postwar Japan (ibid). My observation builds on Tsukimura's juxtaposition.

5. LOST AND FOUND IN THE SOUTH PACIFIC

1. Itō Yūnosuke, who plays Yoshida Ichirō in *Yellow Crow*, is cast as the barge operator.

2. The beach acquired iconic status in Japanese youth culture due in no small part to Ishihara Shintarō's 1955 novella, *Season of the Sun* (*Taiyō no kisetsu*, Tokyo: Shinchōsha, 1956), and the subsequent film adaptation.

3. According to a 2007 newsweekly article, Yokoi's capture was not as peaceful as he reported. One of the hunters actually beat Yokoi unconscious and would have shot him on the spot if it had not been for his companion' intervention. Since Japanese stragglers had killed the hunter's brother and nephew in 1950, he had seen them as enemies ("Yokoi Shōichi san wa korosareru sunzen datta!" *Shūkan asahi*, August 24, 2007, 33).

4. "Kiseki no hito o ningen-girai ni shita 10 kakan," *Shūkan gendai*, February 17, 1972, 27; "Yokoi Shōichi san no kangei no sarekata," *Josei jishin*, February 19, 1972, 36. *Shūkan shinchō* reported that about 300 Japanese media personnel went to Guam to cover the Yokoi story ("Hi ga tatsuni tsurete Yokoi san no datsu Guamu genkōroku," *Shūkan shinchō*, February 19, 1972, 34).

5. "Guamu no moto Nihonhei hakken no hamon, *Asahi shinbun*, January 26, 1972, 13th ed., 23.

6. For example, a special issue of *Shūkan yomiuri* reported responses of various generations: "Mada hatsugen shiteinakatta 'machi no koe,'" and "'Sensō o shiranai sedai wa kō hannōsuru,'" February 18, 1972, 50–51, 52–55.

7. Kishida Junpei, "Kigakarina hito tanken: Yokoi Shōichi san to heikasama to soshite . . . ," *Josei jishin*, February 26, 1972, 166.

8. Yasuoka Shōtarō, "Yokoi san to Nihonjin," *Shūkan yomiuri*, special issue, February 18, 1972, 41.

9. "Guam-tō senyūkai no 'hiirō Yokoi' o miru me," *Shūkan bunshun*, February 21, 1972.

10. Yokoi Shōichi, *Ashita eno michi* (Tokyo: Bungei shunjū, 1974), 9–10.

11. Ibid., 12–13.

12. Ibid., 13.

13. Kōseishō shakai engo kyoku engo 50 nenshi henshū iinkai, *Engo 50 nen-shi* (Tokyo: Gyōsei, 1997), 122.

14. Yokoi, *Ashita eno michi*, 30.

15. Ibid., 67.

16. Ibid., 74–75.

17. Ibid., 13.

18. The official notice of Yokoi Shōichi's death was dated September 30, 1944. In the case of battle death, it was customary to receive a posthumous promotion of two ranks. In Yokoi's case, he was promoted to corporal on September 1, 1944, and finally to sergeant on May 2, 1947 (Omi Hatashin, *Private Yokoi's War and Life on Guam, 1944–1972* [Folkestone, Kent: Global Oriental, 2009], 216–19.

19. Yokoi, *Ashita eno michi*, 82–84.

20. "Nijūroku nen tōkō gumi ga kataru Guamu-tō tōhikō no shin jijitsu," *Shūkan sankei*, February 25, 1972, 17–18.

21. Yokoi, *Ashita eno michi*, 122, 149–50.

22. Ibid., 162.

23. Itō Masashi, *Guamu-tō* (Tokyo: Futami shobō, 1960), 96–101; Minagawa Bunzō, *Nanmei no hateni* (Tokyo: Chōbunsha, 1960), 142–49.

24. In Shimada Kakuo's accounts of his straggler life, the topic of salt appears repeatedly (*Watashi wa makyō ni ikita* [Tokyo: Kōjinsha, 2007], 201, 204, 234–35, 262–65, 269–71, 333–34.

25. Yokoi, *Ashita eno michi*, 126.

26. Ibid., 87.

27. Ibid., 156.

28. Ibid., 184–85.

29. Ibid., 155–57.

30. Yokoi Mihoko, *Chinkon no tabiji: Yokoi Shōichi no sengo o ikita tsuma no shuki* (Osaka: Horusu shuppan, 2011), 183.

31. Yokoi, *Ashita eno michi*, 95. Yokoi kept a rough calendar by observing the moon. But partly because he forgot to count the leap month in the lunisolar calendar, his calendar was off by about six months when he was discovered.

32. According to Minagawa Bunzō, a member of the group at the time, the incident took place around 10:00 A.M. on July 13 (*Nanmei no hateni* [Tokyo: Chōbunsha, 1960], 69–70). Nagao Norio and Fujita Hideo died on the spot; Kamijō Keizo was seriously injured and later committed suicide. Yamauchi Masazumi and Shimizu Shigeo were also seriously injured, and Yamauchi died two days later. Although there is no mention of Yamauchi's fate afterward, *Nanmei no hateni* suggests that he survived the injury (Yokoi, *Ashita eno michi*, 97–99).

33. According to Minagawa's memory, Umino Tetsuo died of illness on July 8, 1954 (*Nanmei no hateni*, 179).

34. Minagawa and another straggler, Itō Masashi, were "captured" by the U.S. forces on May 21, 1960. I discuss their return later in this chapter.

35. Yokoi, *Ashita eno michi*, 163–64.

36. Ibid., 169–70.

37. Ibid., 174–75.

38. Ibid., 185–86.

39. Ibid., 189–90.

40. Ibid., 188.

41. Yokoi is actually referring to Typhoon Karen, the Category 5 storm that hit Guam in November 1962, causing $100 million in damages (Lawrence J. Cunningham and Janice J. Beaty, *A History of Guam* [Honolulu: Bess Press, 2001], 301). Describing the damage the typhoon caused, the authors make an interesting reference to the war: "The navy said that the damage to Guam equaled that of an indirect hit of a nuclear bomb. It was like World War II all over again" (301).

42. Yokoi, *Ashita eno michi*, 203–5.

43. Ibid., 206.

44. Kaji Sōichi, "Watashi ga tachiatta Yokoi, Kozuka, Onoda san no sei to shi," *Sandei mainichi*, March 31, 1974, 28. Yokoi confided in the three *Mainichi shinbun* reporters (Kaji Sōichi, Yokota Saburō, and Shiiya Noriyoshi) about his solitary struggle:

    I'm telling you, the nights in the cave were long. Crying, singing, . . . yelling. . . . I talked to myself. . . . I was losing my grip on myself. I used to pray to the gods and Buddha, often. . . . Scratching the walls. . . . I sometimes banged my head against the walls. . . . My mother's spirit came to visit me often. Very close to me. . . . With my war buddies. . . . Then once I came out of the cave, some of them clung to me, and others threatened me. . . . It was a huge typhoon, wasn't it? Huge. Yet . . . after that, there was absolutely nothing to eat in the mountains. Nobody can understand. (Quoted in Mainichi shinbunsha, *Saigo no ippei: Guamu tō shuzai kishadan no zenkiroku* [Tokyo: Mainichi shinbunsha, 1972], 155)

    In contrast, in his 1974 memoir, Yokoi portrays himself as remaining composed, even in his solitude (*Ashita he no michi*, 226).

45. "Hitori de tatakkata 'himitsu no 28 nen' shijō kanzen rokuon, kiseki no seikan," *Shūkan sankei*, February 26, 1972, 16–17. Yokoi offered a slightly different account to another reporter: "I learned about the end of the war more than twenty years ago. But I was afraid that if I were to come out, I would be treated as a traitor because I didn't die" ("Yokoi genkō roku ni miru 'sei,'" *Shūkan yomiuri*, February 18, 1972, 97). In the Guam police report, Yokoi claimed that he learned of the end of the war in 1952.

46. It is likely Yokoi is referring to *Mariyana jihō*, the propaganda fliers printed in Hawaii by the U.S. Navy.

47. Yokoi, *Ashita eno michi*, 102.
48. Ibid., 107.
49. Ibid., 157–58.
50. Ibid., 192.
51. For example, the special issue of *Shūkan sankei* included the *manga* story "Aa rikugun gochō Yokoi Shōichi ikite ryoshū no hazukashime o ukezu" (Story by Kuchiki Takashi; illustrations by Narushima Sei), which describes Yokoi as being under the control of the *Field Service Code* (*Senjinkun*). This special issue also printed the entire text of the *Field Service Code* (*Shūkan sankei*, special issue, February 26, 1972, 83, 95–103). *Sandei maichini* agreed with this reasoning ("Yokoi gochō o sasaeta? Senjinkun towa," *Sandei maichini*, February 20, 1972, 24–25).
52. Yasuoka, "Yokoi san to Nihonjin," 41.
53. "Nijūhachi nen no kūhaku, 'shinwa no sekai' kara konoyo e," *Shūkan yomiuri*, February 18, 1972, 28.
54. Thirty-five years after capturing Yokoi, one of his captors, Manuel De Gracia, revealed that his brother in law, Jesus Dueñas, beat Yokoi unconscious and was ready to kill him. Dueñas apparently would have killed Yokoi if his companions had not intervened. Dueñas was deeply resentful of the Japanese stragglers because they had killed his brother and nephew in 1950 ("Yokoi Shōichi san wa korosareru sunzen datta," *Shūkan asahi*, August 24, 2007, 33).
55. Despite their strong reluctance to do so, some Japanese soldiers intentionally surrendered to enemy forces. Yokota Shōhei, who also fought in Guam, surrendered shortly after the U.S. landing. For Yokota's psychological justification for his decision, see *Watashi wa gyokusai shinakatta* (Tokyo: Chūōkōron shinsha, 1999).
56. Yokoi, *Ashita eno michi*, 175–76.
57. Historian Beatrice Trefalt has examined the media coverage of the earlier stragglers' return, including Itō's and Minagawa's (*Japanese Army Stragglers and Memories of the War in Japan, 1950–1975* [New York: RoutledgeCurzon, 2003], 49–64, 77–84, 104–9).
58. Marukawa Tetsushi, "Liu Lianren, Yokoi Shōichi, 'Nakamura Teruo' ni totteno sensō," in *Teikoku no sensō keiken*, vol. 4 of Iwanami kōza Ajia Taiheiyō sensō (Tokyo: Iwanami shoten, 2006), 333–34.
59. Yamaguchi Makoto, *Guamu to Nihonjin: sensō o umetateta rakuen* (Tokyo: Iwanami shoten, 2007), 46.
60. Signed by the United States and Japan on September 8, 1951, the treaty recognized the United States' right to station its forces in Japan. In the late 1950s, the Liberal Democratic Party led the efforts to make the treaty a more reciprocal agreement.
61. Yoshikuni Igarashi, *Bodies of Memory: Narratives of War in Postwar Japanese Culture, 1945–1970* (Princeton, N.J.: Princeton University Press, 2000), 132–43.
62. Hatsuda Kōsei, "Tokyo no sengo fukkō to yamiichi," in *Sakariba wa yamiichi kara umareta*, ed. Hashimoto Kenji and Hatsuda Kōsei (Tokyo: Seikyūsha, 2013), 45.

63. Yoshimi Shunya, *Banpaku gensō* (Tokyo: Chikuma shobō, 2005), 59. The total number of admissions reached 64 million.

64. Yamaguchi, *Guamu to Nihonjin*, 78–90.

65. Although the oil shock of 1973 momentarily shattered this expectation, the national optimism returned and persisted once Japan adjusted to the new international economic environment. For a more detailed discussion of how postwar Japanese society struggled to recover from the trauma of war, see Igarashi, *Bodies of Memory*.

66. Toda Hiroshi, "Fushigina hodo ijōna 'nōryoku' kesshō," *Shūkan asahi*, February 11, 1972, 23.

67. "Ikita 'Senjinkun' 28 nenme no konwaku," *Shūkan yomiuri*, February 11, 1972, 23. Edward Tsutsui, deputy director of the Guam Visitors Bureau, told a reporter that he was the one who urged Yokoi to do so ("Yokoi san ga watashi dakeni katatta hitori ikinokotta shinsō," *Shūkan gendai*, February 17, 1972, 22).

68. Yasuoka, "Yokoi san to Nihonjin," 41.

69. Emori Kōyō, " 'Ikinobiru koto wa' haji nanoka," in Yokoi Mihoko, *Chinkon no tabiji*, 224.

70. "Hi ga tatsuni tsurete Yokoi san no datsu Guamu genkō roku," 34.

71. The special issue of *Shūkan sankei* contains a short article about his visit: "Hitori de tatakatta 'Himitsu no 28 nen," 17–18.

72. "Hi ga tatsuni tsurete Yokoi san no datsu Guamu genkō roku," 34.

73. "Yokoi san shuzai no 'ima dakara hanaseru hiwa,' " *Shūkan posuto*, February 18, 1972, 160–61.

74. Mainichi shinbunsha, *Saigo no ippei*, 116–17.

75. One weekly magazine article observed that Yokoi was suffering from "Guam autism" (Guamu *jiheishō*) and wrote about what it would take for him to adjust to modern society (" 'Guamu jiheishō' no shakai fukki ni machikamaeru otoshiana," *Shūkan sankei*, February 18, 1972, 24–27).

76. "Shōgen kōsei kiseki no hito, Yokoi Shōichi san no 'tabidachi,' " *Yangu redii*, February 16,1972, 52.

77. Shiraishi Katsunori, "Yokoi san no 'dōkutsu' de ichiya o sugoshita!" *Shūkan bunshun*, February 14, 1972, 24–27; Yamashita Katsutoshi, "Tsuitaiken, honshi kisha Guamu no janguru ni komoru," *Shūkan asahi*, February 21, 1972, 23–25. Judging from their given names (they both contain the character for "victory"), they were born during the Asia Pacific War, but the naive tone of their articles conveys the cultural distance that separated them from the war.

78. "Yokoi Shōichi san ga kekkon suru hazudatta josei wa Itō Mitsuko san," *Shūkan heibon*, February 10, 1972, 38–42; "Zehi watashi wa 'kon'yakusha' ni aitai . . . ," *Josei jishin*, February 12, 1972, 32–33; "Wasure enu hatsukoi no hito, kon'yakusha wa sudeni naku . . . ," *Josei sebun*, February 16, 1972, 37–38.

79. "Yokoi gunsō no imawanaki kon'yakusha no iji ga kataru 28 nenkan," *Asahi geinō*, February 10, 1972, 15; "Shinseki kaigi de osareta Yamada Sachiko san wa 20 sai," *Shūkan josei*, February 19, 1972, 28–31.

80. Yokoi, *Ashita eno michi*, 223. Some reporters discussed the possibility of asking him about his sexual drive during the interview at Haneda Airport immediately

after he landed. In an effort to keep the interaction respectable, though, they ultimately did not ask him ("Doku o kutteita Yokoi Shōichi san eno 10 no?'" *Shūkan taishū*, February 24, 1972, 147–48). Reporters later asked him similar questions in more private settings. Itō Masashi, who was discovered with Minagawa Bunzō in Guam, openly described his desire for women in the accounts he later published (*Guamu-tō*, 166–70).

81. "Yokoi Shōichi san fūfu omedeta! Daga 3 kagetsu de munen!" *Yangu redii*, January 28, 1974, 27–29; "'Gokainin' sawagi de morashita Yokoi Shōichi fūfu no hagemikata," *Shūkan posuto*, February 1, 1974, 44.

82. "'Guamu-tō 28 nen' ikinokori no kyōi o shusseiji kara tsuiseki suru," *Shūkan posuto*, February 11, 1972, 20. Once back in Japan, he also told reporters that he "want[ed] to return his rifle to the Grand Marshal [the emperor]" ("Yokoi Shōichi san bunmei tono tatakai isshūkan," *Shūkan yomiuri*, February 19, 1972, 24).

83. Iizawa Tadasu, "Reigai wa kihan ni naranu," *Shūkan asahi*, February 11, 1972, 21; Ōoka Shōhei, "Tōbun, hottoite agetai," *Shūkan asahi*, February 11, 1972, 22.

84. Yokoi had a chance to look at the emperor's printed images because a newspaper reporter shoved two graphic magazines into his hands in his hospital room (despite the "No visitors" sign) (Mainichi shinbunsha, *Saigo no ippei*, 43).

85. "Ano suchuwaadesu san no yōna wakai musume san ga iinō," *Shūkan heibon*, February 17, 1972, 39. Yokoi's arrival scene was telecast by NHK for sixty minutes, with the rating of this special coverage as high as 41.2 (Hikita Sōya, *Zenkiroku terebi shichōritsu 50 nen kyōsō* [Tokyo: Kōdansha, 2004], 126).

86. "Hontō ni futari o koroshita noka? Yokoi Shōichi san no misuterii kako," *Shūkan myōjō*, May 21, 1972, 198; "'Mitsurin no himitsu' o kokuhaku shita Shōicchuan no dōyō," *Shūkan taishū*, May 18, 1972, 142–43.

87. "'Mitsurin no himitsu' o kokuhaku shita Shōicchuan no dōyō," 144. In his memoir, Yokoi mentions an episode before the end of the war in which he and other stragglers killed four men who were patrolling and stole their food (*Ashita eno michi*, 97–98).

88. "Sabita teppō mo taisetsu ni," *Asahi shinbun*, January 27, 1972, 13th ed., 3. Yokoi explained that the rot was due to the fact that the wooden part was made with soft lauan wood.

89. Based on the May 1972 exchange rate of $1 = ¥308.

90. According to an article in *Yangu redii*, as of 1974, "he delivers twenty lectures for each month and his schedule is completely full until November." The lecturer's fees were "50,000 yen ($175) in Aichi Prefecture, and 100,000 yen ($350) outside the prefecture" ("Otoko Yokoi Shōichi o hazukashinagara rikkōho saseta 'okusan no chikara'!" *Yangu redii*, July 1, 1974, 32). An article in 1990s shows that the rates rose in later years: "It's been reported: 200,000 yen in the Aichi Prefecture, and 300,000 outside the prefecture" ("Kieta yūmeijin no nikusei, Yokoi Shōichi [75]," *Shūkan hōseki*, May 17, 1990, 49).

91. "Yokoi Shōichi san fusai: rainen 1 gatsu ni kodomo ga dekisōdesu," *Josei sebun*, December 27, 1972, 190.

92. *Asahi shinbun*, February 9, 1972, 13th ed., 23; "Shinseki kaigi de osareta Yamada Sachiko san wa 20 sai," 28.

93. "Yokoi Shōichi san ga terebi de kokuhaku! 'oshikake nyōbo kōho ni komat-temasu,'" *Josei sebun*, September 6–13, 1972, 39.

94. "Daremo ga odoroita! Yokoi Shōichi san genkōroku," *Shūkan josei*, March 24, 1973, 38.

95. "Guam-tō shinkon ryokō de mitazo Yokoi fūfu no sugoude," *Shūkan bunshun*, March 26, 1973, 49. Yokoi was also disappointed that the residents of Guam were not as enthusiastic about his return as he had hoped.

96. "Hazukashi nagara toruko o taikenshimashita," *Gendai*, May 1973, 276–83.

97. "Kyabarei de taishō ni shōshin shiteita Yokoi Shōichi san," *Asahi geinō*, July 26, 1973, 12–13; "Ano Yokoi san ga gunjin ni gyakumodori!?" *Yangu redii*, July 23, 1973.

98. "Yokoi san no risō senkyo sengen," *Shūkan bunshun*, July 1, 1974, 153; "Seiji no karakuri no nioi o kagu inu ni naritai," *Shūkan asahi*, June 28, 1974, 151.

99. "Yokoi san wa tōsen suruka," *Shūkan shinchō*, June 27, 1974, 149–50.

100. "Yokoi san wa tōsen suruka," 151; "Washi wa saitei 100 manbyō wa koeru to omottoru!" *Josei jishin*, July 4, 1974, 34.

101. "Hapuningu ga okotta Yokoi san tono isshūkan," *Shūkan bunshun*, July 8, 1974, 41–42. Itagaki Tadashi, the secretary-general of the Japan Association of the Bereaved Families, commented: "From the very beginning, I didn't think the votes of the bereaved families would go to Mr. Yokoi. Mr. Yokoi is a person who came home alive. I don't think those whose family members died in the war could help having very complex feelings" ("Yokoi gochō ni tōhyō shita hitota-chi no kimochi," *Shūkan shinchō*, July 18, 1974, 155).

102. "Hyakunin no 20 seiki, Yokoi Shōichi," *Asahi shinbun*, August 15, 1999, Sunday ed., WD, B.

103. Ibid., WD, A. Quoting Yokoi Mihoko, the *Asahi* reporter suggests that Yokoi may have starved himself to death—choosing to die in the same way that many of his fellow soldiers died. But Mihoko strongly insisted that his death was completely due to natural causes (Yokoi Mihoko, interview with author, May 27, 2012).

104. Omi, *Private Yokoi's War and Life on Guam*, 214.

6. RESCUED FROM THE PAST

1. From the moment he emerged from hiding, Onoda adhered to the position that he had simply been carrying out his orders in Lubang jungles ("Kyoshu no rei, guntō, dangan, senkyō hōkoku, soshite mangetsu no yoru," *Shūkan yomiuri*, March 23, 1974, 18).

2. For example, according to *Shukan taishū*'s report, "only thirtysome people out of the hundred saw Second Lieutenant Onoda as a 'hero'" ("Onoda moto shōi 'kamubakku geki' ni kakatta gōkei ichioku-en no meisai," *Shukan taishū*, March 28, 1974, 23).

3. Tsuda Shin, "Onoda wa gensō no eiyū da," *Shūkan posuto*, June 24–August 26, 1977. These articles were later published as *Gensō no eiyū: Onoda shōi tono 3 kagetsu* (Tokyo: Tosho shuppansha, 1977).

4. Fujinami Osamu, "Rubangu-tō no izoku," *Shokun*, September 1977, 117–34.

5. The depiction of his early life is based on information found in the following: Onoda Hiro'o, *Waga Ruban tō no 30 nen sensō* (Tokyo: Kōdansha, 1974); Tsuda, *Gensō no eiyū*; and Toi Jūgatsu, *Onoda Hiro'o no owaranai tatakai* (Tokyo: Shinchōsha, 2005). *Waga Ruban-tō no 30 nen sensō* also appeared in English as *No Surrender: My Thirty-Year War* (Tokyo: Kodansha International, 1974). The translation of Onoda's memoirs is mine, as well as the translation in *No Surrender*.

6. After the war, former warrant officers were given the derisive moniker "Potsdam lieutenants" (Potsudamu shōi) (Mikuni Ichirō, *Senchū yōgoshū* [Tokyo: Iwanami shoten, 1985], 204–5).

7. Kōseishō engokyoku, "Rubangu-tō moto Nihonhei sōsa hōkokusho," August 1973, 2.

8. Ibid.

9. Wakaichi Kōji, *Saigo no senshisha, rikugun ittōhei Kozuka Kinshichi* (Tokyo: Kawade shobō-shinsha, 1986), 159.

10. Kōseishō engokyoku, "Rubangu-tō moto Nihonhei sōsa hōkokusho," 2–4.

11. The 1972/1973 search crews interviewed three local people and reached this conclusion (Kōseishō engokyoku, "Rubangu-tō moto Nihonhei sōsa hōkokusho," 140; Wakaichi, *Saigo no senshisha*, 160–80).

12. Besides the Japanese, nineteen members of the Philippine air force and 132 local residents participated in the third phase search alone (Kōseishō engokyoku, "Rubangu-tō moto Nihonhei sōsa hōkokusho," 62, 189–90).

13. For example, the Ministry of Health and Welfare sent three people to Lubang for the first organized search in May 1954 and fourteen for the second search, which lasted from May to December 1959 ("Onoda moto shōi 'kamubakku geki' ni kakatta gōkei ichioku-en no meisai," *Shūkan taishū*, March 28, 1974, 24).

14. Suzuki Norio, *Dai hōrō: Onoda Shōi hakken no tabi* (Tokyo: Bungei shunjū, 1974), 163–64, 185–86.

15. "'Kimi wa sensō no koto o nanimo shiranai na' youyōni Nihongo o shaberi tsuzuketa Onoda moto shōi," *Shūkan asahi*, March 25, 1974, 33.

16. "Gendai no eiyū shiriizu 2: Onoda Hiro'o," *Shūkan bunshun*, March 25, 1974, 140.

17. Suzuki Norio, "Onoda Shōi hakken no tabi," *Bungei shunjū*, May 1974, 167–68; Taniguchi Yoshimi, "Futatsu no meireisho," *Bungei shunjū*, May 1974, 181. The reporter for *Sandei mainichi* describes that although they turned on a tape recorder while reenacting the scene, they failed to record their voices (Kaji Sōichi, "Watashi ga tachiatta Yokoi, Kozuka, Onoda san no sei to shi," *Sandei mainichi*, March 31, 1974, 28).

18. Onoda Hiro'o explains in his memoir that he changed back into combat gear at the Philippine side's request ("Himitsu meirei nashi—watashi no shūsen," *Shūkan gendai*, August 8, 1974, 39; *Waga Ruban tō no 30 nen sensō*, 245). The

English version claims that it was at President Marcos's request (*No Surrender: My Thirty-Year War*, 217). It is highly unlikely that the nation's leader made such a request; at this point, everything was still being handled locally.

19. Kaji, "Watashi ga tachiatta Yokoi, Kozuka, Onoda san no sei to shi," 27.
20. Yamashita Yukihide, "Tekichi no genshu ni saikō no rei de mukaerareta Onoda Shōi," *Shūkan sankei*, April 3, 1974, 21.
21. Nakano Satoshi, "The Politics of Mourning," in *Philippines-Japan Relations*, ed. Ikehata Setsuho and Lydia N. Yu Jose (Quezon City: Ateneo de Manila University Press, 2003), 338.
22. Yamashita, "Tekichi no genshu ni saikō no rei de mukaerareta Onoda Shōi," 22.
23. Onoda Hiro'o and Aida Yūji, "Kangaeteita Nihon, genjitsu no Nippon," *Gendai*, July 1974, 81.
24. Kaji, "Watashi ga tachiatta Yokoi, Kozuka, Onoda san no sei to shi," 29.
25. Ibid.
26. Honda Yasuharu, "Onoda Hiro'o moto Shōi to katari akashita 'Tennō to heitai,'" *Shūkan gendai*, April 1, 1976, 126. Onoda also believed that the emperor should have abdicated the throne to take responsibility for Japan's lost war (Kikuchi Ikuzō, "Burajiru no Onoda Hiro'o Nihonkoku musekinin-ron o kataru," *Asahi jaanaru*, October 3, 1975, 81).
27. "Rubangu ikinokori hei no 28 nen," *Shūkan asahi*, November 3, 1972, 21.
28. "Yappari ita! Rubangu no moto Nihon hei," *Sandei mainichi*, November 5, 1972, 18.
29. Fujinami, "Rubangu-tō no izoku," 120.
30. Tsuda, *Gensō no eiyū*, 80.
31. "Nosaka Akiyuki o kiri-koroshite yaru!" *Shūkan yomiuri*, April 26, 1975, 34.
32. Tsuda, *Gensō no eiyū*, 82.
33. Ibid.
34. "Rubangu-tō 'jūmin 30 nin satsugai' no tsumi wa dōnaru?" *Shūkan sankei*, November 17, 1972, 18.
35. Of the seventy-nine Japanese who received a death sentence in the Philippine war crimes courts, only seventeen were actually executed; the remaining sixty-two received presidential pardons (Nagai Hitoshi, *Firipin BC kyū senpan saiban* [Tokyo: Kōdansha, 2013], 214).
36. "Kodokukan nakatta: Onoda san genchi kaiken no shōhō," *Mainichi shinbun*, March 11, 1974, evening, 4th ed., 5.
37. "Hateshinaki shokku o kataru kakkai 100 nin," *Shūkan bunshūn*, April 8, 1974, 30.
38. Fujiwara Akira, *Uejini shita eireitachi* (Tokyo: Aoki shoten, 2001), 107; Ōoka Shōhei, *Reite senki, ge* (Tokyo: Chūōkōron, 1974), 286.
39. "Bōken zuki Nihonjin seinen no Onoda moto Shōi 'hakken to kyūshutsu,'" *Shūkan sankei*, March 22, 1974, 15.
40. "Hiirō No. 2 Suzuki seinen no 'waga Onoda kyūshutsu sakusen,'" *Shūkan sankei*, March 29, 1974, 11.
41. Onoda Hiro'o, "Ikinokotta yonin," *Shūkan gendai*, May 30, 1974, 31, 45–47; and *Waga Rugangu-tō no 30 nen sensō*, 136–40.

42. The search crew of 1959 left four months' worth of newspapers there: "The stack was more than twenty inches high" (Onoda Hiro'o, "Watashi no Taiheiyō sensō," *Shūkan gendai*, June 20, 1974, 43).
43. Onoda Hiro'o, "Kozuka to futari bocchi 20 nen," *Shūkan gendai*, July 4, 1974, 46–47; and *Waga Rugangu-tō no 30 nen sensō*, 172–74.
44. Onoda, "Watashi no Taiheiyō sensō," 45–47; and *Waga Rugangu-tō no 30 nen sensō*, 136–40.
45. Tsuda, *Gensō no eiyū*, 138–39.
46. Ibid., 146.
47. Onoda Hiro'o, "Kakure goya no seikatsu," *Shūkan gendai*, June 27, 1974, 44–45; and *Waga Rugangu-tō no 30 nen sensō*, 160–61.
48. Onoda, "Kozuka to futari bocchi 20 nen," 46–47; and *Waga Rugangu-tō no 30 nen sensō*, 173–74.
49. He was talking not only about the first twenty years of keeping a calendar until he obtained the radio. When Onoda first met Suzuki Norio, the latter asked him, "What day do you think it is today?" Onoda's answer: "If I count backward, there is a six-day difference. It is probably February 21." This statement reveals that he kept his own calendar in his head, even though he had learned the accurate dates from the radio (Suzuki, "Onoda Shōi hakken no tabi, 157).
50. Yamamoto Shichihei, *Watashi no naka no Nihongun*, jō (Tokyo: Bungei shunjū, 1975), 139.
51. After being rescued from Guam in 1960, Minagawa Bunzō also talked about the strange psychological state he experienced in the jungle. Around 1953, when he saw some newspapers left by the search crew, he "did not trust them, thinking that they are quite elaborate trick, something that the U.S. would do with its money and rich resources." He was, nevertheless, interested in their contents (Minagawa Bunzō, *Nanmei no hateni* [Tokyo: Chōbunsha, 1960], 186–88).
52. Shimada Kakuo, *Watashi wa makyō ni ikita* (Tokyo: Kōjinsha, 2007), 348.
53. Tsuda, *Gensō no eiyū*, 17.
54. Onoda was part of the first class that graduated from the campus (Saitō Michinori, *Rikugun Nakano gakkō* [Tokyo: Heibonsha, 2006], 126).
55. Onoda Hiro'o, "Himitsu senshi no tanjō, *Shūkan gendai*, May 16, 1974, 24.
56. Onoda, *Waga Rubangu-tō no 30 nen sensō*, 27.
57. Onoda, "Himitsu senshi no tanjō, 24; and *Waga Rubangu-tō no 30 nen sensō*, 27.
58. Onoda, "Himitsu senshi no tanjō, 23.
59. Furthermore, the 240 students from Futamata descending on the small city of Hamatatsu to purchase these instruments would have been highly conspicuous and alerted the public that something was up.
60. Onoda, "Himitsu senshi no tanjō, 23. He changed the figure to 230 in *Waga Rubangu-tō no 30 nen sensō* (26), and 226 students graduated as part of the first class (it is not clear how many, if any, dropped out) (Saitō, *Rikugun Nakano gakkō*, 132).
61. Onoda, "Himitsu senshi no tanjō, 25; and *Waga Rubangu-tō no 30 nen sensō*, 29–30.

62. Onoda, "Himitsu senshi no tanjō, 24; and *Waga Rubangu-tō no 30 nen sensō*, 69.
63. Onoda Hiro'o, "Ikinokotta yonin," *Shūkan gendai*, May 30, 1974, 25; and *Waga Rubangu-tō no 30 nen sensō*, 69–70.
64. Onoda, "Ikinokotta yonin," 25; and *Waga Rubangu-tō no 30 nen sensō*, 70. In the magazine version, he stated: "If the enemies had been waiting for us at that particular moment, I might have died in the battle. Luckily, the enemies may have detected our night raid; they retreated beyond our reach." In the book version, Onoda changed "Luckily" to "Luckily or unluckily" [*kō ka fukō ka*], most likely to avoid the impression that he did not want to fight the Americans.
65. Tsuda, *Gensō no eiyū*, 244.
66. Ibid., 245.
67. Onoda, *Waga Rubangu-tō no 30 nen sensō*, 70.
68. Tsuda, *Gensō no eiyū*, 246.
69. Onoda Hiro'o, "Meirei no nakami," *Shūkan gendai*, May 23, 1974, 22; and *Waga Rubangu-tō no 30 nen sensō*, 41–42.
70. Onoda, "Meirei no nakami," 22; and *Waga Rubangu-tō no 30 nen sensō*, 42.
71. Onoda, "Meirei no nakami," 22; and *Waga Rubangu-tō no 30 nen sensō*, 43. "Meirei no nakami" emphasizes this part in boldface.
72. Tsuda, *Gensō no eiyū*, 130.
73. Onoda Hiro'o and Taniguchi Yoshimi, "Onoda kun, watashi o yurushite kure," *Shūkan gendai*, August 22, 1974, 29.
74. Yamamoto, *Watashi no naka no Nihongun*, jō, 138–39.
75. Onoda, "Meirei no nakami," 23; and *Waga Rubangu-tō no 30 nen sensō*, 44.
76. In his conversation with Aida Yūji, Onoda made the following remarks: "Onoda: But in reality, nobody had the right to issue the orders. Aida: Nobody did. Onoda: Then they brought me to Japan by deception" (Aida Yūji and Onoda Hiro'o, "Nihon o suteru watashi no kokoro no kokosoko niwa," *Shūkan gendai*, February 20, 1975, 31).
77. "Onoda san wa fugirimono ka: sono kon'yaku ni kokyō Kainan shimin ga okoru riyū," *Shūkan yomiuri*, December 20, 1975, 151.
78. Aida and Onoda, "Nihon o suteru watashi no kokoro no kokosoko niwa," 29.
79. Tsuda, *Gensō no eiyū*, 59.
80. "Onoda Hiro'o shi wa naze sattaka," *Shūkan bunshun*, February 19, 1975, 20.
81. Onoda told the stories about attacking local residents to the editors of Kōdansha (Tsuda, *Gensō no eiyū*, 80–82, 185). Even after he moved to Brazil, he shared similar tales with Ishihara Shintarō, who visited him there. With praise, Ishihara described Onoda's actions: "At the villagers or patrols who got carried away and stepped too far into the jungle, they fired a shot or two out of their limited ammunition, causing some serious damage and efficiently kicking them out. Their expert selection of advantageous positions, and their decision of when, who, and how to shoot [impressed me]" ("Harukana ikyō Burajiru de watashi wa tatakai owatta otoko no kokoro no soko o mita," *Sandei mainichi*, August 10, 1975, 21). When juxtaposed with Tsuda's accounts, Ishihara's stories use "serious damage" to refer to killing. It also should be obvious that Onoda

and his men were the ones who "got carried away and stepped too far into the jungle," which rightfully belonged to the villagers.

82. Nosaka Akiyuki, "Onoda 'eiyū shuki' o yonde zannen na koto," *Shūkan posuto*, August 16, 1974, 42–43.

83. Tsuda, *Gensō no eiyū*, 272–73.

84. "Nosaka Akiyuki o kiri-koroshite yaru!" *Shūkan yomiuri*, April 26, 1975, 33.

85. Ibid., 34.

86. Aida Yūji, "Kōfuku na futari no Nihonhei," *Bungei shunjū*, December 1972, 182.

87. "Nosaka Akiyuki o kiri-koroshite yaru!" 33–34.

88. Many magazine and newspaper articles used the term *kyūshutsu* (rescue). But as a Canadian reporter pointed out, it was the Lubang residents who needed to be rescued ("Onoda Shōi kikan no kandō to 'Tennō kaiken,'" *Shūkan shinchō*, March 21, 1974, 131).

89. Wakaichi Kōji, the author of Kozuka Kinshichi's biography, describes the growing national interest in rescuing Onoda after Kozuka was shot to death: "The public's demanding the rescue of Lieutenant Onoda gained more support everyday. It began to appear that the search-and-rescue activities were a national mission" (*Saigo no senshisha*, 183).

90. "'Yokoi taiken wa tsūyō shinai' to iwareru Onoda Shōi no kikan dorama," *Shūkan shinchō*, March 14, 1974, 44.

91. In the essay explaining his decision to move to Brazil, Onoda describes his disappointment with the Japanese government: "Since Japan renounced war, I would not ask for compensation. But I felt the government had ignored the thirty years during which I was driven into the war like other 100 million during the war, tossed [into the jungle] with no formal orders for this secret warrior, and forced to fight" ("Yurushite kudasai! Watashi wa Burajiru ni ijūshimasu," *Shūkan gendai*, November 7, 1974, 145). Not just the government but also postwar Japan ignored his war.

92. "Onoda Hiro'o shi wa naze sattaka," 20. An article in *Shūkan gendai* reported that as soon as he returned to his hometown, Onoda had an emotional exchange with his father ("Ryōshin to kyōri o suteru Onoda san no himitsu o toku rokuon teipu," *Shūkan gendai*, April 3, 1975, 166–67). Onoda talked about the subsequent clash with his father in his conversation with Aida Yūji ("Kangaeteita Nihon, genjitsu no Nippon," 83–84).

93. In *Onoda Hiro'o no owaranai tatakai*, Toi Jūgatsu participated in this popular discourse by uncritically reproducing Onoda's claims.

94. Onoda Hiro'o, "Watashi kojin wa makete nakatta," *Shinchō*, August 1990, 37.

95. Onoda Hiro'o, Sakamaki Kazuo, and Muramatsu Takeshi, "Onoda san to Sakamaki san," *Bungei shunjū*, November 1976, 340.

96. Onoda Hiro'o, *Tatta hitori no 30 nen sensō* (Tokyo shinbun shuppankyoku, 1995), 235. The accounts in this book were originally serialized in the *Tokyo shinbun*, the *Chūnichi shinbun*, and the *Hokuriku Chūnichi shinbun* under the title "Kono michi."

97. Reconciliation between the two parties, albeit desirable, should not be the court's primary goal. Such a goal could easily tie the victims' testimony to the

need for national healing and international accord. Richard A. Wilson, for example, critically discusses the nationalistic desire to produce national unity—"a new 'we'"—through the work of reconciliation (*The Politics of Truth and Reconciliation in South Africa: Legitimizing the Post-Apartheid State* [Cambridge: Cambridge University Press, 2001], 13–15).

98. The court proceedings would also have opened a floodgate of emotions concerning Japan's war in the Philippines. Instead, the officials of both countries preferred a quick and easy solution to the messy, prolonged process of working through these difficult memories.

99. As Pricilla B. Hayner observed, the process of giving testimony could not always be therapeutic: the victims could be retraumatized when they were forced to reexperience the traumatic events (*Unspeakable Truth: Transitional Justice and the Challenge of Truth Commissions* (London: Routledge, 2011), 152–55.

100. Tsuda, *Gensō no eiyū*, 62.

7. THE HOMECOMING OF THE "LAST JAPANESE SOLDIER"

1. *Asahi shinbun*, December 27, 1974, 13th ed., 15.
2. "Nakamura Teruo ittōhei no shirarezaru 'sengo' to shi," *Sandei mainichi*, November 11, 1979, 46–49.
3. *Sankei shinbun*, June 16, 1979, 15th ed., 19; *Asahi shinbun*, June 16, 1979, evening 3rd ed., 3; *Yomiuri shinbun*, June 16, 1979, evening 4th ed., 11; *Mainichi shinbun*, June 16, 1979, evening 4th ed., 10.
4. Marukawa Tetsushi, "Liu Lianren, Yokoi Shōichi, 'Nakamura Teruo' ni totte no sensō," in *Teikokuno sensōkeiken*, ed. Kurasawa Aiko et al., vol. 4 of Iwanami kōza Ajia Taiheiyō sensō (Tokyo: Iwanami shoten, 2006), 341.
5. Kawasaki Masumi, *Kaettekita Taiwanjin Nihonhei* (Tokyo: Bungei shunjū, 2003), 72.
6. Narita Ryūichi, "'Hikiage' to 'yokuryū,'" in *Teikoku no sensōkeiken*, ed. Kurasawa et al., 180–82.
7. The following statement that Maruyama Masao made in 1984 attests to the ways in which the presumption of Japanese society's homogeneity made former colonial subjects invisible:

No other highly industrialized nations maintain the level of ethnic homogeneity as Japan does. Some scholars these days claim that the ethnic homogeneity is a mere fiction or ideology. They bring up such examples as the Kumaso or the Hayato that appear in *Record of Ancient Matters* and *Chronicles of Japan*, the Ainu, and the origins of the people who have historically been discriminated against. What I am talking about is not that difficult an argument. In short, it is the matter of comparing Japan with other advanced capitalist nations in relative terms. The "scholars" are so educated that they cannot make a simple observation like this. The first thing that I feel when I come back from a foreign country is that, taking a train, "Aah, the passengers are almost all Japanese." (*Maruyama Masao chosakushū* [Tokyo: Iwanami shoten, 1996], 12:142)

To Maruyama, looking Japanese was the same thing as being Japanese. Maruyama could have been standing right next to some resident Koreans (it is virtually impossible to identify them just by their appearance) in the train car when he said to himself: "Aah, the passengers are almost all Japanese."

8. Morotai senyūkai's *Aa Morotai: Harushima senki* describes in detail the process through which "Taiwan moto Nihonjin heishi no hoshō mondai o kangaeru kai" (a group advocating compensation for the former Japanese soldiers from Taiwan) was established and the group's activities were carried out (Morotai senyūkai, ed., *Aa Morotai: Harushima senki* [Tokyo: Morotai senyūkai, 1978], 448–78). Responding to public demand, which the group helped shape, the Japanese Diet passed the bill that promised to compensate the former Japanese soldiers from Taiwan and their bereaved families. About 30,000 people were eligible for an average compensation of ¥2 million ($14,000) (*Asahi shinbun*, September 10, 1987, 4th ed., 1).

9. Beatrice Trefalt, *Japanese Army Stragglers and Memories of the War in Japan, 1950–1975* (New York: RoutledgeCurzon, 2003), 177; Marukawa, "Liu Lianren, Yokoi Shōichi, 'Nakamura Teruo' ni totte no sensō," 344.

10. Katō Yōko, *Chōheisei to kindai Nihon* (Tokyo: Yoshikawa kōbunkan, 1996), 254–55.

11. Morotai senyūkai, ed., *Aa Morotai: Harushima senki*, 9.

12. Ibid., 74, 131.

13. Ibid., 208.

14. "Nakamura Teruo san "kikan" Morotai-tō moto Nihonhei 13 nin no jinmyaku kenkyū," *Shūkan asahi*, January 17, 1975, 21.

15. Ibid., 22.

16. They actually "returned" to Japan: one of them eventually repatriated to Taiwan, while the rest settled in Tokyo (ibid., 20).

17. His sense of time was also skewed. He was upset with his wife because he believed that she could not have endured the five or six years of his absence and married another man (Satō Aiko, *Suniyon no isshō: Taiwan Takasago zoku giyūtai Nakamura Teruo no higeki* [Tokyo: Bungei shunjū, 1984], 79). In an interview, he insisted that he had lived in the same place since March 1945 (in reality, he probably did not set up camp there until 1952 or 1953). He also made the utterly unrealistic claim that he kept a precise calendar, even though he did not remember the date when he started his solitary life. The reporter who interviewed Nakamura tried to refute the accuracy of his calendar by explaining the convoluted conversion between the solar calendar and the lunar cycle that he used to count the days. But he just insisted that his calendar was amazingly accurate (Takahashi Teruaki, ed., "Ore wa hadaka no gensui da, 4: Koyomi wa 30 nen pitarito atta," *Shūkan sankei*, April 17, 1975, 53).

18. *Sankei shinbun*, December 31, 1974, 15th ed., 13.

19. Satō, *Suniyon no isshō*, 97–98.

20. "Nihon no moto senyū towa dōshitemo aitakunai," *Shūkan gendai*, January 30, 1975, 35.
21. "Tokubetsu intabyū Nihon no minasan e Morotai-tō no moto Nihonhei Nakamura Teruo," *Shūkan bunshun*, January 29, 1975, 33.
22. Takahashi Teruaki, ed., "Ore wa hadakano gensui da, 1: Watashi wa dassōhei dewa nakatta," *Shūkan sankei*, March 27, 1975, 36.
23. *Sandei mainichi*, January 19, 1975, 23.
24. Satō, *Suniyon no isshō*, 96–97.
25. Discussing Japanese society's responses to the indigenous Taiwanese Nakamura Teruo, the writer Inagaki Masami argued that popular fantastic images of the natives from the 1930s survived in postwar Japan and continued to conceal the harsh colonial reality ("Bōken Dankichi to Nakamura Teruo," *Chūōkōron*, April 1975, 212–15).
26. *Lianhebao*, December 28, 1974, 3; *Zhongguoshibao*, December 28, 1974, 3; *Sankei shinbun*, December 28, 1974, evening 5th ed., 6.
27. According to the Taiwanese book *Li Guanghui de shi jie*, someone told him at the hospital that his wife had already remarried, but he refused to believe it. While it helps explain his psychological state at that particular moment, this episode could well have been a later projection. Being produced in extreme haste (in several days), the book appears to reflect the author's intent to portray Nakamura as a decent human being. For example, it completely skips over the scene of his emotional outburst by suggesting that his wife picked up her belongings and left him of her own accord (Zhao Musong, *Li Guanghui de shijie* [Taipei: Jiang jun chu ban shi ye gu, 1975], 134, 144).
28. When he joined the military, his son was only one month old ("Morotai-tō no Nihonhei Nakamura Teruo san 30 nen no mukuware kata," *Shūkan taishū*, January 23, 1975, 24).
29. The writer Suzuki Akira writes that he heard this episode on the NHK's primetime television news show *Nyūsu sentaa 9 ji* ("Rikugun heichō Nakamura Suriyon," *Bungei shunjū*, March 1975, 186).
30. "Saikon shitanara ie ni kaerenai," *Sankei shinbun*, January 15, 1975, 15th ed., 14.
31. On January 12, 1975, *Lianhebao* reported that Nakamura would live with his son's family and that Li Lanyin and Huang Jinmu would continue to live together. The newspaper printed only two brief articles on him before it reported, on March 7, his second marriage with Li Lanyin. *Zhongguoshibao* eagerly covered Nakamura's case until he returned to Taiwan. But the paper stopped carrying articles about him after reporting on January 12 that the family members had been meeting to discuss Nakamura's future, and the paper did not even mention his second marriage.
32. "Nakamura ittōhei no shirarezaru 'sengo' to shi," *Sandei mainichi*, November 11, 1979, 48.
33. "32 nen buri no kokyō de 'bōchūkan," *Shūkan sankei*, March 27, 1975, 8.
34. "Nakamura ittōhei no shirarezaru 'sengo' to shi," 47; Kawasaki, *Kaettekita Taiwanjin Nihonhei*, 84–85.

35. "Jokei shakai ni modotta Nakamura Teruo san wa ima," *Shūkan bunshun*, April 23, 1975, 22.
36. According to the newspaper article that reported Nakamura's death four years later, he was smoking as many as eighty cigarettes a day (*Sankei shinbun*, June 16, 1979, 15th ed., 19.
37. Takahashi, ed., "Ore wa hadaka no gensui da, 4: Koyomi wa 30 nen pitarito atta," 51.
38. "Hanken dokusen Morotai-tō 31 nen 'Nakamura Teruo no tatta hitori no tatakai, 1,'" *Shūkan posuto*, March 14, 1975, 175.
39. Nakamura Teruo and Chen Haoyang, *Nakamura Teruo Morotai-tō 31 nen no kiroku* (Tokyo: Orijin shobō, 1975), 60.
40. Takahashi Teruaki, ed., "Ore wa hadaka no gensui da, 2: Hatsukoi no hito o daku yume o mita," *Shūkan sankei*, April 3, 1975, 52–53; "Ore wa hadaka no gensui da, 4: Koyomi wa 30 nen pitarito atta," 53–54; and "Ore wa hadaka no gensui da, 5: Suichū megane tsukutte unagi tori," *Shūkan sankei*, April 24, 1975, 57–58.
41. At the hospital, the doctors found that Nakamura was beginning to develop cataracts ("Mararia hatsubyō ka," *Sankei shinbun*, January 1, 1975, 15th ed., 22).
42. "Nakamura ittōhei no shirarezaru 'sengo' to shi," 48.
43. "Moto Nihonhei Nakamura Teruo san no 'sonogo,'" *Shūkan gendai*, February 9, 1978, 40.
44. *Sankei shinbun*, June 16, 1979, 15th ed., 19.
45. The Ministry of Health and Welfare announced that Nakamura would receive back pay of ¥38,279 (approx. $128) and a onetime repatriation allowance of ¥30,000 (approx. $100). But since he was no longer Japanese, he was not eligible for a military pension ("Jindōjō tachiba kara shori," *Asahi shinbun*, December 30, 1974, 13th ed., 3). The ministry ruled that the repatriation allowance applied, regardless of the country he returned to ("Nakamura san ni 68,000 yen," *Asahi shinbun*, December 31, 1974, 13th ed., 1).
46. "Morotai-tō no Nihonhei Nakamura Teruo san 30 nen no mukuware kata," 23–26.
47. For example, according to the Taiwanese newspaper *Lianhebao*, the local notables of Nakamura's hometown urged the authorities to facilitate his swift return there. The paper also printed the opinion of an individual in the diplomatic service that Nakamura should return to Taiwan (*Lianhebao*, December 28, 1974, 3). See also *Zhongyanribao*, January 9, 1975, reprinted in "Nihon no hyōban: gaikoku shi ni miru hankyō," *Bungei shunjū*, March 1975, 274.
48. Some Japanese newspapers and magazines printed his signature using the Japanese name "Nakamura Teruo" (*Sankei shinbun*, December 30, 1974, 15th ed., 12; *Asahi shinbun*, December 30, 1974, 13th ed., 14; "Nakamura moto ittōhei kogun 31 nen no kyokugen seikatsu," *Sandei mainichi*, January 19, 1975, 20). Meanwhile, *Zhongguoshibao* carried the Chinese message handwritten by Nakamura: "Li Guanhui is thankful that the people throughout the country have shown great care for him. He is happy to have come home to Taiwan" (Li Gua-

nhui xiexie quanguo tongbao de guanxin hengaoxing huida Taiwan lai). Since he was not literate in Chinese, Nakamura probably copied a message written by a reporter (*Zhongguoshibao*, January 9, 1975, 3).

49. In media representations since the second half of the 1960s, the kamikaze pilots, who were sent off by women, replaced the figures of the repatriated soldiers who either were assimilated into or disappeared from society (or, to extend the metaphor of animals, they flew away as hawks and eagles). In *Yellow Crow*, the repatriated man makes the transition back to his community with the help of the woman who patiently awaited his return (in real life at the time of the film's release, there were still many women awaiting their men's return). In later years, the cultural representations of the Japanese soldiers shifted to the men who would never return and the women who saw them off for their death missions. In a decade or so, the direction of popular concerns seems to have completely reversed.

50. *Asahi shinbun*, July 17, 1973, 13th ed., 1, 3.

51. *Yomiuri shinbun*, July 17, 1973, 4th evening ed., 1, 11: *Mainichi shinbun*, July 17, 1973, 4th evening ed., 1; *Sankei shinbun*, July 17, 1973, 5th evening ed., 7.

52. *Shūkan taishū*, August 2, 1973, 26–29; *Shūkan posuto*, August 3, 1973, 36–39; *Shūkan Asahi*, August 3, 1973, 143–47; *Sandei mainichi*, August 5, 1973, 20–24.

53. *Yomiuri shinbun*, July 21, 1973, 14th ed., 22. The *Sankei shinbun* printed the comments made by one of his "Japanese relatives" who met him: "Although there are some questions—there is a two-centimeter difference in height, and he has no memories before 1944—he seems to be Ryōji" (*Sankei shinbun*, July 21, 1973, 15th ed., 14).

54. "Ima dakara warau, Maboroshi no 'Miki Ryōji sōsaku no kara sawagi," *Shūkan shinchō*, August 9, 1973, 35.

55. "'Kangeki no hōdō' no ato no gonin 'Mindanao no Nihonhei' sōdō," *Shūkan sankei*, August 17, 1973, 168; "Hajime kara ayashikatta Mindanao no 'Moto Nihonhei,'" *Shūkan bunshun*, August 13, 1973, 174. The *Asahi*'s special correspondent, Murakami Yoshio, insisted that Tanao Tao was actually Miki Ryōji, despite the amount of contrary evidence ("Maboroshi ni owatta Nihonhei hakken dorama," *Shūkan asahi*, August 10, 1973, 147).

56. *Sankei shinbun*, July 19, 1973, 15th ed., 15.

57. "Aiji 17 nin to Mindanao ni ikiru!" *Sandei mainichi*, August 5, 1973, 22.

58. The *Asahi shinbun* listed this condition as one of the reasons why there were no strong reactions to Nakamura's discovery in Indonesia (*Asahi shinbun*, December 30, 1974, 13th ed., 14).

59. Murakami Yoshio, "Nihonjin de 'aritaku nakatta' Miki san no 30 nen," *Shūkan asahi*, August 3, 1973, 144.

60. Ibid.

61. Ibid.

62. Ibid.

63. Robert Tierney argues, "The cannibal never became a familiar or prevalent figure of the savage in Japanese colonial discourse" (*Tropics of Savagery: The*

Culture of Japanese Empire in Comparative Frame [Berkeley: University of California Press, 2010], 185). One of the notable exceptions was the popular *manga, Bōken Dankichi,* which portrays the native islanders as cannibals (Shimada Keizō, *Bōken Dankichi manga zenshū* [Tokyo: Kōdansha, 1967], 261–65).

64. As Masaki Tsuneo insists, any image of man-eating natives must be examined against the broader Western discourse on the colonial other. Masaki uses the imaginary cannibal tribe in Burma that Takeyama Michio's *Burmese Harp* (*Biruma no tategoto,* 1947–1948) portrays as a jumping-off point for such an inquiry (*Shokuminchi gensō* [Tokyo: Misuzu shobō, 1995], 13–15).

65. Fujiwara Akira, *Uejini shita eireitachi* (Tokyo: Aoki shoten, 2001), 99–101.

66. Ibid., 137.

67. In 1979, for example, Tomitani Shūkō publicly admitted that he had consumed fellow Japanese soldiers' flesh in New Guinea ("Watashi wa senyū no jinniku de ikinobita," *Shūkan yomiuri,* July 29, 1979, 152–54).

68. We could add to this list Takeda Taijun's novel *Luminous Moss* (*Hikarigoke,* 1954), a fictional account of a real-life event. The story takes place off the coast of Hokkaido, involving an army-commandeered ship and its crew. Cannibal practices also constitute a key motif in Hara Kazuo's documentary *The Emperor's Naked Army Marches On* (*Yukiyukite shingun,* 1987).

EPILOGUE

1. In his drafting notes, Kurosawa wrote: "There is no other way but to keep writing while crying. Actually no tears are coming out, but the face twitches like when it is covered with tears. Even the body trembles" (quoted in Tsuzuki Masa'aki, *Kurosawa Akira no yuigon "Yume"* [Tokyo: Kindai bungeisha, 2005], 36).

2. Bungei shunjū, ed., *Kurosawa Akira "yume wa tensai dearu"* (Tokyo: Bungei shunjū, 1999), 127–28.

3. Historian Ichinose Toshiya discusses the role that families and hometown played in mobilizing the nation, in his provocatively titled book *Furusato wa naze heishi o koroshita ka* (*Why Hometowns Killed Soldiers*) (Tokyo: Kadokawa shoten, 2010).

4. Japan's rapid economic development in the 1960s was a major cause of this change. Philosopher Uchiyama Takeshi posits 1965 as a watershed year for the folk belief's demise in Japan's rural communities. According to the rural residents whom Uchiyama interviewed, foxes—trickster animals in the Japanese folk belief—stopped tricking people around 1965 (Uchiyama Takeshi, *Nihonjin wa naze kitsune ni damasarenaku natta noka?* [*Why Did Foxes Stop Tricking the Japanese?*] [Tokyo: Kōdansha, 2007], 3–31).

5. The issue of rural depopulation was already beginning to receive the media's and policymakers' attention in the 1960s (Fujii Hidetada, "Kayōkyoku no nakano 'kokyō,'" in Narita Ryūichi et al., *Kokyō no sōshitsu to saisei* [Tokyo: Seikyūsha, 2000], 60).

6. Yamada Yōji's film *Musuko* (*Son*, 1991) laments the critical state of home in contemporary Japan at the tail end of its bubble-economy era. After his wife's death, an army veteran lives alone in a country house in the mountains of Iwate Prefecture. He is a problem for his three children, all of whom have moved elsewhere. After surviving a heart attack, he rekindles his familial feelings with his children. But at the end of the film, he sits all alone in the home filled with family memories. It is not hard to imagine the fate of his home as a physical space: it will disappear with the man's death: his house will remain unoccupied and eventually collapse under the weight of the snow.

7. In the actual shooting of the film, an assistant stood in the woods with a paper screen door while another assistant lit a light in it from behind. There was literally no home in this scene (Tsuzuki, *Kurosawa Akira no yuigon "Yume,"* 152). His nonchalant attitude toward Noguchi's home is a striking contrast with Kurosawa's meticulous care with other aspects of the film. For example, it took more than three months for him and his staff to come up with satisfactory fox makeup for the "Sunshine Through the Rain" segment (80–83). Kurosawa was known for his obsessive attention to detail: he once had his staff paint the white walls with black paint first in order to give the white some "depth" (Tasogawa Hiroshi, *Kurosawa Akira vs. Hariwuddo: "Tora, Tora, Tora!" sono nazo no subete* [Tokyo: Bungei shunjū, 2006], 291).

8. While similar trickery was used to bring Onoda Hiro'o back home, in that case, Onoda initiated the move, outsmarting the postwar media and society.

9. Cultural critic Sashida Fumio argues that the fact that Kurosawa dodged military service during the war became a psychological burden on him (*Kurosawa Akira no jūjika: sensō to Tuburaya tokusatsu to chōhei kihi* [Tokyo: Gendai-kikakushitsu, 2013]). The circumstances under which Kurosawa avoided the draft are not clear. Sashida speculates that Tōhō Studios used its political clout to protect him because they regarded Kurosawa as the next great director. Sashida then locates the director's guilty conscience in Kurosawa's film. He offers no documentary evidence and his argument is largely speculative, but his readings of Kurosawa's films are compelling. Extending Sashida's argument, I submit that the tunnel segment in *Dreams* shows not only Kurosawa's remorse but also his sense of closure, in that he is finally freed from his demons.

10. It is widely acknowledged that the tunnel segment is cast in the fantasy nō format, in which a supernatural being appears before a traveler (Bungei shunjū, ed., *Kurosawa Akira "yume wa tensai dearu,"* 119). However, the similarity remains rather superficial. For example, the officer tells the ghosts what happened to them: since having been left in a state of total ignorance, the ghosts have lost their own story and agency. In nō plays, by contrast, the fantastic beings tell stories about themselves and the circumstances that led to their deaths.

11. Kurosawa Akira kenkyūkai, ed., *Kurosawa Akira: yume no ashioto* (Tokyo: Kyōdō tsūshinsha, 1999), 308. The *zuidō deita beisu* (tunnel database) website provides the details of the tunnel: http://tdb.the-orj.org/view.php?no=2744.

12. Kurosawa uses the dog to represent the frightening nature of Japan's militarism and imperialism. But it actually wags its tail excitedly in the scene, sensing the actor Terao Akira's affection. The dark past thus appears to be already pacified (Bungei shunjū, ed., *Kurosawa Akira "yume wa tensai dearu,"* 130).

13. "Shōgensha: sono genba ni watashi wa ita," *Sandei mainichi*, December 31, 1972, 132.

BIBLIOGRAPHY

Abe Gunji. *Shiberia kyōseiyokuryū no jittai: Nisso ryōkoku shiryō karano kenshō.* Tokyo: Sairyūsha, 2005.

Abe Yoshikuni. "Watashi mo keihai datta: 3 nenkan kunan no yokuryū." In *Shiberia keihai: Soren yokuryū no kōishō*, edited by Yamamoto Yasuo, 199–204. Tokyo: Shiberia keihai zenkoku renrakukai, 1983.

Aida Yūji. "Kōfuku na futari no Nihonhei." *Bungei shunjū*, December 1972, 176–82.

Aida Yūji and Onoda Hiro'o. "Kangaeteita Nihon, genjitsu no Nippon." *Gendai*, July 1974, 78–93.

——. "Nihon o suteru watashi no kokoro no kokosoko niwa." *Shūkan gendai*, February 20, 1975, 28–34.

"Aiji 17 nin to Mindanao ni ikiru!" *Sandei mainichi*, August 5, 1973, 20–23.

Akita Ken. *Haha no uta serekushon.* Tokyo: Fūjinsha, 2001.

"Ano suchuwaadesu san no yōna wakai musume san ga iinō." *Shūkan heibon*, February 17, 1972, 38–41.

"Ano Yokoi san ga gunjin ni gyakumodori!?" *Yangu redii*, July 23, 1973, 11.

Anzai Hiroshi. *Ishihara Yoshirō no shi no sekai.* Tokyo: Kyōbunkan, 1981.

Aonuma Yōichirō. *Kikan sezu: zanryū Nihon-hei 60 nenme no shōgen.* Tokyo: Shinchōsha, 2006.

Asahi shinbunsha, ed. *Asahi jinbutsu jiten.* Tokyo: Asahi shinbunsha, 1990.

Asari Atsushi. "Shikisai to seikaku (muishiki no gengo)." *Color*, June 1953, 4–13.

Ayukawa Nobuo and Yoshimoto Taka'aki. "Ishihara Yoshirō no shi: sengoshi no kiki." *Jiba*, spring 1978, 136–56.

Ban Toshihiko. "Tōji no sesō to jiken no keika o otte." *Shinpyō*, August 1971, 228–34.

Bao Ninh. *The Sorrow of War: A Novel of North Vietnam.* New York: Pantheon Books, 1995.

Barshay, Andrew. *The Gods Left First: The Captivity and Repatriation of Japanese POWs in Northeast Asia, 1945–1956.* Berkeley: University of California Press, 2013.

"Bestoseraa no kakureta jōken." *Shūkan shinchō,* August 18, 1958, 34–35.

Biess, Frank. *Homecomings: Returning POWs and Legacies of Defeat in Postwar Germany.* Princeton, N.J.: Princeton University Press, 2006.

——. "Pioneers of a New Germany: Rethinking POWs from the Soviet Union and the Making of East German Citizens, 1945–1950." *Central European History* 32, no. 2 (1999): 143–80.

——. "Survivors of Totalitarianism: Returning POWs and the Reconstruction of Masculine Citizenship in West Germany, 1945–1955." In *The Miracle Years: A Cultural History of West Germany, 1949–1968,* edited by Hanna Schissler, 57–82. Princeton, N.J.: Princeton University Press, 2001.

"Bōken zuki Nihonjin seinen no Onoda moto Shōi 'hakken to kyūshutsu.'" *Shūkan sankei,* March 22, 1974, 12–15.

Borges, Jorge Luis. "On Rigor in Science." In *A Universal History of Infamy.* Translated by Norman Thomas di Giovanni. New York: Dutton, 1972.

Bungei shunjū, ed. *Kurosawa Akira "yume wa tensai dearu."* Tokyo: Bungei shunjū, 1999.

Cunningham, Lawrence J., and Janice J. Beaty. *A History of Guam.* Honolulu: Bess Press, 2001.

"Daremo ga odoroita! Yokoi Shōichi san genkōroku." *Shūkan josei,* March 24, 1973, 38–40.

"Doku o kutteita Yokoi Shōichi san eno 10 no?'" *Shūkan taishū,* February 24, 1972, 146–48.

Drea, Edward. *In the Service of the Emperor: Essays on the Imperial Japanese Army.* Lincoln: University of Nebraska Press, 1998.

Emori Kōyō. "'Ikinobiru koto wa' haji nanoka." In Yokoi Mihoko, *Chinkon no tabiji: Yokoi Shōichi no sengo o ikita tsuma no shuki,* 220–30. Osaka: Horusu shuppan, 2011.

Esaki Masanori. "Sengo ishoku jinbutsu tanken, 2: Kodaira Yoshio, jō." *Shūkan gendai,* January 21, 1962, 68–72.

Figal, Gerald. "How to *jibunshi*: Making and Marketing Self-Histories of Shōwa Among the Masses in Postwar Japan." *Journal of Asian Studies* 55, no. 4 (1996): 902–33.

Fujii Hidetada. "Kayōkyoku no nakano 'kokyō.'" In Narita Ryūichi et al., *Kokyō no sōshitu to saisei,* 37–90. Tokyo: Seikyūsha, 2000.

Fujinami Osamu. "Rubangu-tō no izoku." *Shokun,* September 1977, 117–34.

Fujitake Akira. "Sengo jikenshi no imi." *Shokun,* December 1974, 34–48.

Fujiwara Akira. *Uejini shita eireitachi.* Tokyo: Aoki shoten, 2001.

Fujiwara Tei. *Nagareru hoshi wa ikiteiru.* Tokyo: Chūōkōron, 1994.

——. *Tei: A Memoir of the End of War and Beginning of Peace.* Translated by Nana Mizushima. Tonnbo Books, 2014.

Fukuda Ajio et al., eds. *Nihon minzoku dai-jiten.* Tokyo: Yoshikawa kōbunkan, 1999.

Fukui Hideo. *Seishun no nagai michi.* Tokyo: Kyōikushiryō shuppankai, 1995.

Fukuma Yoshiaki. *"Sensō taiken" no sengoshi: sedai, kyōyō, ideorogii.* Tokyo: Chūōkōron shinsha, 2009.

———. *Shōdo no kioku: Okinawa, Hiroshima, Nagasaki ni utsuru sengo*. Tokyo: Shin'yōsha, 2011.

Futaba Kaname. *Shiberia-horyo no shuki*. Tokyo: Daigensha, 1947.

———. *Shiberia ni iru Nihonjin horyo no jitsujō*. Denver: Saikensha, 1948.

"'Ganpeki no haha' Hashino Ise san (75 sai) mukuwareta shūnen no kiroku." *Shūkan heibon*, July 10, 1975, 53–57.

"Gendai no eiyū shiriizu 2: Onoda Hiro'o." *Shūkan bunshun*, March 25, 1974, 136–40.

Gluck, Carol. "The Human Condition." In *Past Imperfect: History According to the Movies*, edited by Ted Mico, John Miller-Monzon, and David Rubel, 250–53. New York: Holt, 1995.

"'Gokainin' sawagi de morashita Yokoi Shōichi fūfu no hagemikata." *Shūkan posuto*, February 1, 1974, 44.

Gomikawa Junpei. "Genten to shiteno waga 'sensō to ningen.'" *Ushio*, August 1971, 191–95.

———. *Jiyū tono keiyaku*. 6 vols. Tokyo: San'ichi shobō, 1958–1960.

———. "Rekishi no jikken." *Chūōkōron*, January–April 1959.

———. *Rekishi no jikken*. Tokyo: Chūōkōron, 1959.

———. "Seishin no gan." In *Watashi to sensō*, edited by Gomikawa Junpei, Murakami Ichirō, and Yamada Munemitsu, 9–60. Tokyo: Shunjūsha, 1959.

———. *Senki shōsetsu-shū*. Tokyo: Bungei shunjū, 1993.

———. "Waga shōsetsu: Ningen no jōken." *Asahi shinbun*, December 25, 1961, 12th ed., 6.

Gomikawa Junpei and Aratama Michiyo. "Katsumokushite machimashō." *Chūōkōron*, May 1959, 156–63.

Gomikawa Junpei et al. "'15 nen sensō' no imi." *Rekishi hyōron*, January 1972, 2–30.

"Gomikawa-ke honjitsu tabō: wadai no 'Ningen no jōken' sonogo." *Shūkan asahi*, March 16, 1958, 112–13.

Gosho Heinosuke. *Waga seishun*. Tokyo: Ōzorasha, 1998.

"'Guamu jiheishō' no shakai fukki ni machikamaeru otoshiana." *Shūkan sankei*, February 18, 1972, 24–27.

"'Guamu-tō 28 nen' ikinokori no kyōi o shusseiji kara tsuiseki suru." *Shūkan posuto*, February 11, 1972, 20–27.

"Guamu-tō senyūkai no 'hiirō Yokoi' o mirume." *Shūkan bunshun*, February 21, 1972, 136–41.

"Guamu-tō shinkon ryokō de mitazo Yokoi fūfu no sugoude." *Shūkan bunshun*, March 26, 1973, 46–49.

"Hajime kara ayashikatta Mindanao no 'Moto Nihonhei.'" *Shūkan bunshun*, August 13, 1973, 172–175.

"Hanken dokusen Morotai-tō 31 nen 'Nakamura Teruo no tatta hitori no tatakai, 1.'" *Shūkan posuto*, March 14, 1975, 172–76.

"Hapuningu ga okotta Yokoi san tono isshūkan." *Shūkan bunshun*, July 8, 1974, 38–42.

Hasegawa Shirō. *Shiberia monogatari*. Tokyo: Kōdansha, 1991.

Hatashin, Omi. *Private Yokoi's War and Life on Guam, 1944–1972*. Folkestone, Kent: Global Oriental, 2009.

Hataya Fumiyo. *Shiberia yokuryū towa nandatta no ka*. Tokyo: Iwanami shoten, 2009.

"Hateshinaki shokku o kataru kakkai 100 nin." *Shūkan bunshun*, April 8, 1974, 26–32.

Hatsuda Kōsei. "Tokyo no sengo fukkō to yamiichi." In *Sakariba wa yamiichi kara umareta*, edited by Hashimoto Kenji and Hatsuda Kōsei. Tokyo: Seikyūsha, 2013.

Hayano Tōru. *Tanaka Kakuei*. Tokyo: Chūōkōron shinsha, 2012.

Hayashi Ei'ichi. "Onoda Hiro'o to Yokoi Shōichi: Yutakana shakai ni shutsugen shita Nihon hei." In *Nihon rettō kaizō: 1970 nendai*, edited by Sugita Atsushi, 217–43. Vol. 6 of Hitobito no seishinshi. Tokyo: Iwanami shoten, 2016.

——. *Zanryū Nihonhei: Ajia ni ikita ichimannin no sengo*. Tokyo: Chūōkōron shinsha, 2012.

Hayashi Risuke. "Firipin baishō." In *Nihon no sengo baishō: Ajia kyōryoku no shuppatsu*, edited by Nagao Shin'ichirō and Kondō Masaomi, 69–81. Tokyo: Keisō shobō, 1999.

Hayner, Pricilla B. *Unspeakable Truth: Transitional Justice and the Challenge of Truth Commissions*. London: Routledge, 2011.

"Hazukashi nagara toruko o taikenshimashita." *Gendai*, May 1973, 276–83.

Heibonsha, ed. *Gendai jinmei jōhō jiten*. Tokyo: Heibonsha, 1990.

"Hi ga tatsuni turete Yokoi san no datsu Guamu genkōroku." *Shūkan shinchō*, February 19, 1972, 32–35.

"Hiirō No. 2 Suzuki seinen no 'waga Onoda kyūshutsu sakusen.'" *Shūkan sankei*, March 29, 1974, 10–13.

"Hikiagetewa mitakeredo." *Shinsō*, January 1950, 53–56.

Hikita Sōya. *Zenkiroku terebi shichōritsu 50 nen kyōsō*. Tokyo: Kōdansha, 2004.

Hiranuma Gyokutarō. "30 dai to iu jinsei wa nai." In *Namida ni urumu Maizurukō*, edited by Sōkagakkai hansen seinenbu hansen shuppan iinkai, 32–44. Tokyo: Daisanbunmei sha, 1979.

Hirasawa Yoshihiro. *Ekkyō: Okada Yoshiko, Sugimoto Ryōkichi no dabisubitaanya*. Sapporo: Hokkaidō shinbunsha, 2000.

Hirose Saburō. "Jikyū jisoku ni taete." In *Horyo taikenki*, edited by Takahashi Daizō et al., 7:142–45. Tokyo: Soren ni okeru Nihonjin horyo no seikatsu taiken o kirokusuru kai, 1989.

"Hitori de tatakkata 'himitsu no 28 nen' shijō kanzen rokuon, kiseki no seikan." *Shūkan sankei*, February 26, 1972, 16–20.

Hokari Kashio. *Shiberia furyoki: ichi heishi no kakokunaru yokuryūtaiken*. Tokyo: Kōjinsha, 2009.

Honda Yasuharu. "Onoda Hiro'o moto Shōi to katari akashita 'Tennō to heitai.'" *Shūkan gendai*, April 1, 1976, 122–26.

"Hontō ni futari o koroshita noka? Yokoi Shōichi san no misuterii kako." *Shūkan myōjō*, May 21, 1972, 198–99.

Hori Hidehiko. "Seibugeki *Ningen no jōken*." *Shinchō*, July 1958, 66–69.

"Hyakunin no 20 seiki, Yokoi Shōichi." *Asahi shinbun*, August 15, 1999, Sunday ed., WD, A–B.

Ichinose Toshiya. *Furusato wa naze heishi o koroshita ka*. Tokyo: Kadokawa shoten, 2010.

——. *Kōgun heishi no nichijō seikatsu.* Tokyo: Kōdansha, 2009.

"Ikita 'Senjinkun' 28 nenme no konwaku." *Shūkan yomiuri,* February 11, 1972, 23–25.

Igarashi, Yoshikuni. *Bodies of Memory: Narratives of War in Postwar Japanese Culture, 1945–1970.* Princeton, N.J.: Princeton University Press, 2000.

——. "Mothra's Gigantic Egg: Consuming the South Pacific in 1960s Japan." In *In Godzilla's Footsteps: Japanese Pop Culture Icons on the Global Stage,* edited by William Tsutsui and Michiko Ito, 83–102. New York: Palgrave Macmillan, 2006.

Iijima Kōichi. "Kobayashi Masaki to 'Ningen no jōken.'" *Eigahyōron,* January 1961, 74–77.

Iizawa Tadasu. "Reigai wa kihan ni naranu." *Shūkan asahi,* February 11, 1972, 21.

"Ima dakara warau, Maboroshi no Miki Ryōji sōsaku no kara sawagi." *Shūkan shinchō,* August 9, 1973, 32–35.

Inagaki Masami. "Bōken Dankichi to Nakamura Teruo." *Chūōkōron,* April 1975, 208–15.

Inoue Yasumasa. *Enzai no kiseki.* Tokyo: Shinchōsha, 2011.

Ishida Ayuu. *Micchii būmu.* Tokyo: Bungei shunjū, 2006.

Ishihara Shintarō. "Harukana ikyō Burajiru de watashi wa tatakai owatta otoko no kokoro no soko o mita." *Sandei mainichi,* August 10, 1975, 16–23.

——. *Taiyō no kisetsu.* Tokyo: Shinchōsha, 1956.

Ishinomori Shōtarō. *Ningen no jōken.* 4 vols. Tokyo: Bukkusu Tokyo, 1998.

Ishinomori Takeo. *Saihate no nagareboshi.* Tokyo: Kindai bungeisha,1996.

Itō Eiji. "Watashi no taiken keika." In *Horyo taikenki,* edited by Takahashi Daizō et al., 2:237–38. Tokyo: Soren ni okeru Nihonjin horyo no seikatsu taiken o kiroku-suru kai, 1984.

Itō Masashi. *The Emperor's Last Soldiers: The Grim Story of Two Japanese Who Hid for Sixteen Years in the Guam Jungle.* New York: Coward-McCann, 1967.

——. *Guamu-tō.* Tokyo: Futami shobō, 1960.

Iyotani Toshio and Hirata Yumi, eds. *"Kikyō" no monogatari / "Idō" no katari.* Tokyo: Heibonsha, 2013.

"Jokei shakai ni modotta Nakamura Teruo san wa ima." *Shūkan bunshun,* April 23, 1975, 22.

"Kaji no ikikata to shi: Gomikawa *Ningen no jōken* to sono dokusha." *Nihon dokusho shinbun,* June 16, 1958, 1.

Kaji Sōichi. "Watashi ga tachiatta Yokoi, Kozuka, Onoda san no sei to shi." *Sandei mainichi,* March 31, 1974, 25–29.

"Kakureta besutoseraa 'Ningen no jōken.'" *Shukan asahi,* February 16, 1958, 3–9.

Kamata Satoshi. *Hirosaki daigaku kyōju fujin satsujin jiken.* Tokyo: Shinpūsha, 2006.

Kamei Tsutomu. *Shiberia yokuryūsha to izoku wa ima.* Kyoto: Kamogawa shuppan, 1992.

"'Kangeki no hōdō' no ato no gonin 'Mindanao no Nihonhei' sōdō." *Shūkan sankei,* August 17, 1973, 166–69.

Kariyuki Seiji. "Kūfuku no akumu." In *Namida ni urumu Maizurukō,* edited by Sōkagakkai hansen seinenbu hansen shuppan iinkai, 93–101. Tokyo: Daisanbun-mei sha, 1979.

Karpov, Victor. *Sutaarin no horyotachi: Soren kimitsu shiryō ga kataru zenyō.* Translated by Nagase Ryōji. Sapporo: Hokkaidō shinbunsha, 2001.

Kasahara Kazuo. *Hametsu no bigaku: yakuza eiga eno rekuiemu.* Tokyo: Tōgensha, 1997.

Kasuga Taichi. *Nakadai Tatsuya ga kataru Nihon eiga ōgonjidai.* Kyoto: PHP kenkyūjo, 2013.

Kasuya Eiichi. "Ishihara Yoshirō no omoide." In *Techō* Vol. 3 of *Ishihara Yoshirō zenshū,* 1–2. Tokyo: Kashinsha, 1980.

Katasonova, Elena. *Kantōgun heishi wa naze Shiberia ni yokuryū saretaka.* Translated by Shirai Hisaya. Tokyo: Shakai hyōronsha, 2004.

Katō Kiyofumi. *"Dai Nippon Teikoku" hōkai.* Tokyo: Chūōkōron shinsha, 2009.

——. "Dai Nippon Teikoku no hōkai to zanryū Nihonjin hikiage mondai." In *Dai Nippon Teikoku no hōkai to hikiage, fukuin,* edited by Masuda Hiroshi, 13–48. Tokyo: Keiōgijuku daigaku shuppankai, 2012.

Katō Kyūzō. *Shiberia ki.* Tokyo: Ushio shuppansha, 1980.

Katō Nobutada. *Watashi no Shiberia nōto.* Fujisawa: Takeda shuppan, 2007.

Katō Yōko. *Chōheisei to kindai Nihon.* Tokyo: Yoshikawa kōbunkan, 1996.

——. "Haisha no kikan." *Kokusai seiji,* no. 109, May 1995, 110–25.

Kawamoto Saburō. *Ima hitotabi no Nihon eiga.* Tokyo: Iwanami shoten, 1994.

Kawamura Katsumi. *Kuroi tora: Nihongami zukuri ichidai-ki.* Osaka: Fōramu A, 1996.

Kawasaki Masumi. *Kaettekita Taiwanjin Nihonhei.* Tokyo: Bungei shunjū, 2003.

Kazuki Yasuo. *Watashi no Shiberia.* Tokyo: Bungei shunjū, 1970.

"Kieta yūmeijin no nikusei, Yokoi Shōichi (75)." *Shūkan hōseki,* May 17, 1990, 49–50.

Kikuchi Ikuzō. "Burajiru no Onoda Hiro'o Nihonkoku musekinin-ron o kataru." *Asahi jaanaru,* October 3, 1975, 79–83.

"'Kimi wa sensō no koto o nanimo shiranai na' youyōni Nihongo o shaberi tsuzuketa Onoda moto shōi." *Shūkan asahi,* March 25, 1974, 30–33.

Kiridōshi Risaku. *Honda Ishirō: mukan no kyoshō.* Tokyo: Yōsensha, 2014.

"Kiseki no hito o ningen-girai ni shita 10 kakan." *Shūkan gendai,* February 17, 1972, 26–29.

Kishida Junpei. "Kigakarina hito tanken: Yokoi Shōichi san to heikasama to soshite . . . " *Josei jishin,* February 26, 1972, 162–66.

Kishi Nobuhito. *Keizai hakusho monogatari.* Tokyo: Bungei shunjū, 1999.

Kitahara Shigee. *Sakufū no nakano furyo: Shiberia yokuryū seikatsu no kiroku.* Tokyo: Kenkōsha, 1971.

"Kodaira Yoshio no yobichōsho." *Shinpyō,* August 1971, 236–50.

Komatsu Tsuneo et al., eds. "Kakureta besutoseraa 'Ningen no jōken.'" *Shukan asahi,* February 16, 1958, 3–9.

Konno Tsutomu. "Okada Yoshiko no ushinawareta 10 nen." *Chūōkōron,* December 1994, 323–41.

"Kono haha wa mada matteiru!" *Shūkan josei,* December 23, 1972, 40–43.

Kōseishō engo kyoku. "Rubangu-tō moto Nihonhei sōsa hōkokusho." August 1973.

Kōseishō shakai engo kyoku engo 50 nenshi henshū iinkai, ed. *Engo 50 nenshi.* Tokyo: Gyōsei, 1997.

Koyabu Shigeyoshi. "Kokoro no kokyō—Maizuru—hikiage no kiroku." In *Maizuru hikiage kinenkan, Hikiage shuki watashi no hikiage, jō,* 253–62. Maizuru: Maizuru hikiage kinenkan, 1992.

Kubo Sadajirō. "Chichioya no ketsujo matawa fuzai." In *Shikisai no shinri: kodomono eno shinriteki kiroku,* edited by Kubo Sadajirō et al., 15–18. Tokyo: Dai Nihon shuppan, 1956.

Kuchiki Takashi and Narushima Sei. "Aa rikugun gochō Yokoi Shōichi ikite ryoshū no hazukashime o ukezu." *Shūkan sankei,* February 26, 1972, 63–94.

Kurihara Toshio. *Shibeira yokuryū wa "kako" nanoka.* Tokyo: Iwanami shoten, 2011.

Kurosawa Akira. *Gama no abura: jiden no yōnamono.* Tokyo: Iwanami shoten, 2001.

——. *Something Like an Autobiography.* New York: Knopf, 1982.

Kurosawa Akira kenkyūkai, ed. *Kurosawa Akira: yume no ashioto.* Tokyo: Kyōdō tsūshinsha, 1999.

Kusanagi Taiji. "Watashi no Shiberia-ki, shō." In *Horyo taikenki,* edited by Takahashi Daizō et al., 7:106–14. Tokyo: Soren ni okeru Nihonjin horyo no seikatsu taiken o kirokusuru kai, 1989.

Kuwabara Takeo. "Setsujitsuna kansō." *Chūōkōron,* January 1954, 108–9.

"Kyabarei de taishō ni shōshin shiteita Yokoi Shōichi san." *Asahi geinō,* July 26, 1973, 12–14.

"Kyoshu no rei, guntō, dangan, senkyō hōkoku, soshite mangetsu no yoru." *Shūkan yomiuri,* March 23, 1974, 16–19.

Liu Wenbing. "Rekishi o utsusu hizunda kagami no yōni: 'Keimin eiga' ni miru Manshūkoku no hyōshō." In *Fumikoeru dokyumentarii,* edited by Kurosawa Kyoshi et al., 131–53. Vol. 7 of Nihon eiga wa ikiteiru. Tokyo: Iwanami shoten, 2010.

"Mada hatsugen shiteinakatta 'machi no koe.'" *Shūkan yomiuri,* February 18, 1972, 50–51.

Maeno Shigeru. *Ikeru shikabane.* 3 vols. Tokyo: Shunjūsha, 1961.

Mainichi shinbunsha. *Saigo no ippei: Guamu tō shuzai kishadan no zenkiroku.* Tokyo: Mainichi shinbunsha, 1972.

Maizuru hikiage kinenkan. *Hikiage shuki: watashi no hikiage, jō* Maizuru: Maizuru hikiage kinenkan, 1992.

——. *Maizuru hikiage kinenkan zuroku.* Maizuru: Maizuru hikiage kinenkan, 2000.

Maizuru-shi. *Shiberia yokuryūgaten zuroku.* Maizuru: Maizuru hikiage kinenkan, 1995.

"Manshū ni atta Aushubittsu." *Shūkan shinchō,* August 20, 1956, 90–93.

Marukawa Tetsushi. "Liu Lianren, Yokoi Shōichi, 'Nakamura Teruo' ni totteno sensō." In *Teikokuno sensōkeiken,* edited by Kurasawa Aiko et al., 323–50. Vol. 4 of Iwanami kōza Ajia Taiheiyō sensō. Tokyo: Iwanami shoten, 2006.

Maruyama Masao. *Maruyama Masao chosakushū.* Vol. 12. Tokyo: Iwanami shoten, 1996.

Masaki Tuneo. *Shokuminchi gensō.* Tokyo: Misuzu shobō, 1995.

Masuda Hiroshi, ed. *Dai Nippon teikoku no hōkai to hikiage, fukuin.* Tokyo: Keiōgijuku daigaku shuppankai, 2012.

Matsufuji Hajime and Nawata Senrō. *Sengo Soren de keihai ni kakatta Nihonjin furyotachi.* Tokyo: Nihon tosho kankōkai, 1997.

Mikuni Ichirō. *Senchū yōgoshū*. Tokyo: Iwanami shoten, 1985.

Minagawa Bunzō. *Nanmei no hateni*. Tokyo: Chōbunsha, 1960.

Ministry of Internal Affairs and Communications, Statistics Bureau, Director-General for Policy Planning (Statistical Standards) & Statistical Research and Training Institute. *Historical Statistics of Japan*. Chapter 26. http://www.stat.go.jp/english /data/chouki/26.htm.

"'Mitsurin no himitsu' o kokuhaku shita Shōicchuan no dōyō." *Shūkan taishū*, May 18, 1972, 142–44.

Miyazawa Ki'ichi. *Sengoseiji no shōgen*. Tokyo: Yomiuri shinbunsha, 1991.

Mizuki Shigeru. *He no yōna jinsei*. Tokyo: Kadokawa shoten, 2009.

——. *Musume ni kataru otōsan no senki: minami no shima no sensō no hanashi*. Tokyo: Shakai hyōronsha, 1999.

Mizutani Eiji. *Akai tōdo*. Hara shobō, 1969.

Morimoto Yoshio. *Shiberia horyoki: shi to zetsubō karano kikan*. Tokyo: Shunjūsha, 2001.

Morisawa Hiroshi. "Daigo bunsho, tsurushi agerareru made." In *Horyo taikenki*, edited by Takahashi Daizō et al., 4:433–38. Tokyo: Soren ni okeru Nihonjin horyo no seikatsu taiken o kirokusuru kai, 1985.

Morotai senyūkai, ed. *Aa Morotai: Harushima senki*. Morotai senyūkai, 1978.

"Morotai-tō no Nihonhei Nakamura Teruo san 30 nen no mukuware kata." *Shūkan taishū*, January 23, 1975, 23–26.

"Moto Nihonhei Nakamura Teruo san no 'sonogo.'" *Shūkan gendai*, February 9, 1978, 40.

Murakami Yasuhiko. "Watashi no seishun." In Maizuru hikiage kinenkan, *Hikiage shuki: watashi no hikiage*, jō, 95–104. Maizuru: Maizuru hikiage kinenkan, 1992.

Murakami Yoshio. "Maboroshi ni owatta Nihonhei hakken dorama." *Shūkan asahi*, August 10, 1973, 146–47.

——. "Nihonjin de 'aritaku nakatta' Miki-san no 30 nen." *Shūkan asahi*, August 3, 1973, 143–47.

Murase Manabu. *Naze "oka" o utau kakyōkyoku ga takusan tsukurarete kitanoka*. Tokyo: Shunjūsha, 2002.

Murayama Tsuneo. *Shiberia ni ikishi 46300 mei o kizamu: Soren yokuryū shibōsha meibo o tsukuru*. Tokyo: Nanatsumori shokan, 2009.

Nagai Hitoshi. *Firipin BC kyū senpan saiban*. Tokyo: Kōdansha, 2013.

Nagano Shin'ichirō and Kondō Masaomi, eds. *Nihon no sengo baishō: Ajia kyōryoku no shuppatsu*. Tokyo: Keisō shobō, 1999.

Nagaoka Keiji. "300 pon no bohyō o nokoshite." In *Horyo taikenki*, edited by Takahashi Daizō et al., 7:276–86. Tokyo: Soren ni okeru Nihonjin horyo no seikatsu taiken o kirokusuru kai, 1989.

Nagasawa Yoshio. *Shiberia yokuryū to sengo Nihon: kikansha tachi no tatakai*. Tokyo: Yūshisha, 2011.

Nagase Ryōji. *Shiberia yokuryū zenshi*. Tokyo: Harashobō, 2013.

Naikaku sōridaijin kanbō kōhōshitsu, ed. *Zenkoku yoron chōsa no genkyō, Heisei 9 nendo* [1996]. Tokyo: Sōrifu, 1997.

——, ed. *Zenkoku yoron chōsa no genkyō, Heisei 14 nendo* [2001]. Tokyo: Sōrifu, 2002.

——, ed. *Zenkoku yoron chōsa no genkyō, Shōwa 35 nendo* [1960]. Tokyo: Sōrifu, 1961.

Nakahara Toshio. "Watashi no Shiberia monogatari." In *Horyo taikenki*, edited by Takahashi Daizō et al., 4:34–43. Tokyo: Soren ni okeru Nihonjin horyo no seikatsu taiken o kirokusuru kai, 1985.

Nakai Yoshiharu. "Kōshi no nakakara mita Soren." *Chūōkōron*, January 1954, 100–101.

Nakajima Kazuo. *Shūyōjo bungaku-ron*. Tokyo: Ronsōsha, 2008.

Nakamaki Yasuhiro. *Toraware no seishun: Mōhitotsu no Shiberia yokuryūki*. Tokyo: Chōbunsha, 1991.

"Nakamura moto ittōhei kogun 31 nen no kyokugen seikatsu." *Sandei mainichi*, January 19, 1975, 20–26.

Nakamura Teruo and Chen Haoyang. *Nakamura Teruo Morotai-tō 31 nen no kiroku*. Tokyo: Orijin shobō, 1975.

"Nakamura Teruo ittōhei no shirarezaru 'sengo' to shi." *Sandei mainichi*, November 11, 1979, 46–49.

"Nakamura Teruo-san "kikan" Morotai-tō moto Nihonhei 13 nin no jinmyaku kenkyū." *Shūkan asahi*, January 17, 1975, 20–22.

Nakane Hitoshi. "Watashi no yokuryū reki." In *Horyo taikenki*, edited by Takahashi Daizō et al., 4:211–17. Tokyo: Soren ni okeru Nihonjin horyo no seikatsu taiken o kirokusuru kai, 1985.

Nakano Satoshi. "The Politics of Mourning." In *Philippines-Japan Relations*, edited by Ikehata Setsuho and Lydia N. Yu Jose, 337–76. Quezon City: Ateneo de Manila University Press, 2003.

Nakauchi Isao et al. "Onoda shōi to warera Taishō sedai no 30 nen." *Gendai*, May 1974, 108–22.

Nakazawa Masao. *Hibakusha no kokoro no kizu o otte*. Tokyo: Iwanami shoten, 2007.

Narita Ryūichi. "'Hikiage' ni kansuru joshō." *Shisō*, no. 955 (November 2003): 149–74.

——. "'Hikiage' to 'yokuryū.'" In *Teikoku no sensō keiken*, edited by Kurasawa Aiko et al., 179–208. Vol. 4 of Iwanami kōza Ajia Taiheiyō sensō. Tokyo: Iwanami shoten, 2006.

Nenji keizai hōkoku (Keizai hakusho). 1956. http://www5.cao.go.jp/keizai3/keizaiwp/index.html.

NHK "Ryūyō sareta Nihonjin" shuzai han. *Ryūyō sareta Nihonjin: Watashitachi wa Chūgoku kenkoku o sasaeta*. Tokyo: NHK shuppan, 2003.

"Nihon no hyōban: gaikoku shi ni miru hankyō." *Bungei shunjū*, March 1975, 274–75.

"Nihon no moto senyū towa dōshitemo aitakunai." *Shūkan gendai*, January 30, 1975, 32–36.

"Nijū-hachi nen no kūhaku, 'shinwa no sekai' kara konoyo e." *Shūkan yomiuri*, February 18, 1972, 28–33.

"Nijū-roku nen tōkō gumi ga kataru Guamu-tō tōhikō no shin jijitsu." *Shūkan sankei*, February 25, 1972, 16–19.

Nimmo, William F. *Behind a Curtain of Silence: Japanese in Soviet Custody, 1945–1956*. New York: Greenwood Press, 1988.

Nishida Masuo. "Dōro sagyō taiin no kiroku." In *Horyo taikenki*, edited by Takahashi Daizō et al., 2:322–34. Tokyo: Soren ni okeru Nihonjin horyo no seikatsu taiken o kirokusuru kai, 1984.

Nishi'i Kazuo, ed. *Sengo 50 nen*. Tokyo: Mainichi shinbunsha, 1995.

Nishiki Masa'aki. *Yumegaosan ni yoroshiku*. Tokyo: Bungei shunjū, 1999.

Nishio Yasuto. *Tōdo no uta: Shiberia yokuryū 8 nen, Tsume de kaita kiroku*. Tokyo: Waseda shuppan, 1995.

Noge Kei'ichi. *Monogatari no tetsugaku: Yanagita Kunio to rekishi no hakken*. Tokyo: Iwanami shoten, 1996.

Noma Hiroshi. "Nora inu no mondai." *Chūōkōron*, December 1949, 87–89.

——. *Shinkū chitai*. Tokyo: Kawade shobō, 1952.

Nomura Shōtarō. "Watashi no yokuryū taikenki." In *Horyo taikenki*, edited by Takahashi Daizō et al., 4:5–19. Tokyo: Soren ni okeru Nihonjin horyo no seikatsu taiken o kirokusuru kai, 1985.

"Nosaka Akiyuki o kiri-koroshite yaru!" *Shūkan yomiuri*, April 26, 1975, 32–35.

Nosaka Akiyuki. "Onoda 'eiyū shuki' o yonde zannen na koto." *Shūkan posuto*, August 16, 1974, 42–45.

Ochiai Harurō. *Ishihara Yoshirō no Shiberia*. Tokyo: Ronsōsha, 1999.

——. *Shiberia no "Nihon shinbun."* Tokyo: Ronsōsha, 1995.

Odaka Ushimatsu. *Ubawareshi waga seishun*. Tokyo: Kōyō shuppansha, 2008.

Ogawa Mamoru. *Watashi no Shiberia monogatari*. Tokyo: Kōjinsha, 2011.

Ōgiya Shōzō. "Gendai bestoseraa monogatari 46: Gomikawa Junpei *Ningen no jōken*." *Asahi jaanaru*, September 4, 1996, 35–39.

Ōkado Masakatsu. *Sensō to sengo o ikiru*. Vol. 15 of Zenshū Nihon no rekishi. Tokyo: Shōgakkan, 2009.

Okamoto Sei'ichi. "Shuki o yonde." *Chūōkōron*, January 1954, 106–8.

Okumura Waichi and Sakai Makoto. *Watashi wa "ari no heitai" datta: Chūgoku ni nokosareta Nihonhei*. Tokyo: Iwanami shoten, 2006.

Onoda Hiro'o. "Himitsu senshi no tanjō." *Shūkan gendai*, May 16, 1974, 20–32.

——. "Ikinokotta yonin." *Shūkan gendai*, May 30, 1974, 20–32.

——. "Kakure goya no seikatsu." *Shūkan gendai*, June 27, 1974, 36–46.

——. "Kozuka to futari bocchi 20 nen." *Shūkan gendai*, July 4, 1974, 42–49.

——. "Meirei no nakami." *Shūkan gendai*, May 23, 1974, 20–32.

——. *No Surrender: My Thirty-Year War*. Translated by Charles S. Terry. Tokyo: Kodansha International, 1974.

——. *Tatta hitori no 30 nen sensō*. Tokyo: Tokyo shinbun shuppankyoku, 1995.

——. *Waga Ruban-tō no 30 nen sensō*. Tokyo: Kōdansha, 1974.

——. "Watashi kojin wa makete nakatta." *Shinchō*, August 1990, 34–38.

——. "Watashi no Taiheiyō sensō." *Shūkan gendai*, June 20, 1974, 38–48.

——. "Yurushite kudasai! Watashi wa Burajiru ni ijūshimasu." *Shūkan gendai*, November 7, 1974, 142–45.

Onoda Hiro'o, Sakamaki Kazuo, and Muramatsu Takeshi. "Onoda san to Sakamaki san." *Bungei shunjū*, November 1976, 328–44.

Onoda Hiro'o and Taniguchi Yoshimi. "Onoda kun, watashi o yurushite kure." *Shūkan gendai*, August 22, 1974, 26–32.

"Onoda Hiro'o-shi wa naze sattaka." *Shūkan bunshun*, February 19, 1975, 20.

"Onoda moto shōi 'kamubakku geki' ni kakatta gōkei ichioku-en no meisai." *Shūkan taishū*, March 28, 1974, 23–27.

"Onoda san wa fugirimono ka: sono kon'yaku ni kokyō Kainan shimin ga okoru riyū." *Shūkan yomiuri*, December 20, 1975, 150–52.

"Onoda Shōi kikan no kandō to 'Tennō kaiken.'" *Shūkan shinchō*, March 21, 1974, 128–31.

Onoda Yoshiki. "*Norainu* no kinchōkan." In *Bessatsu bungei: Kurosawa Akira*, edited by Nishiguchi Tōru. Tokyo: Kawade shobō shinsha, 1998.

Ōno Kaoru. *8 gatsu 17 nichi, Sorengun jōrikusu: saihate no yōshō Shumushu-tō kōbōki*. Tokyo: Shinchōsha, 2008.

Ōno Shin. "Ishihara Yoshirō ron." *Gendaishi techō*, September 1972, 34–46.

Ono Takamichi. "Tōdo no yokuryūsha no omoi kanketsu." *Asahi shinbun*, August 5, 1998, 14th ed., 26.

Ōoka Shōhei. *Nobi*. Osaka: Sōgensha, 1952.

——. *Reite senki*. 3 vols. Tokyo: Chūōkōron, 1974.

——. *Taken Captive: A Japanese POW's Story*. Translated by Wayne P. Lammers. New York: Wiley, 1996.

——. "Tōbun, hottoite agetai." *Shūkan asahi*, February 11, 1972, 22.

"Otoko Yokoi Shōichi o hazukashinagara rikkōho saseta 'okusan no chikara'!" *Yangu redii*, July 1, 1974, 30–32.

Ōtsuka Shigeru. *Damoi no michi wa tōkatta*. Tokyo: Kokusho kankōkai, 1995.

Prince, Stephen. *The Warrior's Camera: The Cinema of Akira Kurosawa*. Princeton, N.J.: Princeton University Press, 1991.

Rogaski, Ruth. "Nature, Annihilation, and Modernity: China's Korean War Germ-Warfare Experience Reconsidered." *Journal of Asian Studies* 61, no. 2 (2002): 381–415.

"Rubangu ikinokori hei no 28 nen." *Shūkan asahi*, November 3, 1972, 18–29.

"Rubangu-tō 'jūmin 30 nin satsugai' no tsumi wa dōnaru?" *Shūkan sankei*, November 17, 1972, 16–19.

"Ryōshin to kyōri o suteru Onoda san no himitsu o toku rokuon teipu." *Shūkan gendai*, April 3, 1975, 164–67.

Saitō Kunio. *Shiberia yokuryūhei yomoyama monogatari*. Tokyo: Kōjinsha, 2006.

Saitō Michinori. *Rikugun Nakano gakkō*. Tokyo: Heibonsha, 2006.

Sakai Saburō. *Sakai Saburō kūsen kiroku*. Tokyo: Kōdansha, 1992.

Sakamoto Tatsuhiko. *Shiberia ryoshū hanseiki: minkanjin Hachiya Yasaburō no kiroku*. Tokyo: Kōbunsha, 1998.

Sakamoto Yaichi. "Karaganda no tankō chiku de." In *Horyo taikenki*, edited by Takahashi Daizō et al., 5:121–28. Tokyo: Soren ni okeru Nihonjin horyo no seikatsu taiken o kirokusuru kai, 1986.

"Sanjū-ni nen buri no kokyō de 'bōchūkan.'" *Shūkan sankei*, March 27, 1975, 8–9.

Sano, Iwao Peter. *1,000 Days in Siberia*. Lincoln: University of Nebraska Press, 1997.

Sashida Fumio. *Kurosawa Akira no jūjika: sensō to Tuburaya tokusatsu to chōhei kihi*. Tokyo: Gendai kikakushitsu, 2013.

Satō Aiko. *Suniyon no isshō: Taiwan Takasago zoku giyūtai Nakamura Teruo no higeki.* Tokyo: Bungei shunjū, 1984.

Sawachi Hisae. *Shōwa: tōihi chikaihito.* Tokyo: Bungei shunjū, 1997.

——. *Watashi ga ikita "Shōwa."* Tokyo: Iwanami shoten, 2000.

Sawachi Hisae and Sataka Makoto. *Sedai o koete kataritsugitai sensō bungaku.* Tokyo: Iwanami shoten, 2009.

"Seiji no karakuri no nioi o kagu inu ni naritai." *Shūkan asahi,* June 28, 1974, 150–52.

Seki Kiyoto. *Tsuioku no hibi.* Tokyo: Bungeisha, 2001.

Seno Osamu. *Shiberia Yokuryūki.* Tokyo: Kōyūsha, 1947.

"'Sensō o shiranai sedai' wa kō hannōsuru." *Shūkan yomiuri,* February 18, 1972, 52–55.

Seraphim, Franziska. *War Memory and Social Politics in Japan, 1945–2005.* Cambridge, Mass.: Harvard University Asia Center, 2008.

Shibasaki Satoshi. *Ishihara Yoshirō: shibungaku no kakushin.* Tokyo: Shinkyō shuppansha, 2011.

Shiga Kiyoshige et al. *Aa Hairaru, Daihachi kokkyō shubitai tenmatsuki.* Tokyo: Kōjinsha, 1992.

Shimada Kakuo. *Watashi wa makyō ni ikita.* Tokyo: Kōjinsha, 2007.

Shimada Keizō. *Bōken Dankichi manga zenshū.* Tokyo: Kōdansha, 1967.

Shimada Toshihiko. *Kantō gun.* Tokyo: Chūōkōron,1965.

Shimizu Akira. *Sensō to eiga.* Tokyo: Shakaishisōsha, 1994.

Shimizu Ikutarō. *Shimizu Ikutarō chosakushū.* Vol. 14. Tokyo: Kōdansha, 1993.

Shindō Kenzō. "Watashi no Shiberia monogatari: Shuberuta shūyōjo no koro." In *Horyo taikenki,* edited by Takahashi Daizō et al., 7:257–69. Tokyo: Soren ni okeru Nihonjin horyo no seikatsu taiken o kirokusuru kai, 1989.

Shinonaga Nobutaka. "Betonamu baishō." In *Nihon no sengo baishō: Ajia kyōryoku no shuppatsu,* edited by Nagano Shin'ichirō and Kondō Masaomi, 89–104. Tokyo: Keisō shobō, 1999.

"Shinseki kaigi de osareta Yamada Sachiko san wa 20 sai." *Shūkan josei,* February 19, 1972, 28–31.

Shiozawa Minobu. "Shiozawa Minobu no 'Bestuoseraa no haikei' yomigaetta *Ningen no jōken.*" *Gekkan BOSS,* November 2011, 114–15.

Shirai Hisaya. *Dokyumento Shiberia yokuryū: Saitō Rokurō no kiseki.* Tokyo: Iwanami shoten, 1995.

——. *Kenshō Shiberia yokuryū.* Heibonsha, 2010.

Shiraishi Katsunori. "Yokoi san no 'dōkutsu' de ichiya o sugoshita!" *Shūkan bunshun,* February 14, 1972, 24–27.

"Shōgen kōsei kiseki no hito, Yokoi Shōichi san no 'tabidachi.'" *Yangu redii,* February 16, 1972, 46–52.

"Shōgensha: sono genba ni watashi wa ita." *Sandei mainichi,* December 31, 1972, 132–33.

Shūkan asahi, ed. *Sengo nedan shi nenpyō.* Tokyo: Asahi shinbun shuppan, 1995.

Sōkagakkai hansen seinenbu hansen shuppan iinkai, ed. *Namida ni urumu Maizurukō.* Tokyo: Daisanbunmei sha, 1979.

Solzhenitsyn, Aleksandr I. *The Gulag Archipelago.* New York: Harper & Row, 1973.

Spiegelman, Art. *MetaMaus: A Look Inside a Modern Classic, Maus.* New York: Pantheon Books, 2011.

Suga Hidemi. "Komyunikeishion toshiteno 'ue': Ishihara Yoshirō ron." *Gendaishi techō*, November 1989, 140–45.

Sumioka Takashi. "Shi to nichijō to: Ishihara Yoshirō san no koto." *Techō*. In *Ishihara Yoshirō zenshū*, 3:2–4. Tokyo: Kashinsha, 1980.

Suttmeier, Bruce. "Speculations of Murder: Ghostly Dreams, Poisonous Frogs, and the Return of Yokoi Shōichi." In *Perversion and Modern Japan: Psychoanalysis, Literature, Culture,* edited by Nina Cornyetz and J. Keith Vincent, 22–37. New York: Routledge, 2009.

Suzuki Akira. "Rikugun heichō Nakamura Suriyon." *Bungei shunjū,* March 1975, 174–90.

——. *Takasago-zoku ni sasageru.* Tokyo: Chūōkōron shinsha, 1980.

Suzuki Norio. *Dai hōrō: Onoda Shōi hakken no tabi.* Tokyo: Bungei shunjū, 1974.

——. "Onoda Shōi hakken no tabi." *Bungei shunjū,* May 1974, 132–72.

Suzuki Shōzō. "*Raageru*" *no nakano seishun.* Tokyo: Akashi shoten, 1999.

Tachibana Seitarō. *Ningen no jōken.* 4 vols. Tokyo: Horupu shuppan, 1983.

Tachibana Takashi. *Shiberia chinkonka: Kazuki Yasuo no sekai.* Tokyo: Bungei shunjū, 2004.

Tada Shigeharu. *Ishihara Yoshirō "Shōwa" no tabi.* Tokyo: Sakuhinsha, 2000.

——. *Uchinaru Shiberia yokuryū taiken: Ishihara Yoshirō, Kano Buichi, Kan Sueharu no sengoshi.* Tokyo: Shakaishisōsha, 1994.

Tajima Kyōji. *Shiberia no akumu.* Tokyo: Tokyo keizai, 1995.

Takahashi Daizō. "Kaisetsu: hangun, minshuka undo no keika." In *Horyo taikenki,* edited by Takahashi Daizō et al., 8:3–44. Tokyo: Soren ni okeru Nihonjin horyo no seikatsu taiken o kirokusuru kai, 1992.

——. "Kikoku shūketsuchi Nahotoka no koe." In *Horyo taikenki,* edited by Takahashi Daizō et al., 2:3–44. Tokyo: Soren ni okeru Nihonjin horyo no seikatsu taiken o kirokusuru kai, 1984.

Takahashi Teruaki, ed. "Ore wa hadaka no gensui da, 1: Watashi wa dassōhei dewa nakatta." *Shūkan sankei,* March 27, 1975, 32–37.

——. "Ore wa hadaka no gensui da, 2: Hatsukoi no hito o daku yume o mita," *Shūkan sankei,* April 3, 1975, 48–53.

——. "Ore wa hadaka no gensui da, 4: Koyomi wa 30 nen pitarito atta." *Shūkan sankei,* April 17, 1975, 50–54.

——. "Ore wa hadaka no gensui da, 5: Suichū megane tsukutte unagi tori," *Shūkan sankei,* April 24, 1975, 54–58.

Takasugi Ichirō. *Ikite kaerishi hei no kioku.* Tokyo: Iwanami shoten, 1996.

——. *Kyokkō no kageni.* Tokyo: Iwanami shoten, 1991.

Takeda Masanao. *Kokkan Shiberia yokuryūki.* Tokyo: Kōjinsha, 2001.

Takeda Taijun. *Hikarigoke.* Tokyo: Shinchōsha, 1992.

Takeuchi Kikuo. *Shōka, dōyō 1,000 no shinjitsu.* Tokyo: Yamaha, 2009.

Takeyama Michio. *Biruma no tategoto.* Tokyo: Akane shobō, 1959.

Takeya Seikichi. "Shūjin ressha Sutoroipin." In *Nanae no teppi: Nihonjin horyo no Shiberia yokuryūki.* Tokyo: Nikkan rōdō tsūshinsha, 1958.

Tamanoi, Mariko. *Memory Maps: The State and Manchuria in Postwar Japan*. Honolulu: University of Hawai'i Press, 2009.

Tamura Hideo. "Gakusei no eigashitsu: Kiiroi karasu." *Kōkō jidai*, March 1957, 210–11.

Taniguchi Yoshimi. "Futatsu no meireisho." *Bungei shunjū*, May 1974, 175–85.

Tasogawa Hiroshi. *Kurosawa Akira vs. Hariwuddo: "Tora, Tora, Tora!" sono nazo no subete*. Tokyo: Bungei shunjū, 2006.

Tierney, Robert. *Tropics of Savagery: The Culture of Japanese Empire in Comparative Frame*. Berkeley: University of California Press, 2010.

Toda Hiroshi. "Fushigina hodo ijōna 'nōryoku' kesshō." *Shūkan asahi*, February 11, 1972, 18–23.

Toi Jūgatsu. *Onoda Hiro'o no owaranai tatakai*. Tokyo: Shinchōsha, 2005.

"Tokubetsu intabyū Nihon no minasan e Morotai-tō no moto Nihonhei Nakamura Teruo." *Shūkan bunshun*, January 29, 1975, 32–35.

Tomitani Shūkō. "Watashi wa senyū no jinniku de ikinobita." *Shūkan yomiuri*, July 29, 1979, 152–54.

Tomita Takeshi. *Shiberia yokuryūsha tachi no sengo*. Tokyo: Jinbun shoin, 2013.

Trefalt, Beatrice. *Japanese Army Stragglers and Memories of the War in Japan, 1950–1975*. New York: RoutledgeCurzon, 2003.

Tsuda Shin. *Gensō no eiyū: Onoda shōi tono 3 kagetsu*. Tokyo: Tosho shuppansha, 1977.

——. "Onoda wa gensō no eiyū da." *Shūkan posuto*, June 24–August 26, 1977.

Tsukase Susumu. *Manshūkoku: "minzoku kyōwa" no jitsuzō*. Tokyo: Yoshikawa kōbunkan, 1998.

Tsukimura Toshiyuki. "Ishihara Yoshirō: sono kiseki." *Gendaishi techō*, February 1978, 168–83.

Tsurumi Shunsuke. "Maegaki," In *Sengo eiga no tenkai*, edited by Imamura Shōei et al. Vol. 5 of Kōza Nihon eiga. Tokyo: Iwanami shoten, 1987.

Tsutsumi Kizaburō. "Shiberia yokuryū seikatsu." In *Horyo taikenki*, edited by Takahashi Daizō et al., 2:123–37. Tokyo: Soren ni okeru Nihonjin horyo no seikatsu taiken o kirokusuru kai, 1984.

Tsuzuki Masa'aki. *Kurosawa Akira no yuigon "Yume."* Tokyo: Kindai bungeisha, 2005.

Uchimura Gōsuke. *Shitsugo to dannen: Ishihara Yoshirō ron*. Tokyo: Shichōsha, 1979.

——. *Uchimura Gōsuke rongu intabyū*, edited by Suyama Ikurō. Tokyo: Keigadō shuppan, 2008.

Uchimura Yūshi. "Kodaira jiken." In *Nihon no seishin kantei*, edited by Fukushima Akira, Nakata Osamu, and Ogi Sadataka, 193–241. Tokyo: Misuzu shobō, 1973.

Uchiyama Takeshi, *Nihonjin wa naze kitsune ni damasarenaku natta noka*. Tokyo: Kōdansha, 2007.

Uegusa Keinosuke. *Keredo yoakeni: waga seishun no Kurosawa Akira*. Tokyo: Bungei shunjū, 1978.

Uno Kuni'ichi. "Han 'sei-seijigaku' teki kōsatsu." *Shisō*, no. 1066, February 2013, 40–57.

Usui Yoshimi. "Tsuini deta sensō bungaku: Ningen no jōken o yonde." *Shūkan asahi*, February 16, 1958, 9.

Utsumi Aiko. *Sengo hoshō kara kangaeru Nihon to Ajia*. Tokyo: Yamakawa shuppan-sha, 2002.

Wada-Marciano, Mitsuyo. *Nippon Modern: Japanese Cinema of the 1920s and 1930s*. Honolulu: University of Hawai'i Press, 2008.

Wakaichi Kōji. *Saigo no senshisha, rikugun ittōhei Kozuka Kinshichi*. Tokyo: Kawade shobō shinsha, 1986.

Wakatsuki Yasuo. *Sengo hikiage no kiroku*. Tokyo: Tokyo: Jiji tsūshinsha, 1991.

——. *Shiberia horyoshūyōjo*. Tokyo: Akashi shoten, 1999.

"Washi wa saitei 100 manbyō wa koeru to omottoru!" *Josei jishin*, July 4, 1974, 34–35.

"Wasure enu hatsukoi no hito, kon'yakusha wa sudeni naku . . ." *Josei sebun*, February 16, 1972, 37–38.

Watanabe Chiguto. *Aru igakuto no seishun*. Fukuoka: Kaichōsha, 1994.

Watanabe Tokio. *Saihate no Raageru nite: Shiberia yokuryū chinkon no hi*. Kōfu: Yamanashi furusato bunko, 2008.

Watt, Lori. *When Empire Comes Home: Repatriation and Reintegration in Postwar Japan*. Cambridge, Mass.: Harvard University Asia Center, 2009.

Wilson, Richard A. *The Politics of Truth and Reconciliation in South Africa: Legitimizing the Post-Apartheid State*. Cambridge: Cambridge University Press, 2001.

Wilson, Sandra. "War, Soldier and Nation in 1950s Japan." *International Journal of Asian Studies* 5, no. 2 (2008): 187–218.

Winter, Jay M. *Sites of Memory, Sites of Mourning: The Great War in European Cultural History*. New York: Cambridge University Press, 1995.

Yamaguchi Makoto. *Guamu to Nihonjin: sensō o umetateta rakuen*. Tokyo: Iwanami shoten, 2007.

Yamamoto Shichihei. *Watashi no naka no Nihongun, jō*. Tokyo: Bungei shunjū, 1975.

Yamashiro Mutsumi. *Tenkeiki to shikō*. Tokyo: Kōdansha, 1999.

Yamashita Katsutoshi. "Tsuitaiken, honshi kisha Guamu no janguru ni komoru." *Shūkan asahi*, February 21, 1972, 23–26.

Yamashita Shizuo. *Shiberia yokuryū 1,450 nichi*. Tokyo: Dejipuro, 2007.

Yamashita Yukihide. "Tekichi no genshu ni saikō no rei de mukaerareta Onoda Shōi." *Shūkan sankei*, April 3, 1974, 20–23.

Yasuoka Shōtarō. *Tonsō*. Tokyo: Kōdansha, 1957.

——. "Yokoi san to Nihonjin." *Shūkan yomiuri*, February 18, 1972, 40–41.

"Yokoi genkō roku ni miru 'sei.'" *Shūkan yomiuri*, February 18, 1972, 97–98.

"Yokoi gochō ni tōhyō shita hitotachi no kimochi." *Shūkan shinchō*, July 18, 1974, 154–55.

"Yokoi gochō o sasaeta? Senjinkun towa." *Sandei mainichi*, February 20, 1972, 24–25.

"Yokoi gunsō no imawanaki kon'yakusha no iji ga kataru 28 nenkan." *Asahi geinō*, February 10, 1972, 12–15.

Yokoi Mihoko. *Chinkon no tabiji: Yokoi Shōichi no sengo o ikita tsuma no shuki*. Osaka: Horusu shuppan, 2011.

"Yokoi san ga watashi dakeni katatta hitori ikinokotta shinsō." *Shūkan gendai*, February 17, 1972, 20–25.

"Yokoi san no risō senkyo sengen." *Shūkan bunshun*, July 1, 1974, 151–53.

"Yokoi san shuzai no 'ima dakara hanaseru hiwa.'" *Shūkan posuto*, February 18, 1972, 158–61.

"Yokoi san wa tōsen suruka." *Shūkan shinchō*, June 27, 1974, 148–51.

Yokoi Shōichi. *Ashita eno michi*. Tokyo: Bungei shunjū, 1974.

"Yokoi Shōichi san bunmei tono tatakai isshūkan." *Shūkan yomiuri*, February 19, 1972, 22–25.

"Yokoi Shōichi san fūfu omedeta! Daga 3 kagetsu de munen!" *Yangu redii*, January 28, 1974, 27–29.

"Yokoi Shōichi san fusai: rainen 1 gatsu ni kodomo ga dekisōdesu." *Josei sebun*, December 27, 1972, 189–90.

"Yokoi Shōichi san ga kekkon suru hazudatta josei wa Itō Mitsuko san." *Shūkan heibon*, February 10, 1972, 38–42.

"Yokoi Shōichi san ga terebi de kokuhaku! 'oshikake nyōbo kōho ni komattemasu.'" *Josei sebun*, September 6–13, 1972, 38–39.

"Yokoi Shōichi san no kangei no sarekata." *Josei jishin*, February 19, 1972, 34–38.

"Yokoi Shōichi san wa korosareru sunzen datta!" *Shūkan asahi*, August 24, 2007, 32–35.

Yokota Shōhei. *Watashi wa gyokusai shinakatta*. Tokyo: Chūōkōron shinsha, 1999.

Yoshida Isamu. *Chinkon no Shiberia: heishi no damoi eno michi*. Osaka: Shinpū shōbō, n.d.

Yoshida Mitsuru. *Requiem for Battleship Yamato*. Translated by Richard Minear. Annapolis, Md.: Naval Institute Press, 1999.

——. *Senkan Yamato no saigo* in *"Senkan Yamato" to sengo*, edited by Hosaka Masayasu, 11–190. Tokyo: Chikuma shobō, 2005.

Yoshida Yutaka. *Heishitachi no sengoshi*. Tokyo: Iwanami shoten, 2011.

Yoshimi Shunya. *Banpaku gensō*. Tokyo: Chikuma shobō, 2005.

——. "Eigakan to iu sengo: henyō suru Tokyo no sakariba no nakade." In *Miru hito, tsukuru hito, kakeru hito*, edited by Kurosawa Kiyoshi et al., 1–12. Vol. 3 of *Nihon eiga wa ikite iru*. Tokyo: Iwanami shoten, 2010.

Yoshimoto Mitsuhiro. *Kurosawa*. Durham, N.C.: Duke University Press, 2000.

Yoshinaga Haruko. *Sasurai no "mi-fukuinhei."* Tokyo: Chikuma shobō, 1987.

"Zehi watashi wa 'kon'yakusha' ni aitai . . ." *Josei jishin*, February 12, 1972, 29–33.

Zhao Musong. *Li Guanghui di shijie*. Taibei: Jiang jun chu ban shi ye gu, 1975.

Zhongyang danganguan et al., eds. *Riben diguo zhui qinhua dangan ziliao xuanbian: dongbei jingji lüedao*. Vol. 14. Beijing: Zhonghua shuju chuban, 1991.

INDEX

Numbers in italics refer to pages on which illustrations appear

Baikal, Lake, *xi*, 88

Baikal–Amur Mainline (BAM) railway, 93, 116, 117, 119, 121, 132

Bao Ninh, 51

Barshay, Andrew, 16, 247n.78, 252n.15

Biess, Frank, 83–84, 249n.109

Black Rain (*Kuroi ame*; film; Imamura), 231n.7

Blue Mountains (*Aoi sanmyaku*; film), 25

Bodies of Memory (Igarashi), 6, 10

body, 130, 115, 118–19, 121–22, 130, 135, 137–38; anarchic chaos of mind and, 123; divide between mind and, 115; of Gomikawa Junpei, 72, 73; of Ishihara Yoshirō, 117, 137, 139, 142; Kaji's fatigued, in *The Human Condtion*, 70; of Kodaira Yoshio's first murder victim, 28; of Kozuka Kinshichi, 176; of Kurosawa Akira, 272n.1; mind and, 121; of Murakami, in *Stray Dog*, 38; of Namiki Harumi, in *Stray Dog*, 34; tension of mind and, 122; vulnerable, 139; Wang Xiangli's emaciated, in *The Human Condition*, 61; of Yokoi Shōichi, 150, 156, 170

Borges, Jorge Luis, 15, 224

Brazil, 197, 198, 228n.18, 265n.81, 266n.91

British Empire, 151

Burma (Myanmar), peace treaty with Japan, 55, 236n.16

cannibalism, 91, 215–16, 245n.50, 271n.63, 272n.64, 272nn.67–68

capitalism, 67, 104–5, 145, 163

Carmen Comes Home (*Karumen kokyō ni kaeru*; film), 25

Children Hand in Hand (*Te o tunagu kora*; film), 25

China, Nationalist, 29, 151; Japanese soldiers in service of, 42, 238n.28; repatriates from, 5, 228n.10. *See also* Taiwan (Republic of China)

China, People's Republic of (PRC), *x*, *xi*, 2, 3, 73; belated repatriates from, 17, 22, 24, 41–43, 78, 160, 233n.34,

238n.28; diplomatic relations of, with Japan, 204; Patriotic Hygiene Campaign in, 44, 233n.39; postwar fear/dislike of, 250n.122; women repatriates from, 229n.23

Chita, *xi*, 93, 95, 116

Chūōkōron (magazine), 58, 76, 102, 103–4, 229n.21

civilian repatriates, 1, 8–9, 10, 23

Cold War, 16, 108, 211

"Colleges of Cartographers" (Borges), 15

colonialism, 10, 27, 56–57, 217; fantasy of, 216, 231n.6; Japan's past of, in Taiwan, 204, 211

Communists: abandonment of Communist beliefs by repatriates, 84, 243n.17; employers' fear of Communist repatriates, 5, 42, 105; Japan Communist Party (JCP), 101, 104, 168, 242nn.14–15; repatriates from China as, 2, 3; repatriates from Siberia as, 84, 105–6, 242nn.14–15, 243n.16; U.S. Occupation policy in Japan and, 161

conservatives, Japanese, 104–5, 106

consumer society, 10–11

Contract with Freedom (*Jiyū tono keiyaku*; Gomikawa), 240n.58

"Courage of a Pessimist, The" (Peshimisuto no yūki no tsuite; Ishihara), 131–38

criminality, 26–29, 31, 232n.17

Dalian, *xi*, 56, 57

De Gracia, Manuel, 258n.54

Dear Venerable Emperor (*Haikei tennō-heika sama*; film; Nomura), 235n.50

democratization movement, 58, 70, 77, 248n.98; oppressive and fear-inspiring nature of, 99–100, 105, 248n.96; repatriates from Siberia as avid Communists and, 84; traumatic memories of, 247n.78

disease, metaphor of, 27, 44

299

Neither Donkey nor Horse: Medicine in the Struggle Over China's Modernity, by Sean Hsiang-lin Lei. University of Chicago Press, 2014.

When the Future Disappears: The Modernist Imagination in Late Colonial Korea, by Janet Poole. Columbia University Press, 2014.

Bad Water: Nature, Pollution, & Politics in Japan, 1870–1950, by Robert Stolz. Duke University Press, 2014.

Rise of a Japanese Chinatown: Yokohama, 1894–1972, by Eric C. Han. Harvard University Asia Center, 2014.

Beyond the Metropolis: Second Cities and Modern Life in Interwar Japan, by Louise Young. University of California Press, 2013.

From Cultures of War to Cultures of Peace: War and Peace Museums in Japan, China, and South Korea, by Takashi Yoshida. MerwinAsia, 2013.

Imperial Eclipse: Japan's Strategic Thinking about Continental Asia before August 1945, by Yukiko Koshiro. Cornell University Press, 2013.

The Nature of the Beasts: Empire and Exhibition at the Tokyo Imperial Zoo, by Ian J. Miller. University of California Press, 2013.

Public Properties: Museums in Imperial Japan, by Noriko Aso. Duke University Press, 2013.

Reconstructing Bodies: Biomedicine, Health, and Nation-Building in South Korea Since 1945, by John P. DiMoia. Stanford University Press, 2013.

Taming Tibet: Landscape Transformation and the Gift of Chinese Development, by Emily T. Yeh. Cornell University Press, 2013.

Tyranny of the Weak: North Korea and the World, 1950–1992, by Charles K. Armstrong. Cornell University Press, 2013.

The Art of Censorship in Postwar Japan, by Kirsten Cather. University of Hawai'i Press, 2012.

Asia for the Asians: China in the Lives of Five Meiji Japanese, by Paula Harrell. Merwin-Asia, 2012.

Lin Shu, Inc.: Translation and the Making of Modern Chinese Culture, by Michael Gibbs Hill. Oxford University Press, 2012.

Occupying Power: Sex Workers and Servicemen in Postwar Japan, by Sarah Kovner. Stanford University Press, 2012.

Redacted: The Archives of Censorship in Postwar Japan, by Jonathan E. Abel. University of California Press, 2012.

Empire of Dogs: Canines, Japan, and the Making of the Modern Imperial World, by Aaron Herald Skabelund. Cornell University Press, 2011.

Planning for Empire: Reform Bureaucrats and the Japanese Wartime State, by Janis Mimura.Cornell University Press, 2011.

Realms of Literacy: Early Japan and the History of Writing, by David Lurie. Harvard University Asia Center, 2011.

Russo-Japanese Relations, 1905–17: From Enemies to Allies, by Peter Berton. Routledge, 2011.

Behind the Gate: Inventing Students in Beijing, by Fabio Lanza. Columbia University Press, 2010.

Imperial Japan at Its Zenith: The Wartime Celebration of the Empire's 2,600th Anniversary, by Kenneth J. Ruoff. Cornell University Press, 2010.